# Private Law in Theory and Practice

*Private Law in Theory and Practice* explores important theoretical issues in tort law, the law of contract and the law of unjust enrichment, and relates the theory to judicial decision making in these areas of private law. Topics covered include the politics and philosophy of tort law reform, the role of good faith in contract law, comparative perspectives on setting aside contracts for mistake, and the theory and practice of proprietary remedies in the law of unjust enrichment.

Contributors to the book bring a variety of theoretical perspectives to bear on the analysis of private law. They include: economic analysis, corrective justice theory, comparative analysis of law, socio-legal inquiry, social history, political theory as well as doctrinal analysis of the law. In all cases the theoretical approaches are applied to recent case law developments in England, Australia and Canada, and, in the case of tort law, proposals in all these jurisdictions to reform the law.

The book aims to present the theory of private law, and the application of theory to practical legal problems in an accessible form to teachers and students of tort, contract and the law of unjust enrichment, legal researchers and law reformers.

**Michael Bryan** is Professor of Law at the University of Melbourne. He has researched and published extensively in the areas of equity, trusts and restitution, including *The Law of Non-Disclosure* (with A. Duggan and F. Hanks: Longman, 1995) and contributed a chapter to *The Law of Obligations: Connections and Boundaries* (UCL Press, 2003).

# Private Law in Theory and Practice

Edited by Michael Bryan

Routledge·Cavendish
Taylor & Francis Group
LONDON AND NEW YORK

First published 2007 by Routledge-Cavendish
2 Park Square, Milton Park, Abingdon, Oxon OX14 4RN

Simultaneously published in the USA and Canada
by Routledge-Cavendish
711 Third Avenue, New York, NY 10017

*Routledge-Cavendish is an imprint of the Taylor & Francis Group, an
informa business*

© 2007 Michael Bryan

Typeset in Times and Gill Sans by
RefineCatch Limited, Bungay, Suffolk

*First published in paperback in 2011*

*British Library Cataloguing in Publication Data*
A catalogue record for this book is available from the British Library

*Library of Congress Cataloging in Publication Data*
Bryan, Michael.
  Private law in theory and practice / Michael Bryan.
    p. cm.
  ISBN 1–84472–140–X (hardback)
    1. Civil law – England.   2. Civil law – Australia.   3. Civil law –
Canada.   I. Title.
  K623.B79 2006
  346 – dc22                               2006021366

ISBN13:  978–0–41551–636–5 (pbk)
ISBN13:  978–1–84472–140–5 (hbk)

This book is dedicated to the memory of Peter Birks who by precept and practice demonstrated why private law scholarship matters.

# Contents

# List of Contributors

**Susan Barkehall-Thomas** is a Senior Lecturer in Law at Monash University.

**Michael Bryan** is a Professor of Law at the University of Melbourne.

**Kylie Burns** is a Lecturer in Law at Griffith University.

**Peter Cane** is a Professor of Law in the Research School of Social Sciences, Australian National University.

**David Capper** is a Reader in Law at Queen's University, Belfast.

**Elizabeth Cooke** is a Professor of Law at Reading University.

**Tony Duggan** holds the Frank Iacobucci Chair in Capital Markets Regulation at the University of Toronto.

**Nick Hopkins** is a Senior Lecturer at the University of Southampton.

**Harold Luntz** is a Professorial Fellow at the University of Melbourne.

**Jeannie Paterson** is a Senior Lecturer in Law at Monash University.

**Catherine Valcke** is an Associate Professor of Law at the University of Toronto.

**Stephen Waddams** holds the Goodman-Schipper Chair of Law at the University of Toronto.

# Introduction

In 2002 the Faculty of Law at the University of Melbourne celebrated the opening of its new Law School Building by holding a conference on the Law of Obligations. The success of that conference, and of the book of the conference proceedings, *The Law of Obligations: Connections and Boundaries*, 2004 Andrew Robertson, (ed) UCL Press, encouraged the organisers to repeat the venture. The second University of Melbourne Conference on the Law of Obligations demonstrated, if it needed demonstrating, the intellectual vitality of scholarly writing in the law of obligations – which was defined broadly, for the purposes of the conference to include tort, contract, unjust enrichment and property law.

I am grateful to all the participants for their contribution to the success of the conference. The papers benefited from the lively discussion which was a feature of all the conference sessions. I am particularly grateful to Dr Andrew Robertson who co-organised the conference, with his unfailing attention to significant detail, and who has given me wise advice at every stage of the production process of this book. Finally, I am indebted to Anna Severin for her invaluable editorial assistance which helped to pull the book together at a critical juncture.

The papers by Peter Cane and Tony Duggan have appeared in the Oxford Journal of Legal Studies and the Toronto Law Journal, respectively. The publishers of these journals have kindly consented to the inclusion of the papers in this volume.

Michael Bryan
January 2007
University of Melbourne

# Part I

# Principle and policy

# Chapter 1

# Private right and public interest

*Stephen Waddams*

It is common for writers to relate legal concepts to each other in terms of such metaphors as maps and organisational or taxonomic schemes. Distinctions are drawn among contract, tort, and unjust enrichment, and between obligations and property, and, at a higher level of generality, between private rights and public policy. These distinctions are then commonly depicted as distinct areas on a map, or as separate classes, orders, genera, and species in a taxonomic scheme. Metaphors may illuminate a complex subject, but any metaphor, if pressed too far, is apt to distort. The ideas of mapping and taxonomy in law owe their attraction partly to their indeterminacy and variability. Mapping, as applied to law, is not a single metaphor, but multiple metaphors: the idea of a political map is not the same metaphor as the idea of a map of physical geography, and the idea of an urban map differs from the idea of a global map of seas and continents. Any set of ideas may claim its map, but different writers have used the word in different ways. Blackstone spoke of a map,[1] and his map (rights of persons, rights of things, private wrongs, public wrongs) was useful for his purpose but plainly did not seek to set out mutually exclusive categories. Many private law obligations might fall simultaneously into all of his first three books. Modern writers, by contrast, have often envisaged a map that separates obligations rather as a map of physical geography separates places (Ottawa is in Canada, and therefore not in Europe) or as a taxonomical scheme separates biological specimens (an animal is either an insect or a mammal, but cannot be both).

Some maps and taxonomic schemes claim, expressly or by implication, to be descriptive of the past. In that case the accuracy of the map or scheme can be assessed by historical evidence, as a geographical map may be compared with the terrain it depicts, or a taxonomic scheme may be tested by whether it includes all known specimens; in case of discrepancy, of course, it must be the map or scheme, not the terrain or collection of specimens, that is amended.

---

1 Blackstone, W, *Commentaries on the Laws of England*, 1765–69, Oxford: Clarendon Press, i, 35.

Actual assertions about the past should be tested and if they turn out to be false, should be contradicted. So, if it were asserted that every legal obligation has been derived from one only of three or four discrete concepts, this assertion could be contradicted by evidence that some legal obligations have been derived from the concurrent and cumulative operation of several concepts. It is true of many rules of private law that they have not been derived exclusively from a single concept. The law of vicarious liability cannot be derived entirely from the concept of fault, nor can the law of agency be derived entirely from the idea of consent, and so a map or scheme with fault, consent, and unjust enrichment as primary and mutually exclusive categories would not accurately describe the past. If it were sought to marginalise the non-conforming cases by suggesting that instances of vicarious liability and agency had been infrequent or of small importance, the criteria of frequency and importance should be demanded: if testable, the assertions should be tested by historical evidence, and if untestable, this should be pointed out. A statement that could not be falsified by historical evidence might be valid, but it would not be a statement about the past.

Alternatively a map or scheme might depict an ideal. A writer might propose that for reasons (for example) of ethics, utility, logic, elegance or of conformity with a philosophical or political system, or with another legal system (ancient or modern), every legal obligation *should be* derived from one only of three or four discrete concepts. This would be a quite different undertaking. It could not, of course, be refuted by historical evidence, but then neither could it be supported by such evidence. To vindicate such a proposal it would be necessary to identify the rules of existing law that would be altered by it, and to persuade the reader of the superior virtue of the value underlying the proposed scheme (ethics, utility, logic, elegance, etc.). If the rules in question were of long standing and answered to an instinctive sense of fairness or convenience this would be a difficult task – to abolish vicarious liability and the law of agency for the sake of elegance would imply a very high view of elegance as an unqualified and overriding human good – but if the argument succeeded, a persuasive case for reform would have been made out.

Each of these two approaches has been common in legal discourse, and each is valuable, but what is undesirable (I would suggest) is to run them together, using the proposed map or scheme to eliminate or marginalise inconsistent features of the past, and then using the past, so pruned, as evidence in support of the map or scheme. Such an approach tends to assume what is sought to be proved; it confuses description of the past with prescription for the future; it produces assertions about the past that cannot be falsified (or tested) because contradictory evidence is automatically marginalised; and it produces prescriptions for the future that cannot be evaluated because neither the extent to which the law is to be changed nor the underlying reason for making the change is made explicit.

The conclusion I would draw is not that maps and taxonomic schemes are useless, nor that better maps and schemes are needed, but that the metaphors of mapping and taxonomy should not be pressed too far. If we wish to understand Rouen Cathedral (to adopt Calabresi's well-known metaphor, 'one view of the cathedral')[2] we need more views or perspectives, not just a better ground plan, or a catalogue of building materials.

Quite frequently propositions about law combine (by a kind of rhetorical slippage) historical and non-historical assertions, and tend to slide from one to the other: the natural meaning of words suggests the conclusion desired by the writer; with the accompanying suggestions that the law (past, present, and future; here and everywhere) generally conforms, has conformed, should conform, and, properly understood, *must* conform, with the writer's view. Taken in the mass, this mixture of ideas makes the proposition unfalsifiable, and therefore untestable, because any potentially contradictory evidence will automatically have been marginalised as exceptional, anomalous, and unprincipled. If the proposition is to be tested, historical and non-historical propositions must be disentangled, for different tests are appropriate to each.

Put like this, these points seem almost too obvious to be worth making, as non-lawyers – both historians and philosophers – usually tell me when I try to explain it to them. Yet I think that most lawyers will recognise the kind of slippage I have described. I will go further and say that most of us have been guilty of it ourselves, lawyers being particularly susceptible because of the conventions of judicial reasoning (and therefore of forensic argument and of academic commentary) that seek to anchor every innovation in the past. The phenomenon has been pervasive in legal argument, and by no means confined to any particular view of law. Intellectual order in law is desirable, but it is not assisted by misunderstanding the past. The law is an actual social phenomenon with a history that cannot be reconstructed in an academic's study or in a judge's chambers. Let us by all means seek intellectually satisfying justifications for legal results, but let it be on the basis of an accurate understanding of past law. Wishful thinking about the future may be a virtue; wishful thinking about the past is not: it leads to bad history and to the distortion of judgment. In pointing this out I hope it is clear that I am seeking to contribute to, not to disparage, good intellectual order in the law. Good history is never at odds with good intellectual order.

Some have suggested that, since no one could disagree with these propositions, the danger I point to is not real. I have said that most lawyers will recognise the kind of slippage I have described but for those who do not, I would refer (by way of illustration) to a recent (2001) statement by the Supreme Court of Canada on vicarious liability:

---

2   See n 26, below.

In general tort law attempts to hold persons accountable for their wrongful acts and omissions and the direct harm that flows from those wrongs. Vicarious liability, by contrast, is considered to be a species of strict liability because it requires no proof of personal wrongdoing on the part of the person who is subject to it. As such, it is still *relatively uncommon* in Canadian tort law.[3]

This passage, not of great significance in itself, will serve to illustrate the phenomenon to which I seek to draw attention. Throughout the twentieth century, instances of vicarious liability have not been 'relatively uncommon': by any measure, they have been very frequent. No one knows this better than the judges of the Supreme Court of Canada who made the statement just quoted. How is it then that they appear to have asserted the contrary? The answer lies in a slippage, common in legal writing, between conceptual and historical propositions.[4] A variety of words and phrases have tended to blur the distinction. Thus it may be said that instances of liability without fault are 'exceptional', 'anomalous', 'insignificant', 'marginal', 'unusual', 'islands', 'pockets', 'outliers', 'outside the mainstream', 'abnormal', 'deviant', 'departing from the norm', 'aberrant', or repugnant to a 'normative' view of the question – expressions that tend to blur the distinction between conceptual and historical – and, from this it is deduced that therefore in the past such instances must actually have been rare, a proposition that, without being tested historically, in its turn is then implicitly deployed in support of the underlying idea: that liability must depend on fault. Writers who make such statements may quite properly say that they are meant to be conceptual, not historical, but if the distinction is not emphasised, there is a danger (illustrated by the passage just quoted) that confusion of the conceptual with the historical may lead to erroneous conclusions about the past. There is a real danger of serious confusion of thought: there are, no doubt, several cogent arguments that might be made against vicarious liability, but the proposition that it has been relatively uncommon is not one of them.

The sequence of thought just mentioned is closely linked with questions of categorisation and classification, the underlying assumption being that all liability that does not fall into some other recognised category must depend on wrongdoing. Even brief attention to the actual history of Anglo-American law shows that, as a description of the past, such a scheme tends towards oversimplification: the relation of legal concepts to each other, as

---

3   *671122 Ontario Ltd v Sagaz Industries Canada Inc* [2001] 2 SCR 983, 204 DLR (4th) 542, at 551 (emphasis added).

4   See Waddams, S, 'Classification of Private Law in Relation to Historical Evidence: Description, Prescription, and Conceptual Analysis,' in Lewis, A and Lobban, M (eds) *Law and History: Current Legal Issues 2003*, (2003), p 265.

they have operated in practice, is not exactly captured by a two-dimensional diagram.

The topic of our attention is the relation between principle and policy in private law. Peter Cane has observed that 'the word "policy" is one of the most under-analysed terms in the modern legal lexicon'.[5] I agree, and would suggest that there is much uncertainty also in the meaning of the word 'principle'. There is never a single agreed principle that applies to a controversial legal question; principles may be stated and restated at an infinite number of levels of generality; often principles conflict with each other; any legal rule, as Hart pointed out, may be called a principle.[6] As with other legal ideas the meaning of the word varies according to what is contrasted: for example, 'principle and policy', 'principle and precedent', 'principle and authority', 'principle and pragmatism', 'principle and practice', 'principle and utility'. Commonly the word is used to signify a reason or rule framed at a higher level of generality than another: 'general principle' as opposed to a particular rule, instance, or application. Principles confidently asserted by one judge or writer may be equally confidently contradicted by others at another time or place, or by dissenting judges at the same time and place. 'In the law of England, certain principles are fundamental. One is that only a person who is a party to a contract can sue on it,' Lord Haldane asserted confidently in 1915.[7] But the law had been different 50 years earlier, and it has changed subsequently, in some jurisdictions by judicial development and in others by statute. On the same point Viscount Simonds said, in 1962, having quoted Lord Haldane's assertion, 'The law is developed by the application of old principles to new circumstances. Therein lies its genius. Its reform by the abrogation of those principles is the task not of the courts of law but of Parliament.'[8] But, in an uncodified system, it is always a matter of judgment whether a proposed change in the law is an application of an established principle or the creation of a new one. The results in particular cases depend entirely on the level of generality at which principles are framed. The denial of specific performance in a land sale contract, for example, has been called a 'principled approach'[9] on the premise that the principle is that specific performance is only available in sales of unique property. But if the principle were stated at a higher level of generality, for example that contracts should be observed, or that sales of land should normally be enforced, the opposite result would appear to be principled. Neil Duxbury has said, with reference to Pollock's attempt to discover the principles of contract law, that 'jurists,

---

5    Cane, P, 'Another Failed Sterilisation,' (2004) 120 LQR 189, 191.
6    Hart, HLA, *The Concept of Law*, 2nd edn, 1994, New York, Oxford University Press 259–60.
7    *Dunlop Pneumatic Tyre Co Ltd v Selfridge & Co Ltd* [1915] AC 847, 853.
8    *Midland Silicones, Ltd v Scruttons, Ltd* [1962] AC 446, 468 (HL).
9    *Domowicz v Orsa Investments Ltd* (1993) 15 OR (3d) 661 at 683, and see *Semelhago v Paramedavan* [1996] 2 SCR 415.

when they dedicate themselves seriously to determining principles of law, will almost inevitably discover instances where those principles are ambiguous, incoherent, insufficiently developed, or even absent.'[10] Commonly the word is used to mean a reason in support of a legal conclusion that the writer considers persuasive, legitimate, or satisfactory: conclusions that are approved are never called unprincipled. The holding that a racially discriminatory contract is unenforceable is clearly an instance where modern policy (against racial discrimination) has overridden a legal principle (enforceability of contracts), but no one who agrees with the policy would venture to describe the holding as 'unprincipled'.

For a speaker at a conference to cast doubt on the meaning of one of the two operative words in the conference title may be regarded as constructive; to cast doubt on both might look like an excess of zeal. But this kind of linguistic indeterminacy is by no means unusual in legal discourse, and certainly does not imply that the issue is unimportant or misdescribed. I think that the conference title is well chosen, but it does invite careful identification of the question to be addressed. The question addressed here is: from a historical perspective, how significant in the determination of private rights have been the judges' perceptions of the public interest? My (modest) conclusion is that these perceptions have been often influential and sometimes determinative. I do not claim that all or even most cases, or legal issues, have been determined by unmediated perceptions of public interest, and I do not claim to have shown that past practice has been beneficial, or that a continuation of it is either inevitable or desirable in the future.[11]

Many shades of opinion are to be found among judges and academics on the question of the relation between private law and public policy. Three main strands may be discerned. First is the view that the two are separate; legal rules are to be derived or deduced strictly from formal legal sources, the function of private law being not the creation of law in the public interest, but the declaration and application of pre-existing law for the prevention and correction of injustice between the individual parties to each dispute. Second, there is the view that when courts are called upon to create a new rule, or to modify an old one, or to extend it to a new situation, they address the question of whether the proposed rule would be, on balance, beneficial to the community; assessment of this question requires the weighing of the costs and benefits of the proposed rule as it will be applied in the future to parties other than the individual litigants in the current case. Third is the view that an

---

10  Duxbury, N, *Frederick Pollock and the English Juristic Tradition*, 2004, Oxford; New York: Oxford University Press, p 191.

11  The preceding pages are based in part on Chs 1 and 11, and the following pages on Ch 10 of Waddams, Stephen, *Dimensions of Private Law: Categories and Concepts in Anglo-American Legal Reasoning*, 2003, Cambridge, UK: New York; Cambridge University Press.

element of judgment is frequently involved that includes broad social and political considerations. There are many intervening combinations and shades of opinion.

The three main views correspond broadly with what may, for sake of convenience, be epitomised as principle, utility, and policy. These have sometimes been presented as competing 'theories', of which the reader is impliedly invited to choose one and reject the other two. But from a historical standpoint they appear rather as complementary strands in a single rope, or different dimensions of a single phenomenon. They merge into each other, because, where a new legal problem presents itself for decision, it has not been possible to consider what would be a just rule for the particular parties without to some extent considering the consequences of the proposed rule in other cases. Principle and policy, though sometimes contrasted, have been in practice inseparable, for principles have been adopted to give effect to policies, and adherence to principle has been itself a policy. Holmes wrote that judges take into account 'what is expedient in the community concerned', adding that 'every important principle which is developed by litigation is in fact and at bottom the result of more or less definitely understood views of public policy'.[12] Emphasis has varied from time to time and from one jurisdiction to another, but elements of all three dimensions have been consistently present, sometimes on the lips of a single judge in different cases, or even in the same case.[13]

In the important eighteenth-century case of *Omychund v Barker*,[14] where the issue was the admissibility of the evidence of a witness who could not take the Christian form of oath, all three dimensions were evident. Counsel (William Murray, later Lord Mansfield), arguing in favour of admissibility, said that the question was 'whether upon principles of reason justice and convenience this witness ought to be admitted'.[15] His fellow counsel (Dudley Rider, also, like Murray, a future Chief Justice of the King's Bench) said that 'trade requires it [admission of the testimony]; policy requires it'. The Lord Chancellor (Hardwicke) relied both on the principle of justice between the parties and on the overt policy consideration that 'if we did not give this credence, courts abroad would not allow our determinations here to be valid'.[16] This was also the case in which Murray said, in urging judicial reform of the law, that the common law 'works itself pure'.[17] The remark has sometimes been quoted out of context to suggest that Murray favoured a purity of formal legal principle, but it is evident that 'purity' did not, in

12  Holmes, OW, *The Common Law*, [1881] 1963, (ed) Howe, MD, Boston: Little, Brown, p 32.
13  Dr Lushington, the nineteenth-century admiralty and ecclesiastical law judge, is a good example. See Waddams, S, *Law, Politics, and the Church of England: the Career of Stephen Lushington, 1782–1873*, 1992, Cambridge, UK; New York: Cambridge University Press.
14  (1744) 1 Atk 21.      15  Id 32.      16  Id 33.      17  Ibid.

Murray's mind, nor in the Chancellor's, exclude considerations of utility and policy, and it certainly did not require that policy decisions should be left to parliament: Murray's argument was to precisely the opposite effect. All three dimensions (principle, utility, and policy) can derive support from historical evidence. But from this it necessarily follows also that historical evidence cannot support a claim of any one of them to be the *exclusive* explanation of private law.

Judicial statements purporting to exclude considerations of public policy have been very frequent. An example often cited is the assertion of Parke B in *Egerton v Brownlow*[18] that:

> It is the province of the judge to expound the law only; the written from the statutes, the unwritten or common law from the decisions of our predecessors and of our existing courts, from text writers of acknowledged authority, and upon the principles to be clearly deduced from them by sound reason and just inference; not to speculate upon what is best, in his opinion, for the advantage of the community. Some of these decisions [past decisions on public policy] may no doubt have been founded upon the prevailing and just opinions of the public good; for instance the illegality of covenants in restraint of marriage or trade. They have become part of the recognized law, and we are therefore bound by them, but we think we are not thereby authorized to establish as law everything which we may think for the public good, and prohibit everything which we think otherwise.[19]

This passage bears some of the marks of its origin as part of a draft collective opinion of the judges summoned to advise the House of Lords. The case was notorious and controversial, the issue being the validity of a provision in a will leaving a large sum of money conditionally on the acquisition of a dukedom, and the fear being that upholding such provisions would lead to corruption. But the judges were not unanimous, and the House of Lords requested their individual opinions.[20] By a large majority the judges agreed with Baron Parke, but in the House of Lords their views were rejected, and the disputed clause was held to be contrary to public policy.

In recent years a formal approach to private law has received the approbation of distinguished academics, including Peter Birks, pressing the logical claims of classification and taxonomy, and Ernest Weinrib, writing from a philosophical standpoint. These writers have (rightly) reminded us that private law cannot dispense with its own forms and its own framework of thought, for if private law were reduced to a means of effecting some extraneous purpose (social, political, or economic), it would in a sense cease

---

18  (1853) 4 HLC 1.        19  Id 123.        20  4 HLC 63. See *The Times*, 2 Aug 1853, 7f.

to be law, and become a mere tool of the extraneous purpose.[21] Others have also stressed the need for internal coherence and for adherence to form, but none would claim to have established by historical evidence that these have, in the past, been the *exclusive* approaches of Anglo-American private law. If law is to be taken on its own terms its actual past, not just an idealised version of it, must be consulted.

Much evidence supports the view that judges have often been influenced by the perceived probable costs and benefits of legal rules. Dr Lushington, in a matrimonial case, where the husband was alleging cruelty, refused to allow himself 'to be led away, by an anxiety to relieve a hardship upon an individual, to do what might cause an infinitely greater injustice to the interests of the public at large'.[22] He was here giving attention to the costs and benefits, as he perceived them, of the then very narrow rule permitting separation only in case of extreme cruelty. The rules governing separation for cruelty were judge-made, and Lushington did not doubt the judicial power to relax them. But he thought relaxation inexpedient. The fact that public and judicial opinion has changed so radically on this question since his time makes all the plainer the extent to which the judges' estimate of the social costs and benefits of the legal rule were influential.

Other judges have addressed the costs and benefits of legal rules in overtly economic terms. In *Bamford v Turnley*,[23] for example, Bramwell LJ said that a person might be liable to pay damages to those injured by a nuisance even though the defendant's activity was, on balance, for the public benefit, by which he meant 'that if all the loss and all the gain were borne and received by one individual, he on the whole would be a gainer'.[24] But such an individual still ought to compensate those who had suffered the losses, because if the activity really were beneficial the defendant could compensate the plaintiff and still show a profit; if not, the activity was, when its full costs were taken into account, not truly profitable:

> It is for the public benefit that trains should run, but not unless they pay their expenses . . . [U]nless the defendant's profits are enough to compensate [the persons injured] I deny that it is for the public benefit he should do what he has done; if they are he ought to compensate.[25]

This is one of the general arguments for strict liability, and similar arguments, based on 'internalisation' of costs, have been adduced in support of strict liability on other legal issues, for example vicarious liability for acts of employees and agents, and injury caused by defective products.

21  Weinrib, E, *The Idea of Private Law*, 1995, Cambridge, Mass: Harvard University Press.
22  *Furlonger v Furlonger* (1847) 5 Not Cas 422.
23  (1862) 3 B & S 62. See Waddams, *Dimensions of Private Law*, Ch 5.    24  3 B & S 85.
25  Ibid.

The purest forms of economic analysis of private law have insisted on a rigorous exclusion of attention to the re-allocation of wealth between the individual parties to the dispute (on the ground that economics is not concerned with the actual distribution of wealth among individuals) and exclusion also of broad considerations of social policy (on the ground that the economic concept of efficiency is a neutral principle independent of social and political considerations). Whatever may be the merits of such rigorous exclusions from an economic point of view, their effect has been to detach this kind of economic analysis from any links with the actual historical institution of Anglo-American private law, for it cannot be effectively denied that the latter has been very materially concerned with the re-allocation of wealth between the individual parties to disputes, and has been concerned also with broad questions of social policy. A more moderate view, held by such influential scholars as Guido Calabresi and Michael Trebilcock, is that economic analysis illuminates the understanding of private law, but does not exclude considerations of justice between the individual parties nor wider considerations of social policy.[26] Economic considerations, though influential, have not been in themselves determinative. As Robert Sharpe put it:

> While the pursuit of efficiency is ... an important legal goal, it is a pursuit qualified by the concept of rights which may not be superseded merely because the general social welfare would be advanced.[27]

Closely related to such cases as *Egerton v Brownlow*, are questions of public policy in contracts. Contracts are not enforceable if contrary to public policy, nor can restitution of contractual payments be obtained in such cases on grounds of unjust enrichment.[28] As Lord Mansfield recognised in 1775, the consequence is to deprive the plaintiff of a result that justice otherwise would require:

> The objection, that a contract is immoral or illegal as between plaintiff and defendant, sounds at all times very ill in the mouth of the defendant. It is not for his sake, however, that the objection is ever allowed; but it is

---

26  Calabresi's best-known article was subtitled *One View of the Cathedral*, with reference to the many aspects of Rouen Cathedral, Calabresi, G and Melamed, A, 'Property Rules, Liability Rules and Inalienability: One View of the Cathedral', 85 Harvard Law Review 1089 (1972); Trebilcock, M, *The Limits of Freedom of Contract*, 1991, Cambridge, Mass: Harvard University Press.

27  Sharpe, R, *Injunctions and Specific Performance*, 1983, Toronto: Canada Law Book, s 4.550.

28  Goff, R and Jones, G, *The Law of Restitution*, London: 5th edn, 1998, pp 67–72, London: Sweet & Maxwell, 1998, Birks, P, 'Recovery of Value Transferred under an Illegal Contract' (2000) 1 Theoretical Inquiries in Law 155.

founded in general principles of policy, which the defendant has the advantage of, contrary to the real justice, as between him and the plaintiff, by accident, if I may so say.[29]

Although at certain periods the courts, in some jurisdictions, have taken a narrow view of the power to declare new heads of public policy,[30] it cannot be doubted that judicial perceptions of public policy have varied from time to time and from place to place: 'public policy is necessarily variable'.[31]

One example of the variability of public policy is the changing judicial attitude in the nineteenth century to separation agreements between husband and wife. Of such agreements Sir George Jessel said:

Judicial opinion has varied a great deal . . . For a great number of years, both ecclesiastical Judges and lay Judges thought it was something very horrible, and against public policy, that the husband and wife should agree to live separate, and it was supposed that a civilized country could no longer exist if such agreements were enforced by Courts of law, whether ecclesiastical or not. But a change came over judicial opinion as to public policy; other considerations arose, and people began to think that after all it might be better and more beneficial for married people to avoid in many cases the expense and the scandal of suits of divorce by settling their differences quietly . . . and that was the view carried out by the Courts when it became once decided that separation deeds *per se* were not against public policy.[32]

A few years earlier the same judge had in another contractual context rejected an appeal to *overt* considerations of public policy, but this does not show that public policy had in fact no influence, for the conclusion itself rested on the judge's perception of what public policy required:

If there is one thing which more than another public policy requires it is that men of full age and competent understanding shall have the utmost liberty of contracting and that their contracts when entered into freely and voluntarily shall be held sacred and shall be enforced by courts of justice.[33]

---

29 *Holman v Johnson* (1775) 1 Cowp 341 at 343.
30 *Fender v St John Mildmay* [1938] AC 1, HL, at 42.
31 Winfield, P, 'Public Policy in the English Common Law', 42 Harvard Law Review 76 at 93 (1929).
32 *Besant v Wood* (1879) 12 Ch D 605 at 620. See also *Davies v Davies* (1886) 36 Ch D 359 at 364 (Kekewich, J).
33 *Printing & Numerical Registering Co v Sampson* (1875) LR 9 Eq 462 at 465 (Sir George Jessel, MR).

The context of this last case was restraint of trade, a doctrine that has reflected differing views of the importance of a free market in various commodities and services.[34] There are many other instances of changes in perceptions of public policy. The attitude to racially discriminatory contracts, and similar provisions in wills, clearly enforceable until the mid-twentieth century,[35] were (by the end of the century) just as clearly unenforceable.[36] Contracts of financial support between unmarried co-habitants, clearly immoral in the nineteenth century[37] were, by the last quarter of the twentieth century, clearly enforceable in most jurisdictions.[38] In the New Jersey case of *Henningsen v Bloomfield Motors*,[39] (a products liability case) the court said:

> Public policy is a term not easily defined. Its significance varies as the habits and needs of a people may vary. It is not static and the field of application is an ever increasing one. A contract or a particular provision therein, valid in one era, may be totally opposed to the public policy of another.[40]

An English judge said a few years later that 'the law relating to public policy cannot remain immutable. It must change with the passage of time. The wind of change blows upon it.'[41]

An example of the influence of public policy on the enlargement of tort liability is vicarious liability for an employee's deliberate wrongdoing. Both the Supreme Court of Canada (1999) and the House of Lords (2001) have held an employer liable for sexual assaults committed by an employee in children's residences. These results were not reached by purely logical inference which, indeed, tended in the opposite direction. Both courts relied on broad considerations of public policy, and Lord Steyn, who gave the leading speech in the English case, warned that:

> [a] preoccupation with conceptualistic reasoning may lead to the absurd conclusion that there can only be vicarious liability if the bank carries on business in defrauding its customers [with reference to a case of fraud by a bank clerk]. Ideas divorced from reality have never held much attraction for judges steeped in the tradition that their task is to deliver principled

---

34  Trebilcock, M, *The Common Law of Restraint of Trade*, 1986, Toronto: Carswell, pp 1–59.

35  See, for example, *Essex Real Estate Co v Holmes* (1930) 37 OWN 392, affd 38 OWN 69, Div Ct, *Re McDougall and Waddell* [1945] 2 DLR 244, *Re Noble and Wolf* [1949] 4 DLR 375, reversed on other grounds [1951] SCR 64.

36  See *Canada Trust Co v Ontario Human Rights Commission* (1990) 69 DLR (4th) 321, Ont CA.

37  See *Fender v St John Mildmay*, n 30 above, at 42.

38  See *Chrispen v Topham* (1986) 28 DLR (4th) 754, affd 39 DLR (4th) 637, Sask CA.

39  32 NJ 358, 121 A 2d 69 (SCNJ, 1960).        40  Id at 121 A 2d 95.

41  *Nagle v Fielden* [1966] 2 QB 633, CA, at 650 (Danckwerts, LJ).

but practical justice. How the courts set the law on a sensible course is a matter to which I now turn.[42]

The words 'absurd', 'reality' and 'sensible', and the rejection of 'conceptualistic' reasons reflect the influence of broad considerations of judgment and policy. The same may be said of *Fairchild v Glenhaven Funeral Services Ltd*[43] where strict requirements of proof of causation were modified in favour of injured employees who could not prove which of various employers had caused their injuries.

There are many examples of the effect of general policy considerations leading to the denial or abridgement of tort liability. The whole law of defamation has been controlled by considerations of freedom of speech. Liability for negligence has also been controlled in some jurisdictions by general considerations of public policy.[44] Recent examples of denial of tort liability on public policy grounds include the decision of the Supreme Court of Canada in *Dobson v Dobson*.[45] In this case, an expectant mother was involved in a car accident allegedly caused by her negligent driving, and the child was born with injuries caused by the accident. The issue was whether the mother, if proved to be negligent, was liable to the child. The Supreme Court of Canada, reversing the two lower courts, held that she was not. In this case, formal legal reasoning and internal logic tended to support the claim, as previous decisions had established that an unborn child, if negligently injured and subsequently born alive, could bring an action against the person responsible for the injuries, and this was conceded, in relation to any person other than the mother.[46] Economic considerations might also be said to support the claim, for it would seem that the cost to the mother of driving carefully must have been less than the expected (discounted) cost of the injury. Some policy considerations might also be said to support the claim, in that encouraging careful driving is beneficial to the community, and that one of the purposes of compulsory liability insurance is to secure a fund for the compensation of those negligently injured in road accidents; in fact the mother personally favoured the claim in the particular case.

But all these considerations were overridden in the mind of the majority of the court by the argument that if the mother were held liable in this case, pregnant women in the future might be subjected to undue restraints on their freedom. In the words of the majority:

---

42 *Lister v Hesley Hall Ltd* [2002] 1 AC 215 at 224.     43 [2003] 1 AC 32 (HL).
44 *Anns v Merton London Borough Council* [1978] AC 728, HL, rejected in *Murphy v Brentwood District Council* [1991] 1 AC 398, HL, but followed in Canada; *Kamloops (City) v Nielsen* [1984] 2 SCR 2, *Cooper v Hobart* (2001) 206 DLR (4th) 193.
45 [1999] 2 SCR 753, 174 DLR (4th) 1.
46 See Klar, L, 'Judicial Activism in Private Law', (2000) 80 Canadian Bar Review 215.

[t]he determination of whether a duty of care should be imposed must be made by considering the effects of tort liability on the privacy and autonomy interests of women, and upon their families, rather than by reference to a formalistic characterization of the conduct in question . . . The public policy concerns raised in this case are of such a nature and magnitude that they clearly indicate that a legal duty of care cannot, and should not, be imposed by the courts on a pregnant woman towards her foetus or subsequently born child.[47]

This is a judgment, as in *Egerton v Brownlow*, on a very general question of social policy, and the judgment in both cases was evidently influenced by the social and political climate of the times. The opposite result in *Egerton v Brownlow* could readily have been reached by saying that testators had a right to dispose of their property as they wished unless Parliament restricted it, and in the *Dobson* case, as the reasoning of the minority demonstrates, by saying that the injured child had a right to compensation according to established legal principles, unless the legislature declared that it should be removed.

To these instances should be added the many cases where considerations of public policy have played an auxiliary role concurrently with considerations of property, contract, wrongdoing, and unjust enrichment. Together these examples show that judgment, in a broad sense, has played an important part, and sometimes a crucial part, in private law adjudication. On the basis of such evidence it was suggested, in the first half of the twentieth century, by the school of thought loosely known as[48] 'American legal realism'[49] that formal legal reasoning was often fictitious, and this line of thinking was taken up in the second half of the twentieth century, and given a powerful political edge, by the school known (again loosely) as 'critical legal studies', and also by writers who have shown that judgment on matters of social policy has often been influenced by disputable assumptions about race and gender. These lines of thinking have drawn attention to an important aspect of the relation between law and policy, and they support the conclusion that judgment on matters of social policy has often played a significant role in adjudication. Attempts to deny this, if they cannot be effectively supported by historical evidence, are likely to encourage a more radical scepticism than they seek to oppose. The conclusion that policy has played an important part,

---

47  Note 45 above at 790 and 797 (SCR), 27 and 32 (DLR).
48  See Twining, W, *Karl Llewellyn and the Realist Movement*, 1973, London, Weidenfeld and Nicolson pointing out that there was no organised 'movement' and that critics often overstated the case against the realists. Corbin, for example, who was identified as a realist in 1930, was certainly not a radical skeptic, and devoted his life's work to his great treatise on contract law.
49  Pound, R, 'The Call for a Realist Jurisprudence' 44 Harvard Law Review 697 (1931).

however, does not establish that it has been the *exclusive* explanation of private law, or that considerations of principle and utility have not also been important.

Closely related to these questions is the capacity of the law to change by judicial decision. This has important implications for the role of the judge and for the relevance, in judicial decision making, of public policy. Judges in civil litigation have had both an adjudicative and a rule-making function. As Joseph Jaconelli put it, 'the adjudicative process in developed legal systems may be said to possess both a private and a public aspect'.[50] Considerations of public policy have been to some degree inescapable, for the court, in making a new rule, has always, implicitly if not expressly, taken into account the probable costs and benefits to potential future litigants of the proposed change. Many judges have been reluctant openly to avow a rule-making function; hence the 'agreeable fiction',[51] or 'fairy tale'[52] that judges only declare and do not make the law. Some would doubt whether the fiction is agreeable, or the tale innocuous, but the judicial reluctance overtly to assume a law-making power has been strongly associated with perceptions of the proper constitutional role of judges and of the need for legal continuity. The relation between the declaratory and law-making functions is complex, for rules may be stated at many different levels of generality, and it is often impossible, even for the decision maker, to distinguish between the application of an existing rule and the making of a new one, for 'the application of existing law to new circumstances can never be clearly distinguished from the creation of a new rule of law'.[53] There may be good reasons for judges and for advocates to disclaim creativity, but legal historians, whose function is different from both, cannot always accept such disclaimers at face value.

It cannot be doubted that the courts, particularly at the appellate level, do change the law, and there are examples from all areas of private law. In 1998 Lord Goff said, 'we all know that in reality, in the common law as in equity, the law is the subject of development by the judges . . . It is universally recognised that judicial development of the common law is inevitable'. It has often been said that the role of the court in changing the law has been 'interstitial',[54] or 'incremental',[55] but it is not very clear what this has meant in

50 Jaconelli, J, 'Hypothetical disputes, Moot Points of Law, and Advisory Opinions' (1985) 101 LQR 587.
51 Herbert, AP, Jocularly, *Uncommon Law*, 1959, London, Methuen, p 156.
52 Seriously by Lord Reid, 'The Judge as Law Maker' (1972) 12 Journal of the Society of Public Teachers of Law (New Series) 22, *Kleinwort Benson Ltd v Lincoln City Council* [1999] 2 AC 349, HL, at 358 (Lord Browne-Wilkinson).
53 Cross, R, *Precedent in English Law*, 1961, Oxford: Clarendon Press, p 22.
54 Justice Holmes in *Southern Pacific Co v Jensen* 244 US 205, 221 (1917).
55 *Winnipeg Child and Family Services (Northwest Area) v DFG* [1997] 3 SCR 925,152 DLR (4th) 193. See Sunstein, CR, *One Case at a Time: Judicial Minimalism and the Supreme Court*, Cambridge, Mass, 1999.

practice. In *London Drugs Ltd v Kuehne & Nagel International Ltd*[56] the Supreme Court of Canada held that an employee (though not himself a party to the contract) might take advantage of an agreement limiting liability for accidental damage to goods. The court, in admitting an exception to the rule against enforcement of contracts by third parties, several times described the change as 'incremental', indicating a reluctance to make a 'major change in the common law involving complex and uncertain ramifications'.[57] From one point of view the court created a single limited exception, leaving the rule of privity otherwise intact. But from another point of view the decision made a very radical change, abolishing the rule *as a rule*, and inviting courts in the future to admit new exceptions whenever 'consistent with modern notions of commercial reality and justice'.[58] In subsequent decisions the court has introduced into maritime law the rules of contributory negligence and of contribution among tortfeasors, and a scheme of liability to third parties for fatal and non-fatal injuries, including compensation for intangible losses.[59] It may well be thought that these were useful improvements to Canadian maritime law, but most observers would not have described these changes as 'incremental'. It had previously been generally supposed that legislation was necessary to introduce into the law the principle of compensation for fatal accidents, to extend that principle to injury to third parties by non-fatal accidents, to extend it further to cover intangible losses, and to introduce the principles of apportionment for contributory negligence, and of contribution among wrongdoers. Several of these questions have 'complex and uncertain ramifications'. It would appear, therefore, that the assertion by the court that judicial development of the law can only be incremental must be read in the light of a generous interpretation of what is meant by 'incremental'. Changes in the law have been important, and frequent, and have often rested on policy grounds.

A significant factor has been the rise, and in some jurisdictions the subsequent decline, in the second half of the twentieth century of law reform commissions. If it can be confidently expected that private law will be regularly reviewed and reformed by legislative commissions, there is correspondingly less need for active judicial law reform. This was a factor that influenced the House of Lords in *Beswick v Beswick*[60] to refrain from amending the contractual rule of privity. Eventually (though not until 30 years later)

---

56 [1992] 3 SCR 299.        57 Id 453.
58 Id 437. See *Fraser River Pile & Dredge, Ltd v Can-Dive Services Ltd* [1999] 3 SCR 108.
59 *Bow Valley Husky (Bermuda) Ltd v Saint John Shipbuilding Ltd* [1997] 3 SCR 1210, *Ordon Estate v Grail* [1998] 3 SCR 437.
60 [1968] AC 58, HL, at 72: 'If one had to contemplate a further long period of parliamentary procrastination, this House might find it necessary to deal with this matter. But if legislation is probable at an early date I would not deal with it in a case where that is not essential.' (Lord Reid).

the rule was reformed in England by statute.[61] When this question came before the Supreme Court of Canada in 1980[62] no reforming action was taken, but when it arose again in 1992 the court, as we have seen, did take action to alter the law.[63] By that date it was clear that Canadian legislatures were unlikely to resolve the problem either promptly, or on a uniform basis.[64] In federal jurisdictions, like Canada and Australia, reform of private law, including the weighing of policy considerations, has largely fallen in practice to the judges.

Public policy has played an important role in many questions of private law, but in two kinds of case it has operated directly so as actually to impose in litigation between individuals obligations to pay rewards and fines. The law of maritime salvage, though closely associated with unjust enrichment, contains an element that cannot be derived from unjust enrichment, namely, reward for the performance of meritorious service. Somewhat analogously, the law of exemplary (punitive) damages permits the imposition of a fine in order to punish and deter conduct that is the reverse of meritorious. Private law concepts, considered alone, do not explain why the reward element in salvage cases should be owed by the defendant, nor why exemplary damages should be payable to the plaintiff.

By admiralty law, a reward (salvage) is payable for saving property at sea. Modern English scholars differ sharply on whether or not salvage law should be included in the law of unjust enrichment. Some writers have included it,[65] but others have doubted whether it should be included within the subject, partly because the services are rendered voluntarily, and partly because the measure of recovery is not exclusively based on the defendant's enrichment.[66] Francis Rose has accommodated the opposing views by leaving open the question of whether salvage strictly forms part of the law of unjust enrichment, while adding that 'it is clear that many

---

61 Contracts (Rights of Third Parties) Act, 1999.
62 *Greenwood Shopping Plaza Ltd v Beatty* [1980] 2 SCR 228.
63 *London Drugs*, n 56 above.
64 The Ontario Law Reform Commission had proposed reform in 1987, but no legislative action was pending or probable in Ontario. The rule was, however, altered by statute in New Brunswick by Law Reform Act, SNB 1993 c L-1.2, s 4(1).
65 Goff, R and Jones, G, *The Law of Restitution*, 1966, London: Sweet & Maxwell, Chapter 15, Steel, D and Rose, F, *Kennedy's Law of Salvage*, 1985, 5th edn, London: Stevens, chapter 16, Klippert, G, *Unjust Enrichment*, 1983, Scarborough, Ont.: Butterworths, p 46, Burrows, A, *The Law of Restitution*, 1993, London: Butterworths, pp 236–8.
66 Lord Wright, *Legal Essays and Addresses*, 1939, Cambridge: Cambridge University Press, p 55, noting with approval the omission of the subject from the American Law Institute's, *Restatement of Restitution*, Birks, P, 1985, *An Introduction to the Law of Restitution*, Oxford: Clarendon Press: New York; Oxford University Press, pp 304–308, Virgo, G, *Principles of the Law of Restitution*, 1999, Oxford: Clarendon Press, p 321, Burrows, A, *The Law of Restitution*, 1993, London, Butterworths, pp 248–49.

of the principles which govern restitution [unjust enrichment] also operate within salvage . . .'.[67]

Salvage law falls within most definitions of private law, and of the law of obligations, in that it imposes legal obligations on private persons for the benefit of other private persons. But there has always been a strong element of public policy. Dr Lushington, judge of the High Court of Admiralty from 1838 to 1867, said (citing Justice Story, the American scholar and judge) that salvage is 'a mixed question of private right and public policy'.[68] He said that the reward is given 'not merely to remunerate the effort made to save the ship, cargo, and lives of the persons on board, but also to encourage others to make similar attempts'.[69] 'Say what you will,' he said in another case, 'so long as human motives operate on conduct, unless you give a reward, you must take away all incitement to service.'[70] He had no doubt of the beneficial effect of salvage law, describing it as 'of the utmost importance to the safety of shipping',[71] and 'absolutely necessary'.[72]

If public policy were the exclusive source of the obligation then one would expect that merit would be rewarded regardless of success. However, one of the chief characteristics of salvage law has been that merit alone is insufficient:

> However meritorious the exertion of alleged salvors may be, if they are not attended with benefit to the owners they cannot be compensated in this Court; salvage reward is for benefit actually conferred in the preservation of property, not for meritorious exertions alone.[73]

A principal reason was that some property had actually to be in the custody of the court to give it jurisdiction.[74] A further indication that public policy was not the sole consideration is that salvage law, until modified by statute in 1846,[75] allowed no reward for saving of life, unless property was also saved.[76] Moreover the very case in which the most generous award was allowed (traditionally one-half of the value salved) was the case of derelict (property abandoned at sea) where human life was not in danger.

---

67 Rose, FD, 'Restitution and Maritime Law' in Schrage, EJH (ed), *Unjust Enrichment and the Law of Contract*. 2001, The Hague, Kluwer, p 367, at p 380.
68 *The Albion* (1861) Lush 282 at 284. The reference is probably to *The Henry Ewbank*, 1 Sumn 400, 11 F Cas 1166, 1170 (CA, Mass, 1833) ('mixed question of public policy and private right').
69 *The William Hannington*, (1845) 9 Jur 641.        70 *The Rosalie* (1853) 1 Sp 188, 189.
71 *The Albion*, n 68 above.        72 *The Neptune* (1858) 12 Moo PC 346, 350.
73 *The India* (1842) 1 W Rob 406, 408.        74 *The Chieftain* (1846) 2 W Rob 450.
75 Wreck and Salvage Act, 9 & 10 Vic, c 90.
76 See *The Bartley* (1857) Swab 198, *The Fusilier* (1865) Br & Lush 341, *Silver Bullion* (1854) 2 Sp 70, *The Coromandel* (1857) Swab 205.

Salvage law cannot be fully explained on contractual principles. No request for the services was necessary,[77] as the case of derelict also shows. Considerations of unjust enrichment were prominent. Lushington spoke often of 'remuneration',[78] 'recompense',[79] 'compensation',[80] and 'what the services were worth'.[81] 'Salvage is governed by a due regard to the benefit received,' Dr Lushington said, while adding, 'combined with a just regard for the general interests of ships and marine commerce.'[82] In giving a large reward for a brief but efficient service Lushington said that 'it is not the mere time occupied; it is not the mere labour, but the real value of the services rendered'.[83]

Many judges have said that salvage is based on principles of natural justice and equity,[84] but this did not mean equity as administered by the Chancery Court, nor did it imply unfettered discretion. The matter might be summed up by saying that salvage law has been influenced principally, but not solely, by considerations of unjust enrichment, and that it cannot be assigned exclusively to any one part of the law of obligations. From one point of view it may be regarded as a kind of imperfect taxation, imposing a surcharge on owners of ships and cargo saved, in order to maintain, in the public interest, a means of inducing seafarers to rescue those in distress. Since salvage law was not part of the common law, and was administered until 1875 by a court entirely separate from the courts of law and of equity, it is scarcely surprising that it does not fit readily into categories derived from the law of obligations.

The direct award of exemplary or punitive damages has been a persistent feature of Anglo-American law, but it has been difficult to justify solely in terms of correction of wrong between the individual parties to the dispute. Nor can it readily be justified by the kind of economic analysis usually applied to private law: the proper measure of deterrence, from an economic point of view, has been said to be the amount of the claimant's loss adjusted by the improbability of a successful claim.[85] The principal arguments against punitive damages in private law are that punishment and deterrence by penal

---

77  *The Annapolis* (1861) Lush 355.
78  *The Inca* (1858) Swab 371, *The Harriett* (1857) Swab 218, *The Undaunted* (1860) Lush 90.
79  *The Syrian* (1866) 14 LT 833.
80  *The Rajasthan* (1856) Swab 171, *The Mary Pleasants* (1857) Swab 224.
81  *The Mary Pleasants*, note 80 above, *The Africa* (1854) 1 Sp 299 ('reward for services rendered'), *The Otto Herman* (1864) 33 LJPMA 189 (payment for 'services').
82  *The Fusilier* (1865) Br & Lush 341, 347.      83  *The General Palmer* (1844) 5 Not Cas 159n.
84  *The Juliana* (1822) 2 Dods 504, 521 (Lord Stowell), *The Calypso* (1828) 2 Hagg 209, 217 (Sir Christopher Robinson), *The Harriet* (1853) 1 Sp 180, and *Cargo ex Capella* (1867) 1 A & E 356 (Dr Lushington), *The Beaverford v The Kafiristan* [1938] AC 136 at 147 (Lord Wright).
85  Posner, R, *Economic Analysis of Law*, 1972, Little, Brown, Boston, p 77. The fifth edn (New York, 1998) appears to allow a wider scope to punitive damages.

sanctions are proper functions not of private law but of criminal or penal law. The institution of punitive damages enables the court in the course of civil litigation to create and define penal offences, and then to punish them without many of the protections that penal law usually affords to persons accused of crime.[86] From an administrative point of view, ad hoc punishment by civil courts is not an effective means of regulation, and may have the counterproductive effect of punishing conduct that has deliberately been approved in the public interest by a regulatory agency.[87] Where the defendant is a large enterprise or a government agency, the cost of the award will not be borne by any person who is actually guilty of the objectionable conduct, but will in practice be passed on to a large section of the community. There is no reason, from the perspective of private law, why a fine, imposed for purposes of punishment and deterrence in the interest of the community, should go into the plaintiff's pocket. Claims for punitive damages complicate private litigation by making relevant many facts, such as the defendant's motives, overall wealth, and conduct in previous cases, that would normally be irrelevant, and they impede settlement because of the radical uncertainty of the probable amount of the award, especially when this is in the hands of a jury. Cumulatively, these arguments amount to a cogent case against punitive damages.[88] Objections of this sort led the House of Lords in 1963 to limit punitive damages to two kinds of case[89] but not to abolish them entirely.[90] Other Commonwealth jurisdictions have retained and in some cases expanded the scope of punitive damages.[91] American jurisdictions have been notorious for large awards of punitive damages,[92] and, despite some legislative and judicial restrictions introduced in the 1980s and 1990s,[93] they retain an

---

86 Burden of proof, right to remain silent, right to jury trial, right to sentencing by a judge, right to appeal against sentence, protection against double jeopardy.

87 Eg, a pharmaceutical drug that is beneficial to the community but poses an inevitable risk to a few. There is a strong argument here for compensatory damages to the person injured if the drug is defective but not for punitive damages.

88 Beever, Alan, 'The Structure of Aggravated and Exemplary Damages' (2003) 23 Ox JLS 27.

89 Profit made from the wrong, and abuse of government power. A third exception was express statutory provision.

90 *Rookes v Barnard* [1964] AC 1129, HL, *Thompson v Commissioner of Police of the Metropolis* [1998] QB 498, CA. *Kuddus v Chief Constable of Leicestershire Constabulary* [2002] 2 AC 122, HL, exhibits a comparatively friendly attitude to exemplary damages.

91 *Uren v John Fairfax & Sons Pty Ltd* (1966) 117 CLR 118, [1969] 1 AC 590 (PC), *Donselaar v Donselaar* [1982] 1 NZLR 97, *Hill v Church of Scientology of Toronto* [1995] 2 SCR 1130, *Botiuk v Toronto Free Press Publications Ltd* [1995] 3 SCR 3, *Vorvis v Insurance Corp of British Columbia* [1989] 1 SCR 1085, *Royal Bank of Canada v W Gott & Associates Electric Ltd* [1999] 3 SCR 408, *Whiten v Pilot Insurance Co* (2002) 209 DLR (4th) 257 (SCC).

92 Eg, *Grimshaw v Ford Motor Co* (1981) 174 Cal Rptr 348 ($125m reduced to $3.5m), *Texaco Inc v Penzoil Co* 729 SW 2d 768 (Tex CA, 1987) ($3 billion).

93 *BMW of North America Inc v Gore* 517 US 559 (1996). State statutes are collected in Schlueter, L, and Redden, K, *Punitive Damages*, 4th ed (2 vols, New York, 2000), Chapter 20.

important place in American law. The persistence of deterrent and punitive elements in Anglo-American private law shows that no rigid division has in practice been sustained between corrective and compensatory considerations on the one hand, and punitive, deterrent, and public policy considerations on the other.

The evidence, overall, establishes that judicial perceptions of public policy have often played an important (and sometimes a decisive) role in Anglo-American private law. It follows that considerations of formal legal logic and internal coherence have not been everything. But it does not follow that they have been nothing. The two most influential American judges of the twentieth century have stressed the simultaneous presence of formal and policy considerations. Holmes' statement that 'the life of the law has not been logic; it has been experience' has usually been quoted out of its context. Holmes' immediately preceding words were 'it is something to show that the consistency of a system requires a particular result, but it is not all'.[94] Cardozo spoke also of 'the demon of formalism [that] tempts the intellect with the lure of scientific order', but added:

> I do not mean, of course, that judges are commissioned to set aside existing rules at pleasure in favor of any other set of rules which they may hold to be expedient or wise. I mean that when they are called upon to say how far existing rules are to be extended or restricted, they must let the welfare of society fix the path, its direction and its distance.[95]

Cardozo's opinion, like Holmes', was that 'logical consistency does not cease to be a good because it is not the supreme good'.[96] Historical evidence supports these opinions: both principle and policy have, in the past, been influential in Anglo-American private law, and so closely interrelated as to be inseparable. Vicarious liability, for example, is seen to be good policy partly because, by internalising costs, it creates an incentive to avoid (at least some) injuries, but partly also because, as between the injured claimant and the enterprise, justice requires the cost of (at least some) injuries to be borne by the enterprise. Neither of these reasons, standing alone, would be sufficient to justify the current rule of vicarious liability, and neither has been carried to its logical conclusion, but together they support a rule that is perceived to be sound in principle partly *because* it is perceived also as good policy, and vice versa.

It was an important and difficult aspect of vicarious liability that led the

94  Holmes, *The Common Law*, p 1.
95  Cardozo, B, *The Nature of the Judicial Process*, 1921, New Haven: Yale University Press, rep (New Haven, 1963), pp 66–7.
96  Id 32.

Supreme Court of Canada to make, almost simultaneously, the following two statements: 'judicial policy must yield to legal principle,'[97] and 'the best route to enduring principle may well lie through policy.'[98] Though apparently contradictory on their face, each of these statements may be supported, from a historical point of view, as capturing a different dimension of a complex interrelationship, for no clear distinction between policy and principle has, in the past, been sustained. To quote Peter Cane again, '[in a sense] all rules and principles that state individuals' rights and obligations are underpinned by policy arguments because policy arguments are arguments about what individuals' legal rights and obligations ought to be'.[99] Approaching the question from one angle, legal principle has often yielded to policy; looking at the matter from another angle, what was initially a policy reason has often been subsequently recognised as a 'principle' when regularly applied by the courts and approved by commentators.

---

97  *Jacobi v Griffiths* [1999] 2 SCR 570 at 593, 174 DLR (4th) 71, at 89 (Binnie, J, for a majority).
98  *Bazley v Curry* [1999] 2 SCR 534 at 551, 174 DLR (4th) 45, at 58 (McLachlin, J, for the whole court).
99  Note 5 above, at 192.

# Part II

# Tort law policy

Chapter 2

# Taking disagreement seriously: courts, legislatures and the reform of tort law

*Peter Cane* *

## Introduction

> ... Parliaments, motivated by political considerations and sometimes
> responding to the 'echo chamber inhabited by journalists and public mor-
> alists', may impose exclusions, abolish common law rules, adopt 'caps' on
> recovery and otherwise act in a decisive and semi-arbitrary way. Judges, on
> the other hand, have the responsibility of expressing, refining and applying
> the common law in new circumstances in ways that are logically reasoned
> and shown to be a consistent development of past decisional law ... judges
> have no authority to adopt arbitrary departures from basic doctrine
> (Kirby J in *Cattanach v Melchior* [2003] HCA 38 at [137]).

The purpose of this chapter is to reflect on two related topics, namely the relationship between common law and statute, and the relationship between courts and legislatures. These reflections are prompted by two recent developments in tort law. The first is the Australian Commonwealth Government's Review of the Law of Negligence (2002) and its legislative aftermath;[1] and the second is a set of judicial decisions in Australia and the UK concerned with the recoverability of damages for loss arising out of the birth of a child. These two developments, and the two topics I want to discuss, are neatly juxtaposed in the quotation at the head of this chapter. It is taken from a case dealing with liability for damages for the cost of rearing a child born as a result of a failed sterilisation procedure, and in a footnote to the passage Kirby J refers to the *Review* to back up his point about the 'decisive and semi-arbitrary' nature of legislation.

* Law Program, Research School of Social Sciences, Australian National University, Canberra. Thanks to Tony Connolly and Leighton McDonald for stimulating discussion and penetrating comments. This article was first published in (2005) 25 *Oxford Journal of Legal Studies* 393–417 and is reproduced with the permission of Oxford University Press.
1 Commonwealth of Australia, *Review of the Law of Negligence*, (Canberra, September 2002) (hereafter '*Review*'). Declaration of interest: the author was a member of the review panel.

This chapter is structured as follows: first, it provides a brief account of the two developments that will frame the discussion. Next, it draws out of the debates surrounding these developments two somewhat conflicting views about the relationship between courts and legislatures, common law and statute. One is that common law is superior to statute because it is the product of reason not power; and the other is that judges should not base their decisions, and the rules and principles supporting them, on their personal views about what the law ought to be. In the rest of the chapter, I will suggest that if we take seriously the fact of genuine, reasonable and intractable disagreement about values, and pervasive uncertainty about the effects of law, we should reject both views. Other things being equal, we should prefer statute law to common law and allow judges, in developing the common law, to give effect to their personal beliefs and values.

## Two recent legal developments in tort law

### The Review: Courts and Legislatures

In 2001 and 2002 Australia experienced what has been called an 'insurance crisis'. In this period, premiums for public liability and medical indemnity insurance, in particular, rose very sharply, and the supply of these forms of insurance shrank considerably. The causes of these events have been much debated; and in the nature of the case, it is very difficult to be confident about the causal relationships between the crisis and its various suggested triggers.[2] However, a popular target for blame was an alleged increase in litigiousness, associated with a new 'culture of blame' and encouraged by judicial generosity in the form of excessively large damages awards and 'stretching' of tort liability rules in favour of 'undeserving' claimants. The *Review* was established partly to address these popular perceptions of the role of law, lawyers, and the courts in precipitating the insurance crisis.

The *Review* was underpinned by two fundamental propositions. The first was that by making it harder for claimants to recover damages for personal injuries and by reducing the amounts of damages recoverable, the rate of increase of premiums for insurance against liability for personal injuries could be slowed. The second underpinning proposition was that personal injuries law, as it had been developed and applied by courts in the last decades of the twentieth century, struck the balance of responsibility between injurers and the injured too much in favour the latter group. The first proposition is clearly empirical and capable, in theory at least, of being proved or disproved by investigating the link between liability rules and the cost of liability insurance. The second proposition is essentially normative; but it was given an

---

2   For a discussion see Cane, P, 'Reforming Tort Law in Australia (2003) 27 Melbourne ULR 649.

empirical twist by critics of the *Review* who argued that the *Review* was unnecessary because Australian courts – especially the High Court – had already readjusted the law in the desired pro-defendant direction. Both propositions were and are contestable and contested.

The purpose of the *Review* was to propose changes to the law that would be given effect by parliamentary legislation. One strand of the debates surrounding the insurance crisis and the establishment of the *Review* was distrust of courts and a feeling that recent judicial activity had set personal injuries law on the wrong course. Because of the suddenness and severity of the insurance crisis, it was felt that only legislative action offered any hope of relief in the short or intermediate term. And because the insurance situation was perceived to be a crisis, politicians felt that something had to be done about it very quickly. As a result, the *Review* had to be carried out in a very short time. In fact, only about 11 weeks elapsed between the review panel's first meeting and the publication of its final report. Despite the speed with which the *Review* was conducted, its terms of reference were extremely broad, inviting and, indeed, requiring the panel to make recommendations about many of the most fundamental aspects of personal injury law. Because the *Review* was a product of strong political will, all jurisdictions in Australia have enacted legislation to give effect to many of its recommendations. The resulting tapestry of legislative provisions is extremely complex.

As was to be expected, the *Review* generated much controversy. Underlying many of the criticisms was an idea that personal injury law is primarily a matter for the courts rather than for legislatures. This line of argument was powerfully developed by Justice Peter Underwood, writing in 2003,[3] and he deserves to be quoted at length. Although legislatures have concerned themselves with the common law of negligence at least since the enactment of Lord Campbell's Act in 1846,

> the last 12 months or so have seen an unprecedented outburst of legislation effecting major changes to the common law of negligence (54) . . . generally speaking the legislative changes over the last two centuries have been ameliorative. Neither singly nor collectively did they effect wide-ranging changes to the principles that have been gradually and carefully worked out by the courts over time. The legislation that has been enacted over the last few months is a wholesale attack on those principles (55) . . . this is a very dangerous development . . . for . . . the common law. It will become uncertain. No one will know whether a particular aspect of the common law will or will not fall under the legislative knife . . . wielded in accordance with the political beliefs of the party that happens to be

3  The Hon Justice Underwood P, 'Is Mrs Donoghue's Snail in Mortal Peril? (2004) 12 Torts LJ 39. The basic arguments are old. See eg Pound, R, 'Common Law and Legislation' (1908) 21 Harvard LR 383, 404.

in power from time to time. Historically, legislative incursions into the common law have been restrained and largely remedial. Recently all that has changed. Legislation is enacted instantaneously and as an immediate response to perceived, but untested, economic factors . . . [T]here is every danger of . . . judicial development being subject to the unnecessary superior and instantaneous editing of the legislature (60).

The foundation of this complex set of arguments appears to be an implied assertion that prime responsibility for making and developing personal injury law ought to rest with the courts rather than with the legislature. When the legislature interferes with the common law, it should do so in a restrained and incremental way. Legislatures should not act quickly, or on the basis of controversial value-judgments and contestable assertions about the social or economic effects of the common law or of proposed legislative intervention. Nor should governments monitor the work of courts to ensure its consistency with contemporary values, because this would threaten the 'stability' of the common law.

Justice Underwood's preference for judicial over parliamentary law-making, and for the common law over statute is shared by Kirby J. In the passage from which the quotation at the head of this chapter is drawn, Kirby J acknowledges that the basic common law principle, of liability for negligently-caused injury, has to be subject to certain bounds. Where these bounds should be set, he believes, is a matter of 'policy'. Even so, the job of setting them is properly one for courts rather than legislatures because, he says, 'The setting of such bounds by a legislature can be arbitrary and dogmatic.' Then follows the passage I have quoted: parliaments cannot be trusted to set the limits of negligence liability because they are prone to be motivated by 'political considerations' and influenced, by public opinion and the media, to pursue social and economic objectives that may be inconsistent with established common law rules and principles. Because the common law is based on 'reason' and 'logic', legislative departures from it are likely to be 'arbitrary'.

At some risk of misrepresentation and oversimplification, what might be called 'the Underwood/Kirby argument' can be summarised in three propositions:

1   Prime responsibility for making, as well as applying, negligence law should rest with the courts.
2   Therefore, parliamentary law-making in the area of negligence law should be exceptional and incremental, and both consistent with and supportive of the common law.
3   Moreover, such statutory interventions should not be based on contestable assertions about the effects of the law, or on controversial value-judgments about its substance.

*Damages for loss arising from birth: Judicial Law-Making*

The main focus here is on cases in which parents claim damages for the cost of bringing up a child who would not have been born but for the negligence of a medical practitioner. By the late 1990s English case-law favoured the propositions that such damages were recoverable by the parents of an 'unplanned' child, but not by the child personally. The first of these propositions was rejected by the House of Lords in *McFarlane v Tayside Health Board* in 2000.[4] This case concerned a healthy child born to a healthy mother, and was subsequently distinguished in *Parkinson v St James and Seacroft University Hospital NHS Trust*,[5] in which damages were awarded to a healthy parent for such of the costs of rearing a disabled child as were attributable to the disability. In 2003 in *Rees v Darlington Memorial Hospital NHS Trust*[6] the House of Lords was confronted with a case in which a healthy child was born to a seriously disabled mother. The decision in *McFarlane* was unanimously reaffirmed, but the majority also held that general damages of £15,000 were recoverable in recognition of the fact that the mother had suffered a legal wrong (consisting of an interference with her reproductive autonomy). The status of the decision in *Parkinson* was left unclear: three of the seven Law Lords considered that it was correctly decided, two impliedly overruled it, and the other two were somewhat equivocal about its correctness. Meanwhile, the High Court of Australia decided, by a 4–3 majority, that damages were recoverable for the cost of bringing up an unplanned child born as a result of a doctor's negligence.[7] As far as I am aware, no superior court in England or Australia has been confronted with a claim by a disabled parent for damages for the cost of bringing up an unplanned disabled child. However, the New South Wales Court of Appeal has held, by majority, that a disabled child, who would not have been born but for the negligence of a medical practitioner, cannot recover damages on its own account for either pecuniary or non-pecuniary loss attributable to the disability.[8]

Despite his disparaging remarks about legislation, Kirby's J's main concern in *Cattanach v Melchior* was not with the respective roles of courts and legislatures in making negligence law but rather with the respective natures of judicial and 'political' law-making techniques and processes. In order to understand the position in which Kirby J found himself it is necessary first to observe that McHugh and Gummow JJ (with whom Kirby and Callinan JJ agreed in the result) apparently thought that the case presented no novel legal issue, and that a decision in favour of the plaintiff followed from

4  [2000] 2 AC 59.      5   [2002] QB 226.      6   [2004] 1 AC 309.
7  *Cattanach v Melchior* (2003) 215 CLR 1. The decision has been partially reversed by legislation in New South Wales (Civil Liability Act 2002, ss 70,71) and Queensland (Civil Liability Act 2003, ss 49A, 49B).
8  *Harriton v Stephens* (2004) 59 NSWLR 694. This decision has since been affirmed by the High Court of Australia; *Harriton v Stephens* (2006) 226 ALR 291.

straightforward application of well-established rules and principles of tort law. By contrast, Kirby J's view was that neither 'authority'[9] nor established principle provided a clear answer to the question posed to the Court. However, Kirby J considered himself bound by 'authority' of the High Court not to have recourse to 'policy' to resolve a novel question of law even though, in his view, if such recourse is not explicit, it will inevitably be implicit in judicial reasoning. As a result of this self-denying ordinance, Kirby J was led to adopt the strategy of arguing that the rule he favoured was consistent with (even though not required by) established legal principles, while other suggested rules were 'arbitrary' and (perhaps synonymously) 'contrary to ordinary principles', and could only be supported by arguments of policy that should be addressed to the legislature. Judges, he said, have no business appealing to their own 'religious beliefs or "moral" assessments' to resolve novel issues in tort law.

The view, that established legal principles justified and required a decision in favour of plaintiffs, presented Heydon J with a different problem, because he dissented from the majority's decision. His strategy was to look for arguments to support his dissent in what he called 'the policy of the law'. McHugh and Gummow JJ distinguished between the policy of the law and 'legal policy'.[10] Their view seems to be that the policy of the law is a legitimate source of justifications for judicial decisions, whereas legal policy is not. This is because they identify legal policy with individual judges' views about what is 'fair, just and reasonable', whereas they identify the policy of the law with arguments that are in some sense inherent in the existing body of legal materials. This seems to be the sense in which Heydon J uses the term 'the policy of the law'. So understood, policies 'of the law' are abstract legal propositions that explain or rationalise relatively less abstract legal propositions. Heydon J's opinion appears to have been that even if a decision in favour of the plaintiff would have been consistent with rules and principles of tort law, it would have been inconsistent with the 'policy of the law' concerning the obligations of parents towards their children and the sanctity of life, and so could not be justified.

The most noteworthy feature of Heydon J's methodology is the way he goes about identifying relevant policies of the law. We might understand his methodology as exploiting a feature of common law norms pointed out many years ago by Julius Stone, namely that they can be stated at different levels of generality;[11] and the process of stating a common law norm at a level of

---

9  Since the High Court is not bound by its own decisions or those of any other court, as used by Kirby J this term must refer to something like 'a consensus of relevant judicial opinion as reflected in published reasons for decision'.

10  (2003) 215 CLR 1 at [70]–[75].

11  Stone, J, 'The *Ratio* of the *Ratio Decidendi*' (1959) 22 MLR 597.

generality other than that at which it was initially stated is not generally understood to involve generating a new norm. We might think of a common law norm as being like the sound of a bell, which consists not only of a dominant note but also of various less obvious notes that are harmonically related to the dominant. A common law norm, however formulated, is (we might say) the dominant member of a set of related propositions formulated at various levels of abstraction, all of which are part of the law even if some of them have never been explicitly stated: the 'harmonic theory of the common law', if you like.[12] Extending the metaphor, we might describe policies of the law as abstract norms that are harmoniously related to less abstract norms in the sense that the more abstract norms explain and rationalise the less abstract. In this way, such policies may be understood to be part of the law even if they have never been explicitly formulated or recognised as such.

Heydon J takes the argument one step further. His judgment suggests that in his view, policies of the law can be harmonics of statutory rules as well as common law rules. When he talks about the policies of 'the law' he apparently refers to the whole body of legal materials, statutory and common law. Nor is his search for relevant policies constrained by legal taxonomy. So for example, the search for policies relevant to deciding an issue classified as one of tort law is not limited to legal materials that are understood to be part of tort law. Heydon J, we might say, proposes a 'seamless web theory of law'. Moreover, the harmonic understanding of law works in both directions, as it were. Just as more abstract policies are implicit in less abstract norms, so less abstract norms may be implicit in more abstract policies. This means that policies that are abstracted from certain, less abstract norms can be concretised into different, less abstract norms. This is how, for instance, policies about the relationship between parents and children read out of 'family law' materials might be used to justify rules of 'tort law'.

The aim of this sophisticated methodology is, apparently,[13] to enable judges to develop the common law without appealing to their own values or to extra-legal norms. It does this by allowing values to be imported into the common law from statute and by allowing one area of law to be cross-fertilised with values derived from other areas of the law. In terms of traditional common law reasoning, the harmonic theory is quite orthodox, but the seamless-web theory is extremely radical, both in the boldness of its attribution of 'gravitational force' to statutes[14] and in its disregard for legal categories. Of course, the degree of constraint imposed upon judicial creativity by this methodology depends crucially on how much freedom judges have to inject

---

12 Concerning legal melody see Postema, GJ, 'Melody and Law's Mindfulness of Time' (2004) 17 Ratio Juris 203.
13 See the Hon Justice Dyson Heydon, 'Judicial Activism and the Death of the Rule of Law' (2004) 10 Otago LR 493.
14 For a classic discussion see Atiyah, PS, 'Common Law and Statute Law' (1985) 48 MLR 1.

their own values into the processes of abstraction and re-concretisation, and into the identification of policies relevant to particular disputes.

The birth cases neatly illustrate two other techniques for dealing with cases in which the existing legal materials are not considered to require resolution of a dispute one way or the other. Lord Steyn has attracted considerable criticism for his invocation of 'commuters on the London Underground' as a source of relevant value-judgments.[15] Of course, judicial appeal to community values has a long history and is a popular ploy to overcome the democratic deficit under which courts are widely thought to labour.[16] For some, the problem with Lord Steyn's approach is not its recourse to popular views but rather its appeal to the views of a particular social group. Such critics would perhaps not object to judges giving effect to opinions and attitudes that could convincingly be said to have widespread and significant support in the community at large.[17]

A second technique for dealing with novel tort cases is neatly exemplified by the approach of Spigelman CJ in *Harriton v Stephens*.[18] The issue in this case was whether a disabled child could recover damages from a medical practitioner without whose negligence the child would not have been born. A majority of the New South Wales Court of Appeal decided against the plaintiff. Ipp J argued that this decision was required by the application of established legal principles. By contrast, Spigelman CJ thought that the existing legal materials provided no conclusive answer to the question confronting the court. In his view, deciding the case required recourse to ethical principles. However, he observed that the relevant principles were 'highly contestable and strenuously contested',[19] and that there was no widely accepted ethical principle that would have resolved the dispute before the court. He concluded that, *for this reason*, the court should decide against the plaintiff. This approach of 'judicial conservatism in the face of intractable disagreement about values' is fundamentally flawed. Once it is accepted that the existing legal materials do not require a decision one way or the other, a decision either way is, in a significant sense, a development of the legal materials. In such situations, judicial conservatism is no more normatively neutral than judicial 'activism'.[20] Once

---

15 *McFarlane v Tayside Health Board* (2000) 2 AC 59, 82; criticised, eg, by Hoyano, LCH, 'Misconceptions about Wrongful Conception' (2002) 65 MLR 883.

16 For a useful catalogue see Sadurski, W, 'Conventional Morality and Judicial Standards' (1989) 73 Virginia LR 339, 351–4.

17 For a careful statement of such an approach see Eisenberg, MA, *The Nature of the Common Law*, 1988, Cambridge, Mass: Harvard University Press, esp 14–26, 149–153. From my perspective, Eisenberg does not take disagreement seriously enough.

18 (2004) 59 NSWLR 694.      19 Ibid [24].

20 Similarly, as Eisenberg argues, application of a common law rule by a judge who has formal power to develop or change it involves a (typically implicit) reaffirmation of the arguments that supported adoption of the rule: op cit n 17 above, esp 75–6, 151–4. In the common law, the content and justification of rules are inextricably intertwined. It is only by giving the

it is accepted that the law can 'run out', as it were, there is no escape from the conclusion that the judicial obligation, to resolve disputes properly brought before the courts, requires judges to develop the existing body of legal materials by adding normative propositions to it. The important issue concerns the obligations of judges in performing that task.

These various techniques utilised in the birth cases are designed to protect judges from the accusation of appealing to their own beliefs and values.

### Taking stock

The debates surrounding the *Review* and the 'birth cases' reveal two rather conflicting attitudes to the proper role of courts in developing tort law. One is that the common law is superior to statute because it is the product of reason, because it develops incrementally and organically, and because it creates stability. This sort of approach has a long lineage which can be traced back to views about the common law that were developed in the late Middle Ages, celebrated by Blackstone in his *Commentaries on the Law of England* in the late eighteenth century, and savagely attacked by Jeremy Bentham in the nineteenth century.[21] The second attitude expressed in recent debates finds judicial law-making problematic because it lacks the legitimacy that parliamentary law-making derives from principles of representative and responsible government. This approach is neatly stated by McHugh and Gummow JJ in *Cattanach*:

> Much of the maturation of the policy of the law . . . took place in England in cases decided in a period in which the body of statute law was comparatively small, representative and responsible government as now understood was in its infancy, and there was no universal franchise. Much has changed.[22]

Because judicial law-making lacks legitimacy, so the argument goes, it is not appropriate for judges to appeal to 'policy' or to their own values and beliefs in deciding how to resolve cases not covered by existing rules and principles.

The aim of the rest of this chapter is to argue that if we take seriously the

---

formulation of a rule canonical status that this link can be broken. This characteristic of the common law explains the sense in which it is based on reason(ing), and why judges have an obligation to give reasons for their decisions.

21  See generally Postema, GJ, *Bentham and the Common Law Tradition*, 1986, Oxford: Clarendon Press; Lieberman, D, *The Province of Legislation Determined: Legal Theory in Eighteenth-Century Britain* 1989, Cambridge: Cambridge University Press, esp Chs 1 and 11; Lobban, M, *The Common Law and English Jurisprudence 1760–1850*, 1991, Oxford: Clarendon Press, esp Chs 2 and 9.

22  *Cattanach v Melchior* (2003) 215 CLR 1 at [74]. See also [82]–[83].

fact that people often genuinely, reasonably, and intractably disagree about what the law ought to be, we should reject both of these views. The first step will be to explore the implications of disagreement for our understanding of law-making by judges and legislators respectively. Then the two developments just surveyed can be reconsidered.

## Legalization

Law provides reasons for action or, in other words, 'practical reasons'.[23] Typically, these reasons take the form of rules and principles of general application that is 'norms'.[24] Legal norms constitute a subset of the 'universe of norms', which includes moral norms, religious norms, norms of etiquette and so on. Some norms are 'uniquely legal' in the sense that they exist solely by virtue of belonging to the set of legal norms.[25] But many legal norms replicate norms that exist elsewhere in the universe of norms.[26] I will refer to the process of incorporating norms into the body of legal norms as 'legalization' of norms. For present purposes, I prefer this term to 'law making' because it reminds us that legal norms do not come from nowhere.[27] Most legal norms exist outside the law before they are given legal force; and uniquely legal norms typically supplement or elaborate pre-existing, extra-legal norms. The term 'legalization' also emphasises that legal norms are a subset of the universe of norms.

Legalization of norms performs various functions. It makes available institutional resources for interpreting, applying and enforcing[28] norms and for resolving disputes about their existence, interpretation, application and enforcement. Legalization also gives access to resources for refining, elaborating and 'determining'[29] the content of norms. In the case of uniquely legal

---

23  As opposed to 'theoretical reasons', which are reasons for belief.

24  The word 'norm' is sometimes used to refer to court orders as well as to the common law and statutory rules and principles that support them: eg Gardner, J, 'The Legality of Law' (2004) 17 Ratio Juris 168. I will distinguish between them and refer only to the latter as 'norms'.

25  The rule designating the side of the road on which to drive is a classic example.

26  I do not mean to imply by the word 'exist' any particular view about the nature of values, such as 'realism' as opposed to 'conventionalism'. All I mean by saying that a norm exists outside the law is that there are people for whom it provides a reason for action regardless of whether it is a legal norm.

27  For a richly suggestive historical reflection on this theme see Milsom, SFC, 'The Past and the Future of Judge-Made Law' (1981) 8 Monash LR 1.

28  Law is coercive but also, from a different perspective, it regulates the use of coercion ('self-help'). From this latter perspective, although legal coercion certainly needs to be justified, the very fact that its use is regulated by legal norms provides part of the justification, given the alternative of unregulated, extra-legal, 'private' coercion.

29  In the philosophy of St Thomas Aquinas, 'determinatio' refers to the process of giving concrete content to abstract values: Finnis, J, Natural Law and Natural Right, 1980, Oxford: Clarendon Press, 284–9.

norms, it provides a reason to comply with the norm where none may have existed previously; and in the case of 'replicative' legal norms, it can provide an additional reason to act in accordance with the norm. For a person who would comply with a particular norm because they agree with its content, the law can provide an additional 'content-independent' reason to comply – 'just because it is the law'.[30] Moreover, because law can provide content-independent reasons for action for those who respect legal institutions and the legal system, such people may be prepared to comply with legal norms that they do *not* agree with, simply because they are the law. Because the law can give people content-independent reasons to comply with its norms, legalization provides an important technique for managing, if not resolving, intractable, and potentially socially-divisive, disagreements about how to behave.[31] This disagreement-management function of legalization will play a central role in the argument that follows.

There are two basic modes of norm-legalization: adjudicative and legislative. Resolving disputes about the existence, application and enforcement of norms is one of the basic 'law jobs' and one of law's major institutional contributions to the regulation of human behaviour. It may be that this was the first law job to be institutionalised.[32] We might imagine the process of legalization beginning with the referral of disputes to a neutral third party; and we might first identify 'courts' and 'judges'[33] when such third parties are recognised as 'public' or 'state' officials. What we now call 'the common law' can be understood as a response to a demand that courts and judges act consistently by articulating general normative propositions to support 'orders' or 'decisions' made to resolve individual disputes.[34] Common law norms are by-products of resolving disputes consistently.[35] Legalization of norms

---

30 Note that the concept of content-independence I am using is different from that discussed by Markwick, P, 'Law and Content-Independent Reasons' (2000) 20 OJLS 579.
31 Honoré, T, 'The Dependence of Morality on Law' (1993) 13 OJLS 1.
32 There is certainly a theoretical argument for concluding that without dispute-resolving institutions, there can be no legal system: Raz, J, *The Authority of Law*, 1979, Oxford: Clarendon Press, Ch 6.
33 I use both of these terms broadly and generically to signify adjudicative bodies that have the power to legalise norms. Not all adjudicators recognised by the legal system have this power.
34 The historical story is complicated, of course: Baker, JH, *An Introduction to English Legal History*, 2002, London: Butterworths, 4th edn, 196–201; Milson, SFC, *A Natural History of the Common Law*, 2003, New York: Columbia University Press, Ch 1 (and see p 75 for the suggestion that legislation rides on the back of the common law). See also Lord Rodger of Earlsferry, 'What Are Appeal Courts For?' (2004) 10 Otago LR 517, 517–19.
35 On the relationship between consistency (ie norm-governed behaviour) and 'formal' justice see Gardner, J, 'The Virtue of Justice and the Character of Law' (2000) 53 *Current Legal Problems* 1.

through adjudication remains an important governmental technique despite the modern dominance of legislation as a source of law.[36]

Courts resolve disputes when and because they are asked to. In this sense, going to court involves bringing a dispute, which has arisen outside the law, into the legal system. The more disputes the courts resolve, the larger the body of norms generated as a by-product. In the early morning of a legal system, as it were, courts have much work to do turning norms into legal norms.[37] As the body of legal norms grows, courts become increasingly involved in refining, developing, adjusting and altering norms that have already been legalised; but even in mature legal systems, there is an important sense in which disputes about legal norms arise outside the law and are brought to the courts – people still 'go to law'.[38] Moreover, even in highly developed legal systems, courts may be asked to legalise norms as opposed to being asked to refine, alter or develop already-legalised norms.

Making 'legislation' (both primary and secondary) is the process of legalising norms independently of settling individual disputes.[39] Because legislation is not tied to dispute-resolution, the process of 'legislative legalization' is very different from the process of dispute-related or 'adjudicative' legalization. Adjudication is essentially 'triadic', involving the presentation of 'arguments and proofs' to a neutral third party by the disputants or their representatives, who are typically trained lawyers.[40] In multi-member appeal courts, where all of the most obvious adjudicative legalization takes place, disagreement between judges is resolved by majority voting. Multi-member courts vote on decisions, not on reasons for decisions: their voting is 'conclusion-driven', not 'premise-driven'.[41] This reflects both the binary character of legal

36  Witness the debate in US administrative law about the choice that regulatory agencies have between adjudicative and legislative law-making: Strauss, PL, *Administrative Justice in the United States*, 2002, Durham, NC: Durham Academic Press, 2nd edn, 258–262.

37  A good modern illustration is provided by the work of the European Court of Justice over the past 40 years or so in developing the main features of EC law. See eg Shapiro, M, 'The European Court of Justice' in Craig, P and de Búrca, G. (eds), *The Evolution of EU Law*, 1999, Oxford: Oxford University Press.

38  Witness the title of Hazel Genn's recent book: *Paths to Justice: What People Do and Think About Going to Law*, 1999, Oxford: Hart Publishing.

39  Concerning the historical development of legislation and of the functional differentiation of the legislature and the courts see Baker, op cit n 34 above, 204–17.

40  The classic exposition is Fuller, LL, 'The Forms and Limits of Adjudication' (1978) 92 Harvard LR 393.

41  Cane, P, *Responsibility in Law and Morality*, 2002, Oxford: Hart Publishing, 165–7. Premise-driven voting is more likely than conclusion-driven voting to produce coherence and consistency over time. This explains the importance of the principle of *stare decisis* and the concept of the *ratio decidendi*, the effect of which is to apply the principle of majority-voting to premises: even the reasoning of judges who dissent from the majority's conclusion may contribute to the majority premises – the *ratio decidendi*. Voting in legislative assemblies is also conclusion-driven. Whereas the particular dispute before the court provides the focus for

reasoning,[42] and the bipolar legal model of human relationships which, in turn, finds expression in the triadic nature of adjudication: two disputants and a neutral third party.

So far as reasons for decision are concerned, the dominant feature of judicial practice in the Anglo-Australian tradition is individuality. Appellate judges are under no obligation to collaborate with their colleagues to produce a single, or a single majority, set of reasons; and such collaboration is relatively rare. In the American tradition, by contrast, reasons for decision are more often a product of debate and deliberation, and even negotiation and compromise, among appellate judges. Debate and deliberation are certainly features of the Anglo-Australian appellate process; but they take place primarily between individual judges and counsel for the parties rather than between the judges. The model for judicial behaviour is one of personal, private research and reflection. Formal deliberation and debate, let alone negotiation and compromise, between judges would be seen by many as inconsistent with the constitutional responsibilities and role-morality of the judiciary. The importance of these features of Anglo-Australian appellate judicial practice should not be underestimated. Judicial individuality can have an extremely detrimental impact on the process of adjudicative legalization of norms. The common law is found, not in the decisions and orders of appellate courts, but in the reasons for those decisions and orders. The more diverse, individualistic and unco-ordinated those reasons are, the less contribution they make to coherent development of the common law.[43] At the margin, adjudication of a dispute by a multi-member appeal court may produce only a decision and no *ratio decidendi*. A certain degree of collegiality and co-ordination is not inimical to but, on the contrary, essential for adequate performance of the constitutionally-important function of adjudicative legalization of norms; and the larger the court, the greater the need.[44]

judicial voting, the canonical words of the statute provide the focus for legislative voting. This explains why court orders and decisions are canonically formulated whereas the reasons for those decisions are not, any more than are the reasons for the enactment of statutes.

42 Conduct is either legal or illegal: legality is not a matter of degree.

43 The lack of discipline in the statement of the reasons and reasoning supporting legislation provides one of the strongest arguments against interpreting legislation by reference to parliamentary debates and other *travaux pre-paratoires*.

44 This is not to say that there cannot be too much collegiality. The modus operandi of the US Supreme Court puts a premium on building coalitions in favour of particular outcomes; and this may be inimical to consistent and coherent development of the law. It may be easier for individual judges than for groups of judges to tell a consistent and coherent story to support their voting decisions in individual cases over time. The fact that the nine-member US court invariably sits *en banc* may aggravate the problem. The seven-member Australian High Court increasingly sits *en banc*, but the strongly individualistic ethos of its members and its non-collegial mode of operation tend to produce the problems outlined in the text. The UK

Excessive individuality on the part of appellate judges poses a threat to the legitimacy of appellate courts and to rule-of-law values.[45]

By contrast with judicial processes of adjudicative legalization, 'political' processes of legislative legalization are pluralistic and multipolar rather than triadic and bipolar. The relevant models of 'political' process are investigation, consultation, deliberation,[46] debate, negotiation, compromise, bargaining and majority voting. The contrast between judicial and political processes drawn here focuses on the way they respectively generate decisions and norms, not on the ways they are held accountable. So, the model of political processes adopted in this chapter does not entail that they are representative and responsible, and it does not include the apparatus of political parties. In terms of accountability, political processes, as I understand them, may derive their legitimacy from pluralistic participation rather than responsibility and representation. The argument, that increasing involvement of non-parties in adjudication as intervenors and friends of court (*amici curiae*) threatens (or promises, depending on one's perspective) to turn adjudication into a 'surrogate political process', rests on some such participatory model of the political process.

Because of the pluralism of political processes, legislative legalization is a group activity in a way and to an extent that adjudicative legalization is not. This is not only because legislative assemblies typically have many more members than courts, but also because the extra-parliamentary stage of the legislative process typically involves a much wider range of interested parties and groups than is involved in adjudication of a dispute. Majority voting on canonically-formulated statutory provisions is the tip of the iceberg of legislative legalization. Indeed, in Westminster systems at least, the significance of majority voting in legislatures is fundamentally affected (and diminished) by the aggregation of individual votes produced by the party system. This might even lead us to the conclusion that legislatures do not legislate so much as monitor the legislative process,[47] which takes place largely outside the

---

House of Lords sits in shifting panels of roughly half its total membership. This may make it easier for its judges to find a safe passage between the Scylla of excessive individualism and the Charybdis of excessive collegiality. (I am very grateful to Adrienne Stone for stimulating this fruitful line of thought.)

45  This point must not be taken too far. Law in general and the common law in particular is always more-or-less uncertain. Contrary to what judges sometimes say, (moderate) uncertainty in the law does not make planning impossible any more than does (moderate) uncertainty in life generally: Eisenberg, op cit n 17 above, 157–8.

46  For an account of 'deliberative democracy' that takes disagreement seriously see Gutmann, A and Thompson, D, *Democracy and Disagreement*, 1996, Cambridge, Mass: Belknap Press.

47  Tomkins, A, 'What is Parliament For?' in Bamforth, N and Leyland, P (eds), *Public Law in a Multi-Layered Constitution*, 2003, Oxford: Hart Publishing. Jeremy Waldron, who is searching for the 'dignity of legislation' in the activities of legislative assemblies – especially majority

legislature and with relatively little involvement of its (backbench) members. In this account, the vote in the legislature serves only to give the final stamp of approval to legislation, so that it can be formally identified as law.

In forming an image of legislative legalization it is easy, but misleading, to concentrate on the canonical text and to ignore the processes of which it is the final product. The fact that the reasons for, and the reasoning supporting, legislation are not part of the official documentary record of the legislative process, while the reasons for court decisions, and the reasoning supporting common law norms, are part of the official documentary record of the adjudicative process, may mislead people into thinking that common law norms are based on reason(ing) whereas legislative norms are based solely on exercises of (unreasoned) will. Perhaps this is because many lawyers are still in the grip of an unduly positivistic understanding of law as the will and command of a sovereign. Such an understanding is doubly simplistic. Even assuming that the metaphor of the command of a single-minded and all-powerful sovereign was ever anything more than an heuristic device, conceived as an alternative to natural-law theories of the concept of law, there is certainly no such sovereign to be found in complex, pluralistic, democratic societies. Moreover, no lawyer is likely to think about the common law in terms of the command of a sovereign. The concept of sovereignty may contain some truth about the relationship between statute and common law, but it tells us little or nothing about the nature of the legislative process.

### The relationship between legislative and adjudicative legalization

The tasks of adjudicative legalization and legislative legalization respectively are typically assigned to different bodies.[48] In modern constitutional terms, this is because adjudicative legalization is a by-product of dispute-resolution, and dispute-resolution is thought to be an unsuitable job for legislatures. But why? The classic answer is that reposing in one and the same body the tasks of making and applying norms would create the risk of unacceptable conflicts of interest.[49] There are, no doubt, also compelling practical reasons – based on their size, for example – why modern legislative institutions are unsuited to adjudication. But the classic answer is puzzling because courts both legalise norms and apply them. In addition, they have the power to revise legal norms at the point of application, and to apply the revisions retrospectively. It is primarily because of these features of adjudicative legalization – flexibility at the point of application and retrospectivity – that we seek to impose

voting (*Law and Disagreement*, 1999, Oxford: Clarendon Press, Part I; *The Dignity of Legislation*, 1999, Cambridge: Cambridge University Press), seems to me to be looking in the wrong place, at least so far as Westminster systems are concerned.

48 But see n 36 above.     49 This is why acts of attainder are thought problematic.

constraints on adjudicative legalization additional to those imposed on legislative legalization.

There is also a democratic argument against adjudicative legalization: courts are neither representative nor responsible whereas our political processes are part of a system of representative and a responsible government.[50] But this, it seems to me, does not get to the heart of the matter. There is good reason not to combine the making and applying of norms in the same institution regardless of whether the institution is or is not representative and responsible. An institution with the power both to legalise norms, and to modify them at the point of application and give them retrospective effect, needs to be restrained in the interests of fairness and predictability. The need for restraining principles is a function of the interaction between the demand for consistency, and the phenomena of flexibility at the point of norm-application and the retrospectivity of adjudicative legalization. Even if our adjudicative institutions were representative and responsible, their norm-legalization function would need to be restrained in the interests of fairness and predictability.

What are the restraining principles? One is the requirement that newly legalised norms be coherent and consistent[51] with norms that have already been legalised. It is commonly said or implied that whereas courts have an obligation to ensure, as far as is possible and desirable, that the body of legal norms is internally consistent and coherent, legislatures have no such obligation. This is a mistake. Both courts and legislatures have an obligation to develop the law consistently and coherently. The difference is that in the case of courts, the norms of coherence and consistency are themselves considered legal in the sense that lack of coherence or consistency in the body of common-law norms provides a reason for a court to change the common law to improve its internal coherence and consistency; whereas courts have no legal power, and legislators have no legal obligation, to change legislation to make

50  Note that this argument is primarily directed to the norm-legalization element of adjudication. By contrast, one aspect of the constitutional desideratum of judicial independence is that judges should be held accountable for the way they resolve individual disputes by being required to respond publicly and in a reasoned way to the arguments and proofs presented by the parties, and not by being answerable to some person or body outside the adjudicative triad. But because the demands of consistency forge a strong link between resolution of individual disputes and legalization of norms, the argument tends to be applied to judicial activity generally and not just to norm-legalization. At all events, the concept of representativeness is deeply ambiguous. To say that courts are not representative might signify that judges are not popularly elected, or that judges as a group are not a 'representative cross-section' of society. Nevertheless, we might consider judges to be representatives in the sense that they are appointed to perform particular tasks on society's behalf. Each of these different senses of representativeness has different implications for issues such as judicial appointments and accountability.

51  Note that I am using 'consistency' in two different, but related, senses. The consistency that underpins adjudicative legalization of norms is the consistency of treating like cases alike ('formal justice' as it is sometimes called). The consistency in issue here is consistency within the body of common law norms.

the statute book internally more coherent or consistent. This does not mean that coherence and consistency are not values applicable to legislation;[52] but it does mean that legislatures are freer than courts to promote other values at the expense of coherence and consistency.

A second, and perhaps more important, restraint on adjudicative legalization is what I will call the principle of 'the priority of the documentary'. This principle requires courts to look for appropriate disputed-settling norms first in the existing documentary legal materials – both statutes and reports of court decisions. Whether an answer can be found there may be a matter of disagreement. This is partly because people may disagree about what it means to say that the documentary material provides an answer to the dispute at hand,[53] and partly because people who share the same understanding may disagree about whether the documents do actually provide an answer.[54] In appellate courts, such disagreements (to the extent that they affect the decision)[55] are ultimately resolved by majority voting. The possibility of genuine and reasonable disagreement about these and other matters is one reason why decisions of single-member courts are subject to appeal to multi-member courts – i.e., so that the disagreement can be managed, if necessary, by a vote. In cases where the documentary materials do not provide a dispute-settling norm, such a norm must be found outside the documents. Even people who think that 'the law' does not run out accept that the documents may. The principle of the priority of the documentary is not by itself enough to enable all legal disputes to be resolved. But the priority of the documentary is essential to prevent legal reasoning becoming all-things-considered reasoning and to maintain the distinctiveness of law as a subset of the universe of norms. It is also the foundation of the stability and conservatism of the common law. Coupled with the demand that courts resolve disputes consistently (treating like cases alike and unlike cases differently), it dictates, for instance, that previous decisions should only rarely be overruled.[56] The documentary nature of law is one of its most significant distinguishing characteristics.[57]

---

52  Courts may and do attempt to remove incoherence and inconsistency from the statute book by interpretative methods.

53  For instance, people may disagree about when it is appropriate for existing common law norms to be rejected (by 'overruling') or side-lined (by 'distinguishing').

54  Judges vary in the degree of respect they accord to 'precedent'. The priority norm leaves much room for individual judicial choice. This minimises the risk of insoluble conflict between the priority norm and the coherence norm.

55  To the extent that they do not affect the decision, they are resolved by the principles according to which the *ratio decidendi* is identified, which provide a surrogate for majority voting.

56  Schauer, F, 'Is the Common Law Law?' (1989) 77 California LR 455. The increasing willingness of appeal courts to revisit earlier decisions is perhaps the main target of Heydon, op cit, n 13 above. For a different perspective see Lord Rodger of Earlsferry, op cit n 34 above, 529–536.

57  The non-documentary nature of 'morality' may be one reason why there is much disagreement amongst philosophers about 'the nature of morality'. For a helpful survey see Wallace, G

The courts typically resolve any and every dispute that is put before them, because that is their job.[58] It follows that in cases where the documents yield no solution to the dispute at hand, the issue confronting the court is typically not whether to legalise a norm to resolve the dispute, but rather which norm to legalise. At least three types of consideration are relevant to deciding this latter issue: norms about how people ought to behave in their dealings with others;[59] principles about the limits of law – i.e. about when it is appropriate to legalise a norm and which norms it is appropriate to legalise;[60] and facts about the effects of law on human behaviour and states of affairs and other relevant matters.[61] The first two types of considerations are normative in character and may obviously be the subject of disagreement. The effects of law are susceptible of empirical investigation; but if, as is typically the case, evidence is lacking or incomplete, people may disagree about this as well.

In many situations in life, people can agree to disagree. The very act of submitting a dispute to a court indicates that the parties cannot agree to disagree; and it is not open to the court to tell them to live with their disagreement. On the other hand, while going to court may resolve the immediate dispute, it provides no guarantee that the disagreement that gave rise to the dispute will be resolved. Courts provide machinery for resolving disputes and, in this way, for managing, without necessarily resolving, the disagreement that gave rise to the dispute. Dispute-resolution by courts provides a mechanism for preventing disagreement getting out of hand, not for removing it. The success of the mechanism is judged not by whether parties end up in agreement

and Walker, ADM, 'Introduction' in Wallace, G and Walker, ADM (eds), *The Definition of Morality*, 1970, London: Methuen. For recent discussion see Wallace, RJ, 'The Rightness of Acts and the Goodness of Lives' in Wallace, RJ *et al* (eds), *Reason and Value: Themes from the Moral Philosophy of Joseph Raz*, 2004, Oxford: Clarendon Press.

58  Particular courts may, of course, have limited jurisdiction. The statement in the text refers to the court system as a whole; and recall that I am using the term 'the courts' very broadly to refer to legal machinery for resolving disputes by adjudication. In this sense, the job of 'the courts' is to resolve disputes put before them, full stop, without limitation to disputes of any particular type or content. This partly explains why the common law is conceived as the background against which legislation operates, whereas in a 'Code system' the Code provides the background against which adjudication operates (Kennedy, D, *A Critique of Adjudication*, 1997, Cambridge, Mass: Harvard University Press, 241): the common law, like the Code, must 'have an answer for everything'.

59  Often called 'moral' or 'ethical' norms.

60  These principles are related to the functions and resources of law and the legal system. This issue was addressed in one of the most famous jurisprudential debates of the twentieth century between Patrick Devlin and Herbert Hart under the heading 'the legal enforcement of morals': Cane, P, 'Taking Law Seriously: Starting Points of the Hart-Devlin Debate' (2006) 10 Journal of Ethics 21.

61  Such considerations are sometimes referred to as matters of 'policy'; but this word is used in a bewildering number of other ways as well. Perhaps the two most frequently rehearsed policy arguments in tort law are the 'floodgates' and 'overkill' arguments.

about how the dispute ought to have been resolved, but only by whether the loser is prepared to abide by the result even if they do not agree with it.

Taking disagreement seriously means finding ways of managing disagreement that do not depend on turning disagreement into agreement.[62] This can be done by establishing institutions and procedures that produce outcomes which people are prepared to accept even if they do not agree with them. Courts can contribute to the management of disagreement if people are prepared to accept their decisions even if they do not agree with them – in other words, if they have content-independent reasons for compliance with court decisions and common-law norms. The characteristics of courts and legal procedures that enable courts to make such a contribution include judicial independence and impartiality, majority voting in appellate courts, and the revisability of judicial norm-legalising decisions by political processes that are characterised by pluralistic investigation, deliberation, debate, compromise and bargaining, and by majority voting in large-group contexts. This point needs some elaboration.

Judges who support their reasons for decision by appeal to concepts such as 'community values' or 'the views of the ordinary person' perhaps believe that by doing so they are more likely to contribute to the management of disagreement, or even to the transformation of disagreement into agreement, than they would be if they offered precisely the same reasons as being their own genuine and considered opinion. Such a belief is likely to be mistaken because judicial views about the content of community values or about what the ordinary person thinks are typically unsupported by evidence, and because there is often no reason to think that disagreements between disputing parties do not reflect wider disagreements in the community at large. Indeed, appeal to controversial external criteria may prove counter-productive if it fuels suspicion that it is being used to mask a personal assessment by the judge of the various considerations relevant to choosing a norm to resolve the dispute at hand. The best strategy for the individual judge is openly and explicitly to choose (and to give reasons justifying their choice of) the norm that they genuinely think best in terms of the three types of considerations outlined earlier, and to leave it to processes such as majority voting by groups of judges in appellate courts, and to political methods of decision making, to manage disagreement about the norms legalised by courts. We should certainly not impose on judges an obligation to support their reasons by unproven and controversial assertions about what the community values or what ordinary people think.

---

62 For this reason, all laws, whether or not the product of political processes, should be revisable. People are more likely to accept laws they disagree with if they know that their existence will not stop debate about the terms of social co-operation. This is why effectively unamendable constitutional provisions are undesirable. See also Postema, op cit n 21 above, 461–4.

This conclusion is not in conflict with my earlier argument about the disadvantages of excessive judicial individualism. Encouraging judges to rely on their own personal judgment is consistent with also encouraging judges of multi-member courts to identify points of mutual agreement and to present them clearly and univocally. Judges have no obligation to agree amongst themselves if, in good conscience, they cannot do so. But conversely, they surely do have an obligation to express their agreement clearly if they can. Moreover, although judges are under no obligation to generate agreement by compromise, nor do they have an obligation not to do so; and doing so may sometimes be appropriate for the sake of promoting legal values such as clarity, certainty and predictability. These values are aspects of what Lon Fuller called 'the inner morality of law';[63] and being aspects of the morality of law, they are also aspects of the morality of law-making – including judicial law-making (adjudicative legalization, as I am calling it).

## Summary

My basic argument, then, is that if we take disagreement seriously, there is no good reason why individual judges should not openly argue and vote for the results and norms each personally thinks best, any more than individual participants in the political process should refrain from arguing and voting for the legislative provisions each thinks best. In the face of intractable disagreement, judicial appeal to proto-democratic standards, such as the views of ordinary people or community values, is undesirable and may be counterproductive. Adjudicative legalization is adequately and most appropriately constrained by the norms of coherence and consistency, the priority of the documentary, the practice of majority voting in multi-member courts, and the revisability of the common law by legislation. For resolving disputes, courts are preferable to political processes mainly for pragmatic reasons. Separation of powers concerns militate against entrusting both creation and application of norms to one and the same institution, and demand that norm appliers be independent and impartial; but they do not require the use of judicial as opposed to political processes for legalising norms as a by-product of adjudicating disputes. Common law should normally be revisable by legislation because political processes of legislative legalization are more pluralistic and open, and because legislative norms are neither revisable at the point of application nor (typically) retrospective in operation. This is not to say, of course, that the political processes we have are ideal from the point of view of managing disagreement,[64] but only that their pluralism and

---

63  Fuller, LL, *The Morality of Law*, 1969, New Haven: Yale University Press, 2nd edn.
64  I suspect that at least one cause of judicial hostility to legislative 'interference' with tort law is dissatisfaction with the way the political process operates in practice – for instance, by

openness give them a relative advantage (in theory, at least) over judicial processes.

However, I would not want to go so far as to argue that norms made by courts should never be unrevisable by legislation. It may be that in some societies, at some times and on some issues, courts will do a better job of managing disagreement than the political system. If so, there would be good reason to give courts politically non-revisable, conclusive power over such issues. Of course, whether courts are better than the political system at managing disagreement over particular issues is itself a matter about which people might disagree; but that need not worry us because there does seem to be widespread agreement that the issue of whether and when courts should have unrevisable power should be decided by political processes. So we can avoid an infinite regress of disagreement.

### Recent developments reconsidered

In the light of this discussion of legalization, we can now reconsider the tort law developments discussed earlier and the two somewhat conflicting propositions that have emerged from debates around them.

#### The Birth Cases: Judicial Law-Making

Judges are right to feel uncomfortable about deciding the sorts of questions they are being asked to confront in the birth cases. As Spigelman CJ said,[65] the ethical issues involved are both contestable and contested. But these issues have been legitimately presented to the courts, and in the absence of determinative statutory provisions, they have no alternative but to deal with them as a matter of common law. Judges who think that existing common-law rules and principles determine the contested issues, need look no further than the principle of the priority of the documentary for guidance about how to fulfil their judicial obligation in such cases. But judges who find no determinate answer in the existing materials must look to other principles. My belief is that regardless of how they explain what they are doing, most judges in this situation make a good faith assessment of relevant arguments for and against the various possible answers to the questions they have to decide, and pick the norm that each considers best. The matters that judges take into account include the internal coherence and consistency of the common law in particular, and of the whole body of law more generally; how people ought to behave towards one another; the functions and effects of law, and so on. And this, I

according 'too much weight' to the views of pro-defendant lobby groups. Another explanation may be judicial 'rent-seeking'.

65  *Harriton v Stephens* (2004) 59 NSWLR 694 at [24].

would argue, is precisely as it should be, because all these matters are relevant to what the common law should be, just as they are relevant to whether particular norms should be legalised by statute.

Judges need not hesitate to decide cases in the way that seems best to them on the basis of such relevant matters. Individual judges cannot hope, and should not try, single-handedly to manage disagreement about contested and contestable issues. Provided they comply with the norms of the priority of the documentary, and of coherence and consistency, they may and can leave it to procedures, such as the possibility of appeal to and majority voting in multi-member courts, and pluralistic political processes, to manage intractable disagreement about the wisdom and acceptability of common-law rules and principles. The primary obligation of the judge is to do 'justice' (according to law) as he or she sees it. To expect individual judges successfully to manage disagreement about what 'justice' means and requires in individual cases and more generally, is both unrealistic and undesirable. All we can reasonably expect of judges is that they make a good faith attempt to do justice.

It is, however, an important corollary of this argument that judges should state clearly and honestly the real reasons that support their decisions and the norms on which their decisions are based. Judges need not shrink from giving effect to their personal views, but they have a correlative obligation to state and explain those views carefully and clearly, and to expose them to public scrutiny. One of the most common accusations made against judges is that the reasons they give for their decisions and normative choices are not the reasons they personally support. If this accusation is fair, judicial practice in this regard is neither desirable nor necessary. Subterfuge is normally undesirable; and it is attractive only to judges who believe, wrongly in my view, that what they personally think is right and just is an inappropriate basis for decision. Once freed from the tyranny of the idea that, whatever they do, they must not give effect to their own views and opinions, judges would also be free to expose their real reasoning to the sort of public scrutiny needed to make them truly accountable.

It does not follow from what I have said that judges should not appeal to controversial standards such as 'community values' or 'the views of the urban commuter', or to controversial 'policy' considerations such as the risk of 'overkill' and 'opening the floodgates', if they genuinely believe that these provide legitimate reasons for legalising one norm rather than another. Indeed, if a judge does have such a belief, their obligation is to declare it, so that the strength (or weakness) of their reasons can be properly assessed and they can be held properly accountable for what they decide and for the norms they legalise. 'Taking disagreement seriously' does not require judges to refrain from using controversial arguments to support their decisions – how could they? What it requires of judges is an uncompromising honesty about their reasons for decision, an explicit recognition that in the face of intractable disagreement all that any individual (judge) can legitimately do is to say how things look from their personal point of view, and an awareness that as judges, they have no privileged access to 'the objective truth' about community values, the effects of law, whether the legal documents provide a determinate answer to a particular question, or any other relevant issue. Conversely, in the face of such disagreement, all we can legitimately require of any judge is clear, good-faith expression of how things look from his or her own perspective.

### The Review: Courts and Legislatures

I have argued that political processes are preferable to judicial processes as agents of norm-legalization because they are more pluralistic and open. The judicial process is preferable to political processes for resolving disputes between individuals mainly for efficiency reasons, but as a norm-legalization mechanism it suffers from being essentially triadic and closed. By contrast, the Underwood/Kirby argument is to the opposite effect, namely that adjudicative legalization of tort norms should be preferred to legislative legalization, which should be exceptional, incremental, consistent with and supportive of the common law, and uncontroversial. On what basis might adjudicative legalization by judicial processes be preferred to legislative legalization by political processes? Two arguments might be suggested: first, that the political process tends to be partisan and arbitrary and that, as a result, statute law is often unprincipled, the product of power not reason, whim not facts; and secondly, that legislative modification of the common law militates against stability and continuity, thus upsetting legitimate expectations and making it difficult for people to plan their lives.[66]

The first argument apparently rests on the idea that whereas political processes are apt to produce partisan outcomes, judicial processes produce neutral and impartial outcomes. It is only necessary to state this proposition in order to appreciate its falsity. Whatever judicial impartiality might mean, it cannot protect judges from having to make choices between competing normative propositions. Making such choices is the very essence of the enterprise of adjudicative legalization. But, it will be said, whereas judges are required to, and actually do, choose between competing normative propositions on the basis of reason and principle, participants in political processes choose between competing propositions on the basis of self-interest or in order to promote partisan causes. While it is no doubt true that judges typically do not

---

66 A third argument might be that tort law is concerned with interpersonal 'corrective justice', not social 'distributive justice'. For discussion of this argument see Cane, P, 'On the Division of Law-Making Labour' (2004) The Judicial Review 31, 47–9; *Responsibility in Law and Morality*, 2002, Oxford: Hart Publishing, 181–90; 'Tort Law and Distributive Justice' [2001] New Zealand LR 401.

make decisions on the basis of crude self-interest, the assumption that participants in political processes are typically or frequently motivated by self-interest is contestable and contested.[67] Moreover, the process of adjudicative norm-legalization involves preferring the interests of one social group to the interests of another. For example, the decisions in the birth cases involve preferring the interests of parents to the interests of medical practitioners, or vice versa. Although it may well be true, for instance, that the judges who have decided against claimants in birth cases were not motivated by a crude desire to 'line the pockets' of doctors or their employers, it is necessarily the case that those judges promoted the interests of doctors at the expense of the interests of parents and their children.

In fact, making and developing tort law involves striking a balance between the interests we all share in personal and financial security on the one hand, and freedom of action on the other. In this way, tort law establishes a particular pattern of distribution of the risks and costs of the types of harm against which it provides protection. Accusations that legislative modifications of common-law rules are arbitrary and unprincipled typically rest on a normative objection to the particular balance the legislature has struck between competing interests. If there is genuine, reasonable, and intractable disagreement about where that balance should be struck, the question we need to ask is whether such disagreement is better managed by judicial processes or by political processes. I have argued that in principle, political processes ought to be preferred to judicial processes as a way of managing intractable disagreements about values and about the functions and effects of law. Unless we think that judicial processes are likely to do a better job than political processes can of managing current disagreements about tort law, there is no reason to prefer judicial to legislative development of the law, and good reason to prefer the latter.

Concerning the second argument, stability and continuity are undoubtedly two of the most valued characteristics of the common law. The priority of the documentary, and the norms of coherence and consistency, coupled with the unsystematic nature of litigation make the common law about as manoeuvrable as a giant ocean liner. Because legislatures can bring about major change quickly – or so the argument goes – legislative legalization may suffer from short-termism, and wild swings back and forth:[68] a showy speedboat rather than a stately ocean liner.[69] Stability in the law is clearly a value; but it is only

---

67  See, eg, Farber, DA and Frickey, PP, *Law and Public Choice: A Critical Introduction*, 1991, Chicago: University of Chicago Press, Ch 1.

68  Ironically, in the area of negligence law, at least, judicial vacillation in the past 25 years or so has arguably created much more instability than legislative intervention.

69  Note that the objection is to legislative change of existing common law rules rather than to legislative extension and development of the common law by the legalization of norms consistent with existing common law rules or designed efficiently to clean up a mess in the

one value, and the appropriate balance between it and other values may itself be the subject of disagreement. Because people can disagree about how much flexibility is desirable, the fact that the political process can operate more speedily than the judicial process cannot by itself be an argument for preferring judicial processes. Indeed, speedy and efficient production of complex legal regimes is essential to create and sustain both the 'welfare state' and the 'regulatory state'.

There is no doubt, however, that excessive speed can be a disadvantage. As I pointed out earlier, the *Review* was conducted in a very short time; and the shortness of the process detrimentally affected the ability of the review panel satisfactorily to deal with the relationship between its recommendations and the existing body of law with which those recommendations interact. Australian personal injury law is now extremely complex, especially in New South Wales, where the common law has been the subject of many relatively unco-ordinated statutory modifications in the past decade and more. It is also true that the interaction between the relevant provisions of the Commonwealth Trade Practices Act (and equivalents in state legislation) on the one hand, and the common law of tort, as statutorily modified, on the other is extremely complex.[70] The construction of anything approaching an internally coherent and consistent regime of personal injury law would have required much more time and resources than were spent on the *Review* (as well as unimaginable agreement and co-ordination among governments).

On the other hand, it is not clear that the common law has a significant advantage in this respect. Political processes have a greater capacity than judicial processes to take a comprehensive and synoptic approach to legal development and change. The birth cases provide a good illustration of the shortcomings of judicial process in this respect. For instance, there is little doubt that the development of English law in this area would have been much more satisfactory if the cases of *McFarlane, Parkinson,* and *Rees* could have been considered together by a single court. The unsystematic nature of litigation militates against coherent development of the common law, especially when combined (as in *McFarlane* and *Rees*) with a willingness to reopen

---

common law. Note, conversely, that the inflexibility of the common law affects its ability to change direction and to clean up its own mess more than its ability to move forward. Indeed, a commonly-touted advantage of adjudicative over legislative legalization is its capacity to deal sensitively and coherently with new areas of law that regulate activities which may develop in unforeseeable ways. This is one reason why legislation may be drafted effectively to delegate significant law-making power to courts. Another oft-cited motivation is a desire to 'depoliticise' contentious issues. Concerning the converse problem of statutory obsolescence and the role of courts in dealing with it see Calabresi, G, *A Common Law for the Age of Statutes*, 1982, Cambridge, Mass: Harvard University Press.

70  See eg Dietrich, J, 'Liability for Personal Injuries Arising from Recreational Services: The Interaction of Contract, Tort, State Legislation and the Trade Practices Act and the Resultant Mess' (2003) 11 Torts LJ 244.

recent debates and reconsider recently announced rules and principles. At the same time, it must be admitted that the flexibility of the political process can also militate against coherent legal development. The legislative reactions in New South Wales and Queensland to the decision in *Cattanach* perhaps provide a good example.[71] On the whole, however, there is little reason to think that the statute book is significantly more internally incoherent than the common law. Although legislators are not subject to a legal norm of consistency and coherence as judges are, considerations of political propriety and expediency greatly reduce the practical significance of this theoretical difference. It is also true that legislation is not likely to achieve its purposes effectively and efficiently unless it is tailored to fit into the conceptual and institutional structure of the legal system. Legislation necessarily operates against the background of all the law – both judge-made and statutory – existing at the time it is enacted,[72] and this severely limits the extent to which the legislature can afford to ignore considerations of coherence and consistency in drafting any particular statute. The image of powerful governments acting on a whim and manipulating the political process to promote personal and sectional interests is as much an over-simplification as that of totally disinterested judges resolving interpersonal disputes by applying normatively neutral principles.

We might conclude that judicial processes and political processes have contrasting disadvantages, the former being relatively inflexible and dependent on accidents of litigation; and the latter being quite manoeuvrable and as a result, prone to ill-considered and partial reactions to perceived crises. However, I would still want to argue that the balance of advantage lies with political process because lack of flexibility and the unplanned nature of litigation are intrinsic to the common law, whereas the political process at its best can be both flexible and timely but also systematic and comprehensive in its approach to legal development. But above all, political processes are much more pluralistic and open than judicial processes.

## Conclusion

Underlying the approach of this chapter has been an attempt to understand the relative advantages and disadvantages of judicial and political processes, common law and statute, as mechanisms for legalising norms, given the fact of genuine, reasonable and intractable disagreement about values and about the functions and effects of law. Although adjudicative legalization is a by-product of dispute-resolution, I have sought to assess the strengths and weaknesses of courts as norm-legalisers independently of their strengths and

71  See n 7 above.
72  Krygier, M, 'The Traditionality of Statutes' (1988) 1 Ratio Juris 20.

weaknesses as dispute-resolvers. I have also put some emphasis on the historical relationship between dispute-resolution and norm-legalization as governmental techniques, and between courts and legislatures. The fact that courts at the beginning of the twenty-first century operate in a very different constitutional and institutional environment from that which existed up until the nineteenth century, gives us cause us to rethink the relationship between common law and statute, and that between judicial and political processes.

Above all, I have sought to argue that managing genuine, reasonable and intractable disagreement is an important function and capacity of norm-legalization, and that in principle, and usually in practice, open, pluralistic political processes provide better means of performing this function and realising this capacity than relatively closed, triadic, judicial processes. I have, therefore, argued against the view that developing tort law should be left to the judges. I have also argued that beyond respecting the norms of the priority of the documentary, and of coherence and consistency, individual judges would be well-advised not to attempt to simulate political processes by adopting as criteria for deciding novel tort cases controversial concepts such as 'the views of the ordinary person' or 'community values'. Rather each should make a personal assessment of the relevant substantive arguments ('moral', 'political'. 'social', 'economic' and so on) for and against the norms that are in competition for legalization, and leave the task of managing disagreement with those assessments to processes such as rights of appeal to, and majority voting in, multi-member appellate courts, and legislative revision of the common law. Courts necessarily legalise norms because they resolve disputes in accordance with the demand for consistency; and they have the job of resolving disputes because judicial processes are better suited for that purpose than political processes. It does not follow, however, that judicial processes should ever be preferred to political processes for the legalization of norms.

# Chapter 3

# The use of policy in negligence cases in the High Court of Australia

*Harold Luntz* *

## Introduction

The theme of the conference at which the paper on which this chapter is based was originally presented was *Principle and Policy in Private Law*. It is not always easy to distinguish principle from policy, as Jane Stapleton has shown in her address to the High Court of Australia on the occasion of its centenary.[1] Nevertheless, this chapter contends that the High Court must make use of policy, since principle alone will seldom be sufficient, to enable it to decide the cases that come before it. At the outset the chapter refers briefly to the controversy as to whether courts do or do not make law. In agreement with most judges and commentators today, it accepts that they do. It recognises, however, that there are differences between judicial and legislative powers in this regard and that there are limits on what judges can do in this respect. Nonetheless, the High Court, like all appellate courts, has leeways of choice open to it.

The opportunity for choice available in the High Court may be more obvious than with other appellate courts because all appeals from courts in Australia to the High Court require special leave to appeal and the High Court, unlike comparable courts elsewhere, gives brief reasons when it refuses special leave. The chapter therefore next analyses the special leave procedure in the case of the High Court and infers that in the cases granted special leave to appeal, there are at least reasonable grounds for argument that the decision below is wrong and the case raises issues of importance. The room then available in deciding each case is manifest in the frequency of multiple reasons for judgment, often based on different grounds, and in the high number of dissenting judgments. The outcome cannot be determined by principle alone and the court must turn to values and policy.

There follows a mainly chronological discussion of instances of policy

---

* I am grateful to Ian Malkin for his comments on my initial draft.
1 Stapleton, Jane, 'The Golden Thread at the Heart of Tort Law: Protection of the Vulnerable' (2003) 24 Australian Bar Review 135.

influencing the decision in particular cases involving the duty of care in negligence. The chapter describes the high-water mark of the transparent use of
policy during the era when Sir William Deane was a member of the High
Court and the subsequent repudiation of his analysis by a majority of the
court. Despite this repudiation, policy continues to play a significant, if less
openly acknowledged, role.

Policy and values enter into the determination of torts cases not only in
relation to duty of care, but also in relation to causation and remoteness of
damage and the assessment of damages. Brief mention is made of some of
the important cases in these areas. Finally, the chapter raises (without resolving) the difficult question of how the High Court could better inform itself of
the relevant social facts in assisting it to make its policy decisions.

### Do appellate courts make law?

In *Rootes v Shelton*,[2] a waterskier was injured while executing a manoeuvre
known as 'Russian Roulette'. A jury found the driver of the boat that was
towing him negligent in failing to point out a submerged log. The New South
Wales Court of Appeal set aside the verdict in his favour on the ground that
the parties were participating in a sport and the driver owed no relevant duty
of care to the plaintiff.[3] The High Court restored the jury's verdict. Opening
his concurring judgment, Kitto J notoriously said:

> it is a mistake to suppose that the case is concerned with 'changing social
> needs' or with 'a proposed new field of liability in negligence', or that it
> is to be decided by 'designing' a rule. And, if I may be pardoned for
> saying so, to discuss the case in terms of 'judicial policy' and 'social
> expediency' is to introduce deleterious foreign matter into the waters of
> the common law – in which, after all, we have no more than riparian
> rights.[4]

Commenting on this passage in the *Oxford Companion to the High Court of
Australia*, in an entry entitled 'Policy considerations', Sir Anthony Mason, a
justice of the court from 1972 and Chief Justice from 1987 to 1995, states
that judges of this persuasion may have had the declaratory theory of law
in mind.[5] He observes that since Lord Reid's classic lecture, this theory has
been exposed as a fairy tale and, as Lord Reid rightly said, 'we do not believe

---

2   (1967) 116 CLR 383.        3   (1966) 86 WN (Pt 1) (NSW) 94.
4   (1967) 116 CLR 383 at 386–7.
5   Mason, Sir Anthony, 'Policy Considerations' in Blackshield, AR, Coper, Michael and
    Williams, George (eds), *The Oxford Companion to the High Court of Australia*, 2001, South
    Melbourne: Oxford University Press, p 535.

in fairy tales any more'.[6] In a 'personal impression' and writing generally without specific reference to tort, Sir Anthony has said that except for a period in the 1980s and 1990s, the High Court's jurisprudence has not been policy-oriented.[7] According to Sir Anthony, the strongest example of the High Court grappling with policy considerations is provided by cases on the duty of care. He claims that it is widely recognised that the question whether a duty of care exists may entail the examination of a complex of policy considerations, notably in claims for economic loss and claims against public authorities.[8]

One may accept that there are certain principles of the law of tort that are immutable by judges, as opposed to legislatures. Thus there is no doubt that only the legislature can introduce no-fault compensation schemes, whereas liability at common law remains theoretically rooted in fault.[9] When McHugh JA, then in the New South Wales Court of Appeal, said that the standard of care required of an employer 'has moved close to the border of strict liability', he was rebuked by the High Court, which acknowledged that standards had indeed risen in response to social changes, but denied that the underlying principle had changed.[10] Subsequently, McHugh JJ took his place on the bench of the High Court. He was there faced with a situation in which an applicant sought access to her medical records in relation to a product liability claim that she might have wanted to pursue in the United States.[11] The joint judgment of Gaudron and McHugh JJ, having found (like all the other members of the court) that the common law did not give such a right of access, commented that any change in the law was for parliament.[12] 'Any changes in legal doctrine, brought about by judicial creativity, must "fit" within the body of accepted rules and principles.'[13] Although Sir Anthony

---

6  Lord Reid, 'The Judge as Law Maker' (1972–73) 12 Journal of the Society of Public Teachers of Law (New Series) 22.

7  Mason, Sir Anthony, 'The High Court of Australia: A Personal Impression of its First 100 Years' (2003) 27 Melbourne University Law Review 864 at 888.

8  Mason, above n 5, p 536, instancing, in relation to economic loss, *Caltex Oil (Australia) Pty Ltd v The Dredge 'Willemstad'* (1976) 136 CLR 529 and *Perre v Apand Pty Ltd* (1999) 198 CLR 180, and, in relation to public authorities, *Sutherland Shire Council v Heyman* (1985) 157 CLR 424 and *Crimmins v Stevedoring Industry Finance Committee* (1999) 200 CLR 1.

9  Compare Lord Diplock, writing extra-judicially in 'Judicial Developments of the Law in the Commonwealth' [1978] 1 Malaysian Law Journal cviii. Note also the limits imposed on Justices Prudential and Lefft in the fantasy by Hutchinson, Allan C and Morgan, Derek, '*Derek and Charles v Anne and Martin*: The Supreme Court of Canengaustrus' in Hutchinson, A (ed), *Dwelling on the Threshold: Critical Essays on Modern Legal Thought*, 1988, Toronto: Carswell.

10  *Bankstown Foundry Pty Ltd v Braistina* (1986) 160 CLR 301.

11  *Breen v Williams* (1996) 186 CLR 71.

12  See now, eg, Health Records Act 2001 (Vic) s 25; Health Records and Information Privacy Act 2002 (NSW) s 3.

13  *Breen v Williams* (1996) 186 CLR 71 at 115. See also n 87, below.

Mason refers to this passage along with the judgment of Kitto J in *Rootes v Shelton*, it does acknowledge that some changes may be brought about by judicial creativity, but that there are limits to what this can achieve.

Another obvious limit on judicial law-making comes from the fact that courts are not at large in what they can choose to legislate on. They are dependent on the particular vagaries of the litigation that comes before them. Legislatures, on the other hand, are free, subject to constitutional restraints, to legislate on whatever subject they wish. Some further limitations are referred to below.[14]

One remnant of the declaratory theory of judicial decisions in Australia is that it has been held that prospective overruling, so that changes in the law do not affect past events, is inconsistent with judicial power.[15] Legislatures, of course, are free to make their changes to the law either prospective or retrospective. It is noteworthy that in enacting the wave of legislation during 2001–04 (euphemistically called 'tort law reform') some of the Australian legislatures opted to make at least some of the changes retrospective,[16] whereas others made the changes prospective only.[17]

### Leeways of choice

Principles alone cannot solve many of the disputes that reach the courts, particularly the higher courts, mainly because they can be stated at various levels of generality.[18] The Preface to the fourth edition of my *Assessment of Damages for Personal Injury and Death*,[19] quotes the much cited dictum of Windeyer J that '[t]he one principle which is absolutely firm, and which must control all else, is that damages for the consequences of mere negligence are compensatory'.[20] Of course, this principle, being applicable only to 'mere negligence', does not tell us when or on what basis exemplary damages may

---

14 See text nn 79–84.
15 *Ha v New South Wales* (1997) 189 CLR 465. See *Brodie v Singleton Shire Council* (2001) 206 CLR 512 at [215]–[216] per Kirby J (giving it as one of the reasons for not changing the law as to the immunity of highway authorities, which he ultimately rejected); *Gifford v Strang Patrick Stevedoring Pty Ltd* (2003) 214 CLR 269 at [129] per Callinan J (seeing it as a reason for caution against judicial activism). Cf the discussion in *In Re Spectrum Plus Ltd (in Liquidation)* [2005] 2 AC 680 (HL); *Chamberlains v Lai* [2006] NZSC 70 (Unreported, 11 September 2006).
16 Eg, Civil Liability Act 2002 (NSW) s 2; Civil Liability Act 2003 (Qld) s 2; Wrongs Act 1958 (Vic) s 28L.
17 Eg, Trade Practices Amendment (Personal Injuries and Death) Act (No 2) 2004 (Cth) Sched Item 11; Law Reform (Ipp Recommendations) Act 2004 (SA) Sched 1 cl 1; Personal Injuries (Liabilities and Damages) Act 2003 (NT) s 4(2).
18 See Stone, Julius, *Precedent and Law: Dynamics of Common Law Growth*, 1985, Sydney: Butterworths, on the 'leeways of choice' open to courts.
19 4th edn, 2002, Sydney: LexisNexis Butterworths, pp ix–x.
20 *Skelton v Collins* (1966) 115 CLR 94 at 128.

be awarded, an issue that has come before the High Court and ultimate appellate courts in many other jurisdictions in the recent past, with outcomes that are not completely uniform.[21] The preface also lists more than a dozen cases dealing with compensatory damages for personal injury caused by negligence which had reached the High Court of Australia since the previous edition of the book and which had not been able to be answered by reference to this principle alone, or its corollary, that the aim of damages is to restore the plaintiff as far as money can do it to the position he or she would have been in if the wrong had not been committed. When faced with an issue such as whether the assessment of damages is to be made by reference to the law of the place of the wrong (*lex loci delicti*) or the law of the forum, the ultimate appellate court has a choice. Having exercised that choice, it has laid down a subsidiary principle, which lower courts are then bound to follow, subject to legislative intervention and the possible carving out by later courts of exceptions.[22]

Some of the other issues that have come before the High Court in the area of assessment of damages for personal injury or death in recent years and that could not be resolved by reference to principle alone include:

- how damages are to be assessed where the injured party has split his or her income with a partner;[23]
- whether damages for voluntary services are to be valued at commercial rates or according to the cost to the supplier;[24]
- whether damages may be recovered for the value of a deceased parent's services where the services have been replaced by the surviving partner without cost;[25]
- whether compensation received under a workers' compensation scheme that is not repayable to the employer or fund from which it came is to be deducted from the award of damages;[26]
- what allowance, if any, is to be made for the chance that a surviving spouse will receive support from a future relationship.[27]

---

21  Eg, *Gray v Motor Accident Commission* (1998) 196 CLR 1; *Kuddus v Chief Constable of Leicestershire Constabulary* [2002] 2 AC 122 (HL); *Whiten v Pilot Insurance Co* [2002] 1 SCR 595 (SCC); *A v Bottrill* [2003] 1 AC 449 (PC); *State Farm Mutual Automobile Insurance Co v Campbell* 538 US 408 (2003) (US SC).

22  See *John Pfeiffer Pty Ltd v Rogerson* (2000) 203 CLR 503 (interstate accidents); *Regie National Des Usines Renault SA v Zhang* (2002) 210 CLR 491 (international accidents); *Neilson v Overseas Projects Corporation of Victoria Ltd* [2005] HCA 54 (2005) 221 ALR 213 (application of *renvoi* to tort claims).

23  *Husher v Husher* (1999) 197 CLR 138.      24  *Van Gervan v Fenton* (1992) 175 CLR 327.

25  *Nguyen v Nguyen* (1990) 169 CLR 245.

26  *Manser v Spry* (1994) 181 CLR 428; *Harris v Commercial Minerals Ltd* (1996) 186 CLR 1.

27  *De Sales v Ingrilli* (2002) 212 CLR 338.

The prevalence of dissent in the highest court demonstrates that the existing law will seldom compel an answer one way or the other in such cases. In the period 2000 to June 2005, there were 81 torts-related cases in which the court brought down its judgment. In no fewer than 46 of these, or 56.8 per cent, there was at least one judge who dissented. The court was able to agree on a single set of reasons for judgment in only 11 of these cases (13.6 per cent).

The choice made by the ultimate appellate court when faced with cases like these must rest on policy. In the *Oxford Companion* entry on 'Policy considerations', Sir Anthony Mason quotes Neil MacCormick, who states: ' "Policy" has become a hideously inexact word in legal discourse.'[28] A distinction is often made by judges between 'legal policy' or 'the policy of the law' and 'public policy'.[29] I do not accept any such distinction.[30] For present purposes the meaning of 'policy' is clear enough. As Sir Anthony says, policy arguments may come into play when a decision cannot be made according to established rules, which, for reasons to be given in relation to the procedure for special leave to appeal, will be in nearly every case that comes before the High Court. He observes that the new rule laid down will have an application that extends beyond the parties to the case. The judges need to bear in mind that their decision creates a precedent, which affects persons other than the parties themselves. They therefore have to consider whether a decision for or against each of the parties will on balance be beneficial or deleterious for others, that is, for society generally.[31] Part of that policy may be simply to fit the new principle or rule in with broader principles or to reduce anomalies, as, for example, in *Brodie v Singleton Shire Council*,[32] where the High Court by a majority of 4:3 overturned the long-established immunity of highway authorities for non-feasance. In this particular instance, legislatures throughout Australia disagreed with this decision and reinstated the protection for highway authorities, at least

28  Mason, Sir Anthony, 'Policy considerations' in Blackshield, Coper and Williams, above n 5, p 535, quoting MacCormick, Neil, *Legal Reasoning and Legal Theory*, 1978.

29  See, eg, *Cattanach v Melchior* (2003) 215 CLR 1 at [70] per McHugh and Gummow JJ, citing Lord Millett in *McFarlane v Tayside Health Board* [2000] 2 AC 59 (HL) at 108. Their Honours noted that 'the appellants in the present case displayed no enthusiasm for a distinction between "legal policy" and "public policy"; they rightly preferred the term "policy of the law" '. See also *Rees v Darlington Memorial Hospital NHS Trust* [2004] 1 AC 309 (HL).

30  See also the paper presented at this conference by Cane, Peter, 'Taking Disagreement Seriously: Courts, Legislatures and the Reform of Tort Law' (2005) 25 Oxford J Legal Studies 393

31  See Symmons, CR, 'The Function and Effect of Public Policy in Contemporary Common Law' (1977) 51 Australian Law Journal 185 at 189 (essential function of public policy 'is to bring into judicial consideration the broader social interest of the public at large').

32  (2001) 206 CLR 512.

temporarily or to a limited extent,[33] presumably recognising values of greater public importance than coherence of the law. It is always open to the legislature to do this, but the court often has to act first when a problem arises and it should make its choice by taking into account wider matters than the mere harmonising of particular rules with broader principles.

This chapter does not reiterate the sort of concerns that have been enunciated by the courts and collected by Jane Stapleton in her various papers.[34] What this chapter sets out to do is simply to document (mainly chronologically) some of the negligence cases in which the High Court expressly or implicitly took policy into account in the course of its reasoning.

### Special leave procedure

Today, all appeals to the High Court of Australia from State, Territory and Federal courts are subject to the grant of special leave to appeal.[35] The Judiciary Act of 1903 (Cth) s 35A lays down the following criteria for granting special leave:

> In considering whether to grant an application for special leave to appeal to the High Court under this Act or under any other Act, the High Court may have regard to any matters that it considers relevant but shall have regard to:
>
> (a) whether the proceedings in which the judgment to which the application relates was pronounced involve a question of law:
>   (i) that is of public importance, whether because of its general application or otherwise; or
>   (ii) in respect of which a decision of the High Court, as the final appellate court, is required to resolve differences of opinion between different courts, or within the one court, as to the state of the law; and
> (b) whether the interests of the administration of justice, either generally or in the particular case, require consideration by the High Court of the judgment to which the application relates.

---

33  Civil Liability Act 2002 (NSW) s 45; Civil Liability Act 2003 (Qld) s 37; Civil Liability Act 1936 (SA) s 42; Civil Liability Act 2002 (Tas) s 42; Transport Act 1983 (Vic) s 37A (see now Road Management Act 2004 (Vic) Pt 6); Civil Liability Act 2002 (WA) s 5Z; Civil Law (Wrongs) Act 2002 (ACT) s 113.

34  See, in particular, Stapleton, Jane, 'Duty of Care Factors: a Selection from the Judicial Menus' in Stapleton, Jane and Cane, Peter (eds), *The Law of Obligations: Essays in Celebration of John Fleming*, 1998, Oxford: Clarendon Press, p 59.

35  Judiciary Act 1903 (Cth) ss 35(2) and 35AA(2); Federal Court of Australia Act 1976 (Cth) s 33.

Although similar criteria probably exist in other common law jurisdictions,[36] there are two reasons why the application of the criteria is more transparent in Australia than elsewhere. First, the argument on the special leave application is today available on the internet very shortly after it has been heard. It often commences with the judges asking counsel 'what is the special leave point?' and one can see counsel grappling, in the face of often vigorous questioning, with attempts to formulate reasons why the court should grant such leave. Secondly, the High Court gives brief reasons for refusing special leave to appeal. The House of Lords, the Supreme Court of Canada and the US Supreme Court do not, as far as I know, give reasons for refusing to hear appeals under their various procedures.

The High Court of Australia will not ordinarily grant special leave to appeal in cases involving the application of facts to a well-established principle,[37] even if it appears that the application was wrong in the particular circumstances (except occasionally under what it calls its 'visitorial jurisdiction').[38] Its workload is simply too great for it to handle such cases. As McHugh J said on one special leave application,

> This Court . . . is not just another Court of Appeal. It is to determine no more than 100 cases a year at the most and before the Court can entertain a case it must be convinced, not only that it is wrong, but there is something special about the case that takes it outside the general run of cases. And unless you can satisfy that criterion, you do not get leave.[39]

Even if some point of principle does arise, the court will not grant special leave to appeal in cases where the applicant's prospects of success are small. Common phrases in refusing leave are that the decision below 'is not attended

---

36  For a discussion of the criteria laid down in Canada for the Supreme Court to grant leave to appeal and for the similar criteria that should be adopted in the rare case where a provincial court gives leave to appeal to the Supreme Court, see *L(H) v Canada (Attorney General)* (2003) 19 CCLT (3d) 226 (Saskatchewan Court of Appeal).

37  Illustrations include *Summerville v Walsh* S25/1998 (11 September 1998); *Peck v Greater Taree City Council* [2003] HCATrans 360 (12 September 2003); *Cheesman v Bathurst City Council* [2005] HCATrans 298 (29 April 2005).

38  See, eg, the transcript of argument in *Zafer v West Australian Trotting Association* P28/1996 (4 November 1996). A recent example of the court granting leave under its visitorial jurisdiction is *Laybutt v Glover Gibbs Pty Limited t/as Balfours NSW Pty Ltd* (2005) 221 ALR 310: see the transcript of argument on the special leave application, [2005] HCATrans 26 (4 February 2005).

39  *Commissioner of Taxation of the Commonwealth of Australia v Vabu Pty Ltd* S173/1996 (14 February 1997). His Honour reduced the number of cases the High Court could take annually to '50 or 60' in *Ross v The Owners of Strata Plan 63477* [2005] HCATrans 841 (7 October 2005). Ironically, the issue in the *Vabu* case did eventually come before the High Court in a different context in *Hollis v Vabu Pty Ltd* (2001) 207 CLR 21.

with sufficient doubt'[40] or that 'the prospects of success' on the appeal are insufficient to warrant the grant of leave.[41] A case must be truly arguable before special leave will be given. Other reasons why the court will not take on a case include the following:

- It is not a suitable vehicle for determining the point of principle that it raises. This may be because of the way the case was conducted in the lower courts[42] or the facts are not clearly established and the case would require the High Court itself to investigate facts.[43]
- Legislatures have intervened and there is no need for the High Court itself to determine the issue[44] or a legislative solution is called for.[45]
- The principle for which the applicant is contending has recently been laid down by the court and there is no reason to revisit it, even where it is being misapplied.[46]
- The issue turns on legislation that is likely to be of concern to only one state.[47]
- The point on which the applicant seeks to base the appeal was not considered by the lower courts.[48]

From these reasons for refusing special leave to appeal, we can infer that in cases where leave has been granted:

- the intermediate appellate court reached a decision that is arguably wrong; or
- there is a conflict between intermediate appellate courts that the High Court should resolve; and
- the case involves an issue of law, not just of fact;
- the court has the benefit of the views of the lower court on that law;
- the issue is of relevance throughout Australia or at least fairly generally; and

40  Eg, *Macleay-Hastings Area Health Service v Wallaby Grip (BAE) Pty Ltd (in liq)* S31/1999 (19 November 1999).
41  Eg, *NRMA Ltd v Heydon* S26/2001 (14 September 2001).
42  Eg, *Pettersen v Bacha* S37/1995 (13 October 1995); *AAA v Backwell* M25/1996 (5 August 1996); *Prosser v Eagle* S103/1999 (30 November 1999).
43  Eg, *Cowell v British American Tobacco Australia Services Ltd* [2003] HCATrans 384 (3 October 2003).
44  Eg, *Rosniak v Government Insurance Office of NSW* S77/1997 (13 March 1998); *Horvath v State of Victoria* [2004] HCATrans 215 (18 June 2004).
45  Eg, *FAI General Insurance Company v Griffiths and Sons Pty Ltd* B55/1996 (4 April 1997).
46  Eg, *Zafer v West Australian Trotting Association* P28/1996 (4 November 1996).
47  Eg, *Copur v Alcan Australia Ltd* M71/1994 (9 June 1995).
48  Eg, *Cran v State of New South Wales* [2005] HCATrans 21 (4 February 2005).

- the case is one that should allow the court to state a principle applicable to future cases.

These criteria mean that in practice appeals should be confined to cases where the principle to be applied is uncertain or lower courts have held different views on the scope of the relevant principle. In other words, there is room for argument and it is not obvious which side of the argument is right. The ultimate appellate court is then able to formulate the principle in different ways or to select as applicable one of two or more competing principles. This explains why, as we have seen above, there are leeways of choice, frequent dissents and multiple concurring judgments stating the principles involved in different ways. It should be recognised, however, that these characteristics are probably displayed to excess in the High Court of Australia.[49] Be that as it may, the choice that is ultimately made necessarily depends on policy and values.

### Express reference to policy pre-1980

The stance of the High Court prior to the 1980s may not have been policy-oriented, but that does not mean that policy did not play a role; merely that it was less transparent. As early as 1940, we find the High Court carving out an exception to the general principles of negligence liability because '[t]o concede that any civil liability can rest upon a member of the armed forces for supposedly negligent acts or omissions in the course of an actual engagement with the enemy is opposed alike to reason and to policy'.[50] Over 50 years later, the reasons spelt out in this case were accepted as valid and the decision was followed in England in an action by a member of the army who served in the first Gulf War.[51] The issue is still a live one in England. These authorities were recently considered at length, but distinguished, in relation to peace-keeping soldiers performing essentially police duties in Kosovo.[52] The whole matter

49  See Davies, Martin, 'Common Law Liability of Statutory Authorities: *Crimmins v Stevedoring Industry Finance Committee*' (2000) 8 Torts Law Journal 133 at 145–51 (comparing the High Court of Australia with the House of Lords and US Supreme Court). See also the quotation in the text at n 64, below.

50  *Shaw Savill & Albion Co Ltd v The Commonwealth* (1940) 66 CLR 344 at 361–2 per Dixon J. The proceedings in this case arose on the pleadings. When the matter went to trial, the defendant was unable to make out the defence that the collision between the ships occurred while the naval vessel was engaged in active operations against the enemy and the plaintiff's action succeeded: see Dixon J in *A-G (NSW) v Perpetual Trustee Co Ltd* (1952) 85 CLR 237 at 251–2.

51  *Mulcahy v Ministry of Defence* [1996] QB 732 (CA). See also *Multiple Claimants v The Ministry of Defence* [2003] EWHC 1134 (QB) (Owen J, 21 May 2003, unreported).

52  *Bici v Ministry of Defence* [2004] EWHC 786 (QB) (Elias J, 7 April 2004, unreported). The decision drew criticism from the Daily Telegraph (London): Editorial, 'Hobbling Our Soldiers', 9 April 2004.

may be revisited in relation to claims against the British and Australian armed forces in Iraq.[53]

Windeyer J, as so often, may have been ahead of his time in openly recognising the role of policy in 1970. In *Mount Isa Mines Ltd v Pusey*,[54] where the court was concerned with the duty of care to avoid causing psychiatric injury, his Honour expressly agreed with Professor Heuston 'that the question cannot be answered solely by logic and that an issue of policy is involved',[55] but added the caveat:

> it is not for an individual judge to determine the policy of the law according to his own view of what social interests dictate. The field is one in which the common law is still in course of development. Courts must therefore act in company and not alone. Analogies in other courts, and persuasive precedents as well as authoritative pronouncements, must be regarded.[56]

Without referring to policy, but calling on his experience as a general for his metaphors, he had taken a similar line the year before when he said:

> We need not doubt, nor need we disguise, that this movement and development of the law is the result of the creative work of courts making at times a conscious choice between allowing or disallowing a remedy, and thus creating or denying a right. Nevertheless those who insist that the common law is still on the move should remember that it must always march in step. Decisions in cases passing at the moment must be in step with those which have just gone past, although not necessarily with those at the head of the column. Moving the metaphor from the parade ground to the field, it is as sound a maxim for law as for war that operations should be from a firm base, that an advance must be from a position which has been securely established.[57]

One of the cases cited by Sir Anthony Mason as involving consideration of complex policy issues, *Caltex Oil (Australia) Pty Ltd v The Dredge 'Willemstad'*,[58] also arose in the 1970s. This was the first case to allow recovery of damages for what has since been called relational pure economic

---

53 Norton-Taylor, Richard, 'Troops Accused on Iraq Killings: MoD Faces Lawsuits over Deaths of 18 Civilians', Guardian Unlimited, London, 21 February 2004 [accessed 21 February 2004] www.guardian.co.uk/Iraq/Story/0,2763,1153028,00.html; Roberts, Jeremy, 'Soldiers' "Victim" to Sue British Military', *The Australian*, 30 June 2004; Nicholson, Brendan, 'Wounded Iraqi Demands Compensation', *The Age* (Melbourne), 18 March 2005.

54 (1970) 125 CLR 383.    55 *Salmond on Torts* (14th ed, 1965), p 289.

56 (1970) 125 CLR 383 at 396.    57 *Benning v Wong* (1969) 122 CLR 249 at 305.

58 Above, n 8.

loss, but it was marred by the fact that the five judges, while unanimous as to the outcome, were so divided as to their reasons that the Privy Council later claimed to be unable to discern a *ratio decidendi*.[59] Although members of the court did look to the reasons why the law had hitherto denied liability in such cases and held that they were not applicable to the facts of the case, both Gibbs and Stephen JJ refused to adopt the view of Lord Denning in *Spartan Steel & Alloys Ltd v Martin & Co (Contractors) Ltd* that '[i]t seems . . . better to consider the particular relationship in hand, and see whether or not, as a matter of policy, economic loss should be recoverable, or not'.[60] For Stephen J this was too open-ended.

> Policy considerations must no doubt play a very significant part in any judicial definition of liability and entitlement in new areas of the law; the policy considerations to which their Lordships paid regard in *Hedley Byrne*[61] are an instance of just such a process and to seek to conceal those considerations may be undesirable. That process should however result in some definition of rights and duties, which can then be applied to the case in hand, and to subsequent cases, with relative certainty. To apply generalized policy considerations directly, in each case, instead of formulating principles from policy and applying those principles, derived from policy, to the case in hand, is, in my view, to invite uncertainty and judicial diversity. This suggests a need to search for some more positive guidance as to the entitlement, if any, to recover in negligence for solely economic loss than is provided by judicial policy making based upon a case-by-case consideration of whatever factors the particular court may deem relevant.[62]

Subsequent decisions have shown that attempts to define rights and duties in this area are futile and have created as much uncertainty as a case-by-case consideration of policy factors is likely to have done. After the court had decided *Perre v Apand Pty Ltd*,[63] one judge in a lower court had the temerity to say:

---

59 *Candlewood Navigation Corporation Ltd v Mitsui OSK Lines Ltd* [1986] AC 1 (PC) at 22. The headnote of *Caltex* in the CLR attributes the following principle to three members of the court:

> Although as a general rule damages are not recoverable for economic loss which is not consequential upon injury to person or property, even if the loss is foreseeable, damages are recoverable in a case in which the defendant has knowledge or the means of knowledge that a particular person, not merely as a member of an unascertained class, will be likely to suffer economic loss as a consequence of his negligence.

In *Hill v Van Erp* (1997) 188 CLR 159 at 175 Dawson J adopted this as the holding of 'the court'.
60 [1973] 1 QB 27 (CA) at 37.
61 *Hedley Byrne & Co Ltd v Heller & Partners Ltd* [1964] AC 465 (HL).
62 (1976) 136 CLR 529 at 567.    63 (1999) 198 CLR 180.

I wish ... to emphasise the present disgraceful uncertainty in the law dealing with claims for pure economic loss in negligence. [The other two members of the court] refer to having found nothing to change their opposing views in the present matter by reference to the High Court's recent decision in *Perre v Apand Pty Ltd*. Similarly, I have laboured through the 437 paragraphs (and a good deal of the material referred to in the 539 footnotes) of the seven judgments upholding that appeal. With the greatest of respect, there is nothing there in terms of agreement on basic guiding principles to assist with resolution of claims such as the present. I appreciate that these observations will be of no comfort to either the appellant in the present matter or countless future litigants until such time as there is consensus as to the fundamental principles in this branch of the law of tort.[64]

In *Caltex* Stephen J went on to reject one possible factor that might be taken into account in an open-ended inquiry:

The task of the courts remains that of loss fixing rather than loss spreading and if this is to be altered it is, in my view, a matter for direct legislative action rather than for the courts. It should be undertaken, if at all, openly and after adequate public inquiry and parliamentary debate and not worked towards covertly, in the course of judicial decision, by the adoption of policy factors which assume its desirability as a goal and operate to further its attainment.[65]

Yet, shortly afterwards, in *Griffiths v Kerkemeyer*,[66] he was prepared to take such considerations into account 'if theories of loss distribution might be resorted to' in order to test the desirability of a principle.

It is worth pursuing this example a little. In this case the plaintiff, who had suffered severe injuries, received nursing care on a voluntary basis. The court overruled authority to the effect that the plaintiff could recover the cost of nursing care only if under a legal or possibly moral obligation to pay for it. Deriving a principle from a series of English decisions, particularly *Donnelly v Joyce*,[67] the court held that the loss was sustained by the plaintiff, not the provider of the services. Since the defendant had created the need for the services, the plaintiff could recover damages for the value of the loss. This principle was endorsed in *Van Gervan v Fenton*,[68] which was concerned with

---

64 Metal Roofing & Cladding Pty Ltd v Eire Pty Ltd (1999) 9 NTLR 82 (FC) at [24] per Bailey J.
65 (1976) 136 CLR 529 at 580.    66 (1977) 139 CLR 161 at 176.    67 [1974] QB 454 (CA).
68 (1992) 175 CLR 327.

the valuation of the loss.[69] However, the principle was challenged in cases where the provider of the services was also the defendant. The House of Lords in *Hunt v Severs*[70] ultimately held that the principle was wrong and refused to allow recovery in such circumstances. However, the High Court, recognising the reality that the payment of the damages would come from insurance sources and the defendant personally would not be paying twice, and also that there were other policy reasons for allowing the plaintiff to recover,[71] refused to follow *Hunt v Severs*: *Kars v Kars*.[72] The English Law Commission subsequently preferred the reasoning of *Hunt v Severs*, but the policy of *Kars v Kars*, and recommended that legislation be enacted to reverse *Hunt v Severs*.[73] The High Court's policy orientation made that unnecessary.

Another case from the 1970s that is instructive is *State Government Insurance Commission v Trigwell*.[74] The court was faced with a challenge to the rule in *Searle v Wallbank*,[75] where it was held that the owner or occupier of a field abutting on to a highway owes no duty of care to users of the highway to keep in animals. The rule, of course, long predated *Donoghue v Stevenson*,[76] with which it was clearly inconsistent, and had been abrogated by legislation in its country of origin. There were also questions as to whether it had ever been received into Australian law. Murphy J had no hesitation in rejecting it, but the majority of the court disagreed. Mason J, having adduced reasons why the court should not in that case change a settled rule of the common law, concluded that the retention or abolition of the rule called for an assessment and adjustment of conflicting interests and that this was best left to Parliament.[77] Australian legislatures, other than in Queensland and

---

69  In dissenting on how the valuation is to be effected, Deane and Dawson JJ took account of the policy of some legislatures in reacting to the perceived over-generosity of the courts in awarding damages in these circumstances. Their dissenting judgment formed the basis of later legislation in most jurisdictions which places caps and thresholds on the amount that might be recovered. See, eg, Civil Liability Act 2002 (NSW) s 15. For the view that the interpretation of such provisions is to accord with the dissenting judgment of Deane and Dawson JJ, see *Mortimer v Burgess* (1997) 25 MVR 463 (NSW CA) at 467–8; *Finch v Rogers* [2004] NSWSC 39 (Unreported, David Kirby J, 13 February 2004).

70  [1994] 2 AC 350 (HL).

71  The policy reasons for allowing recovery by plaintiffs of damages in respect of services voluntarily provided by relatives and friends include the undesirability of compelling well-advised plaintiffs to enter into formal binding agreements for the provision of such services and the desirability of allowing a seriously injured person to choose to receive intimate care from someone with whom there is an existing relationship instead of obtaining the services from a commercial provider.

72  (1996) 187 CLR 354.

73  Law Commission, *Damages for Personal Injury: Medical, Nursing and Other Expenses; Collateral Benefits*, Law Com No 262, London: The Stationery Office, 1999, paras 3.75–76.

74  (1979) 142 CLR 617.    75 [1947] AC 341 (HL).    76 [1932] AC 562 (HL).

77  See (1979) 142 CLR 617 at 633–6.

the Northern Territory, have in fact abolished or modified the rule.[78] It is noteworthy, however, that in Western Australia, an upper limit of $500,000 was placed on the defendant's liability.[79] This followed a recommendation of that state's Law Reform Commission, which obtained information as to the insurance available to farmers and graziers.[80] It is likely that no court would place a similar limit on liability in a case like this, since once liability is recognised the damage would fall within well-established categories and the court would be concerned merely to restore the plaintiff so far as money could do so to the position that obtained before the accident. The case therefore differs from the judicial legislation indulged in by a majority of the House of Lords, over the strong protests of the minority, in *Rees v Darlington Memorial Hospital NHS Trust*,[81] where the sum of £15,000 was fixed as appropriate compensation for the newly recognised interference with reproductive autonomy.[82] In his dissenting judgment in *Brodie v Singleton SC* Gleeson CJ observed that the legislature could distinguish between property damage and personal injury if it wished to, whereas the court could not.[83] Although the first part of this proposition is unquestionably true, it is at least arguable that if policy reasons called for such a distinction, courts could make it.[84]

Mason J's opinion in *Trigwell* was quoted against him by McHugh J in his dissenting judgment in *Burnie Port Authority v General Jones Pty Ltd*,[85] where the majority held that the rule in *Rylands v Fletcher*[86] had become so riddled with anomalies and exceptions that it should be abolished and absorbed into the law of negligence. McHugh J did note that 'courts in general, and [the High Court] in particular, are more ready to alter the rules of the common law . . . than they were in 1979 when *Trigwell* was decided'. McHugh J, as a

---

78 Animals Act 1977 (NSW) s 7(2)(b); Civil Liability Act 1936 (SA) s 18(4); Law of Animals Act 1962 (Tas) Pt IV; Wrongs Act 1958 (Vic) s 33; Highways (Liability for Straying Animals) Act 1983 (WA); Civil Law (Wrongs) Act 2002 (ACT) s 214.

79 Highways (Liability for Straying Animals) Act 1983 (WA) s 3(5). The amount seems not to have been increased, despite the passage of over 20 years.

80 Report on Liability for Stock Straying on to the Highway, Project No 11, 1981, paras 6.16–21.

81 [2004] 1 AC 309 (HL).

82 Earlier judicial legislation along these lines is to be found in *Benham v Gambling* [1941] AC 157 (HL), where the House of Lords fixed the amount that could be awarded for loss of expectation of life. That decision led to further litigation as to whether the amount could increase with inflation: *Naylor v Yorkshire Electricity Board* [1968] AC 529 (HL). Their Lordships in *Rees* have not offered guidance on this in relation to their new remedy. Compare the Supreme Court of Canada's limit on non-pecuniary loss: *Lindal v Lindal* [1981] 2 SCR 629.

83 (2001) 206 CLR 512 at [44].

84 Compare Atiyah, PS, 'Property Damage, and Personal Injury – Different Duties of Care?' in Simos, T (ed), *Negligence and Economic Torts*, 1980, Sydney: LBC, p 37. See also in relation to remoteness of damage the judgment of Macarthur J in *Stephenson v Waite Tileman Ltd* [1973] 1 NZLR 152 (CA).

85 (1994) 179 CLR 520 at 592–3.     86 (1868) LR 3 HL 330.

party to the joint judgment in *Brodie v Singleton SC*, in turn relied heavily on the reasoning of the majority in *Burnie Port Authority v General Jones* to hold that another ancient rule of the common law, giving immunity to highway authorities for non-feasance, should also be abrogated and absorbed into the law of negligence. His Honour has also given us the benefit extra-judicially of his views as to when it is appropriate for judges to exercise their choices, which he acknowledges, in adapting the common law to changed social conditions.[87]

## The era of Deane J

*Jaensch v Coffey*,[88] a case of psychiatric injury to a woman who did not directly witness the accident in which her husband was seriously injured, gave Deane J the opportunity to commence his judgment with a broad exposition of the tort of negligence.[89] He explained that reasonable foreseeability, though necessary, is not sufficient to establish a duty of care. There must also be present a relationship of proximity between the plaintiff and the defendant, and no overriding rule of statute or common law (he instanced cases of joint illegality) that precluded the implication of such a duty in the circumstances of the case. He subjected the requirement of proximity, stemming from Lord Atkin's 'neighbour principle' in *Donoghue v Stevenson*,[90] to a close analysis, providing it with more content than anyone had previously thought to give it. He admitted that not much attention was given to it in some cases, but he said that was because it was not there in dispute. This tended to happen in well-settled areas of the law of negligence, such as actions for physical injury by employees against employers, where the proximity of the relationship had already been established. However,

> in a new or developing area of the law of negligence, the question whether the relationship between plaintiff and defendant with reference to the allegedly negligent act possessed the requisite degree of proximity is a question of law to be resolved by the processes of legal reasoning by induction and deduction.

To this he added significantly:

> The identity and relative importance of the considerations relevant to an issue of proximity will obviously vary in different classes of case and the

---

87  See McHugh, Hon Justice M, 'The Judicial Method' (1999) 73 Australian Law Journal 37. See also n 13, above and his joint judgment with Gummow J in *Cattanach v Melchior* (2003) 215 CLR 1 at [58]–[83].

88  (1984) 155 CLR 549.      89  Ibid 578–87.      90  [1932] AC 562 (HL) at 580.

question whether the relationship is 'so' close 'that' the common law should recognize a duty of care in a new area or class of case is, as Lord Atkin foresaw, likely to be 'difficult' of resolution *in that it may involve value judgments on matters of policy and degree.*[91]

Having warned, in terms similar to those of Windeyer J referred to above,[92] that it is not for judges to apply their idiosyncratic values in particular cases, he continued:

The identification of the content of the criteria or rules which reflect that requirement in developing areas of the law *should not*, however, *be either ostensibly or actually divorced from the considerations of public policy* which underlie and enlighten it.[93]

Soon afterwards, in *Sutherland Shire Council v Heyman*,[94] a case categorised by him as one of pure economic loss, Deane J reiterated almost word for word what he had said in *Jaensch*, but also took the opportunity to respond to some criticism from the English courts of what he had there said.[95] In the course of doing so, he included 'notions of what is "fair and reasonable" ' as an alternative to 'considerations of public policy'.

Like *Caltex*, both *Jaensch* and *Heyman* were cases in which the High Court was unanimous in relation to the outcome, but hopelessly divided on the reasons for the result. As with Lord Atkin's speech in *Donoghue v Stevenson*, what Deane J said was not adopted by any other member of the court. However, in subsequent cases his Honour won over all the then members of the High Court except Brennan J, who resolutely stood out against acceptance of this concept of 'proximity', which Deane J claimed constituted a 'unifying concept' or 'touchstone' or 'general determinant' of the categories of case in which the common law of negligence recognises a duty to take reasonable care to avoid a reasonably foreseeable and real risk of injury to another.[96] Policy arguments were not ignored, but appeared subservient to the conceptualisation of 'proximity'. Thus in *Bryan v Maloney*,[97] where the issue was whether the builder of a house owed a duty of care not to cause pure economic loss to a subsequent purchaser, the joint judgment of the majority was expressed largely in terms of proximity, but took account of factors such as the cost of purchase often being the most significant expense in the life of an average Australian.

91  (1984) 155 CLR 549 at 585 (emphasis added).    92  See text at n 56, above.
93  (1984) 155 CLR 549 at 585 (emphasis added).    94  (1985) 157 CLR 424.
95  Ibid 495–8.
96  See, eg, *Cook v Cook* (1986)162 CLR 376 at 381–2; *Burnie Port Authority v General Jones Pty Ltd* (1994) 179 CLR 520 at 542–3; *Bryan v Maloney* (1995) 182 CLR 609.
97  (1995) 182 CLR 609.

The attempt to embrace policy arguments within the concept of 'proximity', instead of considering them separately, reached its height in *Gala v Preston*.[98] This was another case of joint illegality involving the theft of a motor vehicle. In *Jaensch*, as we have seen, Deane J mentioned joint illegality as an illustration of an overriding rule of the common law, separate from notions of proximity, that precluded the implication of a duty of care. In *Smith v Jenkins*,[99] however, the court had unanimously denied recovery to a passenger against the driver of a vehicle they had stolen together. Barwick CJ posed the question whether the denial was due to a refusal to erect a duty of care or a refusal of damages on grounds of public policy. He preferred the former basis, though he had 'no doubt considerations of public policy have their place in the decision in the particular case to impose or erect such a duty'.[100] Windeyer and Owen JJ similarly held that no duty of care arose because of the absence of a duty of care, which they attributed to an absence of 'neighbourness' or proximity. Kitto and Walsh JJ seemed to prefer the view that the law simply refused to recognise a cause of action in such cases.

In the course of his judgment in *Smith v Jenkins*,[101] Windeyer J delivered a typically learned disquisition on why the maxim *ex turpi causa* had no relevance to the law of torts. He acknowledged that 'development in the common law of torts today [is] dictated by a sense of existing and inherent policy and principle', and he again endorsed a passage from *Salmond on Torts* that referred to the courts' ability on the grounds of policy to limit the scope of negligence.[102] But he saw it as 'a mistake to approach the case by asking whether the plaintiff is precluded by considerations of public policy from asserting a right of action for negligence', holding instead that the parties were not 'neighbours' in Lord Atkin's sense because they took the risk of each other's conduct, it being irrelevant, in his view, whether the rule was 'founded on the negation of duty, or on some extension of the rule *volenti non fit injuria*, or simply on the refusal of the courts to aid wrongdoers'.[103]

This lack of a firm agreed basis may have accounted for the path that the law of joint illegality took thereafter. In two later cases, the court, over Barwick CJ's dissent in each, allowed plaintiffs engaged in joint illegal activities to recover damages.[104] In *Jackson v Harrison*, Murphy J was typically scornful of the grounds on which *Smith v Jenkins* had been decided, seeing it actually as an application of 'judicial policy'. He proceeded to demonstrate the error of

---

98 (1991) 172 CLR 243.　　99 (1970) 119 CLR 397.　　100 Ibid, 400.
101 Ibid, 409–17.　　102 15th ed, 1969, p 257, cited ibid 418.
103 (1970) 119 CLR 397 at 422.
104 *Progress and Properties Ltd v Craft* (1976) 135 CLR 651 and *Jackson v Harrison* (1978) 138 CLR 438.

such a policy in a transparent presentation of the arguments for not denying a duty of care in cases of joint illegality.[105] But in *Gala v Preston* the court again unanimously denied recovery. Mason CJ, Deane, Gaudron and McHugh JJ delivered a joint judgment, basing the decision on the absence of proximity,[106] which in turn was dependent on the inability of the courts to establish a standard of care in the circumstances. Brennan J maintained his objection to the use of proximity for this purpose, instead resting his decision on the need to maintain coherence with the criminal law. Dawson J, who had gone along with the proximity notion in earlier decisions,[107] also found it impossible in this case to hold that there was an absence of proximity. Certainly, if one considers Deane J's initial explanation in *Jaensch* and *Heyman* of the notion in terms of physical, circumstantial or causal proximity, it is difficult to see why the parties were not here in a relationship of proximity, notwithstanding what was said in *Smith v Jenkins*. Uncertainty as to the true basis of denial of recovery in cases of joint illegality divided the full Federal Court on the issue of onus of proof in *Italiano v Barbaro*.[108] It is suggested that this is another instance where a decision more openly based on policy would have provided more helpful guidance to lower courts than one supposedly based on principle.

We turn to another area of controversy, the liability of advocates for negligence in the conduct of court proceedings and matters intimately associated with such proceedings. Anecdotally, I believe that when Stephen Charles QC, now Charles JA of the Victorian Court of Appeal, was preparing to argue in the High Court the case of the respondent barristers in the appeal from *Wraith v Giannarelli*,[109] he was warned of the need to be ready to answer questions relating to proximity. In the result, the High Court implicitly accepted the argument of Cliff Pannam QC that the 'proximity of the relationship is such that a duty of care would be found to exist unless some

---

105  (1978) 138 CLR 438 at 464–5.
106  It is surprising to find McHugh J a party to this joint judgment based on proximity. Prior to his elevation to the High Court and in more recent times he has been the most trenchant critic of the concept: see, eg, his extra-judicial article 'Neighbourhood, Proximity and Reliance' in Finn, PD (ed), *Essays on Torts*, 1989, Sydney: LBC, p 5; *Hill v Van Erp* (1997) 188 CLR 159 at 210 (acknowledging that he had joined in the judgment in *Gala*, but having found that the present case reinforced his scepticism); *Perre v Apand Pty Ltd* (1999) 198 CLR 180 at [78]; and the joint judgment to which he was a party in *Sullivan v Moody* (2001) 207 CLR 562 at [48]–[49]. Cf. his view of *Gala v Preston* (and of *Cook v Cook* (1986) 162 CLR 376) in *Joslyn v Berryman* (2003) 214 CLR 552 at [29]–[30]. See also his approach to *Bryan v Maloney* (1995)182 CLR 609 in *Woolcock Street Investments Pty Ltd v CDG Pty Ltd* (2004) 216 CLR 515 at [72]–[73].
107  See *Cook v Cook* (1986) 162 CLR 376; *Burnie Port Authority v General Jones Pty Ltd* (1994) 179 CLR 520.
108  (1993) 40 FCR 303. Compare *Hall v Hebert* [1993] 2 SCR 159.
109  [1988] VR 713 (FC).

immunity based on public policy is to be created',[110] but not one of the six[111] substantial judgments mentioned proximity.[112] The four members of the majority all discussed the public policy issues which in their view justified the absence of a duty of care in negligence. Deane J was in dissent and would have held the defendants liable. After the decision of the House of Lords in *Arthur J S Hall & Co (a Firm) v Simons*,[113] those issues were reconsidered in *D'Orta-Ekenaike v Victoria Legal Aid*.[114] The majority of the court refused to overrule its earlier decision and possibly extended it, though many of the policy reasons previously given were seen either as wrong or of marginal importance. In the end the decision of the majority rested on two bases:

(a) the place of the judicial system as a part of the governmental structure; and

(b) the place that an immunity from suit has in a series of rules, all of which are designed to achieve finality in the quelling of disputes by the exercise of judicial power.[115]

Another leading case of the era when Deane J was a member of the court was *March v E & M H Stramare Pty Ltd*.[116] This was not dealt with as a case on duty of care, but of causation, though it is arguable that the issue of causation was in effect determined once it was held, as Deane J did, that the duty of care owed by the defendants was not confined to persons who were careful and sober, but extended to all foreseeable users of the road, including bad and inattentive drivers and those whose faculties were impaired either naturally or by the effect of alcohol. Although insisting that causation is a question of fact to be decided on the basis of common sense and experience, the judgment of Mason CJ, with which Toohey and Gaudron JJ agreed, and that of Deane J, with which Gaudron J also agreed, held that considerations of policy and value judgments necessarily enter into it. McHugh J, too, recognised the reality that limiting rules are 'the product of a policy choice', which he wanted to see openly exposed as part of the reasoning on remoteness of damage, leaving causation to be determined on a simple 'but-for' test.[117] McHugh J's view has since been vindicated. As a result of the acceptance of Jane Stapleton's theories[118] by the

---

110  See *Giannarelli v Wraith* (1988) 165 CLR 543 at 547.
111  Gaudron J merely agreed with the dissenting judgment of Toohey J.
112  *Giannarelli v Wraith* (1988) 165 CLR 543.   113  [2002] 1 AC 615 (HL).
114  (2005) 214 ALR 92.   115  Ibid [25] per Gleeson CJ, Gummow, Hayne and Heydon JJ.
116  (1991) 171 CLR 506.   117  Ibid 531–6.
118  See, eg, Stapleton, Jane, 'Perspectives on Causation' in Horder, J (ed), *Oxford Essays in Jurisprudence (4th Series)*, 2000, Oxford: Oxford University Press, p 61; Stapleton, Jane, 'Cause-in-Fact and the Scope of Liability for Consequences' (2003) 119 Law Quarterly Review 388.

Ipp Committee,[119] legislation has now been enacted in almost all jurisdictions requiring a two-stage approach to the issue, with the 'but-for' test ordinarily applying at the first stage, and a very broad consideration of other factors determining the scope of liability at the second stage.[120]

The use of policy in relation to causation in the High Court was most manifest in the decision of the majority in *Chappel v Hart*.[121] In this case three members of the court held a surgeon who failed to warn the plaintiff of a risk that eventuated liable for the consequences, even though she would have had to undergo the operation at some time and the risk may have been the same.[122] The case has been followed in England by a similar majority in *Chester v Afshar*.[123]

### Post-Deane J

In the latest edition of the casebook that I produce with David Hambly, *Torts: Cases and Commentary*,[124] I wrote: 'Once Deane J left the High Court in 1995 to become Governor General, a reaction set in.' I hasten to assure Michael Kirby, who replaced Sir William Deane, that I meant a reaction to the notion of 'proximity' as the touchstone or determinant of the categories of case in which a duty of care is recognised.[125] The court rapidly abandoned this exaggerated claim for the concept: see *Hill v Van Erp*[126] and *Esanda Finance Corporation Ltd v Peat Marwick Hungerfords (Reg)*.[127] Policy arguments loomed large in both these cases, which were concerned with whether there was a duty of care in two quite diverse instances of pure economic loss. The judgment of McHugh J in *Esanda*, in particular, though finding it unnecessary to come to a final conclusion because the claim had been inadequately pleaded, spelt out at some length, policy considerations that would influence such a conclusion if it became necessary to reach one.[128]

It may be instructive to look at *Hill v Van Erp* in simplified form in order

---

119 Commonwealth of Australia, *Review of the Law of Negligence Report*, Canberra, 2002 [accessed 2 September 2002] http://revofneg.treasury.gov.au/content/review.asp paras 7.25–7.50 and Recommendation 29.

120 Civil Liability Act 2002 (NSW) s 5D; Civil Liability Act 2003 (Qld) s 11; Civil Liability Act 1936 (SA) s 34; Civil Liability Act 2002 (Tas) s 13; Wrongs Act 1958 (Vic) s 51; Civil Liability Act 2002 (WA) s 5C; Civil Law (Wrongs) Act 2002 (ACT) s 45.

121 (1998) 195 CLR 232.

122 See the note on the case by Honoré, Tony, Medical Non-Disclosure, Causation and Risk: *Chappel v Hart* (1999) 7 Torts Law Journal 1.

123 [2005] 1 AC 134 (HL).

124 2002, 5th edn, Sydney: Butterworths LexisNexis, para [2.2.18].

125 Compare Kirby, The Hon Justice Michael, 'Harold Luntz: Doyen of the Australian Law of Torts' (2003) 27 Melbourne University Law Review 635 at 641.

126 (1997) 188 CLR 159.       127 (1997) 188 CLR 241.       128 Ibid 282–9.

to explain the thesis of the present chapter that it is necessary to resort to policy in arriving at decisions in the ultimate appellate courts. The claim in this case was made by a disappointed beneficiary against a solicitor who had failed properly to supervise the execution of a will. The issue had come before the House of Lords not long before in *White v Jones*,[129] where it had been decided by a narrow majority that a duty of care was owed. Lord Mustill dissented strongly on the basis of principle, as did McHugh J in the Australian equivalent. The underlying principle that supports these dissents is that a person who is not a party to a contract cannot ordinarily enforce it. A response to that might be that *Donoghue v Stevenson*[130] 'exploded' the contract fallacy.[131] That might be rebutted by saying that the loss here was purely economic and the *ratio decidendi* of *Donoghue v Stevenson* does not extend to loss of this nature. The majority of the House of Lords found competing principles in cases such as *Hedley Byrne & Co v Heller & Partners*[132] and *Nocton v Lord Ashburton*,[133] which they preferred. However, in choosing to adapt or expand the competing principles, the majority were clearly influenced by the policy argument earlier advanced in *Ross v Caunters*[134] that to deny a remedy here would mean that the only person who could sue as a result of the solicitor's negligence would have suffered no loss and could recover no more than nominal damages, whereas the person who had suffered a real loss would be unable to sue. The High Court, having previously held in *Caltex Oil (Australia) Pty Ltd v The Dredge 'Willemstad'*[135] that damages for pure economic loss could extend beyond the *Hedley Byrne*-type situation, had to decide whether the present situation should be brought within the *ratio* of that case, whatever it was. The majority found additional reasons of policy to bring this type of case within the scope of the expanded duty of care. So emphasis was laid on the reliance the community places on solicitors to see that wills are properly executed, the need to maintain standards among solicitors, the absence of conflict between the duty owed to the client and the new duty to the beneficiary, the knowledge of the solicitor as to the potential claimants, the absence of indeterminacy in the amount of the loss and the continued coherence of the law.

Similarly, policy arguments were advanced at various points in the long judgments in *Perre v Apand Pty Ltd*,[136] another, though different, case raising the issue of duty of care to avoid causing pure economic loss. It is true to say, however, that the court was more concerned to try to find a framework for deciding such cases, a search which, we have seen, failed dismally.[137] What

---

129 [1995] 2 AC 207 (HL).      130 [1932] AC 562 (HL).
131 *Candler v Crane, Christmas & Co* [1951] 2 KB 164 (CA) at 177 per Denning LJ.
132 [1964] AC 465 (HL).      133 [1914] AC 932 (HL).      134 [1980] Ch 297.
135 Above, n 8.      136 (1999) 198 CLR 180.
137 See the quotation in the text at n 64, above.

may have emerged from it was the importance of 'vulnerability' – in the sense of a plaintiff's inability to protect against loss – as a factor in establishing a duty of care.[138]

Criticism directed at the court for failing to provide guidance may have led to the adoption of a unanimous joint judgment of the five Justices then sitting in *Sullivan v Moody*, a case denying a duty of care on child protection authorities towards parents being investigated for sexual abuse.[139] Rejecting the three-stage approach adopted in England since *Caparo Industries Plc v Dickman*,[140] the court jettisoned proximity, perhaps throwing the baby out with the bathwater.[141] This has meant that cases like *Bryan v Maloney*[142] have come under renewed scrutiny, which is at present inconclusive, but the court has said that it can no longer be supported on the grounds that were advanced.[143]

It may be recalled that in *Heyman* Deane J equated what is 'fair and reasonable', then gaining ground as a test in England, with the policy considerations that he said must not be divorced from the other criteria that went to the identification of 'proximity' in a novel area of the law of negligence.[144] The court in *Sullivan v Moody* rejected this too, as it is now found in the third stage of the *Caparo* test. It offered the following criticism:

> The question as to what is fair, and just and reasonable is capable of being misunderstood as an invitation to formulate policy rather than to search for principle. The concept of policy, in this context, is often ill-defined. There are policies at work in the law which can be identified and applied to novel problems, but the law of tort develops by reference to principles, which must be capable of general application, not discretionary decision-making in individual cases.[145]

As we have seen, recognition of the influence of policy does not entail discretionary decision-making in individual cases.[146] The 'policies at work' in

---

138  See Stapleton, above n 1; *Woolcock Street Investments Pty Ltd v CDG Pty Ltd* (2004) 216 CLR 515.

139  (2001) 207 CLR 562. The issue has been decided against the parents also in the Privy Council on appeal from New Zealand (*B v Attorney-General* [2003] UKPC 61; [2003] 4 All ER 833) and in the House of Lords (*D v East Berkshire Community Health NHS Trust* [2005] 2 AC 373 (HL)).

140  [1990] 2 AC 605 (HL).

141  Compare Witting, Christian, 'The Three-stage Test Abandoned in Australia – or Not?' (2002) 118 Law Quarterly Review 214. See now Witting, Christian, 'Duty of Care: An Analytical Approach' (2005) 25 Oxford Journal of Legal Studies 33.

142  (1995) 182 CLR 609; see text at n 97, above.

143  *Woolcock Street Investments Pty Ltd v CDG Pty Ltd* (2004) 216 CLR 515.

144  See text following n 95, above.        145  (2001) 207 CLR 562 at [49].

146  See Windeyer J's statements quoted in the text at nn 56 and 57 and *Jaensch v Coffey* (1984)155 CLR 549 at 585 per Deane J, citing *H C Sleigh Ltd v South Australia* (1977) 136

this case included the need to recognise the statutory framework within which child protection workers functioned; that the best interests of the child must remain paramount; the need not to override the law of defamation, which had struck a balance in the protection of privileged reports; coherence with the law generally applicable to persons performing statutory functions and in particular with the protection given to the police in the investigation of crime; the potential indeterminacy of liability; and the avoidance of instilling a defensive attitude in the minds of the protection workers.

Earlier, in *Perre v Apand*, McHugh J had said that while 'almost everyone would agree that courts should not impose a duty of care on a person unless it is fair, just and reasonable to do so', such a test is of little use for the guidance of others and makes trials expensive because of the increased range of evidentiary materials necessary.[147] It is noteworthy, however, that in *D v East Berkshire Community Health NHS Trust* the House of Lords advanced similar issues of policy to those adumbrated in *Sullivan v Moody* – which was indeed cited with approval in several of the speeches – in deciding that it was not 'fair, just and reasonable' to impose on healthcare and other child protection professionals a common law duty of care owed to parents against whom they had made unfounded allegations of child abuse and who in consequence suffered psychiatric injury.

Kirby J did not sit in *Sullivan v Moody*. In a series of cases he had adapted the framework of the three-stage test of *Caparo* to Australian law and tried to persuade his fellow judges to adopt it.[148] He has on several occasions after *Sullivan* declared himself to be bound by it to abandon his test, but he continues to regret it.[149] Whether as part of the three-stage test or otherwise, he has never concealed his discussion of policy in the cases that have come before him. One may pick up any of his numerous judgments and almost always find the policy arguments for both sides set out, followed by his own reasons. But he has often acknowledged that the courts seldom have available to them evidence on which to base conclusions, particularly economic evidence. Australian courts do not benefit from 'Brandeis briefs' and intervention on behalf of *amici curiae* is limited.[150] Thus, in *Northern Sandblasting*

CLR 475 at 514 per Jacobs J. See also *Travel Compensation Fund v Robert Tambree t/as R Tambree and Associates* (2005) 222 ALR 263.

147 (1999) 198 CLR 180 at [80]–[81].

148 See, eg, *Pyrenees Shire Council v Day* (1998) 192 CLR 330 at [242]–[244]; *Crimmins v Stevedoring Industry Finance Committee* (1999) 200 CLR 1 at [221]–[222].

149 *Graham Barclay Oysters Pty Ltd v Ryan* (2002) 211 CLR 540 at [237]–[244]; *Woolcock Street Investments Pty Ltd v CDG Pty Ltd* (2004) 216 CLR 515 at [159]; *Cattanach v Melchior* (2003) 215 CLR 1 at [121]–[122].

150 See Kenny, The Hon Susan, 'Interveners and Amici Curiae in the High Court' (1998) 20 Adelaide Law Rev 159; Mason, Sir Anthony, 'Interveners and Amici Curiae in the High

*Pty Ltd v Harris*,[151] where he dissented from the majority decision (for different reasons) to hold a landlord liable to the child of the tenant, his reasons included the following passage:

> There are other reasons of legal policy or principle which tend to restrain the creation of a new sub-category of non-delegable duty in this case. . . . the result would still be the introduction of a new burden on landlords which, on legal authority accepted until the recent past, they would not reasonably have anticipated. Such a burden would necessarily have a retrospective operation. Given the wide range of persons who constitute landlords of the proposed class, it could be anticipated that some would not be insured. Even those insured might find their cover limited to established liability, as under the Residential Tenancies Act. *This Court has no way of estimating the economic consequences of inventing a new category of 'special' duty.* Nevertheless such consequences would clearly include the potential costs of imposing new duties of inspection; of withdrawing some low cost accommodation from the market; and of obtaining liability insurance to meet the relatively rare case that the insurance of a qualified contractor, engaged by the landlord, proved insufficient for the peculiar risk in a particular case.[152]

He reiterated reasons of this sort when a member of the majority in *Jones v Bartlett*,[153] a similar case in which special leave to appeal had been given in order to clarify the uncertainty engendered by the divided majority in *Northern Sandblasting*. The comment emphasised in the above passage drew a sympathetic response from Callinan J, who went on to list factors which might influence a decision whether to buy or rent premises.[154]

Kirby and Callinan JJ, however, found themselves on opposite sides of the debate on policy factors in setting the standard of care in *Woods v Multi-Sport Holdings Pty Ltd*,[155] though it was with McHugh J's use of social facts that Callinan J mostly quarrelled. This issue has been analysed by Kylie

Court: A Comment' (1998) 20 Adelaide Law Review 173; Durbach, Andrea, 'Interveners in High Court Litigation: A Comment' (1998) 20 Adelaide Law Review 177; Owens, Rosemary J, 'Interveners and Amicus Curiae: The Role of the Courts in a Modern Democracy' (1998) 20 Adelaide Law Review 193; Neville, Warwick, 'Abortion before the High Court: What Next? Caveat Interventus: A Note on Superclinics Australia Pty Ltd v CES' (1998) 20 Adelaide Law Review 183; Williams, George, 'The Amicus Curiae and Intervener in the High Court of Australia: A Comparative Analysis.' (2000) 28 Federal Law Review 365. See also *Levy v Victoria* (1997) 189 CLR 579 at 650–2 per Kirby J. The call for clarification of the role of interveners and *amici curiae* in the rules of the High Court appears to have gone unanswered in the new rules of the High Court which took effect on 1 January 2005.

151 (1997) 188 CLR 313.     152 Ibid 401–2 (emphasis added).
153 (2000) 205 CLR 166.     154 Ibid [288].     155 (2002) 208 CLR 460.

Burns in an article on the case[156] and she has again considered the matter, with especial reference to the assumptions made in *Cattanach v Melchior*,[157] in a paper originally presented at this conference.[158] These papers demonstrate that the assumptions made may well be inaccurate. Kirby and Callinan JJ differed too on the policy factors to be taken into account in *Liftronic Pty Ltd v Unver*,[159] on contributory negligence of employees. In *Hollis v Vabu Pty Ltd*,[160] the majority, including Kirby J, approved a statement attributing the doctrine of vicarious liability to policy, not analytical jurisprudence,[161] and accepted the policy-oriented approach of the Supreme Court of Canada in *Bazley v Curry*;[162] whereas Callinan J dissented, drawing attention to the possible falsity of the assumptions on which the policy arguments were based and contending that the matter was one for Parliament and not the courts.[163] In *Cattanach v Melchior* Callinan J made the apparently disingenuous statement:

> I cannot help observing that the repeated disavowal in the cases of recourse to public policy is not always convincing. Davies JA in the Court of Appeal in this case was, with respect, right to imply that it would be more helpful for the resolution of the controversy if judges frankly acknowledged their debt to their own social values, and the way in which these have in fact moulded or influenced their judgments rather than the application of strict legal principle.
>
> In substance, almost all of the arguments that can be made against the awarding of damages for the costs of rearing a child consequent upon . . . a wrongful pregnancy, do involve emotional and moral values and perceptions of what public policy is, or should be.[164]

He then purported to put these values aside and to decide the case, with some distaste for the conclusion, on legal principle.

There is a further irony in *Cattanach v Melchior*, the judgments in which are looked at more closely in Peter Cane's paper presented at this conference.[165] The three dissenting judges, Gleeson CJ, Hayne and Heydon JJ, are normally associated with the conservative side of the court, which prefers to

---

156  Burns, Kylie, 'It's Just Not Cricket: The High Court, Sport and Legislative Facts' (2002) 10 Torts Law Journal 234.

157  (2003) 215 CLR 1.

158  Burns, Kylie, 'The Way the World Is: Social Facts in High Court Negligence Cases' (2004) 12 Torts Law Journal 215.

159  [2001] HCA 24; (2001) 179 ALR 321.        160  (2001) 207 CLR 21.

161  Ibid [34], approving Fullagar J in *Darling Island Stevedoring and Lighterage Co Ltd v Long* (1957) 97 CLR 36 at 56–7.

162  [1999] 2 SCR 534.        163  (2001) 207 CLR 21 at [116]–[119].

164  (2003) 215 CLR 1 at [291]–[292].        165  Above, n 30.

decide cases on the basis of principle rather than policy;[166] yet in essence they had to resort to policy to deny recovery of damages for the cost of bringing up a healthy child.[167] Hayne J's judgment contained the most open acknowledgment that '[p]ublic policy has long played a key role in the development of the common law'.[168] Having considered its role in some other areas of law, he observed that it had been given less prominence in the law of torts.[169] He went on to consider some of the cases and dicta that we have already looked at. He concluded his general discussion of public policy with the words:

> it must be recognised, . . . that 'it may be that Judges are no better able to discern what is for the public good than other experienced and enlightened members of the community'. But as Pollock LCB went on to say, 'that is no reason for their refusing to entertain the question, and declining to decide upon it'.[170]

Whether or not one agrees with the conclusion to which he then came by weighing up the arguments of policy he discerned as applicable to the facts of the case, one should applaud this approach.

Kirby J, who, as already mentioned is normally open about his reliance on policy, contended that obedience to *Sullivan v Moody* bound him not 'to confront directly, and even more explicitly, the competing issues of policy', which the third stage of the *Caparo* test would have required him to do.[171] Nevertheless, there is a good deal of policy in his reasoning. McHugh and Gummow JJ were prepared to accept that 'the underlying values respecting the importance of human life, the stability of the family unit and the nurture of infant children until their legal majority [are] an essential aspect of the

---

166  Since this was Heydon J's first judgment after his elevation to the High Court, one has to rely for this on his judgments when a member of the New South Wales Court of Appeal and, more particularly, on his address to a Quadrant dinner, 'Judicial activism and the rule of law', published inter alia in (2003) 23 Australian Bar Review 110. Kirby J has responded to this in the Hamlyn Lectures for 2003 (*Judicial Activism: Authority, Principle and Policy in the Judicial Method*, London: Sweet & Maxwell, 2004) and in the article, 'Judicial Activism? A Riposte to the Counter-Reformation' (2004) 24 Australian Bar Review 219. See also Hutchinson, Allan C, 'Heydon' Seek: Looking for Law in All the Wrong Places (2003) 29 Monash University Law Review 85, who points out that it was the conservative dissenting justices in *Brodie v Singleton SC* who had to resort to policy reasons in order to justify preserving the status quo (see 92–6).

167  Compare Ackland, Richard, 'Putting Labels on Court Rulings That Don't Suit', Sydney Morning Herald (Sydney), 25 July 2003.

168  (2003) 215 CLR 1 at [223].       169  Ibid [236].

170  (2003) 215 CLR 1 at [242], citing Pollock LCB in *Egerton v Brownlow* (1853) 4 HL Cas 1 151.

171  (2003) 215 CLR 1 at [122].

corporate welfare of the community',[172] but, applying a stringent test of 'general recognition in the community', found that it was not generally recognised:

> that those values demand that there must be no award of damages for the cost to the parents of rearing and maintaining a child who would not have been born were it not for the negligent failure of a gynaecologist in giving advice after performing a sterilisation procedure.[173]

The decision in *Cattanach* provoked a storm of public criticism[174] and some support.[175] As Underwood J has pointed out, much of the response could not have been based on a reading of the judgments.[176] Three legislatures have leapt in to reverse it,[177] but others have not, at least so far. Perhaps McHugh and Gummow JJ were right that there is no *general* recognition of the need to deny such damages.

### Conclusion

The High Court of Australia, like all appellate courts, has leeways of choice open to it when deciding the cases that come before it. The transparency of the special leave to appeal procedure in Australia reveals that in virtually every case there are at least reasonable grounds for argument that the decision below is wrong and that the case raises issues of importance. The frequency of dissent in the High Court shows the room that the judges have in deciding each case. Principle alone cannot determine the outcome and in choosing between competing principles or expanding or narrowing the *ratio* of a previous decision, the court must turn to values and policy. Instances of this before the 1970s are to be found, but it is only thereafter that these matters came to be brought out into the open.

Important in this regard was the analysis of the tort of negligence in the

---

172  For a feminist critique of the assumptions underlying the judgments, both majority and minority, see Golder, B, 'From *McFarlane* to *Melchior* and beyond: Love, sex, money and commodification in the Anglo-Australian law of torts' (2004) 12 Torts Law Journal 128. See also Burns, above n 158.

173  (2003) 215 CLR 1 [76]–[77].

174  Eg, Shanahan, Dennis, Saunders, Megan and Agencies, 'Anderson Criticises Baby Damages', *The Australian*, 18 July 2003; Shanahan, Angela, 'A Child Should Never Be Seen as Damage', *The Age* (Melbourne), 22 July 2003.

175  Eg, Graycar, Reg, 'A Loved Baby Can't Cancel out a Clear Case of Negligence', *Sydney Morning Herald* (Sydney), 21 July 2003.

176  Underwood, P, 'Is Ms Donoghue's Snail in Mortal Peril?' (2004) 12 Torts Law Journal 39 at 59–60.

177  In order of enactment, the legislation, which varies in its wording, is Civil Liability Act 2003 (Qld) s 49A; Civil Liability Act 2002 (NSW) s 71; Civil Liability Act 1936 (SA) s 67.

judgments of Deane J in *Jaensch v Coffey* and *Sutherland Shire Council v Heyman*, where values and policy were recognised as playing a role in determining duty of care in novel situations at the stage of deciding whether the relationship between the parties possessed the required degree of proximity. Deane J's analysis also recognised the role of policy in relation to possible overriding rules. His Honour's claims for the concept of proximity as a universal determinant of the categories of case in which a duty of care was recognised were adopted by almost all members of the High Court while he himself was a member of the Bench, but fell into disfavour thereafter.

Deane J's successor on the High Court, Kirby J, has kept the flag flying for open recognition of and consideration of issues of policy, while acknowledging that the limited materials before the court often makes it impossible to decide on true policy grounds. Other members of the court claim to prefer principle to policy, but policy reasoning permeates many of their judgments. This is most apparent in the dissenting judgments by three conservative Justices in the recent decision of *Cattanach v Melchior*.

Policy and values enter into the determination of torts cases not only in relation to duty of care, but also in relation to causation and remoteness of damage and the assessment of damages. *Cattanach* may be seen as an instance of remoteness of damage;[178] *Chappel v Hart* and *Kars v Kars* provide illustrations of policy factors entering into decisions on causation and damages respectively.

This chapter does not attempt to resolve the problem of how the High Court could better inform itself of the relevant social facts in assisting it to make its policy decisions. Brandeis briefs, intervention by non-parties and additional expert evidence at trial all have costs. Who is to bear those costs requires careful consideration. But the consequence of not allowing the High Court to have the benefit of the information they could provide is that the inevitable law-making by the highest court in the country is likely to be flawed.

---

178 As Lord Hoffmann has observed, it is a matter of taste whether issues such as there arose are considered under the scope of the duty of care or remoteness of damage: *Jolley v Sutton London Borough Council* [2000] 3 All ER 409 (HL) at 418.

# Chapter 4

# The High Court and social facts: a negligence case study

*Kylie Burns* *

## Introduction

Negligence cases in the High Court by nature present difficult policy choices and take place against the context of judicial recognition of the nature of Australian society, social values and human behaviour. This has been particularly evident in recent high profile and contentious cases such as *Cattanach v Melchior*.[1] The High Court continues to struggle with its role as policy maker and policy utiliser. Some judges, notably Justice Kirby, have long advocated a more frank acknowledgement of policy concerns in negligence cases.[2] However, at least officially, the majority of the High Court has shied away from considering 'public policy' as an explicit factor in determining liability in all negligence cases.[3] Whether or not the High Court officially recognises that it explicitly considers policy matters in all cases (be they called legal policy,[4] public policy, principle, community values, enduring values or whatever),[5] in

---

* Kylie Burns BA LLB (Hons) LLM Solicitor of the Supreme Court of Queensland, Lecturer Griffith Law School. I particularly thank Professor Sandra Berns for her comments on previous drafts of this chapter and my colleague Lillian Corbin for her input particularly into part 4 of the chapter. I also thank Professor Jane Stapleton, Professor Peter Cane, Professor Harold Luntz and Professor Rosemary Hunter for their helpful comments on previous versions of this chapter.

1 (2003)215 CLR 1. A version of Parts 1–3 of this chapter has previously been published as Kylie Burns, 'The way the world is: Social Facts in High Court Negligence Cases' (2004) 12(3) Torts Law Journal 215.

2 *Cattanach v Melchior* (2003) 215 CLR 1 [121]–[122] and [152].

3 See *Sullivan v Moody* (2001) 207 CLR 562. However, note the comments in *Cattanach v Melchior* (2003) 215 CLR 1 by Callinan J at [291], McHugh and Gummow JJ at [65] and [73]–[76] and Hayne J at [219] and [223]–[242] regarding the role of public policy in tort law and the necessity for judges to make choices. Kirby J at [121] identifies all judges of the High Court in *Cattanach* making express reference to both principle and policy.

4 The unsatisfactory and misleading description adopted by Lord Millett in *McFarlane v Tayside Health Board* [2000] 2 AC 59 at 108.

5 See Stapleton, Jane, 'The golden thread at the heart of tort law: Protection of the vulnerable' (2003) 24 Australian Bar Review 135. I agree with Stapleton's argument that often there is

negligence cases it is clear that the judges inevitably make assumptions about their society, world and human behaviour. These assumptions flavour the interpretation, creation and adoption of doctrinal principles. They create the background context against which a judge's reasoning and decision is formed. They function as rhetorical devices that persuade the reader that a particular interpretation of the law is correct. This affects not only the manner in which principles are applied to the parties of a particular case, but also the development of the general principles of Australian tort law and perhaps even contributes to the construction of particular general social norms.[6] In this chapter these assumptions are referred to as 'social facts'.

This chapter will explore the High Court's use of social facts in Australian negligence cases. The first part of this chapter will discuss the meaning of the concept of 'social fact'. The second part, titled 'Reception of Social Facts in Australia', will discuss the evidential rules relating to the reception of social facts in Australia. The third section will provide a case study of the use of social facts in the High Court in negligence cases in 2003[7] including the frequency of the use of social facts, the nature of social facts, the source of social facts, the use of social scientific evidence and the use of social facts in *Cattanach v Melchior*. Finally, this chapter will discuss the implications of the use of social facts. I will argue that this analysis demonstrates that the High Court has frequent recourse to social facts in the determination of negligence cases. This raises questions not only about the place of policy in High Court negligence cases but perhaps contributes more widely to the refreshed debate regarding legalism and judicial activism in Australian judicial decision-making

little meaningful difference between the nature of principles and policy as used by judges in tort cases, and that often the term 'principle' is used in a misleading way which 'masks the substance of a judge's reasoning process' and suggests that a particular concern is 'trumps' when it may not always be so (at 136). Stapleton advocates using the neutral term 'legal concerns' to describe the concerns taken into account by judges in torts cases (at 137).

6   See for example discussion in Golder, B, 'From *McFarlane* to *Melchior* and beyond: Love, sex, money and commodification in the Anglo-Australian law of torts' (2004) 12 Torts Law Journal 128.

7   The 11 cases considered are *New South Wales v Lepore* (2003) 212 CLR 511, *Cattanach v Melchior* (2003) 215 CLR 1, *Gifford v Strang Patrick Stevedoring Pty Ltd* (2003) 214 CLR 269, *Joslyn v Berryman* (2003) 214 CLR 552, *Fox v Percy* (2003) 214 CLR 118, *Shorey v PT Ltd* (2003) 197 ALR 410, *Suvaal v Cessnock City Council* (2003) 200 ALR 1, *Whisprun Pty Ltd v Dixon* (2003) 200 ALR 447, *Hoyts Pty Ltd v Burns* (2003) 201 ALR 470, *Dovuro Pty Ltd v Wilkins* (2003) 215 CLR 317 and *Amaca Pty Ltd v State of New South Wales* (2003) 199 ALR 596. I do not consider cases in 2003 relating to limitation of actions, insurance, victims' compensation or workers' compensation matters. For a discussion of these cases see Luntz, H, 'Round-up of cases in the High Court of Australia in 2003', (2004) 12 Torts Law Journal 1.

processes.[8] Overall, the chapter will argue that there is no coherent method in Australian law for determining reliable social facts, and that this results in the adoption of conflicting and potentially inaccurate assumptions in High Court cases.

## The nature of social facts

### Traditional categories

The work of Kenneth Culp Davis[9] is widely referred to as the starting point for a consideration of how legal decision-makers refer to non-legal extra-record facts. His work proceeds on the premise that 'no judge can think about law, policy or discretion without using extra record facts'.[10] Davis' work identifies a distinction between two uses of extra-record facts as legislative or adjudicative facts.[11] Where a 'court or an agency finds facts concerning the immediate parties – who did what, where, when, how and with what motive and intent – the court or agency is performing an adjudicative function' so that the relevant facts are 'adjudicative facts'.[12] Where a 'court or an agency develops law or policy, it is acting legislatively; the courts have created the common law through judicial legislation'.[13] The use of facts in this context is referred to as 'legislative facts'.[14] Legislative facts 'help the tribunal to determine the content of law and policy and to exercise its judgment or discretion', are usually general in nature and are utilised 'in the creation of law or policy'.[15]

Davis identified shortcomings in the way judges approach legislative facts, with 'more conventional opinion purporting to rest exclusively upon the record but which in reality is heavily dependent upon the assumption of unproved facts that are left vague and identified'.[16] He also exposed anomalies

---

8 See for example Stapleton above n 5; Justice Heydon, JD, 'Judicial activism and the death of the rule of law' (2003) 23 Australian Bar Review 1; The Hon Kirby, M, 'Judicial activism? A riposte to the counter-reformation' (2004) 24 Australian Bar Review 1; Carrigan, F, 'A Blast from the past: The resurgence of legal formalism' (2003) 27 Melbourne University Law Review 163; Gava J, 'Another Blast from the Past or why the left should embrace strict legalism: A Reply to Carrigan,' Frank (2003) 27 Melbourne University Law Review 186; and Hutchinson, AC '[Dyson] Heydon seek: looking for law in all the wrong places' (2003) 29(1) Monash University Law Review 85.

9 Davis, KC, 'An Approach to the Problems of Evidence in the Administrative Process' (1942) 55 Harvard Law Review 364; Davis KC, 'Judicial Notice' (1955) 55 Columbia Law Review 945.

10 Davis, KC, 'Judicial, Legislative and Administrative Lawmaking: A Proposed Research Service for the Supreme Court' (1986) 71 Minnesota Law Review 1 at 7.

11 Davis, 'Judicial Notice', above n 9 at 952–3. A distinction later drawn on by McHugh J in *Woods v Multi-Sport Holdings Pty Ltd* (2002) 208 CLR 460.

12 Ibid 952.      13 Ibid.      14 Ibid.      15 Ibid.      16 Ibid 953.

in rules of evidence, which did not adequately distinguish between the two kinds of 'facts'.[17]

In a series of articles during the late 1980s, Monahan and Walker sought to take the existing scholarship on the use of social scientific material in judicial decision-making further.[18] Monahan and Walker note the influence of Davis' work, and accept the 'Davis' insight that empirical information can play *two* different roles in legal decision-making.[19] However, they critique his work on the basis that the adjudicative/legislative fact distinction perpetuated 'the old pre-Realist boundaries of the distinction between "fact" and "law" '.[20] They argue that Davis' notion that facts used to create a rule of law should be treated differently from other facts is a 'largely negative proposal'.[21] It provides no 'clear direction regarding how courts should obtain social science data', evaluate social science data or what 'effect they should give to the evaluation of other courts'.[22]

Monahan and Walker categorise the use of social scientific material by judges, by considering 'three possible legal functions of any knowledge about how the world works'.[23] The first function, most closely connected to Davis' notion of legislative fact, is the use of facts like legal authority in the determination of legal rules or policy. This is described as 'social authority'.[24] Such facts are 'general, apply beyond the case at bar, and often are treated by judges as if they were legal authority'.[25] The second function reflects the use of 'social science knowledge' used to determine a particular disputed issue in the case at hand.[26] The third function reflects the use of social scientific evidence relevant to issues in the case at hand. This is referred to as 'social fact'.[27] Monahan and Walker propose a particular process for obtaining and

---

17  Ibid, at 953–60. As a direct result of his critique the US *Federal Rules of Evidence* adopted the distinction between adjudicative and legislative facts with the doctrine of judicial notice expressed only to apply to adjudicative as opposed to legislative fact finding (see rule 201).

18  Monahan, J and Walker, L, 'Social Authority: Obtaining, evaluating and establishing social science in law' (1986) 134 University of Pennsylvania Law Review 477; Monahan, J and Walker, L, 'Social Frameworks: A new use of social science in law' (1987) Virginia Law Review 559; and Monahan, J and Walker, L, 'Social Facts: Scientific methodology as legal precedent' (1988) California Law Review 879.

19  Monahan and Walker, 'Social Authority', ibid 485.

20  Ibid.       21  Ibid.       22  Ibid.

23  Saks, Michael J, 'Judicial attention to the way the world works' (1990) 75 Iowa Law Review 1011 at 1018.

24  Monahan and Walker, 'Social Authority' above n 18 at 488.

25  Saks, above n 23 at 1019.

26  Ibid 1020; Monahan and Walker, 'Social Frameworks' above n 18 at 559. For example, the use of psychological evidence on the reliability of identification evidence, to resolve whether identification testimony should be admitted in a particular case discussed by Saks, ibid 1020.

27  Saks, above n 23 at 1021; Monahan and Walker, 'Social Facts' above n 18. Monahan and Walker's use of the term 'social fact' should be distinguished from my more general definition of the term discussed below.

evaluating social scientific material relevant to each function.[28] Accordingly, Monahan and Walker present not just a critique of current judicial practices, but a positive reformist 'functional' account of how to address the shortfalls in judicial process.[29]

While both the works of Davis, and Monahan and Walker are useful background to a discussion of the meaning and content of the term 'social fact' in this chapter, it is ultimately unhelpful to be too prescriptive or strictly categorical in searching for meaning. The work of Davis, and Monahan and Walker tend to take a categorical approach (for example, Davis' binary approach) to definition with particular emphasis on the function of such 'facts' or the manner in which ultimate evidential rules should be crafted for particular kinds of social scientific evidence. However, often there is significant difficulty[30] in clearly appropriating particular kinds of statements to the existing categories identified by either Davis or Monahan and Walker, with many judicial statements of 'social fact' being mixed statements that could be attributed to more than one 'existing' category or sometimes to none.[31] In addition, Monahan and Walker tend to focus on social facts supported by social scientific evidence; while in Australia (as will be illustrated below) this is a rarity. The approaches of Davis and Monahan and Walker may be useful when the aim is to ultimately identify new rules of evidence and practice for the reception of social facts. However, this tends to place the cart before the horse when the main aim (as mine is) is to examine more generally the statements judges make about the way they perceive the world to operate, particularly when those statements have no social scientific support.

### What is a social fact?

A 'social fact' in this chapter is not a factual finding that is directly descriptive of the facts of the trial matter.[32] A 'social fact' is not a pure statement of law,

---

28  For example they propose that judges should approach social authority in much the same way as they approach legal authority. They argue that evidence of social authority should be presented in a brief rather than given by testimony and judges should be able to source their own research relating to social authority. Monahan and Walker go on to provide extensive guidelines for the methods courts should use to evaluate empirical studies, and how courts should approach the evaluation of social authority by other courts. See Monahan and Walker, 'Social Authority' above n 18 at 495–516.

29  Saks, above n 23 at 1027 and 1030–31. For critique of reformist approaches see Woolhandler, Ann, 'Rethinking the judicial reception of social facts' (1988) 41 Vanderbilt Law Review 111.

30  At least in my own analysis of High Court negligence cases decided in 2003 discussed below.

31  For example, general background statements of social context by judges, although not directly relevant to a legal rule or issue. It is unclear, for example, where the general statement by Gleeson CJ in *De Sales v Ingrilli* (2002) 212 CLR 338 at [26] that 'there are probably just as many work-shy or extravagant, or unreliable men now as there were in 1968' would fit within existing categories.

32  For example, Mrs Melchior was a 46 year-old housewife.

legal rules or legal reasoning.[33] However, past that point there is a continuum of assumptions about society, the world and human behaviour that courts, including the High Court, make in an appellate case. All of these are 'social facts' within the meaning of this chapter. At one end of the spectrum, there are general assumptions a court makes that allow them to interpret adjudicative facts. For example, assumptions about the effect of alcohol on human beings or how people act when intoxicated may be made to determine the adjudicative fact of how drunk a particular party to an action may have seemed at the relevant point in time.[34] Social fact statements may also be made as part of a judge's creation of the background context or social setting of a case. For example, a judge may describe the traditional nuclear family unit as the central and most important foundation group of society.[35] At the other end of the spectrum, social fact assumptions may be made about the wider social effect or consequences of particular findings of liability in a case. These kinds of arguments would traditionally have been described as public or social policy arguments. For example, a judge may make statements about the psychological effects on children born following a failed sterilisation, on later learning of litigation against the relevant medical professional.[36]

As Stapleton points out, there is a difficulty in categorising some kinds of statements as either principle or policy.[37] These include statements that indicate underlying 'legal values' such as respect for human life or indeterminacy. It is probably also impossible that there can ever be a strict definition of the difference between legal principle (law) and factual finding (fact).[38] Many statements made by judges include elements of both. For the purposes of the definition of social fact in this paper, statements framed as bare general legal propositions[39] are excluded (for example, the law does not encourage indeterminacy or the law values life). However, positive statements of

---

33  For example that a cause of action in negligence requires that causation between the breach of duty and the damage be shown.

34  See for example *Joslyn v Berryman* (2003) 214 CLR 552 at [75]–[76]. See also the judicial discussion of the effects of alcohol and community knowledge of the effects of alcohol in the recent case of *Cole v South Tweed Heads Rugby League Football Club Limited* (2004) 217 CLR 469 at [10], [12], [13], [17], [85], [103] and [131].

35  For example see *Cattanach v Melchior* (2003) 215 CLR 1 at [35]. Of course, these 'context' social facts are often far from the neutral statements they may seem and arguably can play a crucial role not only in the determination of the case at hand but in the wider construction of social norms and understandings. See for example Golder, above n 6. This is significant, as context facts would not usually be considered 'policy' matters or perhaps even legislative facts.

36  For example see *Cattanach v Melchior* (2003) 215 CLR 1 at [384]–[386].

37  Stapleton above n 5.

38  Others have long considered the traditional distinction between law and fact to be 'flawed'. See for example the discussion in Monahan and Walker, 'Social Authority', above n 18.

39  Even though they may include underlying implicit assumptions of social fact.

consequence framed in terms of 'values'[40] are included (for example, legal rules providing for school liability for sexual abuse cases by teachers will encourage deterrence, due administration of justice, fulfilment of legitimate expectations for compensation and will not lead to an indeterminate number of claims; or society accepts that all human lives have value) as are identification of policy assumptions underlying the law (for example, the underlying assumption of the law is that children will be harmed by litigation).

Social facts have previously been defined by Mullane in a study of 1990 Family Court cases as a statement 'concerning human behaviour'.[41] He indicates the basis for 'social facts' may be 'revealed' by social scientific disciplines such as 'history, psychology, sociology, anthropology, political science and related fields'.[42] I define the term social fact in wider terms to include not just statements about human behaviour but statements about the nature of society and social values, and the nature and behaviour of social institutions including legal institutions.[43] In addition, while it is true to say some social fact statements may (at least notionally) have a basis in a social scientific or other scientific discipline, this is certainly not true of all social fact statements made by judges. As will be described below, it is rare for any social scientific or other empirical evidence to be cited in support of social fact statements. Social fact statements made by judges may be highly contentious by scientific standards or unsupported by available empirical evidence. Statements are most often not stated in a way that is falsifiable in scientific terms[44] and there is relatively little evidence of any explicit (or even implicit) interdisciplinary approach in judgments. Finally, social facts in judgments may be sourced or unsourced, and may be drawn from submissions of the parties to an action or, often, from a judge's own experience or intuition.[45]

---

40  Even when framed very generally.
41  Mullane, Graham R, 'Evidence of Social Science Research:Law, Practice and Options in the Family Court of Australia' (1998) 72 Australian Law Journal 434 at 434.
42  Ibid.
43  For example I include statements that describe the nature of the state of the court system, the general conduct of legal actors such as judges, lawyers, litigants and expert witnesses, and the general nature of litigation. I would describe as social facts statements about the workload of judges, the stressful nature of litigation, and the practical benefits trial courts have in scrutinising evidence over appellate courts.
44  Many social fact statements are not even capable of being scientifically tested. For example, how could we test a value statement such as 'Human life is inherently valuable'?
45  Or sometimes even from a judge's extra record research. See for example the discussion by McHugh J in *Woods v Multi-Sport Holdings* (2002) 208 CLR 460 at [62] of social scientific research in relation to the frequency of accidents.

### Reception of social facts in Australia

As I have previously argued,[46] judges appear to adopt three main approaches when they perceive a gap in knowledge (which must be filled to reach judgment) between legal principle and adjudicative facts in a particular case. Frequently there is no explicit reference in judgments at all to the underlying social facts or assumptions which judges have relied on in determining legal principle, or such matters are described as legal principle or legal values. Second, judges will make social fact statements which may be unreferenced or referenced generally to case law, legislation or general academic articles.[47] Finally, and far less frequently, judges will cite social scientific or other empirical material in support of their statement of relevant social facts.[48] All of these options have their own difficulties.[49]

The use of social fact material whether sourced or unsourced, provided by the parties or sourced by the judge, or supported by social scientific or empirical material is not adequately provided for in the Australian law of evidence or practice. The reference to such material has apparently developed without any guiding principles as to authenticity, notice or necessary evidential support. The Australian rules of evidence appear to have been designed to support and reflect the adjudicative fact finding function of judges without any significant consideration of how to respond to the wider role of social facts in judicial decision-making.[50] While it may be that after consideration of the issue, policy makers may decide that restrictive evidential rules about

46 Burns, K, 'It's just not cricket: The High Court, sport and legislative facts' (2002) Torts Law Journal 234 at 248.
47 For example see the extensive discussion by McHugh J of the effects of increasing liability of auditors in *Esanda Finance Corporation Limited v Peat Marwick Hungerfords* (1997)188 CLR 241 at 282–9. Many of the 'auditor liability' social facts referred to by McHugh J were referenced to Siliciano, JA, 'Negligent Accounting and the Limits of Instrumental Tort Reform' (1988) 86 Michigan Law Review 1929.
48 See for example *Jones v Bartlett* (2000) 205 CLR 166 at [106]–[111] (McHugh J) where several references are made to a study of environmental health in the home, and a further reference is made to Cassell and Ozanne-Smith (Monash University Accident Research Centre), *Women's Injury in the Home in Victoria*, 1999 regarding the incidence of broken glass injury.
49 For example when there is no statement of the assumptions relied upon there is no opportunity to debate or question the underlying premises of the judgment. However, the use of referenced or unreferenced social facts raises evidential issues relating to permissibility and admissibility.
50 The US Federal Rules of Evidence Rule 201 on Judicial Notice was specifically designed to apply only to the traditional category of adjudicative facts with a deliberate decision to leave the reception of legislative facts within the inherent and unfettered discretion of the judicial decision-maker. This was in response to the work of Kenneth Culp Davis discussed above. See the notes to Rule 201, *Notes of Advisory Committee on Rules*.

social fact reception are inappropriate, on the other hand a totally unregulated judicial use of social facts has many problems.[51]

The common law doctrine of judicial notice has traditionally applied to allow the admission of notorious facts, or facts which are so well known that every ordinary person may be said to be aware of them.[52] It operates as an exception to the general rule of evidence that the parties must prove all facts to a case by the means of relevant and admissible evidence.[53] Courts may judicially notice a fact either with or without enquiry.[54]

However, the very essence of a social fact seems contrary to the basis of the doctrine of judicial notice.[55] The vast majority of social facts are not notorious or commonly known.

A number of Australian states have statutory provisions, which allow courts to refer to authoritative published works.[56] In addition s 144 of the Evidence Act 1995[57] governs the reception of extra-record material federally and in New South Wales. 'Proof is not required of knowledge that is not reasonably open to question', and is common knowledge in the relevant locality or generally, or is 'capable of verification by reference to a document' where the authority of the document cannot be reasonably questioned.[58] Judges may acquire knowledge of those matters in any way they see fit,[59] but

---

51  Interestingly, there appears to be judicial uncertainty about whether social fact material may or may not be admissible before the High Court when not part of the original evidential record of adjudicative facts. In *Cattanach v Melchior* (2003) 215 CLR 1 at [152] Kirby J indicates that if liability is to be denied on public policy grounds it is 'essential that this policy be spelt out so as to be susceptible of analysis and criticism. Desirably it should be founded on empirical evidence, not mere judicial assertion'. However, at [153] he refers to the social fact material introduced by the state intervenors before the High Court relating to costs of actions and effect of liability on state health care systems as being not admissible to supplement the evidentiary record citing the authority of the criminal cases *Mickelberg v The Queen* (1989) 167 CLR 259 (in which Kirby J dissented) and *Eastman v The Queen* (2000) 203 CLR 1. These cases hold that fresh evidence is not admissible before the High Court. This appears to greatly restrict the admission of possible social fact material (including social scientific evidence) or arguments by parties before the High Court on the basis that the material is not adjudicative fact introduced at trial, which seems to contradict the 'policy' role of such material encouraged by Kirby J at [152] and to unnecessarily limit the usefulness of intervenors. This raises the important question of whether the authority of *Mickelberg* and *Eastmann*, both criminal cases where the particular new evidence sought to be adduced was clearly of an adjudicative kind affecting the substantive issues relating to the accused, extends to disallowing social fact arguments and evidence before the High Court when the arguments relate to general law-making functions. If so, the bizarre situation may arise of the parties themselves or intervenors not being able to raise such material or refer to relevant social scientific evidence, but judges being able to do so independently and unfettered.

52  See Heydon, JD, *Cross on Evidence*, Butterworths On-Line, http://Butterworthsonline.com at <3005>; *Holland v Jones* (1917) 23 CLR 149 at 153.

53  *Woods v Multi-Sport Holdings* (2002) 208 CLR 460 at 157 (McHugh J).

54  Ibid.       55  Mullane, above n 41 at 441–2.

56  Evidence Act 1929 (SA) s 64; Evidence Act 1910 (Tas) s 67; Evidence Act 1906 (WA) s 72.

57  (Cth) and (NSW)       58  s 144(1).       59  s144(2).

they must give parties an opportunity to make submissions in relation to the relevant knowledge or refer to other relevant information to avoid unfair prejudice.[60] Once again, however, the very features of s 144 seem to exclude the possibility of application to social facts. Social facts will almost never be matters which are 'not reasonably open to question', or 'capable of verification by reference to a document the authority of which *cannot be reasonably questioned*'.[61] In addition, it appears that the High Court takes a restrictive view of the operation of s 144 which would appear to vastly restrict its operation to social facts. In the recent case of *Gattellaro v Westpac Banking Corporation*,[62] all members of the High Court held that the doctrine of judicial notice encapsulated in s 144 did not allow reception of the fact that banks such as Westpac use a standard form of guarantee.[63] This was on the basis that such knowledge was not common knowledge in the locality, was not capable of verification by a document whose authority could not reasonably be questioned and it had not been demonstrated that the Court of Appeal had given the Gattellaros an opportunity to make submissions on the question of judicial notice.

Recently in *Woods v Multi Sport Holdings*[64] McHugh J and Callinan J debated the use of extra-record social scientific material in judgments.[65] Justice McHugh supported his reference to extra-record social scientific materials[66] on the basis 'that a court may judicially notice and use to define the scope or validity of a principle or rule of law'.[67] This, he argued, was 'legitimate and in accordance with long-standing authority and practice'.[68] Callinan J strongly disagreed that it is generally legitimate for judges to refer to statistical extra-record material as part of their decision, or that the doctrine of judicial

---

60  s 144(4).        61  Mullane above n 55. Italics added.

62  (2004) 204 ALR 258. The case was originally given special leave on the question of whether the doctrine of judicial notice allowed reception of the fact that 'banks such as Westpac used a standard form of guarantee and that it could be inferred that the appellants had signed it' which was held to be a 'far-reaching proposition of great importance in the conduct of commercial litigation', at [55]. This turned out to be of far less importance upon the argument of the actual appeal of the matter before the High Court due to concessions made by Westpac.

63  Gleeson CJ, McHugh, Hayne and Heydon JJ at [15]–[18] and Kirby J at [69]. The joint judgment suggested that in NSW where s 144 applied there appeared to be no room for the application of the common law, while Kirby J indicated the result would be the same whether approached by reference to the common law or statute.

64  (2002) 208 CLR 460.

65  See more detailed discussion in Burns above n 46.

66  Apparently without notice to the parties see Hoey, M, 'The High Court and Judicial Notice: Woods v Multi-Sport Holdings Pty Ltd' (2002) 27(3) Alternative Law Journal 130 at 132.

67  (2002) 208 CLR 460 at [62].

68  Ibid. McHugh J's comments have since been relied on by Wallwork J in *Wood v R* (2002) 36 MVR 94; 130 A Crim R 518 to support the reference to extra-record social scientific material in relation to rates of imprisonment in the determination of a sentencing appeal.

notice generally allows the reception of legislative facts.[69] However, both justifications seem insufficient. As outlined above, traditionally the doctrine of judicial notice has only allowed the admission of notorious or commonly known facts. The reports cited by McHugh J clearly did not fall into that category or even into the statutory categories, and on the authority of *Gattellaro v Westpac Banking Corporation* would clearly not satisfy either common law or statutory tests of judicial notice. However, on the other hand a refusal to allow admission of facts on the basis they are not adjudicative facts, or that the reception of such material does not come within the traditional ambit of the doctrine of judicial notice is unnecessarily restrictive. It fails to address the fact that judges, particularly of the High Court, perform a law-making as well as an adjudicative role.

As will be discussed below, High Court judges do frequently refer to social facts in their judgments. It appears, as suggested by Davis, and Monahan and Walker in the American context as discussed above, there is a need to craft rules which recognise the law-making aspect of judicial decision-making and respond to the needs of judges for social fact material. Given the apparent lack of guiding principles in Australia[70] for the reception of social fact material in the rules of evidence and practice (leaving such matters, it seems, to judicial discretion), it is unsurprising that there are disparities between the use of social facts by judges. There are often no references provided for social fact statements (particularly contentious statements) and there are often difficulties with the veracity and nature of social facts stated. The relatively rare use of intervenors or *amicus curiae* in the High Court, and the lack of any requirement for parties to provide references to any relevant social scientific studies in their appellate briefs[71] probably also compound the problem.

### The Australian High Court and social facts in negligence cases 2003

In the Amercian context Davis identified 'weak spots' in US appellate cases including 'insufficient factual or scientific base' for legislative facts and 'the lack of a democratic base when one is needed'.[72] He identifies predominantly unsuccessful methods the US Supreme Court has used to address these weak spots including:[73]

---

69  (2002) 208 CLR 460 at [165]–[168].
70  This matter is discussed in the recent ALRC Report on Uniform Evidence Laws, ALRC 102 (2006) Chapter 17. The ALRC do not, however, recommend changes to s 144 to deal with judicial notice of social facts.
71  As might be done in a Brandeis brief in America.
72  Davis, KC 'Judicial, Legislative and Administrative Lawmaking', above n 10 at 6.
73  Ibid 9–11.

- sending the case back to the trial court;
- simply asserting an 'emphatic view of legislative facts with nothing to support its view';[74]
- relying on 'common experience' with no reference to facts and 'in the face of . . . convincing evidence to the contrary';[75]
- referring to a published source and finding 'what is not there';[76]
- completely ignoring the need to address a relevant legislative fact;
- imposing the burden of proof on a party to prove a legislative fact; and
- referring to extra-record research in support of legislative facts without giving the parties a chance to respond to, or challenge the research.

My research of the approach of the Australian High Court in negligence cases in 2003 confirms that many of the same things could be said of the Australian High Court.

## Frequency of the use of social fact assumptions

Eleven negligence cases were heard by the High Court in 2003.[77] There were 325 social fact statements[78] made by the judges of the High Court in total in these cases. Some cases displayed very low numbers of social fact statements. For example, the contribution case of *Amaca Pty Ltd v State of New South Wales*[79] had only a single social fact statement.[80] However, this was (unusually) a very short case of only 27 paragraphs and (even more unusually) was a unanimous decision of Justices McHugh, Gummow, Kirby, Hayne, and Callinan. Similarly, the relatively short and factually based[81] case of *Shorey v PT Limited*[82] (89 paras) revealed only a single social fact statement.[83] This case also involved a joint judgment (Gleeson CJ, McHugh

---

74 Ibid 9.      75 Ibid.      76 Ibid.      77 See above n 7.

78 Database on record with author. Social fact statements which fulfilled the criteria discussed in section one of this chapter were identified and entered into an access database recording for each social fact statement (amongst other variables) social fact text, judge(s), case name, paragraph number, whether the social fact was referenced in any way, and the references provided. Where a reference was provided for any part of a social fact statement the social fact was counted as referenced even though other parts of a social fact statement were not supported by the reference. Statements which were on the same social fact topic within a particular single paragraph of a judgment were counted and recorded as a single record. Social facts repeated in additional paragraphs of a judgment were counted as new social fact records.

79 (2003) 199 ALR 596.

80 '*The making of assumptions and the acceptance of concessions for the purpose of litigation is sometimes an appropriate and efficient way to proceed.*' Ibid [20].

81 Focused on the interpretation of trial findings of adjudicative fact.

82 (2003) 197 ALR 410.

83 '*An expert would normally welcome the chance to elaborate the recorded history and to clarify questions and doubts stated, or hinted, in cross-examination.*' Ibid [40].

and Gummow JJ of only 10 paras) with single judgments by Kirby J and Callinan J.

However, at the other end of the spectrum in perhaps one of the most dense examples of social fact use available in Australia, *Cattanach v Melchior*[84] had 169 statements of social fact. This may be explained on a number of bases. First, the case is extremely lengthy (414 paras, and 606 fns). Second, the case involves (as is common in the current High Court in more complex cases) multiple judgments[85] with separate judgments given by Gleeson CJ, Kirby J, Hayne J, Callinan J and Heydon J with a joint judgment by McHugh J and Gummow J. Third, the case involved the highly contentious and novel issue of the recovery of the costs of upbringing of a child following a failed sterilisation surgery. This gave rise to significant policy issues with, as Justice Kirby pointed out, all judges discussing policy matters in their judgments.[86] Finally, Heydon J made very extensive references to social facts (79 instances) in his judgment[87] including references to 'a consideration of matters that would seem better described in moral, social or scientific terms such as: basic legal assumptions about human life in families; the psychology of litigants, parents and children; a parent's moral duties even though these are not enforceable by the law; and the 'disquieting possibilities' in relation to other much more ambitious claims of a type not before the court that might create "an odious spectacle" '.[88]

Overall, the large number of social fact statements in the 2003 cases demonstrates that judges do find the need to refer frequently to knowledge that is neither adjudicative fact nor legal principle.[89] In other words, judges (particularly in appellate courts) tend to find gaps in knowledge needed to make a final decision. This is especially so in 'hard' cases where there is not a clear application of legal principle available, and where the case turns ultimately on issues of policy and values rather than issues of adjudicative fact.

### Nature of the social facts

As outlined above in section one of this chapter, there is a spectrum of the different kinds of social facts that ranges from statements made to assist in judicial evaluation or interpretation of adjudicative facts, to context

---

84 (2003) 215 CLR 1.     85 Six in this case.     86 (2003) 215 CLR 1 at [121].

87 Somewhat surprisingly, given earlier pre-appointment comments in Justice Heydon, JD, 'Judicial activism and the death of the rule of law' (2003) 23 Australian Bar Review 1 regarding judicial activism and legalism. See his comments on the excessive use of citations and footnotes, and on the use of judicial opinions on extraneous matters in judicial decisions at 10–12. See also his warnings about the judicial use of community values at 22.

88 Stapleton, above n 5 at 133.

89 This has also been demonstrated of judges of the Family Court in Mullane's study. See Mullane above n 41 at 452–4.

statements, to consequence statements, to statements that merge from legal value into social fact. All of these kinds of social facts were identified in the analysis of the 2003 cases. For the sake of brevity, only several examples of each kind of social fact are outlined by way of illustration:

## INTERPRETATION OF ADJUDICATIVE FACT

In *Joslyn v Berryman*, Kirby J discussed the effect of alcohol on parties to the litigation (an adjudicative fact) by reference to an assumption about the effect of alcohol on seasoned drinkers:

> Both Mr Berryman and Ms Joslyn were found to have been seasoned drinkers. *This would have reduced somewhat the effect of alcohol consumption on their cognitive and motor capacities.*[90]

In *Cattanach v Melchior*, Gleeson CJ assessed the parental financial obligations of the plaintiff parents by reference to an assumption about the obligations of 'ordinary' parents:

> They have a loving relationship with a healthy child. It does not involve any special financial or other responsibilities that might exist if, for example, the child had an unusual and financially burdensome need for care. The financial obligations which the respondents have incurred, legal and moral, [*are of the same order as those involved in any ordinary parent–child relationship.*][91]

In assessing the accuracy of the recall of the particular events by a party to the action (an adjudicative fact) in *Suvaal v Cessnock City Council*, McHugh and Kirby JJ indicated that:

> Common experience teaches that elements in the recall of past events can be accurate even if elaboration (prompted perhaps by subconscious desires or interests) adds detail that is unreliable, incorrect or unprovable. There may remain at the heart of the matters recalled a core of truth that is accurate and sufficiently established.[92]

---

90  *Joslyn v Berryman; Wentworth Shire Council v Berryman* (2003) 214 CLR 552 at [88]. Italics added.
91  *Cattanach v Melchior* (2003) 189 ALR 131 at [36]. Italics added.
92  *Suvaal v Cessnock City Council* (2003) 200 ALR 1 at [82]. While no doubt common experience may be useful in relation to understanding human memory and recall, this is also an area where equally the process of the construction of human memory is a matter contrary to common experience and where scientific knowledge would suggest that care needs to be taken, for example in such areas as repressed memory and identification testimony.

CONTEXT STATEMENTS

The analysis of the 2003 negligence cases revealed a wealth of social fact statements which were used to paint the background context or picture of society, against which the court or judges discussed principle or policy. These included:

- *The nature of the legal system in Australia.*

  Litigants are represented in our courts by advocates of differing skills. Litigants are sometimes people of limited knowledge and perception.[93]

  Litigation beyond a trial is costly and usually upsetting.[94]

- *The nature of contemporary Australian society and contemporary Australian social values.*

  It is a feature of affluent societies that children remain financially dependent upon their parents for longer periods. Many children are supported by their parents well beyond the age of 18.[95]

  In the 1960s, and thereafter, social attitudes to various forms of contraception, including sterilisation, began to change in Australia as in other like countries.[96]

  Such thinking (like the earlier notion of enforced adoption) bears little relationship to reality in contemporary Australia. That reality includes non-married, serial and older sexual relationships, widespread use of contraception, same-sex relationships with and without children, procedures for 'artificial' conception and widespread parental election to postpone or avoid children.[97]

- *The nature of human relationships and human behaviour.*

  The relationship between two friends who have lived together for many years may be closer and more loving than that of two siblings.[98]

  The value of human life, which is universal and beyond measurement, is not to be confused with the joys of parenthood, which are distributed unevenly.[99]

93 *Whisprun Pty Ltd v Dixon* (2003) 200 ALR 447 at [120].
94 *Fox v Percy* (2003) 214 CLR 118 at [29].
95 *Cattanach v Melchior* (2003) 215 CLR 1 at [20].      96 Ibid [105].      97 Ibid [164].
98 *Gifford v Strang Patrick Stevedoring Pty Ltd* (2003) 214 CLR 269 at [48].
99 *Cattanach v Melchior* (2003) 215 CLR 1 at [6].

But with an ageing population, and increasing pressure on welfare resources, the financial aspects of caring for parents are likely to become of more practical concern.[100]

For some, confronted with an unplanned pregnancy, there is no choice which they would regard as open to them except to continue with the pregnancy and support the child that is born. For others there may be a choice to be made. But in no case is the 'choice' one that can be assumed to be made on solely economic grounds. Human behaviour is more complex than a balance sheet of assets and liabilities. To invoke notions of 'choice' as bespeaking economic decisions ignores that complexity.[101]

## CONSEQUENCE STATEMENTS

It was common in the analysis of 2003 cases to find classic policy or consequence statements. These included statements about loss distribution, possible deterrence value and the general social effect of liability:

To hold a school authority, be it government or private, vicariously liable for sexual assault on a pupil by a teacher would ordinarily give the victim of that assault a far better prospect of obtaining payment of the damages awarded for the assault than the victim would have against the teacher.[102]

That being so, any deterrent or prophylactic effect that might be said to follow from extending the non-delegable duty of care of a school authority to include liability for intentional trespasses committed by teachers would, at best, be indirect.[103]

The various assumptions underlying the law relating to children and the duties on parents created by the law would be negated if parents could sue to recover the costs of rearing unplanned children. That possibility would tend to damage the natural love and mutual confidence which the law seeks to foster between parent and child. It would permit conduct inconsistent with a parental duty to treat the child with the utmost affection, with infinite tenderness, and with unstinting forgiveness in all circumstances, because these goals are contradicted by legal proceedings based on the premise that the child's birth was a painful and highly inconvenient mistake. It would permit conduct inconsistent with the duty to nurture children.[104]

---

100  Ibid [34].      101  Ibid [222].
102  *New South Wales v Lepore; Samin v Queensland; Rich v Queensland* (2003) 212 CLR 511 at [240].
103  Ibid [267].      104  *Cattanach v Melchior* (2003) 215 CLR 1 at [404].

## VALUE STATEMENTS/MIXED PRINCIPLE AND SOCIAL FACT STATEMENTS

The most difficult social facts to identify or analyse are those which embody mixed value statements or mixed fact/principle statements. Examples of statements which were identified as social facts by the definition in the first part of this chapter, included statements that predicted consequences such as disrespect for the law, inhibition of the administration of justice, or indeterminate liability, or that indicated the underlying policies of particular legal principles:

> Further, if vicarious liability is to be imposed so that a person is to be held liable in damages for injury suffered without fault on his or her part, it ought to be imposed only in circumstances where it can be justified by reference to legal principle. To do otherwise is to invite disrespect for the law.[105]
>
> If negligence law is to serve any useful social purpose, it must ordinarily reflect the foresight, reactions and conduct of ordinary members of the community or, in cases of expertise, of the experts in that particular community. To hold defendants to standards of conduct that do not reflect the common experience of the relevant community can only bring the law of negligence, and with it the administration of justice, into disrepute.[106]
>
> The indeterminate nature of the financial consequences, beneficial and detrimental, of the parent-child relationship has already been noted.[107]
>
> The physical integrity of an individual's person and property has always been treated as of central importance in the law of negligence. Likewise the autonomy of the individual called on to make decisions affecting that physical integrity has been given great weight.[108]

### Sources of social facts

The majority of social facts stated in the 2003 cases were unsourced.[109] Of the 325 social fact statements made, only 81 were referenced in any way.[110] The references provided were predominantly case citations with 69 references

---

105 *New South Wales v Lepore; Samin v Queensland; Rich v Queensland* (2003) 212 CLR 511 at [28].

106 *Dovuro Pty Limited v Wilkins* (2003) 215 CLR 317 at [34].

107 *Cattanach v Melchior* (2003) 215 CLR 1 at [38].       108  Ibid [190].

109 No direct reference or footnote was provided for the social fact statement. Where a reference was provided, it did not always provide a basis for the entire social fact statement. However, for the purposes of this analysis where a reference was provided for any part of a social fact statement this was counted as referenced.

110 Statements were counted as referenced where a footnote was provided for at least part of the social fact statement identified.

including case citations. Occasionally references were made to a text, journal article, international instrument or legislation.[111] Only three direct references were made to any form of social scientific or empirical evidence to support social fact statements made. These references were all given by Kirby J. In *NSW v Lepore*, Kirby J cited English Home Office statistics in support of the social fact that there had been an 'increase in the reported instances of physical and sexual assaults upon children by employees of organisations to whose care the parents and guardians of the children have entrusted them'.[112] In *Cattanach v Melchior* Kirby J cited the Kinsey Reports[113] in support of the social fact that social 'changes have come about as a result of greater knowledge of, and discussion about, human sexuality'.[114] In the same case, Kirby J cited an insurance report[115] for the social fact statement that 'calculation of the cost of rearing a child is, by comparison, relatively straightforward. Such calculations are regularly performed for insurance and other purpose'.[116] In addition to these direct references to social scientific support for propositions of social fact, there were three instances where the references indicated that underlying social scientific support may exist for a proposition although the evidence was not directly cited.[117]

Several conclusions may be drawn from this analysis of the sources cited for social fact statements in High Court negligence cases in 2003.

1.   The majority of social fact statements were not referenced in any way,

---

111   Sixteen references referred to secondary sources (including references which also provided case law or other citations) and eight references included references to legislation or international instruments. For the discussion of the use of secondary material citations generally in the High Court see Smyth, Russell, 'Academic Writing and the Courts: A Quantitative Study of the Influence of Legal and Non-Legal Periodicals in the High Court' (1998) 17 *University of Tasmania Law Review* 164; Russell Smyth, 'Other Than "Accepted Sources of Law"?: A Quantitative Study of Secondary Source Citations in the High Court' (1999) 22 UNSW Law Journal 19.

112   *New South Wales v Lepore* (2003) 212 CLR 511 at [276] and see fn 301.

113   Kinsey, AC et al, 1948 *Sexual Behavior in the Human Male*, Philadelphia: Saunders; *Sexual Behavior in the Human Female*, 1953, Philadelphia: Saunders.

114   *Cattanach v Melchior* (2003) 215 CLR 1 at [103] and see fn 137.

115   AMP-NATSEM, Income and Wealth Report, Issue 3, October 2002.

116   *Cattanach v Melchior* (2003) 215 CLR 1 at [144] and see fn 226.

117   Kirby J referred generally to evidence given in *Cattanach* ibid [153] by the state intevenors in relation to the number of failed sterilisation claims in particular states and the possible economic effects of litigation on state health care systems, but dismissed this evidence as inadmissible. See discussion above in fn 51. In *Fox v Percy* (2003) 214 CLR 118 Gleeson CJ, Gummow J and Kirby J (at [31]) and in *Suvaal v Cessnock City Council* (2003) 200 ALR 1 McHugh J and Kirby J (at [75] and fn 55) referred to scientific evidence cited in *Trawl Industries of Australia Pty Ltd v Effem Foods Pty Ltd* (1992) 27 NSWLR 326 at 348 (Samuels JA) that threw light on the limitations of making credibility assessments of witnesses based on appearances.

and accordingly were likely products of judicial experience, intuition and values, with the limitations these bring.

2.   Where references were given, they were predominantly to case law or legal texts and journals. This tends to simply reproduce social facts which are borne out of lawyers' and judges' intuition, experience and values rather than provide any objective, scientific or diverse basis for social facts.

3.   There is very little use of social scientific or other empirical material to support social fact findings in High Court negligence cases.[118] There may be many social facts where social scientific or empirical evidence may either simply be unnecessary (for example, where judges draw from their own experiences of litigation and judicial practice to make social fact statements about the litigation process or the experience of being a judge) or unavailable. However, the very low incidence of such evidence does tend to suggest that there are impediments to the use of such material in the High Court where it might be appropriate and available. This may stem from the constraints of the existing rules of evidence which are designed for adjudicative fact finding discussed above, discomfort within the judiciary and the legal profession regarding the use and utility of social scientific or empirical evidence because of lack of experience and training or legalistic views of the judicial decision-making process, and from practical constraints related to availability, time and cost.[119]

### The case of the (miss)ing social fact

As discussed above, the most prolific 'social fact' case delivered by the High Court in 2003 was *Cattanach v Melchior*.[120] As noted by Kirby J,[121] despite the

---

118  Of course it may be argued that, given a larger sample of cases, a greater incidence of the use of social scientific or empirical evidence may be found. Nevertheless similar findings were made in Mullane's study of the Family Court, above n 41 at 453. Mullane noted that his study of the custody cases decided by the Family Court of Australia in 1990 (302 judgments using a 50% sample) showed that 65% of social fact statements had no source stated or the source was stated as undefined research, 32% of social fact findings were sourced from expert evidence, 2% from previous findings of the Full Court and 1% from research nominated and specified by the judge. As noted in part 1 of this chapter this study also used a much narrower and more specific definition of the term 'social fact'. The family law custody context and the use of trial judgments may also explain the relatively high incidence of expert evidence findings.

119  For example see Heydon, JD, *Cross on Evidence*, Butterworths On-Line, http://Butterworthsonline.com at [3200] where the editors argue that if the general empirical material relied on by judges was not distinct from that which could be judicially noticed this would result in 'an extremely cumbersome and time consuming process of giving the parties warning as to what material the court was relying on, which is not at present engaged in'.

120  (2003) 215 CLR 1.      121  Ibid [121].

currently binding position of the majority of the High Court discouraging explicit reference and reliance on social policy matters (at least at the duty stage)[122] in High Court negligence cases, all members of the court (most prolifically the minority judges)[123] referred to 'policy' matters (or in the context of this chapter, social facts) in the course of their judgments. The nature of the social facts was rich and varied. They included, particularly in the minority opinions of Gleeson CJ, Hayne J and notably Heydon J, statements about the inherent social values of human life especially the lives of children, the nature of the nuclear family as the central unit of our society, the effects of commodifying children, the nature and incidents of the parent/child relationship in modern Australian society, the possible psychological reactions of parents, children and lawyers involved in wrongful birth litigation, the stressful nature of wrongful birth litigation and the financial strategies adopted by Australian families.

Many of these social fact statements were by their very nature value-laden, highly contentious and contestable. For example, Heydon J predicted that if such litigation was allowed to proceed it would encourage, amongst other consequences, parents either to denigrate or create false expectations for their children[124] as part of the litigation process, aided by their lawyers. This, it was argued, would result in the emotional bastardisation of children who would be psychologically damaged upon later learning of the litigation.[125] On the other hand, Kirby J described the 'notion that parents would be encouraged in court or out, to treat such a child as an unwanted "brute"' as a 'sheer judicial fantasy'.[126] Apart from the citations by Kirby J of the Kinsey Reports and the AMP report noted above, no social scientific or other empirical evidence was provided for any social fact statements in *Cattanach* and many

---

122 *Sullivan v Moody* (2001) 207 CLR 562. Note however the comments in *Cattanach*, ibid, by Hayne J at [233]–[242] regarding the role of policy in the law. In particular Hayne J notes at [242], adopting the words of Pollock LCB, that although judges are 'no better able to discern what is for the public good than other experienced and enlightened members of the community . . . that is no reason for their refusing to entertain the question, and deciding to decide upon it'. Similarly, at [291] Callinan J indicated that 'I cannot help observing that the repeated disavowal in the cases of resort to public policy is not always convincing . . . Davies JA in the Court of Appeal in this case was right with respect to imply that it would be more helpful for the resolution of the controversy, if judges frankly acknowledged their debt to their own social values and the way in which these have in fact moulded or influenced their judgments rather than the application of strict legal principle.' In addition, policy issues now appear to be explicitly relevant to determining both factual causation and scope of liability in difficult cases. For example, see the discussion and determination of common law causation in the recent NSWCA case of *Harvey v PD* (2004) 59 NSWLR 639. Tort reform legislation has also incorporated normative considerations into the determination of both factual causation and scope of liability. See for example Civil Liability Act 2003 (Qld) s 11.
123 Gleeson CJ, Hayne J and particularly Heydon J.
124 (2003) 215 CLR 1 at [341]–[346], [363]–[371].       125 Ibid [372]–[392].
126 Ibid [145].

statements were made with no reference at all. Those social fact statements which were sourced were drawn predominantly from existing precedent, simply repeating previous unsourced judicial assumptions of social fact.

There are real dangers in the use of highly contentious or outdated social fact statements which are stated as proven without adequate acknowledgement of contemporary social scientific or other empirical material, where such material is available. There are also dangers in the use of legal statements of social facts which make assumptions about matters which exist outside the realm of law, for example in psychology. In these circumstances, the danger of judicial error about the accuracy of a social fact statement is magnified. For example, in *Cattanach* Heydon J makes the statement sourced to a 1965 law review article[127] (and supported by earlier discussion of 1964 Queensland adoption legislation)[128] that 'the confidentiality which surrounds adoption suggests a perception by the legislature of the damage which can flow to children from learning that their parents regard them as a burden'.[129] This is used as an analogous argument to support a rejection of liability in wrongful birth cases in order to perpetuate secrecy and to protect children from the knowledge that they were unplanned and litigated about. However, this social fact statement is clearly contestable, contentious and reflective of

127 RJL, 'The Birth of a Child Following an Ineffective Sterilization Operation As Legal Damage', (1965) 9 Utah Law Review 808 at 812 n 23. The reasons identified by the author of this article as quoted by Heydon J, ibid [384], for secrecy in adoption include to protect the child from public knowledge or their own knowledge of adoption, to assist the child to feel a 'natural' child of the adoptive parents, and so that the child will not be discriminated against in the adoptive home, and will not know he was unwanted by the natural parents.

128 (2003) 215 CLR 1 at [337] referring to the Adoption of Children Act 1964. It should be noted that since 2002 Queensland has been reviewing the Adoption of Children Act 1964, with a view to developing new legislation which better reflects current social views and understandings about adoption. This is the first major review of the legislation in thirty years. The review recognises the significant social changes that have occurred since 1964. Recent consultation with interested groups has shown strong support for the principles the Queensland Government proposes to use to inform new legislation, including that 'a child has a right to information about family background and cultural heritage and to develop a positive cultural identity' and that 'all parties involved in adoption have a right to engage in information exchange and contact'. See *Adoption Legislation Review Public Consultation*, Overview of Key Issues, Queensland Government Department of Families, March 2003, p 2. See also *Adoption Legislation Review Public Consultation Paper*, Queensland Government Department of Families, 2002, Ch 3 'The concept of adoption and general principles' and Ch 4 'Open Adoption Practice', which notes at 32 that 'since the mid-1970s, there has been a move away from confidential adoption arrangements, closed adoption records and the assumption that such arrangements are in the best interests of children requiring adoption and birth or adoptive parents. Adoption practice reflects social, political, economic and moral changes in society and the move towards more open adoption practice is part of a trend towards more openness in society generally'. The Queensland review is currently delayed pending an assessment of the Federal parliament report of November 2005, 'Overseas adoption in Australia: Report on the inquiry into adoption from overseas.'

129 (2003) 215 CLR 1 at [384].

social values of the 1960s as opposed to modern research and practice in adoption services. Modern adoption research and practice recognises the significant damage that old practices of secrecy in adoption inflicted on birth parents and adopted children (including feelings of loss of family and culture) and advocates a more open approach to adoption.[130] Many Australian legislatures including Queensland and New South Wales have either reviewed or are reviewing their adoption legislation in line with modern research and practice in adoption, particularly in relation to the right to knowledge and the damage inflicted on all parties to adoption by practices of secrecy.[131]

In addition, Heydon J refers repeatedly[132] to the so-called 'emotional bastard' social fact which in effect states that children will be psychologically damaged by the knowledge they were not only unplanned by their parents but were the subject of litigation. This social fact appears to have originated in the United States of America in the late 1950s[133] and Heydon J refers to a number of American cases in support of it.[134] However, there are a number of

130  See the discussion in fn 128 above of the Queensland review. See also the NSW Law Reform Commission, *Review of the Adoption of Children Act 1965 (NSW)*, Report 81 (1997). At para 7.1 the Commission indicates that 'one of the most distinctive features of recent thinking and practice in adoption is the view that adoption law should not facilitate deception or secrecy, but should promote honesty and openness. This mode of thinking developed from research into the long-term effects of adoption and the needs of consumers of adoption services. Research and experience both in Australia and overseas shows that this is in the best interests of the child and should, therefore be encouraged'. For a background of the outdated social notions (including for example the shame of unmarried parenthood and illegitimacy) underlying notions of secrecy see NSW Law Reform Commission, *Review of the Adoption of Children Act 1990: Summary Report*, Report 69 (1992) Ch 2. The report notes at [2.4] social changes away from secrecy and notes that 'at least by the mid 1960s adoptive parents were being advised by adoption agencies to tell children of their adoptive status'. In New South Wales 'after 1977 adoptive parents had to agree to tell their children of their adoptive status' at [2.8]. In discussing the changes in social values and the incidence of adoption since the 1960s Graycar and Morgan also note 'furthermore the social and emotional consequences of giving up babies for adoption are now widely discussed'. See Graycar and Morgan 'Unnatural rejection of womanhood and motherhood: Pregnancy, Damages and the Law' (1996) 18 Sydney Law Review 323 at 340. See also the objectives of the Adoption Act 2000 (NSW) in s 7 which provides among other things that the objectives of the Act include: 'to ensure that adoption law and practice assist a child to know and have access to his or her birth family and cultural heritage' and 'to encourage openness in adoption'.
131  Ibid.
132  For example, see (2003) 215 CLR 1 at [372]–[384], [390]–[391], [392], [399], [410].
133  See the discussion in *Sherlock v Stillwater* 260 NW 2d 169 (Minn, 1977) at 173–4 which refers to the 1957 case of *Shaheen v Knight* 6 Lyc. 19, 23, 11 Pa. D & C. 2d 41, 45 (1957). The argument seems to have been first rejected in 1967 in *Custodio v Bauer* 251 Cal. App. 2d 303, 59 Cal. Rptr 463, 27 ALR 3d 884, noting the new 'modern' social attitudes to such matters.
134  For example, see (2003) 215 CLR 1 at [374]–[380] where Heydon J discusses *Sherlock v Stillwater Clinic* 260 NW 2d 169 (Minn, 1977); *Wilbur v Kerr* 628 SW 2d (Ark, 1982); *Boone v Mullendore* 416 So 2d 718 (Ala, 1982); *McKernan v Aasheim* 687 P 2d 850 (Wash, 1984); *University of Arizona Health Services Center v Superior Court of the State of Arizona* 667 P 2d 1294 (Ariz, 1983) and *Burke v Rivo* 551 NE 2d 1 (Mass, 1990).

major difficulties with this social fact. First, there appears to be no social scientific support for this essentially social scientific fact (knowledge that would potentially stem from the discipline of psychology) either available or stated in the relevant case law sources.[135] Second, a number of the American cases cited by Heydon J[136] positively source the veracity of the social fact to two law review articles.[137] However, neither of those articles appear to verify affirmatively the existence of the 'emotional bastard syndrome' but simply restate it as a theory referred to in case law as a policy against recovery. Ultimately both law review authors reject the legitimacy of the argument as a basis for rejecting liability.[138] The upshot is that the emotional bastard social fact was probably never a proven psychological effect at all but rather a construction by judges which reflected and/or constructed the social norms and values at the time of its inception during the 1950s. This was a time when openness in families was not necessarily encouraged, and when fertility issues were clouded in secrecy and shame. Even the use of the term 'emotional bastard'[139] in the cases and American law review articles harks to old attitudes about the stigma of illegitimacy and the lack of control of individual fertility and reproduction. It seems, that the very genesis of the 'emotional bastard' social fact (and its close relative the 'secrecy in adoption' social fact) in wrongful birth cases is that by analogy with the position of the illegitimate child, the adopted or unplanned child (when the fact of adoption or lack of planning is known) would and should feel social stigma and shame, and accordingly would suffer psychological harm. This kind of assumption should not be encouraged today.

Perhaps the most striking aspect of *Cattanach* is not the social fact assumptions made, but the 'missing' social facts the High Court never considers. *Cattanach* is a case that essentially concerns the reproductive autonomy of women, and the effect on women's lives of childbearing. The issue of

---

135 See Kirby J comments in *Cattanach v Melchior*, ibid at [79] and McHugh and Gummow JJ, ibid at [79]. Certainly I have not identified any social scientific evidence in support of the social fact cited in either the American cases or the relevant academic articles.

136 For example *Wilbur v Kerr* 628 SW 2d 568 at 573; *Boone v Mullendore* 416 So 2d 718 at 722; *McKernan v Aasheim* 687 P 2d 850 at 852; and *University of Arizona Health Services Center v Superior Court of the State of Arizona* 667 P 2d 1294 at 1302.

137 See Robertson, Gerald, 'Civil Liability Arising from "Wrongful Birth" Following an Unsuccessful Sterilization Operation' 4(2) American Journal of Law and Medicine 131 at 153. Robertson, while disposing of the 'theory', does appear to recognise the possibility of some psychological damage to children. He does not, however, advocate this as a sufficient reason to reject wrongful birth actions but as a reason for providing separate representation for children. See also McDonough, Brian, 'Wrongful Birth: A Child of Tort Comes of Age' (1981) 50 University of Cincinnati. Law Review 65 at 74.

138 Ibid.

139 A term used for example in quotes from the American cases, used by Heydon J in *Cattanach v Melchior* (2003) 215 CLR 1 at [375] and [376].

work and family balance, women's reproductive autonomy, childcare and the effect of bearing children on the lives of women are huge issues affecting Australia. As Lord Bingham recently noted in the House of Lords in *Rees v Darlington Memorial Hospital NHS Trust*:[140]

> The spectre of the well-to-do parents plundering the National Health Service should not blind one to the other realities: that of the single mother with young children, struggling to make ends meet and counting the days until her children are of an age to enable her to work more hours and so enable the family to live a less straitened existence; the mother whose burning ambition is to put domestic chores behind her and embark on a new career or resume an old one. Examples can be multiplied. To speak of losing the freedom to limit the size of one's family is to mask the real loss suffered in a situation of this kind. This is that a parent, particularly (even today) the mother, has been denied through the negligence of another, the opportunity to live her life in the way that she asked and planned.[141]

However, the social facts surrounding these issues are virtually absent in *Cattanach* with only Kirby J generally noting the relevance of the effect of children on Australian women's lives.[142] For the rest of the court, the role of 'mother' and the effect of children on the lives of 'mothers' is simply silenced. Mothers are simply considered one half of the generic parental duo and effects on the lives of parents generally (mothers and fathers) are ascribed to women.[143] However, social scientific research has made it clear that the effects of parenthood are not generic, and impact more greatly on the lives and careers of mothers than fathers. There is a rich literature of social scientific material that may have been relevant and accessible to the court.[144] Characterisation

---

140  [2004] 1 AC 309.
141  Ibid [8]. However disappointingly, Lord Bingham joined the other Law Lords in the majority, Lord Nicholls of Birkenhead, Lord Millett and Lord Hope, in thinking that £15,000 was a sufficient 'conventional sum' to match this 'injury and loss'. It is hard to imagine that this sum represents even one year of the true value of mothering a child.
142  (2003) 215 CLR 1 at [162]. He also notes generally that there have been social changes affecting women and marriage at [105].
143  See the discussion in *Cattanach* of effects on the lives of 'parents' ibid [9], the incidence of the parent-child relationship ibid at [36], the effects of parenthood at ibid [196] and the consequences of parenthood ibid at [247]. See also Heydon J's description of fundamental assumptions about 'parenthood' at [323]–[346]. See also discussion in Golder, above n 6.
144  See for example Craig, Lyn, 'The Time Cost of Parenthood: An Analysis of Daily Workload', SPRC Discussion Paper No 117, October 2002; Lyn Craig Caring Differently: A Time Use Analysis of the Type and Social Context of Child Care Performed By Fathers and Mothers' SPRC Discussion Paper No. 116, September 2002. Craig notes that her research adds to the body of work that shows that 'domestic work and the family have different

of wrongful birth cases as if the birth of an unplanned child has an equal and neutral effect on both mothers and fathers misconceives the very nature of these kinds of cases.

Why was there silence on such important social facts? Perhaps some mixed gender on the bench or at the bar may have contributed to more discussion in the judgments (or at least some discussion) of social facts applicable to the lives of women.[145] All members of the current then High Court were male, and all counsel[146] who argued *Cattanach v Melchior* on appeal before the High Court were male.[147] As Hoyano has recently noted of the judgment of Hale LJ (a female judge) in the English judgment of *Parkinson v St James and Secroft University Hospital NHS Trust*:[148]

> In a tour de force, Hale LJ wrote an extended essay on the physical, psychological, practical and legal implications of pregnancy, child birth and motherhood for a woman's personal autonomy, possibly a deliberate

impacts on men and women' (at 18). Her first report finds the time cost of motherhood higher than fatherhood (at 18) with mothers working part-time having the highest overall workload (at 18). Her second report confirms that the nature of childcare is also qualitatively different for mothers with fathers 'more likely to have someone to take over, to be able to avoid the less pleasant and more urgent tasks, and rarely do other tasks at the same time as child care' (at 18).

145 I make this argument cognisant of the fact that membership of a particular gender group does not equate to sharing a viewpoint on all issues, or a shared common experience of gender, with other members of that gender group. There are many factors including culture, race, education, sexuality, religion and social status that influence and shape life experience. Mixed gender on the bench should not automatically equate to a change in overall judicial perception of a particular social fact. However, a total lack of one gender on the bench of the High Court and in any speaking roles before the High Court certainly diminishes the opportunity for developing an understanding of social facts, perceptions and life experiences directly connected to the female gender, for example birth and motherhood, and the effects of mothering on a woman's life and career. Justice Susan Crennan, only the second woman in history to be appointed to the High Court, was sworn in on 8 November 2005 following the retirement of Justice McHugh.

146 Except for one junior counsel appearing for one of the intervenors, the Attorney General for Western Australia. See *Cattanach v Melchior* B22/2002 (11 February) HCA Transcript.

147 For a discussion on the necessity for reform of judicial appointment procedures to allow more female appointments to the bench, see Davis and Williams 'Reform of the Judicial Appointments Process: Gender and the Bench of the High Court of Australia' (2003) 27 Melbourne University Law Review 820. See also the discussion at 828 of the fact that women are 'largely absent from the ranks of lawyers who appear and speak before the High Court'. Davis and Williams refer to speeches given by Justice Kirby that estimate that only 2–3 per cent of the total number of counsel appearing before the court (during the periods discussed in the speeches) were women in speaking roles. See Justice Kirby, M, 'Women Lawyers – Making a Difference' (1998) 10 Australian Feminist Law Journal 125 at 129–34 and Justice Kirby, 'Women in the Law – What Next' (2002) 16 Australian Feminist Law Journal 148.

148 [2002] QB 266.

'reality check' to the panegyrics to parenthood in which all of the (male) Law Lords indulged in *McFarlane*.[149]

In addition, reliance on the rule that the court should focus on legal principle only or at the most legal policy may have had the effect of discouraging the use of relevant social facts generally, including those relating to the effect of children on women's lives.[150] For example, Senior Counsel for the plaintiff respondent when making submissions during the hearing of the High Court appeal responding to judicial questions relating to the relevance of particular matters of 'public policy' commented that:

> In our submission, if public policy is to be used from time to time in the shaping of the common law . . . then it ought never to be by choice of a kind which could realistically and fairly be called partisan during a current or raging controversy. In our submission, that is exactly what would be happening in this case. And all the judges, or most, regardless of the side they line up with on this issue, observe that there is much to be said on either side.[151]

That said, of course it is clear that judges in *Cattanach* clearly did make statements about an array of social facts – just not to those relating to the specific and relevant life experiences of women. It would appear that recognition of social facts relating to the effect of parenting children on the lives of women would have supported a policy argument in favour of the recovery of damages in the case. While I do not argue here that social facts concerning the effects of children on the lives of women are necessarily trump arguments in wrongful birth cases they do at least warrant some attention and recognition, particularly in preference to unproven social facts like the 'emotional bastard' argument.

### Implications of the use of social facts

A number of implications flow from the above social fact analysis. It is apparent that judicial decision-making does not involve the pure application of legal principles to adjudicative facts. A close examination of the cases included in this chapter supports this conclusion. The analysis of the 2003 negligence cases demonstrates that High Court judges do find the need to

---

149  Hoyano, L CH, 'Misconceptions about Wrongful Conception' (2002) Modern Law Review 883 at 897.

150  Although of course, it did not discourage reliance on other social facts such as those relating to the importance of children and the nuclear family unit.

151  See Walker, Mr BW, SC, *Cattanach v Melchior* B22/2002 (12 February) HCA Transcript at 55.

refer to knowledge that is neither adjudicative fact nor legal principle, in other words a knowledge gap is often encountered. Judges who might be considered more conservative,[152] as well as judges who might be considered more activist or instrumental,[153] all made statements about social facts in the course of their judgments. This suggests that the models of judicial decision-making currently in vogue in Australia (included the revived version of legalism) do not adequately explain, predict or describe the role of social facts in judicial decision-making.[154] Likewise, social facts are not purely (or perhaps even predominantly) used in an instrumental way[155] by judges to predict or prefer particular policy outcomes. Social facts are used in the whole spectrum of ways discussed earlier in this chapter.

Americans who study the judicial decision-making methodology of the United States Supreme Court would be surprised at the very rare use of social scientific or empirical materials by the High Court of Australia. Even the three references to social scientific material identified in the analysis could not be described as having any real significance in the overall scheme of the relevant judgment and constituted more passing contextual references. While the Australian High Court occasionally does refer to empirical material[156] it is relatively rare and could not be said to form a major part of the Court's jurisprudence. The tradition developed in the United States following the landmark case of *Brown v Board of Education*[157] of frequent and often meaningful reference to empirical material in United States Supreme Court judgments has not been duplicated in Australia.[158] The High Court has never decided a case, such as *Brown*, where particular social scientific or empirical material has played a significant role. Australia has not adopted or encouraged Brandeis brief procedures[159] to enable the introduction of empirical material by parties. The use of amicus curiae in the Australian High Court is relatively rare and tightly regulated by the High Court.[160]

---

152 For example Gleeson, CJ, Callinan J and Heydon J.    153 For example Kirby J.

154 Although there are some indications in the analysis that judges may be taking an attitudinal approach to decision making, this has not been explored in detail in this chapter.

155 For example, as John Gava has suggested that judges do when they refer to law review articles. Gava discourages the use of law review articles by judges on the basis that judges should not engage in instrumentalist judging. See Gava, J, 'Law Reviews: Good for Judges, Bad for Law Schools?' (2002) 26 Melbourne University Law Review 560.

156 See for example the discussion by McHugh J in *Woods v Multi-Sport Holdings* (2002) 208 CLR 460 at [62] of social scientific research in relation to the frequency of accidents.

157 347 US 483, 495 (1954).

158 There may be a number of reasons for this including the more significant realist tradition in the United States.

159 For a recent advocacy of greater use of Brandeis briefs in the United States see Margolis, Ellie, 'Beyond Brandeis: Exploring the uses of Non-Legal Materials in Appellate Briefs' (2000) 34(2) University of San Francis Law Review 197.

160 See discussion in Williams, George, 'The amicus curiae and intervener in the High Court of Australia: a comparative analysis.' (2000) 28 Federal Law Review 365.

In 2003, there were 74 decisions handed down by the Australian High Court.[161] However, *amici curiae* were involved in only two cases – *Attorney-General (WA) v Marquet*[162] and *Appellant S395/2002 v Minister for Immigration and Multicultural Affairs; Appellant S.*[163] A further 17 cases[164] involved intervenors,[165] although only one intervenor was not a state or federal government interest or authority. By contrast, referring to only two cases decided during the relevant US Supreme Court term, the 2003 United States Supreme Court case of *Grutter v Bollinger*[166] involving the constitutionality of the University of Michigan Law School admission policy which sought to achieve diversity of the student body, drew 102 *amicus* briefs. A number of these briefs were cited by the opinion of the court and were considered to be particularly influential. These included the briefs of the retired military, as

161 This is taken from the cases recorded as decided by the High Court of Australia in 2003 accessed [2 May 2005] www.austlii.edu.au/au/cases/cth/HCA/2003/
162 *Attorney-General (WA) v Marquet* (2003) 202 ALR 233. Amicus (jointly represented by a single counsel) were the Liberal Party of Australia (WA Division) Incorporated, the National Party of Australia (WA) Incorporated, the Pastoralists and Graziers Association of Western Australia (Incorporated), the Western Australian Farmers Federation (Inc), One Nation (Western Australian Division) Incorporated and Judith Ann Hebiton. The amicus in this case were the effective contradictors in the action and, unusually, were allowed to make oral submissions to the High Court.
163 *Appellant S395/2002 v Minister for Immigration and Multicultural Affairs; Appellant S* (2003) 216 CLR 473. The amicus was Amnesty International Australia.
164 *Re Minister for Immigration and Multicultural and Indigenous Affairs; Ex parte Applicant* (2003) 211 CLR 441; *Plaintiff S157/2002 v Commonwealth of Australia* (2003) 211 CLR 476; *Austin v the Commonwealth of Australia* [2003] HCA 3 (5 February 2003); *New South Wales v Lepore; Samin v Queensland; Rich v Queensland* (2003) 212 CLR 511; *The Queen v Gee* (2003) 212 CLR 230; *Fittock v The Queen* (2003) 197 ALR 1; *Ng v the Queen* (2003) 197 ALR 10; *Cattanach v Melchior* (2003) 215 CLR 1; *Re The Maritime Union of Australia & Ors; Ex parte CSL Pacific Shipping Inc* (2003) 214 CLR 397; *News Limited v South Sydney District Rugby League Football Club Limited* (2003) 215 CLR 563; *British American Tobacco Australia Ltd v Western Australia* (2003) 217 CLR 30 ; *Chief Executive Officer of Customs v Labrador Liquor Wholesale Pty Ltd* (2003) 216 CLR 161 ; *Purvis v New South Wales (Department of Education and Training)* (2003) 217 CLR 92; *Paliflex Pty Limited v Chief Commissioner of State Revenue* (2003) 202 ALR 376; *South Sydney City Council v Paliflex Pty Limited* (2003) 202 ALR 396; *Attorney-General (WA) v Marquet* (2003) 202 ALR 233; *Blunden v Commonwealth of Australia* (2003) 203 ALR 189. The only intervenor that was not representative of state or federal interests or was not a governmental authority was People with Disabilities (NSW) Inc intervening in *Purvis v New South Wales (Department of Education and Training)*.
165 Intervenors are treated differently in Australian law to *amici curiae*. Intervenors are normally required to show a particular individual interest in the resolution of a matter, and once allowed to intervene effectively have the rights of a party. State and Federal Governments intervene as of right in certain matters in the High Court of Australia including constitutional cases. The vast majority of interventions involve governments or governmental authorities given a right of intervention by statute.
166 539 US 306, 343 (2003).

well as major corporations.[167] The 2003 Supreme Court case of *Lawrence v Texas*,[168] concerning the constitutionality of statutes criminalising private consensual homosexual sexual acts, also drew a large number of *amicus* briefs.[169] Material provided by *amicus* briefs was also cited in the opinion of the court and appeared influential. It is clear that the use of *amicus* briefs and social science in the United States Supreme Court generally is prolific.[170] By contrast, the use of both amicus briefs and social science in the Australian High Court is extremely limited and of little influence.

There is much literature regarding the use of social science in American Courts and in particular the utility and influence of *amicus* briefs in the US Supreme Court,[171] and some of this criticises the use by the US Supreme Court of social science and the proliferation of amicus briefs.[172] Justice Scalia, for example, recently scathingly criticised the use of social science by the majority opinion, in his dissenting opinion in the juvenile death penalty case of *Roper v Simmons*.[173] He accused the majority of looking 'over the heads of the crowd' and only picking 'out its friends'.[174] However, it is apparent that good amicus briefs, providing the court with unique and reliable information not provided by the parties, has proved to be of assistance to the United States Supreme Court.[175] Given the very apparent use by the Australian High Court of social fact material, there is a clear potential for greater use in Australia of *amicus curiae* to assist the Court with reliable social fact material. This would require both a more robust attitude by the Australian High Court to the admission and encouragement of *amicus curiae* briefs,[176] but also a change of culture in Australian professional and public interest groups.[177] The High Court could also encourage parties to provide a

---

167 For example, see Brief for *Amici Curiae* 65 Leading American Businesses in Support of Respondents, Grutter (No 02–241) and Consolidated Brief for Lt Gen J W Becton et al as *Amici Curiae* in Support of Respondents at 8, Grutter (No 02–241).

168 539 US 558 (2003).

169 See discussion in Christopher LR, 'Lawrence v Texas as the Perfect Storm', (2005) UC Davis Law Review 509.

170 For example see Alger, Jonathan and Krislov, Marvin, 'You've Got To Have Friends: Lessons Learned From The Role Of Amici In The University Of Michigan Cases' (2004) 30(3) Journal of College and University Law 503 at 503–5.

171 For example see discussion at ibid at 503–507.     172 Ibid.     173 125 S.Ct. 1183 (2005).

174 Ibid.

175 See Kearney, JD, and Merrill, TW, 'The Influence of *Amicus Curiae* Briefs on the Supreme Court' (2000) UPA Law Rev 743. For a discussion of hostility by courts to the use of social science in federal courts see Fradella, HF, 'A content analysis of Federal Judicial Views of the Social Science "Researcher's Black Arts" ' (2003) 35 Rutgers Law Journal 103.

176 See discussion in George Williams, above n 161.

177 There does not appear to be the same culture in Australia of interest groups seeking to appear as *amicus curiae*. For example, no public interest groups attempted to appear as amicus in *Cattanach* despite the obvious gender and family values issues inherent in the case.

summary and reference to any relevant empirical material in their appellate brief, in the manner of a Brandeis brief. Both of these options may also require a review of Australian evidence rules, which may prevent such material being introduced at appellate level either because of the fresh evidence rule or because of a potentially restrictive definition of judicial notice.[178] In addition, there are clear implications for greater diversity in judicial appointments, and for the need for judicial education, particularly in relation to the use of interdisciplinary material and scientific methodology.

While I suggest here that there is clearly a greater potential for the use of social science to assist social fact finding by courts including the High Court, this does not mean ignoring the potential difficulties or challenges faced by courts in the admission of social scientific and other empirical material. Clearly, there are issues in relation to the appropriateness of methodology adopted in studies, the potential use of 'junk science', the possible misuse or misunderstanding by lawyers and judges of this kind of material and the possible increases in costs to parties of the provision of such material. I also do not intend to suggest that social science or other sciences have some kind of greater claim to ultimate 'truths', than the law itself. Obviously, there are also many assumptions of social fact made by courts where there simply is no social scientific or other empirical material available that could assist the court. Or multiple competing evidence may be available to a court. In this chapter I do not intend to discuss these issues or difficulties in detail. However, in the final analysis, the potential value of social science to more accurate and reliable social fact finding outweighs the challenges the law faces in dealing with such material. In addition, many of the critiques of the use of social science in law (for example, those relating to misuse of findings, or the resolution of multiple competing findings) can equally apply to the way in which courts use legal principles themselves, and the law has always taken those difficulties in its stride. Pragmatically, if judges are going to refer to social facts (and they do) and refer to them frequently, anything that will improve the accuracy of the statements and the diversity of the views adopted seems desirable.

## Summary and Conclusion

Social fact statements are very commonly used by judges in High Court negligence cases. This, of itself, appears to throw doubt on the proposition that judges in the High Court do not or should not refer to explicit policy

---

In addition, there were clear issues at stake for both medical and insurance interest groups. This may of course be in reaction to difficulties experienced by groups attempting to appear as amicus, or intervenors in the past and for costs reasons.

178  See above n 51 and n 70.

matters in negligence cases. However, the use of social facts in the judgments demonstrates much more than this. Many social fact statements are used to provide a background social context for judgments. This contextual use of social facts falls outside the traditional understanding of 'policy' and perhaps is not considered by judges to be caught by 'anti' policy rules. Yet the setting of the background context to a judgment can be a very powerful persuasive and rhetorical device in the justification of the adoption of particular legal principles. In addition, in a wider context the extensive use of social facts in judgments tends to throw doubt on any description of judicial decision-making that describes the process of decision making as one that rests only upon strictly applying legal principles to adjudicative facts. As a result, there is a strong argument that as a starting point to better use of social facts in legal decision-making, we need to accept that there is often a 'gap' in judicial knowledge that judges need to fill, and will fill,[179] in order to reach a judgment.

The social facts referred to by judges in High Court negligence cases are generally unsupported by any citation of reference at all, and when references are provided they are most often to existing case law which simply reproduces judicial experience and intuition. This may often be of little consequence, for example when judges are describing social facts (as they frequently do) within their own special expertise such as the nature of legal institutions, litigation or legal actors. However, there are very significant issues raised where the social fact statements are highly contentious and debateable, or involve the discussion of 'facts' that are inherently outside the discipline of the law and which ostensibly draw on the expertise of other disciplines. In these circumstances, there is a clear potential for the greater use of reliable social scientific evidence in the High Court. There appears to be no clear rationale either in individual judgments or among the High Court bench as a whole, as to when the use of social facts may be acceptable, where restraint ought to be adopted, or what evidence should support social facts. This demonstrates the need not only for a greater acceptance that judicial gaps in knowledge occur, but also the need to consider how judicial practice, legal professional practice and the rules of evidence ought to respond to these gaps in some coherent fashion.

Finally, we need to acknowledge that social facts used by judges may not just reflect society and social values (if indeed they do) but rather that they may contribute to the construction of social norms. And perhaps it is here that the most damage may be done, where the social facts referred to by judges are incorrect, incomplete and out of date, or tell the story of some members of society, but shut out the reality of the lives of others.

---

179 No matter what commentators' theoretical views are on whether this is an acceptable judicial decision-making technique.

# Part III

# Issues in contract law

# Chapter 5

# Reconfiguring mistake in contract formation

*David Capper**

## Introduction

The English law of contract is reluctant to grant relief against the consequences of mistaken assumptions in the formation of contracts. In contrast to other vitiating factors like misrepresentation, duress, undue influence and unconscionable dealing,[1] the party seeking relief from the mistake is not clearly the victim of the other's wrongdoing.[2] The hesitant attitude towards mistake in contract law may also reflect a perception that the party seeking relief is at fault in making the mistake and that the risk of misassumptions grounding the request for relief should be allocated to that party.[3] It may also be due to the stark consequences of a finding that mistake has vitiated the contract. In English law at least the effect of mistake is to make the contract void so that remedial flexibility to mitigate the dire consequences of unscrambling the contract is extremely limited.

Relief from mistake may be granted where the party seeking to enforce the contract according to its terms has no legitimate or reasonable expectation that the contract be so enforced. 'Reasonable expectations' is a commonly cited theoretical basis explaining why contracts should be enforced; but

* The author gratefully acknowledges the support of the British Academy whose research grant facilitated the research upon which this chapter is based.
1  As expounded by the High Court of Australia in *Commercial Bank of Australia Ltd v Amadio* (1983) 151 CLR 447.
2  See Cartwright, J, 'Defects of Consent and Security of Contract: French and English Law Compared', in Birks, P and Pretto, A (eds), *Themes in Comparative Law, in Honour of Bernard Rudden*, 2002, Oxford: Oxford University Press, 153, at 158. Relief may be granted more readily in respect of mistaken gifts or where money is paid under the mistaken belief that it is owed. In such transactions the sanctity of contract is not a factor militating against granting relief.
3  See Atiyah, PS and Bennion, FAR, 'Mistake in the Construction of Contracts' (1961) 24 MLR 421, at 436–37, where the authors argue that relief may be more readily granted in the case of frustration because that is a supervening event and thus more difficult to make contingency for.

where some serious mistake has occurred in forming the contract reasonable expectations may suggest a different result. As Steyn J put it in *Associated Japanese Bank International v Credit du Nord*:

> Throughout the law of contract two themes regularly recur – respect for the sanctity of contract and the need to give effect to the reasonable expectations of honest men. Usually, these themes work in the same direction. Occasionally, they point to opposite solutions. The law regarding common mistake going to the root of a contract is a case where tension arises between the two themes.[4]

Professor Waddams has expressed the case for relief in similar terms[5] and Professor Perillo in terms of the shared assumption of mutual gain.[6] As the latter has explained contracts are usually avoided because that shared assumption is induced by the wrongful conduct of one party distorting the other's judgment. That wrongful conduct makes it unconscionable for the wrongdoer to hold the other party to the contract. Although transparently wrongful conduct is usually absent from cases of mistake this paper will argue that the undermining of the shared assumption of mutual gain is sometimes so serious that it would be unconscionable to uphold the contract. To this extent unconscionability can be seen as the grounding principle of relief against all contracts vitiated at inception.

This chapter will take the position that where a contract is vitiated by mistake the contract should be voidable at the instance of the party adversely affected by the mistake. The contract should not be void and the court should have a measure of remedial flexibility to adjust relief to take account of circumstances which have occurred since the contract was formed and to protect the interests of bona fide third parties who have become interested in the subject matter of the contract. In this regard English law has taken two potentially unhelpful turnings in recent years. First, in *Great Peace Shipping Ltd v Tsavliris Salvage (International) Ltd* (hereafter *The Great Peace*)[7] the Court of Appeal cast very considerable doubt upon the doctrine of mistake in equity (which rendered a contract voidable) first recognised by Lord Denning in *Solle v Butcher*.[8] Secondly, in *Shogun Finance Ltd v Hudson*[9] the House of Lords (by a 3:2 majority) decided that in the particular circumstances of that case the seller's mistake as to the buyer's identity rendered the contract void. But before going further with this analysis it must first be

---

4   [1989] 1 WLR 255, at 257.
5   Waddams, SM, *The Law of Contracts*, 1999, Toronto: Canada Law Book, 4th edn, paras 341 and 355.
6   *Corbin on Contracts*, Vol 7 (revised edn, 2002, Matthew Bender), para 28.1.
7   [2002] EWCA Civ 1407; [2003] QB 679.       8   [1950] 1 KB 671.
9   [2003] UKHL 62; [2004] 1 AC 919.

acknowledged that sometimes events occur which make a contract void. In this sense the contract is void because no contract is actually formed. There may be a failure of the parties' respective offer and acceptance to correspond so that they make no agreement at all, or the parties may have assumed circumstances to exist without which the entire basis of their agreement is undermined.[10] The next section of this chapter will consider cases like these for the purpose of eliminating them from the reconfigured doctrine of mistake which makes the contract voidable. The section following on from this will consider those cases where a common mistake of both parties should be seen as making the contract voidable and it will be argued there that unconscionability is the fundamental basis on which relief from mistaken assumptions should be granted. The final substantive section will consider cases of unilateral mistake, where it is clearer that the contract is voidable and that unconscionability is the basis for avoidance. It will be contended that this supplies a reason for treating common mistake similarly.

Before turning to the first substantive section of this chapter two further preliminary matters should be addressed. First, where a contract is indisputably formed, that is in those situations not covered in the next section, an important role should be recognised for contractual allocation of risk. Where the contract indicates, either expressly or by reasonable implication, that one party is to bear the risk of some misassumption, then that party should not be entitled to relief from mistake. In the *Associated Japanese Bank* case previously mentioned[11] Steyn J stated that the first question in any mistake case is whether the misassumption that has come to light has been dealt with by the contract itself.[12] As explained in the next paragraph this creates some tension with the unconscionability doctrine but it is nonetheless the logical first question because mistake deals with issues that the contracting parties have assumed would not affect them. If they have made some provision for it, even by implication, there is no justification for relief inconsistent with that provision unless there is some other ground on which a mistaken party can rely. One consequence of respecting the allocation of risk is probably to reduce considerably the scope for the doctrine of mistake to operate. Given the absence of really transparent wrongdoing by the party against whom relief is sought, mistake should only be a factor in the most exceptional of circumstances.

---

10  Half a century ago Sir Christopher Slade wrote an article entitled 'The Myth of Mistake in the English Law of Contract' (1954) 70 LQR 385 in which he argued that most cases of mistake either prevented a contract from being formed or could be resolved through construction of the contract. To the same effect see also Atiyah, PS and Bennion, FAR, 'Mistake in the Construction of Contracts' (1961) 24 MLR 421. In the remainder of this paper efforts will be made to explain why this theory does not best explain all cases of mistake in contract law and why mistake should be recognised as a vitiating factor in some cases.

11  [1989] 1 WLR 255, n 4 above.        12  Ibid 268.

The other preliminary matter is where common mistake should be placed on the map of the law of contract. The argument here is that all cases of mistake should be placed among the vitiating factors – misrepresentation, duress, undue influence, and unconscionable dealing. But another possibility is that common mistake should be paired along with frustration.[13] The basis for this is that both common mistake and frustration deal with misassumptions by the contracting parties, as to circumstances at the time of contracting in the case of mistake and as to the future in the case of frustration.[14] The absence of clear wrongdoing by the party against whom relief is sought also tends to make mistake resemble frustration as opposed to other vitiating factors resting more clearly on unconscionability. Allocation of risk is also a meaningful question in relation to frustration but not for unconscionability as courts are not likely to look with favour on terms permitting parties to commit fraud[15] on one another.

Against this are the following more persuasive arguments. First, it is more realistic to recognise that in cases of common mistake a defective contract is formed instead of no contract at all. While the discharge of a frustrated contract and the rescission of a voidable contract both bring the contract to an end they do so in very different ways. Discharge operates prospectively only whereas rescission cancels the contract from inception and allows for the parties' respective performances to be reversed so far as reasonably practicable.[16] The equation between common mistake and frustration would work much better if common mistake rendered a contract void but it is argued below that this should not be the consequence of a common mistake. Secondly, as unilateral mistake clearly makes a contract voidable and rests upon the unconscionable conduct of the non-mistaken party, it would be mapped in a different place from common mistake. Thirdly, the consequences of holding a contract void (necessarily following from the equation with frustration) are so severe (as shown later in 'Common Mistake undermining the Contract') that this outcome should be avoided if there is any alternative. The arguments stemming from unconscionability and allocation of risk are answered in the next paragraph.

13  This is the approach taken by Farnsworth, EA, 1999, *Contracts* (3rd edn, New York: Aspen Law and Business).
14  An analysis of two cases concerned with the hiring of rooms to view the coronation procession of King Edward VII illustrate this. In *Krell v Henry* [1903] 2 KB 740 the procession was cancelled after the booking had been made and hence frustrated the contract. In *Griffith v Brymer* (1903) 19 TLR 434 the procession had already been cancelled when the booking was made in ignorance of this. The contract was held to be void for common mistake although this paper will argue that it should have been voidable.
15  Including for this purpose equitable fraud.
16  There may be relief from the consequences of performance rendered before the frustrating event both at common law and under the Law Reform (Frustrated Contracts) Act 1943.

Common mistake as a vitiating factor is different from misrepresentation, duress, undue influence and unconscionable dealing because the contract has not been *procured* by unconscionable conduct. Even so the link is stronger with the vitiating factors than it is with frustration. Something went wrong in the formation of the contract and has come to light, thus making it unconscionable to enforce the contract. Allocation of risk is the first question to ask in cases of frustration too[17] and might point towards greater symmetry with the contract being void because there would then be no apparent allocation of the right to behave unconscionably. The answer to this is that unconscionable conduct in making a contract is not dealt with by common mistake, only unconscionable conduct in enforcing the contract. If the risk of the mistake has been allocated there can be nothing unconscionable about upholding the contract.

## Mistakes preventing contract formation

These kinds of mistakes fall into two broad categories; although in relation to the second of these it will be argued that frequently what prevents formation of the contract is not actually the mistake itself. The two categories are:

1.   Misunderstanding – where no agreement is made.
2.   Where the entire basis of agreement is undermined by the non-occurrence of some fact or circumstance integral to the formation of the contract.

### Misunderstanding

In these cases the parties are not *ad idem*, their minds have not met as their purported offer and acceptance are inconsistent. Probably the most celebrated example is *Raffles v Wichelhaus*[18] where seller and buyer had two different ships called *Peerless* in mind for the delivery of a cargo of cotton. The buyer meant the ship arriving at Liverpool in October, whereas the seller meant the *Peerless* arriving in December. Sometimes this case is presented as the victory of subjectivism over objectivism in contract formation but even applying the strict objectivist approach of *Smith v Hughes*[19] an answer had to be found to the question '[W]hich *Peerless*?' Professor Waddams has analysed these cases in terms of legitimate expectation.[20] Thus neither party had a legitimate expectation that its *Peerless* was the agreed ship in *Raffles v Wichelhaus*. The contract was incomplete for failure to agree an essential matter. In *Smith v Hughes* the questions to be resolved were whether the buyer reasonably

---

17 See *Ocean Tramp Tankers Corp v VIO Sovfracht (The Eugenia)* [1964] 2 QB 226.
18 (1864) 2 Hurl & C 906.        19 (1870–71) LR 6 QB 597.
20 See Waddams, above n 5, p 355.

believed that the seller was offering to sell old oats and whether the seller reasonably believed the buyer was accepting this offer. *Scriven Brothers & Co v Hindley & Co*[21] can be explained as a case where the parties were not *ad idem* because the seller had no reasonable basis for a belief that the buyer was bidding an extravagant price for tow. Whatever the precise theoretical basis for these decisions, they are instances where no contract was formed because the parties misunderstood one another about an element essential to the contract's very existence. Consequently the doctrine of mistake as a vitiating factor has no role to play.

### Basis of agreement undermined

The subtitle may be slightly unfortunate in that this concept has been used to explain those mistakes which the next section of this chapter will argue should make the contract voidable. What is meant here is that the parties have outwardly made an agreement which ultimately comes to no agreement at all because, e.g., it has no subject matter or it is an agreement to do the impossible. The contract is void, not because of mistake, but simply because in the circumstances it was not possible to make a contract.

A respectable body of opinion would solve all of these problems, as well as those discussed in the next section, within the contract itself. This approach would look for express or implied terms within the contract to indicate what happens in the event that some fundamental assumption on which the contract is based proves to be unfounded. Sometimes the contract will be void because this assumed fact is a condition upon which its existence depends. Sometimes the assumed fact is part of the bargain and its non-occurrence is thus a breach of contract.[22] This chapter accepts that where there is an express or implied contractual promise that some thing exists or that some fact occurs, its non-existence or non-occurrence is properly a case of breach.[23] But where the contract contains no such promise it is circular to argue that the contract is void because the contract says it is. 'Void' means that the 'contract' is a nullity, that there is no contract. Three categories of vitiation – 'no contract', 'void', and 'voidable' is a surfeit of categories and a source of confusion.

Alternatively it may be arguable that the contract is terminable on the ground of failure of basis. This at least avoids arguing that there is no

21 [1913] 3 KB 564. See also *Falck v Williams* [1900] AC 176.
22 This is the approach taken in the articles by Slade and by Atiyah and Bennion, above n 10. Professor Smith takes the same approach in Smith, JC, 'Contracts – Mistake, Frustration and Implied Terms' (1994) 110 LQR 400. To similar effect is McTurnan, LB, 'An Approach to Common Mistake in English Law' (1963) 41 Can Bar Rev 1.
23 This was the approach taken by the High Court of Australia in *McRae v Commonwealth Disposals Commission* (1951) 84 CLR 377.

contract because the contract says there is no contract. Examples may be afforded by some of the cases arising out of the postponed coronation procession of Edward VII. In *Clark v Lindsay*[24] and *Griffith v Brymer*[25] contracts for the hire of rooms overlooking the procession route were concluded in ignorance of the fact that the procession had been cancelled a short time before. The basis for excusing the plaintiffs from their obligation to pay for the rooms was that the entire basis of the agreement, viewing the coronation procession, had been undermined. The plaintiffs were thus allowed to terminate the contracts because of the common mistake of both parties. The difficulty with this approach is that it ultimately depends upon a fiction. If the parties have made a misassumption about something they are not likely to have thought about, what is to happen should their assumptions prove unfounded? A better basis for relief would be to allow an adversely affected party to rescind for common mistake, along the lines suggested in the next section. The problem was one occurring in the formation of the contract. Greater coherence in the law would be fostered if all such problems were treated as vitiating factors.

### RES EXTINCTA

Where the subject matter of the contract does not exist the contract is void because there is nothing to contract about.[26] The parties may have made a mistaken assumption about the existence of the subject matter but the mistake is not the reason why the contract is void. An early example is *Strickland v Turner*.[27] The plaintiff bought an annuity on the life of one Edward Henry Lane. Before the purchase was completed Lane died. The plaintiff recovered the purchase money because the consideration for its payment had totally failed. It seems tolerably clear that Pollock CB treated the contract as void because the subject matter (the annuity) did not exist at the time of completion of the contract. Another case of *res extincta* is *Galloway v Galloway*[28] where the parties made a separation agreement to end their 'marriage' in ignorance of the fact that the defendant's 'former' wife was still alive. Ridley J said:

> The law clearly was that if there was a mutual mistake of fact which was material to the existence of an agreement the agreement was void. In the present case, looking at the terms of the deed, there could be no doubt that its basis was the belief of both parties that they were respectively husband and wife.[29]

---

24 (1903) 88 LT 198.    25 (1903) 19 TLR 434.
26 This is the way it is put in Furmston, M, *Cheshire, Fifoot and Furmston's Law of Contract*, 14th edn, 2001, London: Butterworths, p 256.
27 (1852) 7 Ex 208.    28 (1914) 30 TLR 531.    29 Ibid 532.

The implication of this is that if the parties had knowingly contracted a biga-mous marriage their separation agreement would have been valid. This simply cannot be right so the true basis of the decision has to be the non-existence of the marriage the separation agreement depended on.[30]

*Res extincta* sometimes arises in connection with contracts for the sale of goods. An often quoted example is *Couturier v Hastie*,[31] although what that case actually decided remains something of a mystery to this day.[32] Although mistake probably did not render the contract void in that case it nonetheless illustrates that the non-existence of the goods to be sold *can* render a contract for the sale of goods void. But as the High Court of Australia decided in *McRae v Commonwealth Disposals Commission*,[33] transactions accompanied by any appreciable risk of destruction or non-existence of subject matter are usually cases of implied contractual promise by the seller that the goods exist.[34] Section 6 of the Sale of Goods Act 1979 will not be considered in any depth here although it should be recognised that this provision applies where the goods have *perished* rather than where they never existed at all.[35] Like other cases of *res extincta* it is not the mistaken assumption that is determinative. The contract is either void because of the absence of anything to contract about, or breached where there is a contractual promise that the subject matter does exist.

## RES SUA

Where A contracts to sell an interest in property X to B and B already has an interest in property X equal to or greater than the interest A is selling there is again no subject matter for the contract and the latter is accordingly void. It is an unlikely scenario but something like it occurred in the famous case of *Cooper v Phibbs*.[36] Doubts have been expressed as to whether the contract

---

30  Had the subject matter been the financial support of one of the partners by the other there would have been no failure of subject matter. A similarly woolly approach was taken by the Court of Appeal in *EIC Services Ltd v Phipps* [2004] EWCA Civ 1069; [2004] 2 BCLC 589, a case about the issue of bonus shares. The contract was void because in the circumstances the directors had no power to issue the shares, not because they mistakenly believed they had.

31  (1856) 5 HL Cas 673.

32  A convincing analysis may be found in Atiyah, PS, '*Couturier v Hastie* and the Sale of Non-Existent Goods' (1957) 73 LQR 340.

33  (1951) 84 CLR 377.

34  This solution was not considered in *Couturier v Hastie* because that case concerned a claim by the sellers for the price, not a claim by the buyers for non-delivery. It should not be thought that solutions like these are confined to sale of goods cases. In *Shaw v Shaw* [1954] 2 QB 429 the defendant, already married, was held to be in breach of an implied contract that he could legally marry a woman he proposed to.

35  The article by Atiyah, above n 32, makes a convincing case that section 6 can be excluded by the parties.

36  (1867) LR 2 HL 149. The contract purported to lease property X to B, the tenant-in-tail.

could have been void in that case as the petitioner sought to rescind it. But this is immaterial because the case was pre-Judicature Acts and there were other complicating features of the transaction that required the assistance of the Court of Chancery to unscramble. None of this alters the fact that the contract was void.[37] Neither does it alter the fact that it is the impossibility of selling to B what B already owns that makes the contract void, not the parties' mistaken belief about the ownership of the property.[38]

A related and more likely scenario is where A attempts to sell to B property which A cannot sell, either because A is not the owner or has no authorisation from the owner to sell. The contract will usually be void in these circumstances although B may acquire title to the property as a bona fide purchaser or via some exception to the *nemo dat* rule. A may also be in breach of an express or implied term in the contract that she is able to sell to B.[39] Once again any mistaken belief in the parties is immaterial.

### IMPOSSIBILITY

A contract to do the conceptually impossible should be seen as void. An example is *Hall v Cazenove*[40] where a covenant in a charter party required a ship to sail on or before a date that had already passed. Where some other date is intended and the mistake is one of transcription rectification may be possible but if the date transcribed is intended then the contract is voided by the impossibility rather than the mistaken belief that the date is right. There is again no subject matter to this contract.

*Sheikh Bros Ltd v Ochsner*[41] was treated as a void contract case. The Indian Contract Act 1872 s 20 provided that: 'Where both parties to an agreement are under a mistake as to a matter of fact essential to the agreement, the agreement is void'. The contract required the respondents to cut and supply to the appellants 50 tons of sisal per month but the land was physically incapable of producing that amount of sisal. The Privy Council appear to have advised that the mistaken belief of the parties as to the land's capacity voided the contract as a matter of English law, not just under the Indian Contract Act. This approach is, with respect, misconceived. In farm-output

---

37 The story of *Cooper v Phibbs* is comprehensively told in Matthews, P, 'A Note on *Cooper v Phibbs*' (1989) 105 LQR 599. See also Goodhart, AL (1950) 66 LQR 169.

38 Where there is doubt as to where the title to property lies, the parties may enter into a quitclaim deed, under which the seller promises to convey whatever title (s)he has. The contract would not be void if the buyer is already the owner of the property because (s)he obtains precisely what was contracted for, clarification of the title.

39 This is the position for sale of goods contracts under section 12 of the Sale of Goods Act 1979. If a quitclaim deed is used the contract would be valid because the buyer buys the risk that the seller has nothing to sell.

40 (1804) 4 East 477.    41 [1957] AC 136.

contracts the occupier should be held to assume the risk that the land will produce the promised quantity. Relief may be justifiable where there is a transcription error or a unilateral mistake by one party of which the other is aware.

### Common mistake undermining the contract

In this scenario the parties have 'outwardly' made a contract. There is an identifiable offer and acceptance and the contract has a genuine subject matter. However, the parties share a common (or mutual) misassumption about something important and would not have made the contract they actually made (or maybe would have made no contract at all) had they been aware of this circumstance. Ever since *Bell v Lever Brothers Ltd*[42] English law has taken the position that if the common mistake makes the contract as made essentially different from the contract the parties intended to make then the contract is void. Conceptually it is not clear whether this means anything different from a failure to make any contract at all. What value lies in the concept of making 'something' which is actually 'nothing' because it is a nullity and can create no enforceable rights, is far from clear. If there is no distinction in theory between contracts void in this sense and contracts not formed at all it looks counter-intuitive to suggest that in these situations there is no contract. Instinctively one is bound to feel that a defective contract has been created, rather than no contract at all. Consequently either party, but more likely the party that suffers adverse consequences from the mistake, should have a right to treat the contract as voidable and to seek to rescind it.

The first two sub-sections of this part of the chapter will consider English law on this question. The first sub-section will deal with the conventional doctrine, and the second with the doctrine of mistake in equity which held that for mistakes less fundamental than those of the conventional doctrine the contract could be voidable. Then the approach to common mistake in other common law jurisdictions, principally the United States and Canada, will be compared to English law, together with some brief mention of approaches in Australia and New Zealand as well as some international approaches. Finally, the shape of a reconfigured doctrine of common mistake will be outlined.

### Conventional English law doctrine

Before *Bell v Lever Brothers*[43] there was some indication that common mistake might make a contract voidable. In *Scott v Coulson*[44] the defendant bought a life insurance policy from the plaintiff. Between the date of the

---

42 [1932] AC 161.    43 Ibid.    44 [1903] 2 Ch 249.

contract and the date of assignment of the policy the defendant received information indicating that the assured had been dead at the time of the contract. After the assignment it was confirmed that this information was true. Thus the defendant was assigned a policy at the considerably higher maturity value than the surrender value the parties had mistakenly assumed at the time of the contract. In upholding the plaintiff's right to rescind the contract two members of the Court of Appeal expressly stated that the defendant should not be allowed to benefit from his inequitable conduct.[45] This suggests that common mistake renders a contract voidable and that unconscionability is the basis of relief. The earlier decision in *Huddersfield Banking Co Ltd v Henry Lister and Son Ltd*[46] is consistent with this approach. A consent order in insolvency proceedings was set aside because the agreement on which it was based was vitiated by the mistaken belief of both parties that certain power looms in a factory were not fixtures.[47]

Although a 3:2 majority decision that the contract in that case was not void *Bell v Lever Brothers* was actually unanimous that common mistake made a contract void. Most weight seems to be attached to the speech of Lord Atkin who stated[48] that mistake negatives or nullifies consent. The mistake must relate to some fundamental matter such as the identity of the contracting parties, the existence of the subject matter of the contract, or the quality of the subject matter. In relation to the latter, Lord Atkin said that 'mistake will not affect assent unless it is a mistake which makes the thing without the quality essentially different from the thing as it was believed to be.'[49] The majority of the House of Lords took the view that the contracts to terminate the services of Messrs Bell and Snelling were not rendered essentially different from what they were believed to be just because of the parties' ignorance or forgetfulness that Lever Brothers had a right to dismiss them summarily. That this is a very narrow test is confirmed by some of the examples Lord Atkin gave of contracts that would not be void for mistake.[50]

One reason for the narrowness of the test in *Bell v Lever Brothers* may be the drastic consequences of holding that a contract is a complete nullity. This

---

45  Ibid, at 253 (Romer LJ), 253–254 (Cozens-Hardy LJ). Vaughan Williams LJ, at 252, thought that the contract was unenforceable at law and that the intervention of equity was unnecessary.

46  [1895] 2 Ch 273.

47  The clearest indication that the agreement grounding the consent order was voidable and not void came from Kay LJ who said, at 284: 'Of course, if the order had been acted upon, and third parties' interests had intervened and so on, difficulties might arise; but nothing of that kind occurs here.'

48  [1932] AC 161, at 217.        49  Ibid 218.

50  Eg, the purchase of an unsound horse believed to be sound (p 220), or of a picture believed to be by some master but in fact a copy (p 224), or of an uninhabitable furnished house (p 224). Professor Smith has stated that it is very difficult to understand how Lord Atkin's test was not satisfied – see n 22 above, at 412–415.

may account for the relative popularity of the doctrine of mistake in equity discussed in the next sub-section. The next case where mistake making the contract void was a serious issue was not until the 1980s, *Associated Japanese Bank (International) Ltd v Credit du Nord.*[51] Steyn J held that the non-existence of the four machines Bennett had sold and leased back from Associated Japanese Bank (AJB) made the contract of guarantee between the two financial institutions essentially different from what it was believed to be. As Professor Smith has pointed out this is difficult to accept. The guarantee related to Bennett's obligations under the leaseback part of his contract with AJB. Those obligations were intact despite the non-existence of the machines. As Bennett had sold the machines to AJB he had impliedly promised the machines' existence and any risk to the contrary was allocated to him.[52] Steyn J was probably trying to create room for the doctrine of mistake at common law to breathe. He rejected AJB's argument that the mistake had to result in a total failure of consideration because this would leave no meaningful and independent scope for the doctrine.[53] The fact remains, however, that *Bell v Lever Brothers* comes very close to this position, at least in the application of the rule to the facts. A more recent case, *Grains and Fourrages SA v Huyton,*[54] recognises common mistake as making the contract void, but the question was insignificant and the judgment contains no discussion of the matter.

The doctrine of *Bell v Lever Brothers* is unsatisfactory for the following reasons.

(1) First, as explained above, the argument that no contract is formed because the parties did not consent to it is deeply implausible. What effectively happens in a case of mistake is that the parties make a defective contract and the party who suffers the more adverse consequences of the mistake seeks to have the contract rescinded. If the theory that the contract is void is correct, technically there would be no contract to rescind, but there would be no other way to unscramble those actions of the parties carried out on foot of the contract believed to exist. The other party seeks to resist rescission on the ground that the mistake, if any, was insufficiently fundamental to merit any relief. Requiring proof of vitiation to the extent that the contract is void is one way to keep the floodgates tight but this comes at the cost of almost denying relief altogether.

(2) Secondly, as illustrated more clearly in the unilateral mistake section later, void contracts sometimes involve injustice to third parties. Where the contract is voidable rescission can obviate some of these problems.

---

51 [1989] 1 WLR 255.
52 See n 22 above, at p 411. For other expressions of scepticism about this case see Treitel (1988) 104 LQR 501, and Carter (1990–91) 3 JCL 237.
53 [1989] 1 WLR 255 at 264.        54 [1997] 1 Lloyds Rep 628 (Mance J).

(3) Thirdly, the consequences of holding the contract void as opposed to voidable are extremely and quite unnecessarily drastic. This can be seen in two cases decided after *Bell v Lever Brothers*. In *Nicholson and Venn v Smith Marriott*[55] the plaintiffs bought a set of linen napkins and table-cloths described as bearing the crest and arms of Charles I. Two years later they were discovered to be Georgian and worth considerably less. Hallett J held that there had been a breach of section 13 of the Sale of Goods Act 1893 (sale of goods by description) but that the right to reject had been lost. The judge went on to hold that Georgian linen was essentially different from Carolean and that the contract was consequently void for common mistake. It was unnecessary to decide whether the contract had to be rescinded or whether it was too late to rescind if this was required[56] because the buyer was happy to settle for damages for breach. With respect, if the contract is void there is nothing to rescind, and therefore no way to prevent the unsatisfactory consequence that the buyer can effectively reject the goods at any time of its choosing. In *Frederick E Rose (London) Ltd v William H Pim Jnr and Co Ltd*[57] the plaintiffs were seeking the rectification of a contract for the purchase of horsebeans. They had been asked by their Egyptian house for 'feveroles' and on enquiring of the defendants what 'feveroles' were they were told 'horsebeans'. So the plaintiffs purchased horsebeans from the defendants and supplied these to their Egyptian house. Since the horsebeans were not feveroles the plaintiffs were required to pay damages to their Egyptian house and then sought unsuccessfully to recover these from the defend-ants. Following this failure the plaintiffs sought rectification of their contract with the defendants to specify 'feveroles' instead of 'horse-beans'. In the course of these proceedings the defendants argued that the contract was void for common mistake. The Court of Appeal rejected this argument and held that the contract could not be rectified because the parties had accurately transcribed the contractual subject matter as 'horsebeans'. But Denning LJ said that the defendants' counsel shud-dered at the consequences of his argument and went on to suggest that the contract might possibly have been voidable.[58] Consider what the con-sequences of holding the contract void might have been. The plaintiffs would have acquired no title to the horsebeans and in the absence of an exception to the *nemo dat* rule could have conferred no title on their Egyptian house. Even supposing that a *nemo dat* exception applied, the plaintiffs' Egyptian house contract might still have been void so that the

---

55  (1947) 177 LT 189.
56  His Lordship inclined to the view that it was not too late to rescind.
57  [1953] 2 QB 450.        58  Ibid, at 459–461.

Egyptian house would have been restricted to recovery of the price and no consequential damages for breach.[59]

How has the law got into this unsatisfactory condition? It has been suggested that the influence of Pothier[60] may have been significant here.[61] Pothier treated mistakes nullifying consent as making the contract void. But there seem to have been two significant misconstructions of Pothier in the application of his treatise to the English law of mistake. One was a failure to understand that what Pothier meant in saying that a contract was void was often that a mistaken party could seek to make the contract void, not that it was void *ab initio*.[62] The other was the assumption that mistake always vitiated consent. Where there was no true consent, as in the *Raffles v Wichelhaus* situation above, the contract was void in the sense that no contract was formed. Common mistake, however, is not truly a case where no contract is formed.

A full understanding of the law's unsatisfactory condition in this area requires a full appreciation of *Bell v Lever Brothers* itself. The story of this case and the context in which the ruling of the House of Lords needs to be seen is impressively told by Catharine MacMillan.[63] In this article two factors are particularly emphasised. Firstly, the case was actually about fraudulent misrepresentation and concealment of the defendants' breaches of fiduciary duty; mistake was not raised until nearly the end of the trial and in Lord Blanesburgh's speech he said he would not have allowed that issue to be raised at that stage. Secondly, a majority of the House of Lords did not wish to see Bell and Snelling suffer disproportionately for breaches of fiduciary duty that seemed minor compared to the sterling work they had done in reviving the fortunes of the Niger company. Absolutely nothing turned on the question whether the contract was void or voidable. It was all about liability and for the reasons outlined a majority of the House of Lords did not want to make the defendants liable.

Before proceeding to 'Mistake in Equity' it is worth briefly mentioning a recent case, *Brennan v Bolt Burdon*,[64] which supports the argument that the

59 See Shatwell, KO, 'The Supposed Doctrine of Mistake in Contract: A Comedy of Errors' (1955) 33 Can Bar Rev 164, at 172, where attention is drawn to this unsatisfactory feature of holding contracts void.

60 Pothier, RJ, *A Treatise on the Law of Obligations or Contracts*, 1806, London: Evans, WD, translation.

61 See Ibbetson, DJ, *A Historical Introduction to the Law of Obligations*, 1999, Oxford: Oxford University Press, 225–229.

62 See Fuller, HL, 'Mistake and Error in the Law of Contracts' (1984) 33 Emory LJ 41, at 49–51; Sabbath, E, 'Effects of Mistakes in Contracts' (1964) 13 ICLQ 798, at 805–806.

63 MacMillan, C, 'How Temptation Led to Mistake: An Explanation of *Bell v Lever Brothers Ltd*' (2003) 119 LQR 625.

64 [2004] EWCA Civ 1017; [2004] 3 WLR 1321.

abolition of the mistake of law rule in restitution[65] extends into the law of contract. Morland J had held that an agreement compromising litigation was void because entered into on the faith of a decision subsequently reversed on appeal. In allowing the appeal the Court of Appeal emphasised that the parties were legally represented and aware that doubts had been expressed about the correctness of the decision forming the basis of their compromise. The assumption of risk and the public interest in upholding compromises dictated that this agreement should be upheld. The decision does not turn in any way on whether common mistake makes a contract void or voidable but the judgment of Maurice Kay LJ makes significant reference to *The Great Peace*[66] discussed in the next sub-section. His Lordship stated that this case 'effects a conceptual assimilation between common mistake and frustration',[67] and that for common mistake to vitiate a contract it must render performance of the contract impossible.[68] With respect, this conceptual assimilation simply does not work. A contract validly formed can be frustrated if it subsequently becomes impossible to perform it. A contract that is impossible to perform from inception is void but not because of a mistaken belief that it could be performed. It is void because it is impossible to perform it.

### Mistake in equity

This doctrine first appeared in the judgment of Denning LJ in *Solle v Butcher*.[69] It applies to cases of mistake insufficiently fundamental to make the contract void under the conventional English law doctrine. Mistake in equity takes a contract outwardly made but vitiated by mistake. It treats the contract as voidable and gives a party adversely affected by the mistake the right to seek rescission of the contract. The doctrine requires a fundamental common misapprehension as to the facts or the parties' relative and respective rights. The party seeking rescission must not be at fault and it must be unconscientious (unconscionable) for the other party to avail of the advantage gained.[70] This doctrine has been applied in a number of subsequent decisions although the result has usually been accompanied by controversy.[71]

---

65  *Kleinwort Benson Ltd v Lincoln City Council* [1999] 2 AC 349.
66  [2002] EWCA Civ 1407; [2003] QB 679.
67  [2004] EWCA Civ 1017 at [10]; [2004] 3 WLR 1321 at 1327.        68  Ibid [17], 1331.
69  [1950] 1 KB 671. Bucknill LJ agreed in substance and Jenkins LJ dissented with regret.
70  Ibid, at 690–693.
71  (1) *Grist v Bailey* [1967] Ch 532 (Goff J). This was a house sale under the mistaken belief that a protected tenant still lived in the house. The protected tenant had died. The contract was rescinded. Arguably the vendor was at fault, or at least assumed the risk, of occurrences like these. (2) *Magee v Pennine Insurance Co Ltd* [1969] 2 QB 507. A compromise insurance claim was rescinded because of a common mistake as to whether the insured had any claim under the policy. The insured was in breach of his duty of *uberrimae fides* in making the insurance

The authority of the 'mistake in equity' doctrine was cast into very considerable doubt by the decision of the Court of Appeal in *The Great Peace*.[72] In a sterile judgment occupying 38 pages of law report and containing 741 lines of verbatim quotation from previous judgments but precious little discussion of principle or policy, the Court of Appeal convincingly demonstrated that 'mistake in equity' is inconsistent with *Bell v Lever Brothers*.[73] Less convincingly, the court also held that if common mistake affects a contract in any way it makes it void, and consistently with frustration performance of the contract must be rendered impossible. In many cases this simply flies in the face of the facts. Performance cannot be impossible when it has been rendered. It may, however, be premature to write off 'mistake in equity' just yet. The Court of Appeal is bound by the doctrine of precedent to follow its previous decisions.[74] Two of the 'mistake in equity' cases are decisions of the Court of Appeal[75] and the doctrine has received support in Commonwealth jurisdictions as later sub-sections of this paper will show.[76]

Despite treating common mistake as making the contract voidable and basing the doctrine on unconscionability principles, 'mistake in equity' is an unsatisfactory doctrine. It cannot be reconciled with *Bell v Lever Brothers* and even if it could it makes little sense to have two doctrines occupying such essentially similar ground.[77] There is no sufficient basis for determining when

---

contract. In his dissenting judgment Winn LJ thought that the facts and issues were indistinguishable from *Bell v Lever Brothers*. (3) *Laurence v Lexcourt Holdings Ltd* [1978] 1 WLR 1128 (Brian Dillon QC). A business lease was rescinded because of a common mistake that planning permission had been granted. Arguably the lessees should have searched and discovered this. (4) *Associated Japanese Bank (International) v Credit du Nord* [1989] 1 WLR 255 (Steyn J). Mistake in equity was an alternative ground for the holding in this case but arguably there was no fundamental mistake because the lessee's obligations were still intact. (5) *Clarion Ltd v National Provident Institution* [2000] 2 All ER 265 (Rimer J). The judge declined to apply the doctrine because the party seeking to rely on it had simply made a bad bargain.

72 Above, n 7.   73 See Reynolds, FMB, (2003) 119 LQR 177.

74 *Young v Bristol Aeroplane Company* [1944] KB 718. See the discussion of this issue in Midwinter, SB (2003) 119 LQR 180. Note, however, that in *EIC Services Ltd v Phipps* [2004] EWCA Civ 1069; [2004] 2 BCLC 589 both Neuberger J and the Court of Appeal assumed the correctness of *The Great Peace*.

75 As indicated at n 69 above Bucknill LJ agreed with Denning LJ. In Cartwright, J, '*Solle v Butcher* and the Doctrine of Mistake in Contract' (1987) 103 LQR 594, the view was expressed that Fenton Atkinson LJ's concurring judgment in *Magee v Pennine Insurance Ltd*, n 71 above, treated the compromise as void, but a better view, it is submitted, is that it was a straightforward concurring judgment.

76 Whatever the view taken of 'mistake in equity', *The Great Peace* was clearly correctly decided. The risk was allocated to the defendants who sought to rely on mistake as a defence. See Cartwright, J, 'Re-writing the Law on Mistake' (2003) 11 RLR 93.

77 See Waddams, S, above n 5, para 354, where it is cogently argued that either relief should be granted or it should not. A contrary view was expressed by Steyn J in *Associated Japanese Bank (International) Ltd v Credit du Nord* [1989] 1 WLR 255 at 267–268.

'mistake at common law' ends and 'mistake in equity' begins. The argument that *Bell v Lever Brothers* applies where no contract is made is unsustainable and there is no other way of delineating when a mistake is insufficiently fundamental for mistake at common law but where relief may be afforded in equity.

That said, the wrong turning identified in the Introduction is, in truth, a failure to repair the damage done in *Bell v Lever Brothers*, and this is something only the House of Lords or Parliament can accomplish. Although the void or voidable question did not have to be addressed in *Bell v Lever Brothers*, the House of Lords clearly laid down that common mistake makes a contract void. Their Lordships did not fail to recognise an independent doctrine of mistake in equity for no such doctrine ever existed. As Professor Blackburn has put it:

Equity judges, with their deeply ingrained tradition of acting as a Court of conscience, very often [did] not analyse precisely the grounds for their decisions. Where the facts raised, say, an element of mistake, an element of misrepresentation, and an element of undue influence, the contract [could] be set aside with no precise analysis of the grounds for doing so.[78]

What the House of Lords failed to do, however, was to forge a post-Judicature Act doctrine of common mistake which owed anything at all to the experience of the Court of Chancery prior to the Judicature Act. Had they produced a modern doctrine of common mistake like the mistake in equity doctrine expounded by Lord Denning and then decided that the mistake was insufficient to justify rescission they would have got much closer to a functional doctrine of common mistake.[79]

The parameters of this functional doctrine of common mistake will be explained later in this section but one issue should be confronted at this stage. It might be argued that substituting voidable for void while still refusing relief in circumstances similar to those indicated in *Bell v Lever Brothers* would be no improvement on the current situation. *Bell v Lever Brothers* prescribed a test which elevated the sanctity of contract to a point where relief from mistake was hardly ever granted. 'Mistake in equity' was invented to provide a measure of relief but has arguably been too loose and afforded insufficient weight to the sanctity of contract. The way forward, it is submitted, is to focus less on the fundamentality of the mistake and more on the unconscionability

---

78  Blackburn, RA, 'The Equitable Approach to Mistake in Contract' (1955) 7 Res Judicatae 43, at 49.

79  Other commentators have favoured replacing 'mistake at common law' with 'mistake in equity'. See Harris (1969) 32 MLR 688; Marston (1989) 48 CLJ 173; Phang, Andrew BL, 'Common Mistake in English Law: the proposed merger of common law and equity' (1989) 9 LS 291; Phang [2003] Conv 247.

of the advantage gained by the party seeking to uphold the contract and on the allocation of risk between the parties. Applied to *Bell v Lever Brothers* it would not be unconscionable for Messrs Bell and Snelling to retain the advantage they gained in the light of the relatively minor breach of fiduciary duty they had committed and the sterling work they had done while employed by Lever Brothers. The risk of the employment contracts being terminable without compensation is one that, in the circumstances of that case, should be allocated to Lever Brothers.

## Mistake in the United States

Mistake is usually treated as a vitiating factor. Its location in contract law texts is usually adjacent to other vitiating factors like misrepresentation, duress and undue influence. In the *Restatement 2d of Contracts* mistake appears in Chapter 6, with misrepresentation, duress and undue influence in Chapter 7. In *Corbin on Contracts*[80] all four of these doctrines appear in Chapter 28. *Murray on Contracts*[81] places mistake at the end of Chapter 5 on 'Operative Expressions of Assent' and the other three doctrines in Chapter 6. Farnsworth is different,[82] grouping mistake with frustration and impossibility of performance in Chapter 9 and the other doctrines in Chapter 4. There is full agreement, however, that common mistake makes a contract voidable, save for circumstances like *Raffles v Wichelhaus*[83] and *res extincta*[84] where no contract is formed.

The basic contours of the American doctrine of common (or mutual) mistake may be found in ss 152 and 154 of the *Restatement 2d of Contracts*.[85] To avoid a contract on the ground of common mistake it must be shown:

1. that the mistake relates to a basic assumption on which the contract is made;
2. that it has a material effect upon the agreed exchange of performances. Comment *c* to s 152 states that the imbalance must be so severe that the party seeking relief cannot fairly be required to carry out the contract;[86]

80 Above, n 6.
81 Murray, JE Jr, *Murray on Contracts*, 1990, 3rd edn, Charlottesville: The Michie Company.
82 Farnsworth, Allan E, *Contracts*, 3rd edn, 1999, Aspen Law and Business, New York.
83 *Restatement 2d of Contracts*, s 20.      84 Ibid s 266.
85 See *Corbin on Contracts*, above n 6, para 28.27, describing the *Restatement* as a useful guide.
86 According to section 152 comment *b*, the first two elements, both derived from section 152, are usually examined together as the essence of the contract. Several famous American authorities are among the principal cases cited for these propositions – *Sherwood v Walker* 33 NW 919 (1887, Supreme Court of Michigan); *Wood v Boynton* 25 NW 42 (1885, Supreme Court of Wisconsin); *Smith v Zimbalist* 38 P 2d 170 (1935, California Court of Appeals);

3. that the risk of the mistake has not been allocated to the party seeking relief under s 154. This may occur because the contract expressly or impliedly allocates the risk, or that party assumes it by entering into the contract knowing that his or her knowledge of the circumstances is limited, or where the court allocates the risk because it is reasonable in the circumstances.

The fundamental basis of relief under the American doctrine of mutual mistake appears to be unconscionability.[87] As the Illinois Appeals Court put it in *John Burns Constr Co v Interlake Inc*,[88] to justify relief the mistake must be 'of such grave consequence that enforcement of the contract would be unconscionable'.[89] In addition there is a substantial body of case law that grounds relief against mutual mistake in equity.[90]

The unconscionability and equitable bases of American mutual mistake can be seen in three principal facets of the doctrine outlined above. First, there is the emphasis placed on contractual imbalance being of an order that the party seeking relief cannot fairly be required to carry out the contract. In the absence of more overtly unconscionable behaviour from the other party, e.g., misrepresentation, duress or undue influence, severe imbalance is needed to prove unconscionability. Second, where the party seeking relief bears the risk of mistake under s 154, courts have stated that refusing relief is not unconscionable.[91] Third, the exercise of discretion to grant or withhold relief is dependent to a large extent on the good conscience of the party seeking it. Relevant factors are the normal ones applying to rescission of

---

*Dover Pool and Racquet Club v Brooking* 322 NE 2d 168 (1975, Supreme Judicial Court of Massachusetts); *Lenawee County Board of Health v Messerly* 331 NW 2d 203 (1982, Supreme Court of Michigan). Incidentally in *Lenawee* the Michigan court repudiated its decision in *Sherwood v Walker* without departing in any way from the doctrine outlined in the paragraph above.

87  Ricks, Val D, 'American Mutual Mistake: Half-Civilian Mongrel, Consideration Reincarnate' (1998) 58 La L Rev 663.

88  433 NE 2d 1126, 1130 (1982).

89  Further support for the unconscionability thesis may be found in *Romine Inc v Savannah Steel Co* 160 S E 2d 659, 660 (1968), Georgia Court of Appeals; *Fulghum v Kelly* 340 SE 2d 589, 591 (1986), Georgia; *Keller v State Farm Ins Co* 536 NE 2d 194, 200 (1989), Illinois Appeals Court; *Ramsey v Coloned Life Ins Co of America* 12 F 3d 472, 479–480 (1994, 5th Circuit).

90  See *Diffendarfer v Dicks* 11 NE 825, 828 (1887, New York) – '[T]he jurisdiction of chancery to rescind contracts for . . . mutual mistake of material facts, is one of the best settled and most beneficent powers of a court of equity.'; *UT Communications Credit Corp v Resort Dev Inc* 861 SW 2d 699, 707 (1993, Missouri Court of Appeals) – 'Equity may grant relief against . . . a mutual mistake of both parties.'; *Brookside Memorials Inc v Barre City* No. 96–429, 1997 WL 357862 (1997, Vermont) – 'Equity affords relief against mutual mistake.'

91  See *Tarrant v Monson* 619 P 2d 1210 (1980, Nevada); *Nelson v Rice* 12 P 3d 238 (2000, Arizona Court of Appeals).

contracts but, significantly, s 157 of the *Restatement of Contracts 2d* states that relief should not be refused because of the claimant's fault unless the latter 'amounts to a failure to act in good faith and in accordance with reasonable standards of fair dealing'.

The American doctrine of common (or mutual) mistake is clearly broader than English law. Professor Treitel has commented that the fact that American rules on this subject are much closer to English equity than English common law does not seem to have caused much inconvenience.[92] Undoubtedly there have been cases where relief was granted where it probably should not have been,[93] but the greater certainty of English law comes at the excessive price of virtually eliminating relief from this category of case altogether. This absolutist position should not be accepted.

### Mistake in Canada

The fundamental principles are not laid down in any particular source like the *Restatement of Contracts*. However, the authorities to be discussed below indicate that common mistake makes a contract voidable and that the basic principle on which relief is granted is unconscionability.

In *Ivanochko v Sych*,[94] a contract for the sale of a house and furniture provided for monthly payments of principal less interest. The purchase price would never have been paid off. The Saskatchewan Court of Appeal (Woods J A) held that a contract had been formed and so could not be regarded as void. The contract was voidable in equity pursuant to Lord Denning's principle in *Solle v Butcher*. In *Hyrsky v Smith*[95] a vendor sold land only slightly in excess of 50 per cent of the land described in the contract. In ordering rescission because of *error in substantialibus*, Lieff J said: 'In equity, a contract is subject to rescission if the parties suffered from a common fundamental misapprehension as to the facts which went to the very root of the contract.'[96] In *Marwood v Charter Credit Corp*[97] a contract for sale of land conveyed the lot next door to the one the parties thought they were contracting about. The lot actually sold was vacant and the one the parties intended to contract about contained a house. Rescission was ordered on the basis of *Solle v Butcher*, *Grist v Bailey*, and *Hyrsky v Smith*. *Toronto-Dominion Bank v Fortin (No 2)*[98] was very similar to *Magee v Pennine Insurance Ltd*.

---

92  Treitel, G, *The Law of Contracts* 10th edn, 1999, London: Sweet & Maxwell, p 286.
93  The famous case of *Sherwood v Walker*, above n 86, is one such example. A heifer was sold on the footing that she was barren. After the sale she was found to be with calf and worth ten times the sale price. The seller was allowed to rescind but surely the risk of the heifer being able to breed was one he had assumed.
94  (1967) 60 DLR (2d) 474.       95  (1969) 5 DLR (3d) 385 (Ontario High Court).
96  Ibid 391.       97  (1971) 20 DLR (3d) 563 (Nova Scotia Supreme Court).
98  (1978) 88 DLR (3d) 232 (British Columbia Supreme Court).

Fortin agreed to buy a group of companies from the receiver/manager. He subsequently repudiated the agreement and paid $10,000 in compromise for his default. When the British Columbia Supreme Court subsequently held that the receiver/manager never had power to sell the companies Fortin sought restitution of the money paid on the basis that the compromise was void. Andrews J held that the compromise was void but appears to have meant voidable because the judge went on to say: 'it being the basis of the later compromise that compromise, following *Magee*, though not a nullity at law is liable to be set aside in equity.'[99]

Two other authorities are worth mentioning although relief was granted on a different basis in each of them. In *R v Ontario Flue-Cured Tobacco Growers' Marketing Board, ex parte Grigg*[100] a contract for the sale of land was held to contain an essential condition that the land contain 14 acres of tobacco growing quota. As the land contained no such quota the contract was held void on the authority of Lord Atkin's alternative ground in *Bell v Lever Brothers*.[101] There are clear parallels here with the coronation cases of *Clark v Lindsay* and *Griffith v Brymer*[102] and once again a better basis would have been a right to rescind for common mistake. In *McMaster University v Wilchar Construction Ltd*[103] Thompson J held that a contract was void because the parties were not *ad idem*. His honour said *obiter* that where a contract is formed, mistake might make it voidable in equity. Where there is mistake as to the promise or some material term of the contract, then provided the mistake is honest, relief will be afforded 'in any case where [the court] considers that it would be unfair, unjust or unconscionable not to correct it'.[104]

The approach taken in Canadian cases appears to be in accord with this paper. Usually relief is granted on the basis that the contract is recognised as formed but voidable at the instance of a party adversely affected by the mistake where it would be unconscionable for the other party to be allowed to enforce it. The main support for any void contract thesis comes from cases where clearly no contract is formed. One improvement would be to end any notion that the contract is valid at common law but voidable in equity. As Professor Waddams has put it, either relief should be granted or it should not.[105]

---

99  Ibid 237. Compare *Brennan v Bolt Burden*, above nn 64–68 and text, another vitiated compromise case.
100  (1965) 51 DLR (2d) 7 (Ontario Court of Appeal).
101  See [1932] AC 161, at 224, where Lord Atkin put this in terms of an implied condition precedent.
102  See nn 24–25 above and text.
103  (1971) 22 DLR (3d) 9 (Ontario High Court); affirmed by Court of Appeal without written reasons 12th March 1973, noted (1977) 69 DLR (3d) 400.
104  Ibid 19.        105  Above n 5, para 354.

## Mistake in Australia

The approach to common mistake in Australia appears to be essentially similar to that advocated in this chapter. As explained in the leading text,[106] contracts tend only to be void where they are not formed at all. Implied condition precedent cases are not cases of initial failure but of termination because the failure of the condition prevents the contract from going on. Where the contract is formed common mistake may result in the contract being avoided in equity but it is most unlikely that any court would find the contract void.[107] Both *Bell v Lever Brothers* and *Associated Japanese Bank (International) Ltd v Credit du Nord* are treated with some scepticism.[108] *Solle v Butcher* received approval in the judgment of McTiernan, Williams and Webb JJ in *Svanosio v McNamara*[109] and in the majority judgments in *Taylor v Johnson*.[110] The basis for granting relief appears to be that it is unconscionable for the party seeking to uphold the contract to have it enforced.[111] It is difficult to believe that the law in Australia is much altered by the unconvincing obiter comments of the Queensland Court of Appeal in *Australia Estates P/L v Cairns City Council*.[111a] It goes too far to say, as that court did, that the reasoning in *The Great Peace* is persuasive and that *Solle v Butcher* has been overruled, at least in Australia where *Bell v Lever Brothers* does not have to be followed. References made by Anderson J to the treatment of *Solle v Butcher* in the High Court judgments discussed above underestimate the degree of support that decision actually received.

## Common mistake in New Zealand

The enactment of the Contractual Mistakes Act 1977 shows that New Zealand has chosen to adopt something similar to the theory of this chapter in its approach to common mistake. In s 6(1)(b) inequality of exchange is specified as an essential condition of granting relief against common mistake, mirroring the argument here that this makes up for the absence of obvious wrongdoing. In s 7, which sets out a wide and flexible range of relief that the

---

106   Carter, JW and Harland, DJ, *Contract Law in Australia*, 2002, 4th edn, Sydney: Butterworths, paras 1206, 1224, 1226, and 1231.

107   The same argument in the text at n 105 could be made here.

108   See Carter (1990–91) 3 JCL 237.          109   (1956) 96 CLR 186.

110   (1983) 151 CLR 422. This was a case of unilateral mistake discussed in the next section.

111   As it was put in Carter and Harland, above n 106, para 1231 – 'Therefore, not only is it clear that there is a jurisdiction in Australia to set aside a contract on the ground of common mistake, but also *Solle v Butcher* can be taken as a valid illustration of the jurisdiction. However, in order for the contract to be liable to be set aside there must be circumstances which render it *unconscionable* for the party who seeks to uphold the contract to have it enforced.'

111a   [2005] QCA at [51]–[62]. There was no operative common mistake in this case so the precedent value is limited. See Seddon, N, 'Mistake Mistake' (2006) 80 ALJ 95.

court may grant, the idea of the contract being void appears nowhere. The 1977 Act somewhat diminishes New Zealand's contribution to the development of the common law[112] in this area, although in one pre-1977 Act case, *Waring v SJ Brentnall Ltd*,[113] Chilwell J preferred 'voidable in equity' to 'void at common law'. Significantly Chilwell J interpreted Denning LJ's statement from *Solle v Butcher* that the party seeking relief must not be at fault as meaning that this party's behaviour must not have been unconscionable.[114]

### International approaches to common mistake

*The Principles of European Contract Law (PECL)*[115] allows a party to avoid a contract for mistake of fact or law existing when the contract was made. The specific grounds are:

(a) (i)   the mistake was caused by information given by the other party; or

   (ii)   the other party knew or ought to have known of the mistake and it was contrary to good faith and fair dealing to leave the mistaken party in error; or

  (iii)   the other party made the same mistake; and

(b)   the other party knew or ought to have known that the mistaken party, had it known the truth, would not have entered the contract or would have done so only on fundamentally different terms.

Two observations should be made about this provision. First, it deals mainly but not exclusively with unilateral mistake. To the extent that greater emphasis is placed on the latter this is a welcome signal that relief against common mistake will be rare. Secondly, the detailed grounds for relief rest upon a clear notion of unconscionability, specifically set forth in (b) which requires contractual terms so disadvantageous to the mistaken party that they would not have been agreed to had the truth been known.

*PECL* denies relief to a party whose mistake was inexcusable or where the risk was assumed by it or should be borne by it. By Art 4.115 avoidance is defined in terms making it essentially similar to rescission. Partial avoidance is allowed by Art 4.116 and by Art 4.105 the party not seeking to avoid may indicate its willingness to perform the contract in accordance with the understanding of the party seeking to avoid. *PECL* does not seem to observe the dichotomy maintained here between mistakes or other events preventing the formation of a contract and those allowing for avoidance. By Art 4.102 both are subject to the Art 4.103 rules. Other than providing wider relief and applying to additional cases, the approach taken by *PECL* is on all fours with

---

112 Including equity.        113 [1975] 2 NZLR 401.        114 Ibid 409.
115 Lando and Beale (eds), *Principles of European Contract Law*, Parts I and II, The Hague: Kluwer Law International, 2002.

this chapter. Art 3 of the UNIDROIT *Principles of International Commercial Contracts* takes an essentially similar approach.

### Shape of the reconfigured doctrine of common mistake

At the beginning of this paper it was said that English law had taken a wrong turning in *The Great Peace*. This is true in the sense that there now appears to be no effective way of providing relief against the adverse consequences of a common mistake. But before *The Great Peace* English law had the impossible task of reconciling 'mistake in equity' with *Bell v Lever Brothers*, and was also maintaining the unsatisfactory dichotomy of 'valid at common law' but 'voidable in equity'. The truth is that the real wrong turning took place in *Bell v Lever Brothers*. That decision has failed to win acceptance in jurisdictions outside England, did not need even to deal with the question of whether common mistake rendered a contract void or voidable, and so far as it establishes that contracts so vitiated are void involves the deeply implausible proposition that the parties created nothing as well as several unjust and inconvenient consequences. It should be statutorily reversed or overruled by the House of Lords on this point at the earliest opportunity presented.

The new doctrine thus created should give a party adversely affected by a common mistake the right to seek to rescind the contract.[116] In what circumstances should this be permitted? The mistake should be fundamental or really serious but this should not be the only question the court has to determine. Too much concentration on whether the contract as made was essentially different from the contract the parties believed they were making is likely to lead to extreme reluctance to grant relief and to bewildering distinctions between cases where relief is granted and those where it is refused. An example of the kind of confusion that could be caused here is the impossible distinction between 'identity' and 'attributes' of contractual subject matter that led the Michigan Supreme Court to repudiate its earlier decision in *Sherwood v Walker*.[117] The mistaken assumption that the cow was barren when she was with calf was held to go to the identity of the cow as a breeder rather than her attributes. This could so easily have gone the other way, hence the subsequent repudiation of the identity/attributes distinction in *Lenawee County Board of Health v Messerly*[118] comes as no huge surprise. The Michigan Supreme Court's new test of case by case adjudication looks initially like an exercise in palm tree justice but is considerably better when integrated with s 152 of the *Restatement 2d*. Two questions must be addressed here. The first is a threshold question of whether the mistake is serious and therefore poten-

---

116 An interesting side question, beyond the scope of this chapter, is whether rescission is the act of the party or the decision of the court. On this, see O'Sullivan, Janet, 'Rescission as a Self-Help Remedy: A Critical Analysis' (2000) 59 CLJ 509.

117 See n 93 above.    118 331 NW 2d 203 (1982).

tially reviewable. Secondly, there is the crucial question of whether enforcing the contract would be unconscionable, and in this regard the inequality of the exchange is particularly important. The question is much more about whether enforcing the contract would be unconscionable than the size or quality of the mistake. The latter is too closely tied to the question of whether a contract is formed and it is tolerably clear that in the typical case of common mistake a contract has been formed.

It cannot be contended that this new doctrine would be free from uncertainty. But it would probably be no more uncertain than the other vitiating factors of misrepresentation, duress, undue influence and unconscionable dealing. The current law provides uncertainty by virtually denying relief altogether. The reconfigured law rests on a theory of unconscionability where wrongdoing in the procuring of the contract is not a feature. The floodgates should not open to excessive relief provided the courts properly use the tools at their disposal. They should be hard to convince that relief should be granted, it should be clearly unconscionable for the party resisting relief to enforce the contract, and it must be clear that the risk of the mistake has not been allocated to the party seeking rescission.

### Unilateral mistake

In this section only one party to the contract is mistaken. Where unilateral mistake is operative it generally makes the contract voidable at the instance of the mistaken party. It is also clear that the basis for rescission of the contract is unconscionability. The first sub-section deals with the general rule and the second and third sub-sections with two difficult problems, unilateral mistake as to identity and *non est factum*, where some reorientation of approach would appear to be called for.

### The general rule

Where A enters into a contract with B, and B either knows or should know that A is mistaken about an important aspect of the contract then relief (either rescission or rectification) may be afforded to A. Whatever the nature of the relief claimed, the basis has usually been the unconscionable conduct of the non-mistaken party. In *Hartog v Colin and Shields*[119] Singleton J denied the buyers' claim for damages because they were aware that the sellers were mistaken in their offer. Rescission of an option contract for the purchase of land was allowed by the High Court of Australia in *Taylor v Johnson*,[120] where the purchaser was aware of circumstances indicating that the vendor

---

119 [1939] 3 All ER 566. The judgment does not say that the contract was rescinded but this seems to be an underlying assumption.
120 (1983) 151 CLR 422.

had made a serious mistake about the terms of the contract and deliberately set out to prevent her from discovering that. It was stressed that B's reliance on the contract and the interests of any third parties would have to be taken into consideration. In *Commissioner for the New Towns v Cooper (GB) Ltd*[121] the Court of Appeal approved *Taylor v Johnson* in a case where B had set out to mislead A and A was misled. It appeared that B did not actually know that it had succeeded in misleading A although it was found to have suspected this. This was equitable fraud and unconscionable conduct. Rectification of the contract to accord with A's understanding was the remedy afforded.[122] In *Agip S p A v Navigazione Alta Italia S p A, The Nai Genova*[123] rectification was refused ostensibly because the defendants had no actual knowledge of the plaintiffs' mistake. It might be said of this case that the law had not developed to the point where something less than actual knowledge would constitute unconscionable conduct. A better basis for that decision, however, is that the contract was concluded after lengthy negotiations and contained a provision mistakenly inserted by the defendants. There had been no unconscionable conduct on their part and the cause of the problem was the plaintiffs' failure to examine the contract carefully enough before binding themselves to it.

From the perspective of this chapter the general rule about unilateral mistake is satisfactory but it is nonetheless worth considering two issues briefly before moving on. First, as Professor Kronman has highlighted in a classic article,[124] there is a fine dividing line between cases where B has to point out A's mistake and cases where B is entitled to take advantage of superior knowledge. Kronman's argument that where B has acquired this knowledge in order to exploit it economically there is no duty of disclosure but where B has come upon it casually A's non-awareness should be pointed out, is a suitable approach. The typical example of the first case is where B, a buyer of land, has surveyed the locality and discovered a high degree of probability that valuable mineral reserves lie beneath the surface. Having acquired this information through personal endeavour, B is not obliged to plug A's information gap about the existence of those minerals. The typical example of the second case is where B becomes aware of A's mistake during the course of contractual negotiations.

Secondly, American jurisprudence provides some support for the theory

---

121   [1995] 2 All ER 929.
122   Rectification had been recognised as a legitimate remedy in *A Roberts and Co Ltd v Leicestershire County Council* [1961] Ch 555; *Riverlate Properties Ltd v Paul* [1975] Ch 133 (relief denied because the lessee did not know and could not reasonably have been expected to know of the lessor's mistake); and *Thomas Bates and Son Ltd v Wyndham's (Lingerie) Ltd* [1981] 1 WLR 505.
123   [1984] 1 Lloyds Rep 353.
124   Kronman, Anthony T, 'Disclosure, Information, and the Law of Contracts' (1978) 7 J Legal Studies 1.

that relief may be granted in the absence of overtly unconscionable conduct by the non-mistaken party so long as enforcement of the contract itself would be unconscionable.[125] An instructive recent example is *Donovan v RRL Corp.*[126] The plaintiff saw a 1995 Jaguar XJ6 Vanden Plas advertised in a newspaper at $25,995. After test-driving it he told the salesperson he would take it at the advertised price of $26,000. The salesperson replied 'that's a mistake' and offered to sell for the proper price of $37,000. A transcription error had occurred and the price of a 1994 model appeared in place of the price of the 1995 model. It was held that a contract had been formed, the plaintiff accepting the defendants' offer that appeared in the advertisement.[127] The defendants were allowed to rescind even though the plaintiff was held to have no reason to know of their mistake.[128] It was held to be unconscionable for the defendants to make a $9,000 loss and the plaintiff a $12,000 windfall.[129] This approach is consistent with common (or mutual mistake) where unconscionability is found in the harshness of enforcing a very unequal exchange.

### Unilateral mistake as to identity

This phenomenon can be illustrated as follows. A sells a good to B under the mistaken belief that B is X. B gives A a worthless cheque for the good and then sells it to C who buys in good faith and without knowledge of the circumstances in which B acquired the good. A then discovers the fraud and, knowing that suing B for damages would be a fruitless exercise, attempts to recover the good from C. In most of these cases B has misrepresented his identity and the contract between A and B would thus be voidable. But by the time A discovers the fraud C has acquired rights over the good and consequently A cannot rescind the contract with B and trace the good through to C. In those circumstances A may try to argue that the contract with B was void due to mistake. If A succeeds in this argument the good can be recovered

---

125  See Restatement of Contracts 2d, s 153; *Corbin on Contracts*, above n 6, para 28.39. Performance of the contract must be 'unduly burdensome' – see *Boise Junior College Dist v Mattefs Constr Co* 450 P 2d 604 (Idaho 1969).

126  27 P.3d 702 (Supreme Court of California, 2001).

127  The advertisement was an offer only because otherwise the California Vehicle Code would have been violated. Advertisements are normally regarded as invitations to treat, eg, *Partridge v Crittenden* [1968] 1 WLR 1204.

128  This may be open to some doubt because the plaintiff had visited another Jaguar dealership the day before and seen 1995 models going for $8,000–10,000 more.

129  It cannot be stated with complete confidence that this decision represents more than California law. *Mariah Investments Ltd v McCabe* 986 P 2d 1209 (Oregon Court of Appeals, 1999) appears to require that the non-mistaken party at least *should* have been aware of the other's mistake. However Professor Perillo inclines towards the view that unconscionability in the exchange is sufficient – see *Corbin on Contracts*, above n 125.

from C because B can acquire nothing under this void contract to pass on to C.[130] To show that the contract is void for mistake, A has to demonstrate that the mistaken belief that B was X was essential to the contract with the person who claimed to be X. In essence A has to show that A intended to make the contract with X alone and not with the person A believed to be X.

There are several variations upon the above scenario and these have contributed much to the complexity that attends this area of contract law. In the most common case, where B buys the good in the presence of A, the approach of the courts is usually to treat the identity of B as X as a non-essential matter. B is thus guilty of nothing more than a misrepresentation and the A-B contract is voidable.[131] However, where the contract is not made face-to-face the courts are more likely to regard the identity of the person A contracts with as essential. Thus, in *Cundy v Lindsay*[132] B (whose name was Blenkarn) wrote to A from an address in the same street as that of a business called Blenkiron and Co that A had heard of and signed his name to make it look like *Blenkiron and Co*. A sent goods to the address given believing it was *Blenkiron and Co* they were dealing with. B did not pay for the goods and sold them on to C. A were allowed to recover the goods from C because they had never intended to contract with B. B had accepted an offer that he knew had been intended for *Blenkiron and Co*, although it might plausibly have been argued that A intended to deal with the proprietor of the business at the address supplied by B because A believed that person to be *Blenkiron and Co*.

Enough has been said to indicate the real nature of these disputes. Both A and C have been defrauded by B. Each can sue B for damages for the loss suffered. But frequently a damages remedy will be worthless and the only way of obtaining an effective remedy is against the good itself. The question of whether A can recover the good or C can keep it depends on fine distinctions and fact-intensive enquiries as to whether the identity of B as X is essential to the contract ostensibly made between A and B. It rests on a misreading of Pothier who meant that the contract could be made void in the event of a mistake as to identity, not that it was void *ab initio*.[133] There should be one simple rule for these cases and this should be that the A-B contract is vitiated by misrepresentation and is voidable at the instance of A.[134] To the extent that this means C is preferred over A it should be pointed out that more often than not A is better placed to avoid the loss. A is the owner of the good, creates the

---

130  This is the essence of the decision in *Cundy v Lindsay* (1877–78) LR 3 App Cas 459.

131  See *Lewis v Averay* [1972] 1 QB 198. Contrast *Ingram v Little* [1961] 1 QB 31. The latter was effectively overruled by the House of Lords in *Shogun Finance Ltd v Hudson* [2003] UKHL 62 [2004] 1 AC 919.

132  Above n 130.

133  See Fuller, Hoffman L, 'Mistake and Error in the Law of Contracts' (1984) 33 Emory LJ 41, at 49–50.

134  In support of this approach may be cited Hare, C, 'Identity Mistake: A Missed Opportunity' (2004) 67 MLR 993, a comment on *Shogun Finance Ltd v Hudson*, n 135 below.

risk that B acquires title fraudulently, and before parting with possession should take care that the identity of the buyer is checked, or that payment is secured. This is the position taken in the USA by Article 2–403 of the Uniform Commercial Code. If the A-B contract is voidable for misrepresentation then these cases would not fall under the reconfigured doctrine of mistake proposed in this chapter.

In light of the above, the decision of the House of Lords in *Shogun Finance Ltd v Hudson*[135] may be viewed with some disappointment. This case concerned a scenario where the contract was not made in the presence of the contracting parties. A rogue wished to buy a car on hire-purchase. He presented a dealer with a driving licence belonging to a Mr Patel of Leicester. The dealer faxed the licence and other relevant personal details to the finance company, which carried out a credit check on Mr Patel. On finding him satisfactory it authorised the dealer to let the rogue, whom the finance company and the dealer both believed to be Mr Patel, take possession of the car. The rogue sold the car to Mr Hudson and defaulted on the hire-purchase instalments. By a three to two majority the House of Lords decided that the finance company could recover the car from Mr Hudson. The majority's reasoning was to the effect that as the finance company had checked the credit history of Mr Patel, it intended to make a contract with him and not the rogue. The rogue could not accept a contractual offer he knew was meant for someone else. This was a *Cundy v Lindsay* situation. It was also emphasised (by Lord Hobhouse of Woodborough in particular) that the contract was in writing and named Mr Patel as the hirer. The certainty and predictability that written contracts provide would be undermined if a decision inconsistent with the writing (that the contract was made with the rogue) were made. The first argument has some measure of plausibility to it because the finance company clearly would not have made the contract had it known the rogue's real identity. It is also true that the rogue knew that the finance company wanted to hire only to Mr Patel. It just does not follow that the finance company *did not* enter into a contract with the rogue. In dissent Lord Nicholls convincingly argued that in these cases, just like the face-to-face transactions, A makes the contract with B because she believes that B is X.[136] The second argument appears to be a misuse of the parol evidence rule, which is primarily used today to prevent departures from the writing where the writing contains all the contractual terms. It is not really designed to resolve disputes as to identity.[136a]

---

135 [2003] UKHL 62, [2004] 1 AC 919. The reaction of commentators has generally been unfavourable. See Phang *et al* (2004) 63 CLJ 24; Elliott (2004) JBL 381; MacMillan (2004) 120 LQR 369.

136 Ibid paras 26–31.

136a See the convincing analysis of Professor McLauchlan in McLauchlan, DW, 'Parol Evidence and Contract Formation' (2005) 121 LQR 9.

*Shogun Finance Ltd v Hudson* should have been treated as a misrepresentation case. The finance company's checks on the identity and creditworthiness of the proposed hirer were useless. Unless the law is to take the position that private sales of motor vehicles (the sale by the rogue to Mr Hudson in this case) are almost by definition suspicious, it must be more efficient to place the risk of fraud in these transactions on finance companies and dealers. These parties have the resources and the expertise to make the necessary checks. If, in spite of all their best endeavours, a rogue gets away with fraud, they are better able to absorb the loss than innocent private buyers like Mr Hudson. Where the A-B contract is a private sale these considerations will not apply, but there is no justification for a different rule. To the extent that private sales are more risky A takes the greater risk than C because she parts with possession without being sure that it is safe to do so.

An alternative analysis of this problem has been provided by William Swadling.[137] Essentially this article suggests that the passing of property between A, B, and C depends on an act of delivery and has nothing to do with contract. Consequently A cannot revest the property in himself by rescinding the contract with B.[138] Rescission has no proprietary consequences, notwithstanding section 23 of the Sale of Goods Act 1979, because the latter is only a codification of what the common law was believed to be. If Parliament mistakenly assumed that there was such a thing as a voidable title this cannot be taken as enacting this concept into existence. The passing of property thus depends on whether the delivery by A to B is either valid or invalid. This appears to depend on a similar test as above, i.e., whether the identity of the buyer as X is so critical that A would have sold to nobody else. It is no criticism of Swadling's impressive analysis that this would leave the law in essentially the same unsatisfactory condition.

Attention should be given to an alternative solution proposed by Professor Sutton and Professor Waddams.[139] Focusing on the 'real' nature of the dispute, namely how to allocate the loss between A and C, the argument is that A should recover the good on condition that C's reliance loss is compensated. Where C has paid something close to the true price of the good, this will not produce a result radically different from misrepresentation. Where, as sometimes happens, the goods have been sold to C for something less than their true value, this has the merit of ensuring C does not receive a windfall.[140] Accomplishing this result using available legal tools might be difficult. Leaving aside Swadling's theory the current position is that

---

137  Swadling, W, 'Rescission, Property and the Common Law (2005) 121 LQR 123.
138  If the A-B contract is void it would be similarly irrelevant.
139  See Sutton, RJ, 'Reform of the Law of Mistake in Contract' (1976) 7 NZULR 40, at 61–65; Waddams, SM, above n 5, at paras 305–306.
140  Arguably C did receive a windfall in *Lewis v Averay*. The car was worth £330, B's cheque was for £450, and the sale to C was for £200.

misrepresentation is regarded as making the A-B contract voidable so that C's good faith purchase defeats rescission altogether. Mistake would make the A-B contract void so C acquires no rights at all. It would be necessary to adjust the rule that the contract cannot be rescinded once a third party's rights have intervened so that the contract can be rescinded so long as C's reliance loss is compensated. This could be accomplished as part of any legislative reform or perhaps through acceptance of Janet O'Sullivan's argument that rescission is the order of the court.[141] It would not be possible to achieve this outcome on Swadling's theory as it rejects any role for rescission in this area. Before leaving this problem of mistake as to identity reference must be made to further work that has been done by Catharine MacMillan and Professor David McLauchlan. In an illuminating historical analysis of this problem Ms MacMillan has shown how several of the most significant early cases on mistaken identity, particularly *Cundy v Lindsay*, were heavily influenced by B's conviction for obtaining property by false pretences.[141a] A decision in the subsequent civil case that a voidable title had passed to B would have been inconsistent with the conviction as the latter depended on proof that B's acquisition of possession of the good was invalid. Later cases, e.g. *King's Norton Metal Co Ltd v Edridge, Merrett & Co Ltd*[141b] and *Phillips v Brooks Ltd*,[141c] which held that B did acquire a voidable title, came after significant legislative amendments that made conviction no longer dependent on proof that the A-B contract was void. Clearly this analysis supports the approach taken in this paper.

Professor McLauchlan's analysis, however, offers a perspective that favours the A-B contract being void.[141d] Adopting a conventional offer and acceptance analysis Professor McLauchlan points out that B often accepts an offer from A which B knows A means to make to X, and where A is the offeree B knows the acceptance is meant for X. How then can a contract be formed between A and B? There is little room for argument that about the hypothetical example of A writing to B making her a contractual offer and B's twin visiting A and purporting to accept. In that situation A's offer is indisputably made to B and not the twin. But it is seriously arguable that in many other mistaken identity cases the identity of the person A deals with as X is immaterial. If so, can it really be said that the contract is not made with B? Is this not the situation Lord Nicholls was thinking of when he said that A makes the contract with B in the belief that B *is* X.[141e] Professor McLauchlan's analysis, though impeccably orthodox, would require the very closest

---

141 See n 116 above.
141a MacMillan, C, 'Rogues, Swindlers and Cheats: the Development of Mistakes of Identity in English Contract Law', (2005) 64 CLJ 711.
141b (1897) 14 TLR 98.    141c [1919] 2 KB 243.
141d McLauchlan, DW, 'Mistake of Identity in Contract Formation', (2005) 21 JCL 1.
141e Supra n 137.

examination of the importance of B's identity being what A believed it to be. This is unrealistic and for policy reasons this paper favours adoption of the simple rule that the contract is always voidable for misrepresentation.

## Non est factum

This ancient principle enables someone who signs a document under a complete misunderstanding of its nature or contents to claim that the signing was literally not his deed. Since a successful plea of *non est factum* makes a contract void, its effects upon innocent third parties who rely on the document, *for example*, by lending money on the security of it, can be devastating. Hence, in the major recent English cases on the doctrine, *Saunders v Anglia Building Society*[142] and *Norwich and Peterborough Building Society v Steed*,[143] the courts have shown themselves most reluctant to grant relief. Essentially the plea is not likely to succeed in the presence of any trace of negligence on the part of the person signing the document. By contrast the decisions of the High Court of Australia in *Petelin v Cullen*[144] and of Gallen J in the New Zealand High Court in *Landzeal Group Ltd v Kyne*[145] indicate that where only the parties to the contract are involved, carelessness on the part of the mistaken party is virtually irrelevant. This is not a particularly satisfactory distinction to draw. The better approach to *non est factum* would be to treat it as a historically recognised class of unilateral mistake where the contract is voidable because it would be unconscionable to enforce it. Third parties who have relied upon the document can be protected by the refusal to set aside the deed where their interests have intervened.

## Conclusion

Save for situations where no contract is formed, the effect of a serious mistake in the process of forming a contract should be to make the contract voidable. The 'void' theory is unrealistic, unjust and inconvenient. The basis for finding a contract voidable on the ground of mistake should be that enforcement of the contract would be unconscionable. An alternative basis might be that a party adversely affected by the mistake has a right to terminate the contract. A right to rescind is better for two reasons. First, it is more realistic. Something has gone wrong in the making of the contract. One or more of the parties has entered into the contract under some fundamental misassumption. Rescission is the way to deal with this, not termination, because the latter operates prospectively. Second, the 'voidable' theory, based on unconscionability, blends mistake with the other vitiating factors touched

142 [1971] AC 1004.    143 [1993] Ch 116.
144 (1975) 132 CLR 355.    145 [1990] 3 NZLR 574.

upon in this chapter. These can be seen as all derived from the same common root – unconscionability. Integration of mistake with these other vitiating factors makes the law more coherent and avoids unnecessary doctrine. Integration of mistake with frustration is not a suitable solution for the reasons stated in the introductory section of this chapter.[146]

This chapter has made some other more concrete proposals. *Bell v Lever Brothers* should be legislatively overruled as should *Shogun Finance Ltd v Hudson*. This latter phenomenon should be placed in the law of misrepresentation rather than mistake. 'Mistake in equity' as an independent doctrine should be buried but its approach should rule us from the grave in the new doctrine of common mistake making a contract voidable. The ancient principle of *non est factum* should come in from the cold as a historically recognised category of unilateral mistake.

In most parts of the common law world the doctrinal developments advocated here can be accomplished through judicial development. Unfortunately, in England, the doctrine of precedent (a good doctrine) means that legislative reform will be necessary to overcome the burden of entrenched and misconceived decisions of the superior courts.

146 See above nn 13–17 and text.

## Chapter 6

# The standard of good faith performance: reasonable expectations or community standards?

*Jeannie Marie Paterson* *

## Introduction

1. Buyer and seller enter into a contract for the sale of land. The contract is made subject to approval by the relevant regulatory authorities of the development proposed for the land. The buyer decides that he does not want to proceed with the sale. Accordingly, the buyer does not apply for approval of the development and terminates the contract on grounds of failure of the condition precedent.

2. Principal and builder enter into a construction contract. The contract provides that the principal may terminate the contract following any specified breach of the contract by the builder, subject to the builder being given opportunity to 'show cause' to the 'satisfaction' of the principal why the contract should not be terminated. The builder breaches the contract. A show cause hearing is organised. In the meantime the principal is quoted a better price for the work than under the original contract with the builder. In order to escape from the original contract, the principal claims that the cause shown was unsatisfactory. The principal terminates the contract.

3. Lender and borrower enter into a loan agreement. The lender provides the borrower with an overdraft facility to a limit of £10,000. Amounts outstanding under the overdraft are agreed to be repayable 'on demand'. The lender decides to reduce its exposure in the borrower's industry. The lender accordingly demands repayment of the loan.

It has sometimes been suggested that the common law of contract would benefit from the recognition of a duty of good faith applying generally to the performance of commercial contracts.[1] Traditionally good faith has only had

---

* Dr Jeannie Paterson is senior lecturer in law at Monash University.
1 See eg, Brownsword, R, ' "Good Faith" in Contracts Revisited' (1996) 49 Current Legal Problems 111; Finn, P, 'Equity and Commercial Contracts: A Comment', *AMPLA Yearbook* 2001, Lücke, H, 'Good Faith and Contractual Performance' in Finn, P (ed), *Essays on*

a very specialised application in contract law. For example, duties of good faith apply to contracts of insurance and in circumstances where the parties are in a fiduciary relationship. What is usually contemplated in suggestions that the common law contract law recognise a duty of good faith performance, is a general implied term that would supplement the express terms of a contract by requiring some degree of fair and co-operative conduct by the parties in performing their contract.[2] The development of such a duty is controversial.[3] However, given there is considerable interest in such a duty, this chapter is concerned not with whether the common law of contract should have a duty of good faith but the standard by which compliance with any such duty would be measured.

In this chapter I suggest that there are two main types of approach to the standard of good faith performance.[4] Under the 'reasonable expectation' approach, good faith requires the parties to conform to their own reasonable expectations at the time of contracting as to the manner in which their contract will be performed. Under a 'community standards' approach the duty is measured by reference to moral standards of conduct deemed appropriate by a judging community external to the parties. I advocate the reasonable expectations approach to good faith and argue that the community standards approach is neither desirable nor likely to succeed in its aims. In so doing, I effectively defend the traditional conception of contract over one reformed to show a more communitarian flavor. I also argue that the relevance of 'relational norms' in governing the relationship of contracting parties does not change this preference.

This chapter begins by considering the meaning of good faith as honesty and the need for an objective standard. Part two describes the two approaches

---

*Contract*, 1987, Sydney: Law Book Company, Mason, A, 'Contract, Good Faith and Equitable Standards in Fair Dealing' (2000) 116 Law Quarterly Review 66, O'Byrne, S, 'Good Faith in Contractual Performance: Recent Developments' [1995] 74 Canadian Bar Review 70, Powell, R, 'Good Faith in Contracts' (1956) 9 Current Legal Problems 16, Taylor, V, 'Contracts with the Lot: Franchises, Good Faith and Contract Regulation' [1997] New Zealand Law Review 459.

2   But cf Peden, E, *Good Faith in the Performance of Contracts*, 2003, Australia: Butterworths, conceiving good faith as a principle of construction.

3   See eg Bridge, M, 'Does Anglo-Canadian Law Need a Doctrine of Good Faith?' (1984) 9 Canadian Business Law Journal 385, 426; McKendrick, E, 'Good Faith: A Matter of Principle?', in Forte, A, *Good Faith in Contract and Property*, 1999, Oxford: Hart Publishing, 41.

4   See also Brownsword who distinguishes between approaches which treat good faith as the 'exception' or supplementary 'requirement' and good faith as 'the rule' or 'regime': Brownsword, R, 'Two Concepts of Good Faith' (1994) 7 Journal of Contract Law 197; ' "Good Faith" in Contracts Revisited', (1996) 49 Current Legal Problems 111; 'Positive, Negative, Neutral: The Reception of Good Faith in English Contract Law' in Brownsword, R, Hird, N, and Howells, G (eds) *Good Faith in Contract: Concept and Context*, 1999, Aldershot: Dartmouth Publishers 13.

for measuring the duty of good faith performance. Part three explains the difference between the approaches. Part four considers their relative merits. Part five focuses on the argument that the duty of good faith should be used to incorporate the insights of relational contract theory into a new, more contextual law of contract.

### Honesty and an objective standard of good faith

A duty of good faith in contract performance is generally agreed at least to require honesty from contracting parties. This is a subjective standard which looks at the actual state of mind of the parties to the contract. The requirement of honesty has a somewhat limited application. Under a strict approach, it will only be relevant where the contract requires some belief to be held by one or other of the parties. For example, consider problem 2 at the beginning of this chapter. Where there is a requirement of 'dissatisfaction' before a party, the principal, can exercise certain contractual powers; then clearly that party must be honestly (which means genuinely) dissatisfied before claiming that the conditions to the exercise of the power have been fulfilled. The party will not be able to claim dissatisfaction if he is really acting for some other, extrinsic reason. By contrast, consider problem 1 where a contractual power is conditioned on events external to the parties, such as development approval being granted. In such a case the subjective state of mind of the parties will not be relevant to determining whether the power can be exercised. Either the event has occurred or it has not.

The honesty aspect of good faith might also be interpreted more widely to require a belief by each of the parties that they have acted consistently with the objectives of the contract.[5] However, even this type of approach will not necessarily resolve the type of concerns good faith is generally envisaged to address. A party might honestly believe in the legitimacy of her actions yet behave in a way that is unfair or oppressive to the other party to the contract. Consider again the first problem above. The conduct of the buyer in seeking to rely on the failure of condition as a reason for ending the contract might be considered reprehensible but that is not because the buyer has been dishonest. The buyer has not lied or cheated in any way and may not even consider that he is acting contrary to the contemplated purpose of the condition, as opposed to protecting his own business interests. The objection to the buyer's conduct is that he has failed to take reasonable steps to co-operate in ensuring that the conditions to performance were satisfied.

Courts commonly describe good faith in terms that go beyond mere

---

5   Carter, J, and Peden, E, 'Good Faith in Australian Contract Law' (2003) Journal of Contract Law 155; C P Gillette, 'Limitations on the Obligation of Good Faith' (1981) *Duke Law Journal* 619.

honesty.[6] Consistently, most commentators consider that a duty of good faith in contract performance should be measured by reference to some objective standard of conduct.[7] There is however little agreement as to the proper objective standard. Courts commonly describe the duty in general terms, for example, as requiring 'loyalty', 'co-operation' or as prohibition on acting 'arbitrarily', 'capriciously', for an 'improper or extraneous purpose' or 'unreasonably'.[8] While these terms give some indication of the flavour of the duty envisioned by courts, they give little guidance as to how good faith will be measured by the courts in any particular case. What degree of co-operation is required? What purposes under a contract are proper?

The lack of a clear standard of good faith might be explained by reference to the excluder analysis proposed by Professor Summers. Summers argues that the duty of good faith is best understood by identifying the conduct excluded by the duty rather than attempting to define a positive standard of required conduct.[9] According to Summers:

> [good faith] is a phrase without general meaning (or meanings) of its own and serves to exclude many heterogeneous forms of bad faith. In a particular context the phrase takes on specific meaning, but usually this is only by way of contrast with the specific form of bad faith actually or hypothetically ruled out.[10]

It may be accepted that, at least to some extent, the jurisprudence of a duty of good faith probably will consist of categories of excluded conduct. Nonetheless, the excluder analysis is unsatisfactory because it provides no reason for characterising certain types of conduct as contrary to good faith.[11] While

6 See, eg, *Renard Constructions (ME) Pty Ltd v Minister for Public Works* (1992) 26 NSWLR 234; *Empress Towers Ltd v Bank of Nova Scotia* (1990) 73 DLR (4th) 400.
  In the United States, references to good faith and fair dealing in parts of the Uniform Commercial Code and the *Restatement (2d) Contracts* is seen as reinforcing the relevance of an objective standard of good faith, see Farnsworth, EA, *Farnsworth on Contracts*, Vol II, 1990, Boston: Little Brown, 331.
7 See, eg, Farnsworth, EA, 'Good Faith Performance and Commercial Reasonableness under the Uniform Commercial Code' (1963) 30 University of Chicago Law Review 666; Summers, R, ' "Good Faith" in General Contract Law and the Sales Provisions of the Uniform Commercial Code' (1968) 54 Virginia Law Review 195.
8 See further Paterson, J, Robertson, A, Heffey, P, *Principles of Contract Law*, 2nd edn, 2005, Sydney: LBC, Ch 16.
9 Summers, R, ' "Good Faith" in General Contract Law and the Sales Provisions of the Uniform Commercial Code' (1968) 54 Virginia Law Review 195, 206.
10 Ibid, 195, 201.
11 See also Burton, S, 'More on Good Faith Performance of a Contract: A Reply to Professor Summers' (1984) 69 Iowa Law Review 497, 508–11; Patterson, D, 'Wittgenstein and the Code: A Theory of Good Faith Performance and Enforcement Under Article Nine' (1988) 137 University of Pennsylvania Law Review 335, 346–52.

the results reached in particular cases may seem correct, instinct and intuition provide little real justification for a result. Moreover, such a method provides little guidance for deciding new cases. It is suggested that it is possible to give greater guidance as to what good faith performance will require in any particular case and moreover that there are two main categories of approach to the proper standard of good faith in contract performance.

### Reasonable expectations and community standards

A reasonable expectations approach bases the duty of good faith on the reasonable expectations of the parties at the time of making the contract as to the manner in which their contract will, as a matter of obligation, be performed.[12] The approach is predominantly contractual, treating the duty as consistent with established contract doctrine. In a common law system courts are commonly asked to give effect to the 'presumed intentions'[13] or 'reasonable expectations' of the parties.[14]

How should courts implying a duty of good faith attempt to replicate the parties' reasonable expectations as to the future course of performance of their contract? Most proponents of the reasonable expectations approach give little guidance on this issue. This is perhaps understandable given that the approach merely asks courts to fulfil their traditionally stated function. Nonetheless, it is possible to describe the process in a little more detail.[15] Importantly, a 'reasonable expectation' will be a presumed or hypothetical expectation not necessarily an actual expectation.[16] Courts do not have reliable access to the private or subjective expectations of the parties. Rather,

---

12 A number of theories are consistent with this approach, see eg Burton, S, 'Breach of Contract and the Common Law Duty to Perform in Good Faith' (1980) 94 Harvard Law Review 369, 373, 391; Burton, S, and Anderson, E, 'The World of a Contract' (1990) 75 Iowa Law Review 861; Easterbrook, F, and Fischel, D, 'Contract and Fiduciary Duty' (1993) 36 Journal of Law and Economics 425, 438; Posner, R, *Economic Analysis of Law*, 4th edn, 1992, Boston: Little, Brown, 91; T L Muris, 'Opportunistic Behaviour and the Law of Contracts', (1981) 65 Minnesota Law Review, 521, 521. Also *Market Street Associates Limited Partnership v Frey*, 941 F.2d 588, 595–6 (7th Cir, 1991); *Kham & Nate's Shoes No 2 Inc v First Bank of Whiting*, 908 F.2d 1351, 1357 (7th Cir, 1990).

13 See, eg, *BP Refinery (Westernport) Pty Limited v President, Councillors and Ratepayers of the Shire of Hastings* (1977) 180 CLR 266, 283.

14 See, eg, Baker, J, 'From Sanctity of Contract to Contractual' (1979) 32 Current Legal Problems 17; Steyn, J, 'Contract Law: Fulfilling the Contractual of Honest Men' (1997) 113 Law Quarterly Review 433.

15 On reasonable expectations see also Mitchell, C, 'Leading a Life of its Own? The Roles of Reasonable Expectation in Contract Law' (2003) 23 Oxford Journal of Legal Studies 639, 642; Bigwood, R, *Exploitative Contracts*, 2003 Oxford: Oxford University Press, esp pp 50–57.

16 See further Williams, G, 'Language and the Law – IV' (1945) 61 Law Quarterly Review 384. Also Paterson, J, 'Terms Implied in Fact: the Basis for Implication' (1998) 13 Journal of Contract Law 103.

courts will attempt to replicate the expectations the parties probably would have held if they had considered the issue in question when making their contract. In this process, courts will consider both the terms of the contract and the surrounding circumstances.[17] The surrounding circumstances will be important in giving content to the duty of good faith in any particular case because they will have shaped the parties' expectations about how their contract is to be performed. However, consistently with established doctrine, the reasonable expectations approach would demand a reasonably persuasive case for qualifying the express terms on the basis of extrinsic factors. The parties' private or subjective hopes for a successful contractual relationship will not be sufficient.

The community standards approach to good faith bases the measure of the duty on standards judged fair by a 'judging community' external to the parties.[18] There are a number of possible 'communities' which might be used to assess the requirements of a duty of good faith. One might be the business community in which the parties are dealing.[19] Under this approach, ascertaining good faith may involve taking evidence from members of the relevant business community. The standard of good faith might also be grounded in the general community, in which case it is possible judges might seek some sort of sociological evidence as to those standards.[20] Commonly, however, proponents of this approach envisage the measure of good faith being found not in the standards of an actual community but in some idealised concept of community. Under this approach good faith embodies standards of neighbourhood and co-operation thought desirable in contracting.

Particularly in its most abstract version, the community standards approach reflects an aspiration to reform the moral basis of contracting. Proponents consider that since society facilitates the enforcement of contracts through the law, society should also demand that contracting parties behave according to the standards of conduct considered appropriate

---

17 The better view is that a court may have regard to the surrounding circumstances when considering whether or not a term should be implied in a contract: *Codelfa Construction Pty Ltd v State Rail Authority of NSW* (1982) 149 CLR 337, 347–53. On construction generally see also *Investors Compensation Scheme Ltd v West Bromwich Building Society* [1998] 1 WLR 896, 912–13; *Bank of Credit and Commerce International SA v Ali* [2001] 2 WLR 735, 739, 749.

18 See, eg, Reiter, B, 'Good Faith in Contracts' (1983) 17 Valparaiso University Law Review 705, 717.

19 See, eg, the Uniform Commercial Code (US) s 2–103(1)(b).

20 See, eg, Farnsworth, E, 'Good Faith Performance and Commercial Reasonableness Under the Uniform Commercial Code', (1963) 30 University of Chicago Law Review 666, 671–2. See also *Restatement (2d) Contracts* § 205, comment a; Reiter, B, 'Good Faith in Contracts' (1983) 17 Valparaiso University Law Review 705, 706.

by the community. Generally, the standards promoted by proponents of this approach are communitarian in flavour. Proponents of the community standards approach generally demand that parties to a contract are to some extent responsible for protecting the interests of their contracting partner.[21]

### Comparing the approaches

In many cases there will be little substantial difference between the reasonable expectations and community standards approaches to measuring good faith performance. In most cases unco-operative or unfair conduct is likely to be inconsistent both with the expectations of the parties and the standards of the community.[22] Consider, again the first and second problems above. In problem 1, under a duty of good faith, and also the more established duty to co-operate, the buyer would be required to take reasonable steps to obtain the development approval before terminating the contract on grounds of failure of the condition.[23] This result can be justified under either approach to the duty of good faith. The discretion granted by the condition ensures the buyer is not bound to perform the contract for the sale of the land unless the buyer can also proceed with the development contemplated to take place on the land. However, the buyer has avoided satisfaction with the condition in order to terminate the contract for reasons unrelated to the purpose of the condition. Under a reasonable expectations approach it might persuasively be argued that the parties would not envisage performance of the contract being impeded by this type of unreasonable lack of co-operation. For similar reasons, the conduct might be precluded as contrary to community standards under the community standards approach.

In problem 2, under a duty of good faith, or indeed as a matter of construction, the principal would be required to be honestly dissatisfied with the builder's performance before exercising the power to terminate the contract.[24]

---

21  See, eg, Brownsword, R, 'Two Concepts of Good Faith' (1994) 7 Journal of Contract Law 197; ' "Good Faith" in Contracts Revisited' (1996) 49 Current Legal Problems 111, Finn, PD, 'The Fiduciary Principle' in TG Youdan (ed), *Equity, Fiduciaries and Trusts*, 1989 Toronto: Carswell, 1; Smith, KJ, 'Themes in the Liability of Banks and Lending Institutions' (1990) 64 Australian Law Journal, 331; M Patterson 'Good Faith, Lender Liability, and Discretionary Acceleration: Of Llewellyn, Wittgenstein and the Uniform Commercial Code' (1989) 68 Texas Law Review 169, 210.

22  See also *Tymshare Inc v Covell* 727 F.2d 1145 (DC Cir, 1984).

23  *Mackay v Dick* (1881) 6 App Cas 251, 263.

24  See, eg, *Canada Egg Products Ltd v Canadian Doughnut Co Ltd* [1955] 3 DLR 1; *Meehan v Jones* (1982) 149 CLR 571; *Renard Constructions (ME) Pty Ltd v Minister for Public Works* (1992) 26 NSWLR 234; *Marshall v Bernard Place Corporation* (2002) 58 OR (3d) 97.

The principal would be precluded from terminating where its dissatisfaction with the builder's cause is feigned. There has also been some suggestion in English courts that a discretionary power under a contract should be exercised in a way that is not 'arbitrary, capricious or unreasonable'.[25] Under this type of approach the principal's decision as to satisfaction would have to relate to the cause presented by the contractor and not be made on the basis of irrelevant factors, such as, for example, a view about the colour of the builder's hair[26] or on the basis of biased or prejudicial information.[27]

Once again these results can be justified under either approach to the duty of good faith. The principal's conduct in terminating is likely to be contrary to the reasonable expectations of the parties. In including a show cause clause in the contract, the parties have attempted to balance their rights in a situation of breach. The principal is entitled to terminate the contract but only if the builder cannot show cause to the contrary to the satisfaction of the principal. The builder has a right to present a case for continuation of the contract and the principal has the right to assess whether that case is persuasive. The show cause procedure is meaningless if the principal can claim dissatisfaction for reasons unrelated to the builder's conduct and use the condition to escape a contract which has become undesirable for other reasons. For similar reasons, to terminate for reasons unrelated to the builder's case might be characterised as unfair and contrary to community standards under a community standards approach to good faith.

Despite their common convergence, the two approaches to the standard of good faith in contract performance reflect very different views about the role of contract law. The reasonable expectations approach is consistent with the emphasis traditionally placed by the law of contract on the preferences of the parties themselves. Contract law obviously constrains the choices made by contracting parties. There are rules about how contracts must be made, are interpreted and about what the parties may contract about. Nonetheless, within these boundaries, the law of contract has traditionally given parties the space themselves to determine how they will manage their contractual relationship. The reasonable expectations approach to the duty of good faith performance accepts the existence of this space for party autonomy. In determining what the duty of good faith requires in any particular case, the reasonable expectations approach tries to replicate the parties' probable expectations as to their preferred course of performance by considering both

---

25  *Abu Dhabi National Tanker Co v Product Star Shipping Ltd (The Product Star)* (No 2) [1993] 1 Lloyds Rep 297, 404; *Gan Insurance v Tai Ping Insurance* [2001] 2 All ER 299, 322.

26  See *Paragon Finance plc v Stauton* [2002] 2 All ER 248, 261.

27  See *Renard Constructions (ME) Pty Ltd v Minister for Public Works* (1992) 26 NSWLR 234.

the express terms and the circumstances surrounding the parties' contract. Moreover, the approach allows the parties to shape the scope of the duty of good faith through the express terms of the contract.

By contrast, being based on an aspiration to reform the moral basis of contracting, the community standards approach to the duty of good faith shows a more interventionist approach to regulating contract performance. The extent to which the express terms of a contract may be qualified by this version of good faith is not precisely clear. However, the approach does appear to contemplate that the parties' own preferences will be curtailed by the co-operative or communitarian values inherent in the community standards approach to good faith.

The difference between the approaches becomes apparent when considering more difficult categories of case than presented by the first and second problems. Problems 1 and 2 involve qualified discretions. In problem 1 performance of the contract is qualified by the occurrence of an outside event: regulatory approval of the development. In problem 2 the power to terminate is qualified by a requirement that the principal be dissatisfied by the cause shown by the contractor. Being qualified powers, it is relatively straightforward in both cases to identify good faith qualifications on the scope of the powers. An unqualified or absolute contractual power raises more directly the extent to which a duty of good faith should override the expectations of the parties as expressed in their contract.

Consider, for example, problem 3 in which a lender demands repayment of a loan under an express power in the loan contract without there being any default by the borrower triggering the right to bring the contract to an end. A reasonable expectations approach would be likely to accept the apparent meaning of the words in the contract, which is that a lender can demand repayment at any time.[28]

As noted earlier, some English cases have suggested that a discretionary contractual power may be subject to qualifications, which might be described as ensuring the fairness of the decision-making process. For example, it has been suggested that a discretion to vary interest rates 'should not be exercised dishonestly, for an improper purpose, capriciously or arbitrarily'.[29] It is uncertain whether this qualification would apply to a power to demand repayment under an overdraft facility. Assuming that the qualifications do apply, then under a reasonable expectations approach the range of proper

---

28 Courts have accepted that 'a debtor required to pay a debt on demand must be allowed a reasonable time to meet the demand': *Bunbury Foods Pty Ltd v National Bank of Australasia Limited* (1984) 153 CLR 491, 502–3; *Bank of Baroda v Panessar* [1987] 1 Ch 335, 348. See further Paterson, JM, 'Limits on a Lender's Right to Repayment on Demand: Construction, Implication and Good Faith?', (1998) 26 Australian Business Law Review 258–727.

29 *Paragon Finance plc v Stauton* [2002] 1 WLR 685, 702.

purposes for which a demand for repayment might be made would be very widely interpreted. A demand clause would allow a lender to demand pre-payment of the loan for any business reason or even possibly for no reason. It would be difficult for the parties to express their arrangement any more clearly. Moreover, there are good business reasons for the broad power envis-aged by a demand clause. Lenders may favour lending on demand because the arrangement gives considerable flexibility in responding to contingencies affecting any aspect of the transaction.[30] The price of the loan to the borrower will have reflected this flexibility.

By contrast, some proponents of a community standard approach see the role of the duty of good faith as qualifying the decision to exercise broadly expressed contractual powers in cases where that exercise would have harsh consequences for the other party to the contract.[31] Proponents of this approach might accordingly argue that in a case such as problem 3, the purposes for which a lender may decide to terminate a contract should be interpreted narrowly. Thus, where the lender is not acting for reasons related, and indeed proportionate, to the borrower's performance, the lender's appar-ent right to terminate should be restricted.[32]

### Which approach?

There is no clear judicial preference for either of the approaches to the measure of good faith in any of the common law jurisdictions. It is submitted that the reasonable expectations approach is preferable to the community standards approach for three reasons.

The first reason relates to the issue of certainty. Under the reasonable expectations approach, it may sometimes be difficult, reliably, to replicate the parties' reasonable expectations as to the manner in which their contract will be performed. However, courts have considerable experience in this process in construing contracts and implying terms in fact. The reasonable expectations approach has the advantage of dictating a focused line of inquiry; it requires a court to consider the terms of the contract and circumstances in which the parties were dealing and to assess what expectations as to the performance of their contract might reasonably be based on those factors.

By contrast, it is suggested that the community standards approach is likely to become increasingly uncertain the further it moves away from the stand-ards of the parties. If, under the community standards approach, good faith is measured by reference to reasonable business standards, then, in a

---

30 See also Waddams, SM, 'Good Faith, Unconscionability and Reasonable Expectations' (1995) 9 Journal of Contract Law 55, 63.

31 See eg Brownsword, R, 'Two Concepts of Good Faith' (1994) 7 Journal of Contract Law 197.

32 See *KMC Co v Irving Trust Co* 757 F.2d 752 (6th Cir, 1985).

homogenous business community or industry, it may be possible to identify the standards of conduct considered appropriate by that industry. Indeed, such standards may be very good evidence of what the parties were likely to have expected at the time of making the contract. However, in broader business contexts there may be a variety of views about what type of conduct should or should not be prohibited as contrary to good faith in contract performance. If the measure of the standard of good faith is that of the general community, the difficulties are likely to magnify. The general community is likely to hold many different, and inconsistent, views about appropriate commercial behaviour. Some members of the community might support a highly individualistic ethic in contracting, others might not. The version of the community standards approach which relies on the standards of an idealised community avoids the problem of identifying common standards in an actual community but is open to concerns about highly discretionary justice.

The second reason for preferring the reasonable expectation approach lies in it being consistent with established contract doctrine and hence respectful of the autonomy of contracting parties. This is valuable in its own right and may also promote more efficient outcomes in contracting. Judges will usually have less experience in commercial matters than the parties to a contract and parties are likely to be better at making business decisions than courts.[33]

The third reason for preferring a reasonable expectations approach over a community standards approach is pragmatic. There is some doubt as to whether the attempt envisaged by the community standards approach to reform the morality of contracting parties is likely to be successful. Basing a duty of good faith performance on community standards of fairness will not make contracting parties believe that they ought to act in accordance with those standards. Primarily, law regulates conduct not character. If contracting parties predict that the requirements of a duty of good faith are unlikely to accord with the parties' own perceptions of their best interests, the parties will attempt to reduce the impact of those terms on their contracts.[34]

### Relational contracting

The argument put thus far might be challenged by some proponents of relational contract theory.[35] Supported by empirical evidence, relational

---

33 See also *Market Street Associates Limited Partnership v Frey 941* F.2d 588, 595 (7th Cir, 1991).

34 See, eg, Brickley, JA, and Dark, FH, 'The Economic Effects of Franchise Termination Laws' (1991) 34 Journal of Law and Economics 101.

35 The concept of a relational contract is difficult to define. Many commentators argue that most contracts have relational features, in that they involve a relationship, not merely an exchange between the parties. It may be argued that the insights of relational contract theory

contract theorists argue that the behaviour of parties to all but the most discrete and one-off transactions is guided by a network of social and business norms that assist in maintaining the relationship between them.[36] As explained by Feinman '[t]he substantive core of relational contract theory proceeds from two propositions: that contract is fundamentally about cooperative social behavior, and that contracts containing significant relational elements are the predominant form of contracting'.[37] Relational contract theorists suggest that parties to relational contracts may place more reliance on 'relational norms' than the written text of their contract. Relational norms may dictate that parties work to continue their relationship rather than enforcing the terms of their formal contract. Indeed, recourse to the legal rights specified in the formal contract may be avoided by contracting parties as likely to sour their relationship.[38]

Relational norms have some similarities with good faith in that they embrace open-ended and flexible concepts promoting the successful performance of a contract.[39] Some proponents of a community standards approach to good faith may argue that, once recognition is given to the role of relational values in contracting, concern about a conflict between their approach and the expectations of contracting parties will disappear.[40]

are applicable as a general contract theory to all but discrete, one-off transactions. See eg, Campbell, D, 'The Relational Constitution of the Discrete Contract' in Campbell, D, and Vincent-Jones, P (eds), *Contract and Economic Organisation*, 1996, Aldershot: Dartmouth Publishers, Ch 3; Eisenberg, MA, 'Why there is No Law of Relational Contracts' (2000) 94 Northwestern University Law Review 805, 816–7. See also Collins, H, *Regulating Contracts*, 1999, Oxford: Oxford University Press, 141–3.

36  See also Macneil, I, 'Values in Contract: Internal and External' (1983) 78 North Western University Law Review 340, 367–82.

37  Feinman, JM, 'Relational Contract Theory in Context' (2000) 94 Northwestern University Law Review 737. 743.

38  Beale, H, and Dugdale, T, 'Contracts Between Businessmen: Planning and the Use of Contractual Remedies' (1975) British Journal of Law and Society 45; Macaulay, I, 'Non-Contractual Relations in Business: A Preliminary Study' (1963) 28 American Sociological Review 55. Also Hadfield, GK, 'Problematic Relations: Franchising and the Law of Incomplete Contracts' (1990) 42 Stanford Law Review 927, 928I McNeil, R, 'Contracts: Adjustment of Long-Term Economic Relations Under Classical, Neo-classical and Relational Contract Law' (1978) 72 Northwestern University Law Review 854; Speidel, RE, 'The Characteristics and Challenges of Relational Contracts' (2000) 94 Northwestern University Law Review 823.

39  See, eg, Lücke, HK, 'Good Faith and Contractual Performance' in Finn, PD (ed), *Essays on Contract*, 1987, Sydney: Law Book Company, 179; Hadfield, GK, 'Problematic Relations: Franchising and the Law of Incomplete Contracts' (1990) 42 *Stanford Law Review* 927; Reiter, BJ, 'Good Faith in Contracts' (1983) 17 Valparaiso University Law Review 705, 725–729; Collins, H, *Regulating Contracts*, 1999, Oxford: Oxford University Press, 181.

40  See, eg, Hadfield, GK, 'Problematic Relations: Franchising and the Law of Incomplete Contracts' (1990) 42 Stanford Law Review 927; Patterson, M, 'Good Faith, Lender Liability, and Discretionary Acceleration: Of Llewellyn, Wittgenstein and the Uniform Commercial Code'

Proponents might argue that relational contract theory shows that the values usually associated with the community standards approach can also be attributed to the expectations of the parties themselves. For example, in problem 3, proponents of this approach might argue that the lender's right to demand repayment should be restricted not merely because the lender's conduct in terminating is unfair from the perspective of the borrower but also because demanding repayment would be contrary to the parties' expectations about the conduct of their relationship. Thus, whether a reasonable expectations or a community standards approach is applied, good faith should promote values of co-operation and fairness in contracting and a reappraisal of the moral basis of contract law.

Certainly, contract interpretation should be sensitive to the possibility of understandings between parties that are not embodied in their formal legal contract. The relationship between parties, particularly in a long-term contract, may be complex and dynamic. A modern and relevant contract law must be alive to these possibilities. A highly formal system of contractual interpretation which gave effect only to the strict letter of the terms in the written contract might have some attractions of certainty but these advantages would probably be overshadowed by the failure of such an approach to recognise the 'real deal' between contracting parties.[41]

However, accepting the relevance of relational norms in structuring a contractual relationship does not mean that these norms should be translated substantive qualifications on the exercise of contractual rights. A reasonable expectations approach would credit the written terms of the parties' contract as good evidence of the parties' reasonable expectations. While the express terms of a contract might be qualified by reference to the surrounding circumstances, industry custom and other considerations, a reasonably strong case for such a course of action would have to be established. The reasonable expectations approach would be unlikely to qualify the express terms of a contract merely by reference to abstract notions of fairness supposedly inherent in the parties' relationship.

Partly this is a pragmatic position; courts do not have the expertise or indeed resources to engage in extensive investigation into the conventions and customs of the business circumstances surrounding a particular dispute. This approach is also likely to be consistent with the expectations of contracting parties. The likelihood that relational norms are a strong influence on the conduct of contracting parties does not mean that the parties expected relational norms to be incorporated into their contract with the status of

---

(1989) 68 Texas Law Review 169; Smith, KJ, 'Themes in the Liability of Banks and Lending Institutions' (1990) 64 Australian Law Journal 331.

41 See further Campbell, D, Collins, H, and Wrightman, J, *Implicit Dimensions of Contract* 2003, Oxford: Hart Publishing.

legal rules. To the contrary, parties may be quite aware that there is a difference between the social norms that guide their approach to the contractual relationship and the legal rights embodied in the contract. They may moreover consider it useful to maintain the distinction between relational norms and legal rights.[42]

While contracting parties may generally conduct their relationship by reference to the relational norms relevant to their relationship, the legal rights specified in the parties' contract also have an important role in regulating the parties' relationship. For example, the strict rights specified in the contract may provide a means of exiting a deal where the relationship has broken down. Analysing this function in terms of game theory, Bernstein argues that the parties may not want relational norms applied to resolve a dispute where they view their relationship as being at 'an end-game stage'.[43] The legal rights specified in a contract may also provide an incentive to strict performance of that contract. Bernstein also applies game theory to this type of situation. Bernstein argues that the concept of end-game may affect a party's decision to rely on his strict contractual rights even where he does not intend to end the relationship. She explains that a party 'might follow a strategy of seeking application of [the terms of the written contract] . . . in order to maintain the credibility of his threat to do so in similar situations in the future'.[44]

### The standard of good faith

A duty of good faith performance need not cause great disruption to the common law of contract if it is applied in a way that is consistent with existing contract doctrines, that is to promote rather than reform the expectations of contracting parties. To this end I have argued that if a general duty of good faith performance is recognised in the common law of contract, the standard of good faith performance should be based on the parties' reasonable expectations rather than an abstract notion of community standards. Recognition of the role of relational norms in regulating the parties' relationship does not change this view. Parties to commercial transactions invest considerable resources in preparing formal contracts. To suggest that parties do not give any real credence to the terms of the contract and that these rights should be qualified by relational norms renders that effort redundant. This is not a step which should lightly be taken.

42 See also Goddard, D, 'Long-term Contracts: A Law and Economics Perspective' (1997) New Zealand Law Review 423, 448; Feinman, JM, 'The Significance of Contract Theory', (1990) 58 University of Cincinnati Law Review 1283, 1302–3.

43 Bernstein, L, 'Merchant Law in a Merchant Court: Rethinking The Code's Search for Immanent Business Norms' (1996) 144 University of Pennsylvania Law Review 1765, 1796.

44 Ibid 1765, 1797.

Chapter 7

# Some thoughts on the comparative jurisprudence of mistakes in assumption

*Catherine Valcke* *

## Introduction

The object of the present contribution is to provide an illustration of comparative law as comparative jurisprudence. It is a view of comparative law that I and others have defended elsewhere.[1] The issue that I propose to use for that purpose is the objective/subjective theory of contract, as revealed through a comparative study of the French, German, and English law of mistakes in assumption. The issue is a complex one deserving of much fuller treatment than can be given here. My aim is only to provide the reader with a sense of how one would go about conducting such a study from the perspective of comparative law as comparative jurisprudence.

Comparative law as comparative jurisprudence entails trying to understand foreign law from the inside, from the perspective of the participants in the foreign legal system; it involves exploring how foreign jurists conceive of law more generally. In turn, this requires understanding the broader intellectual and political context in which these jurists have been operating. So in order to understand the German law of mistakes in assumption from the perspective of German jurists, for example, it is necessary to understand how German jurists view law more generally, and that in turn requires us to familiarise ourselves with the intellectual and political history of the German legal system.

The following chapter is structured accordingly. Following some preliminary remarks on definition, I will examine the French, German, and English law of mistakes in assumption with a view to detecting whether and to what extent contract is perceived objectively or subjectively in each of these legal systems. I will then try to relate these different perceptions of contract to the different intellectual and political environments that bred French, German, and English law.

---

* Professor of Law, University of Toronto.
1 Ewald, W, 'Comparative Jurisprudence (I): What Was It Like to Try a Rat?' (1994–95) 143 U Pa L Rev 1898; Valcke, C, 'Comparative Law as Comparative Jurisprudence: The Comparability of Legal Systems' (2004) 52 Am J Comp L 713.

## Preliminaries

### 'Objective' and 'subjective'

By the terms 'objective' and 'subjective', I mean what is usually meant by these terms in the context of contract, that is, as a reference to the extent to which a party's internal thoughts, ideas and intentions, even if undisclosed, matter from a legal standpoint; in other words, matter for purpose of fixing the parties' rights and obligations.[2]

So if one were to think of this in terms of a spectrum ranging from pure objectivity to pure subjectivity, legal systems that attach full significance to internal ideas, regardless of whether these have been manifested to the outside world, would stand at the subjective end of this spectrum. Legal systems that attach no significance whatsoever to internal ideas per se, and instead consider only what legal agents say and do, would stand at the objective end; and legal systems that attach significance both to internal ideas and their external manifestations would stand somewhere in the middle of the spectrum.

A typical middle-position – and one that is to some extent shared by all three of the legal systems studied here – would be to attach legal significance to manifestations of intention, but only insofar as these have been truly intended, that is only insofar as these can truly be considered manifestations of intention. In such a case the manifestation of intention does count legally speaking, but only insofar as this manifestation can properly be demonstrated to be supported by an internal intention.

### 'Mistake in assumption'

As the title suggests, not all cases of contractual mistake are relevant for our purposes. Take for example, cases of mistake 'as to terms', also known as 'correspondence mistakes'.[2a] In contrast with mistakes 'in assumption', mistakes as to terms involve disputes as to the content of the contract. Cases involving a mistake as to terms thus require the court to choose between two competing versions of what it is that the parties agreed to or, in other words, two competing versions of the parties' mutual *declaration* of intention. German scholars indeed refer to such cases as cases of mistake 'going to the declaration'. So in the famous case of *Smith v Hughes*,[3] when the jury was asked to determine whether the oats had been warranted old, the issue was one of mistake as to terms. In cases of mistaken assumption, in contrast – which German scholars aptly call 'mistakes in motive' – the parties agree as

---

2   See, eg, Waddams, SM, *The Law of Contracts*, 1999, Toronto: Canada Law Book, 105–109.

2a   See Sefton-Green, R, 'General Introduction,' in Sefton-Green, R, *Mistake, Fraud and Duties to Inform in European Contract Law*, Cambridge University Press, 2005, 17–30.

3   (1871) LR 6 QB 597.

to the terms of the contract, but at least one of them claims that this declaration does not reflect her true intention. So in *Smith v Hughes* the issue is one of mistake in assumption (if the jury is asked to determine) not whether or not the oats had been warranted old, but whether or not the buyer believed that the oats had been warranted old. Only in such cases is the court faced with having to choose between the objective, outside manifestation of intention and the subjective, internal intention itself. As a result, only such cases – cases of mistaken assumption or mistake in motive – are informative for purpose of assessing how objective or subjective a legal system really is. Accordingly, only these French, German and English cases on mistake are examined for the purpose of making this assessment.

### The French, German, and English law of mistakes in assumption

#### French law

French private law is often described as among the most subjective of Western legal systems.[4] If this were the case the mere fact that one party to a contract could prove that she was mistaken as to a material aspect of the contract would suffice under French law to have the contract set aside. So in the case of *Smith v Hughes*, it would be enough, in order for a French court to allow the buyer to avoid the contract, to demonstrate the buyer's belief that the oats had been warranted old, quite apart from what the contract actually provided and from any issue of reliance on that belief. For if the buyer never had the intention to buy new oats, no contract for new oats could have ever been formed from a subjective perspective.

Is this an accurate description of the state of French law on the issue? The answer varies depending upon which legal materials one considers. If one considers merely *la doctrine* – what French authors have written on the issue – one might very well be justified in concluding in the affirmative. Indeed, the French treatise typically is more an account of French law as the author wishes it to be, based on logic and principle, than an account of French law as it actually is, based on French judicial practice; and the majority of French authors clearly are of the view that a subjective understanding of contract is more consistent with French legal values and ideals.[5] When one considers

4   Zweigert, K, and Kötz, H, *Introduction to Comparative Law*, Vol II, 1987, Oxford: Clarendon Press, 83–94; Harris, D, and Tallon, D, *Contract Law Today – Anglo-French Comparisons*, 1991, Oxford: Clarendon Press; New York: Oxford University Press, 1–5; Nicholas, B, *The French Law of Contract*, 1992, Oxford: Clarendon Press; New York: Oxford University Press, 83–4; Cartwright, J, 'Defects of Consent and Security of Contract: French and English Law Compared' in Birks, P, and Pretto, A (eds), *Themes in Comparative Law in Honour of Bernard Rudden*, 2002, Oxford: Oxford University Press, 156–57.

5   See, eg, Chabas, J, *De la déclaration de volonté en droit civil français*, 1931, Paris: Sirey, 81–2.

only *la doctrine*, therefore, it seems as if French judges both should and do favour a subjective understanding of contract, and thus also should and do set the contract aside in cases of mistake in assumption.

But closer scrutiny of the judicial decisions cited in support of this conclusion reveals that French law is not nearly so straightforward. In order to void the contract in cases of mistake in assumption, French courts indeed insist that the non-mistaken party must have been aware of the importance which the mistaken party attached to the missing quality – the 'awareness' condition.[6] So in a case like *Smith v Hughes* a French court typically would refuse to void the contract unless it was satisfied that the seller knew that the oats being old was essential to the buyer. What is more, it is nowadays clear that the court would require that the buyer establish not just that the seller knew that the buyer wanted old oats, but in fact that the parties were explicitly or implicitly agreed that the oats would be old. In other words, that the seller had in some way warranted the oats to be sold. This is the 'warranty' condition.[7] One indeed would be hard pressed to find a single mistake case in which a court has set aside a contract despite the non-mistaken party having had no way of knowing that the missing quality was decisive for the mistaken party. Without even one decision of this kind the claim of so many French authors that French law is premised on a subjective understanding of contract is puzzling, to say the least.

In recent times, some French authors have admitted that this claim is difficult to sustain in light of French judicial practice.[8] Most, however, have attempted to explain away the awareness/warranty condition as an exception, one that they reluctantly concede to be necessary for purpose of accommodating certain 'practical' considerations of evidence and fairness to the non-mistaken party.[9] Quarantined among the exceptions, the awareness/warranty condition in their view no longer poses a threat to the integrity of the subjectivist logic that continues to rule on the level of principle. Of course, the warranty condition in reality is far more than just an exception.[10] From the moment that it is accepted that the oats be warranted old in order for the contract to be set aside, nothing is left of the subjectivist principle. The rights and obligations of the parties are entirely determined by these parties' agreement – their objective, common declaration – and not by any subjective, private intention of theirs. The great majority of French authors, however, apparently still refuse to acknowledge this.

It thus seems that French *doctrine* generally holds fast to a view of contract

---

6  Weill, A, and Terré, F, *Droit civil: les obligations*, 1980, Paris: Dalloz, 3rd edn, §176, at 195.

7  Ghestin, J, *La notion d'erreur dans le droit positif actuel* (thèse), 1963, Paris, §526, 489.

8  Vivien, G, 'De l'erreur déterminante et substantielle' (1992) 91 Rev trim drt civ 305 at 306.

9  See, eg, Demolombe, C, *Cours de Code Napoléon*, 1872, Paris: Dalloz, 5th edn, §103; E. Gaudemet, *Théorie générale des obligations*, 1937, Paris: Sirey, 57.

10 For a fuller version of this argument, see my: 'Objectivisme et consensualisme dans le droit français de l'erreur dans les conventions' (2005) XXX Revue de la Recherche Juridique 661.

that is at odds with French judicial practice on mistakes in assumption. Whereas the majority of French authors cling to a view that is very close to the subjective end of our spectrum, judicial practice on mistake suggests one that is closer to the middle of this spectrum.

### English law

As the reader will most likely be familiar with the English law of contract, I will be even briefer here. In many ways, the English understanding of contract is the exact opposite of the French. Since Blackburn J's famous *obiter dictum* in *Smith v Hughes*,[11] English courts have often reaffirmed the objective understanding of contract, whereby contracts are formed through words and actions, not private thoughts. It is only relatively recently in English law that mistakes in assumption came to be recognised as grounds for voiding otherwise valid contracts.[12] Early on, the only contractual mistakes deemed sufficiently serious to constitute such a ground were those known at Roman law as cases of *res sua* and *res extincta*. In cases of *res sua*, the thing which a party purported to acquire through the contract already belonged to her; in cases of *res extincta*, the thing had ceased to exist by the time that the contract was formed. As both the French and the Germans long realised, these cases have more to do with a lack of consideration than with a lack of consent proper. At French and German law, they are respectively treated as cases of 'non-existent contractual object' and cases of 'contractual impossibility'.

It nonetheless is by analogy to cases of *res sua* and *res extincta*, that an error *in substantia* first came to be considered as a possible ground for voiding a contract at English law as in *Bell v Lever Brothers Ltd*.[13] It is still debated to this day whether the effect of that case was to open or close the door to claims of error *in substantia* at English law.[14] On the one hand, the law lords suggested that such a claim was theoretically possible, but on the other hand they formulated a definition of 'substance' that is so strict as to effectively reduce cases of error *in substantia* to cases involving non-existent contractual objects.[15] If *Bell* marks an overture towards a subjective theory of contract, therefore, it is a very hesitant one at best. Indeed, the fact that the justification for the theoretical possibility of claims of error *in substantia* is offered in tandem with an argument in terms of risk allocation between the two parties

---

11 'If whatever a man's real intention may be, he so conducts himself that a reasonable man would believe that he was assenting to the terms proposed by the other party, and that other party upon that belief enters into the contract with him, the man thus conducting himself would be equally bound as if he had intended to agree to the other party's terms', Blackburn J at 607.
12 *Bell v Lever Brothers Ltd* [1932] AC 161 (HL).      13 Ibid.
14 Cheshire, GH, and Fifoot, C, *Law of Contract*, 3rd edn, 1952, London: Butterworth, 179–180.
15 At 218.

(very much in line with the warranty condition of French law) is further ammunition to the many commentators[16] who have insisted that *Bell* has done little, if anything, to modify the traditional, objective understanding of contract.

Nonetheless, English law has at times shown signs of a willingness to move towards the subjective end of the spectrum. Cases in equity, such as *non est factum* cases, clearly involve the courts looking to the parties' subjective intentions.[17] In *Solle v Butcher*,[18] moreover, Lord Denning invoked a line of cases that, he argued, established an equitable doctrine of mistake in order to set aside a lease concluded in the mistaken belief that rent-control legislation did not apply. Lord Denning went as far as to suggest that *Smith v Hughes* might have been decided differently had it been considered in equity. Here again, however, the subjectivist pull of these developments should not be exaggerated. For one, the binding force of *Solle* was seriously called into question in the recent case of *Great Peace Shipping Ltd v Tsavliris*.[19] But even if *Solle* were to remain good law, the case also confirms that relief would never even be considered in cases involving unilateral mistake.[20]

The understanding of contract suggested by the English law of mistake in assumptions thus appears to be the mirror opposite of French law. Whereas French jurists only reluctantly acknowledge the objective dimension of contract which emerges from French judicial practice, English jurists cling to a view of contract that is more objective than judicial practice suggests.

## German law

In contrast to both French and English law the understanding of contract that emerges from the German law of mistake in assumptions – mistake in motive – is not characterised by a preference for one end of the spectrum, and a reluctant movement towards the other end. Rather, it can be described as a happy marriage of equal doses of subjective and objective interacting with one another.[21] For the importance of both intention and declaration in contract formation has never been lost on the Germans. The relative importance of these two elements was debated in the German legal literature long before the German civil code was enacted, and the conscious efforts by the drafters of this code to steer a middle course between pure subjectivism and pure

---

16  See, eg, Stoljar, SJ, 'A New Approach to Mistake in Contract' (1965) 28 Mod L Rev 265 at 278–9; Tylor, T, 'General Theory of Mistake in the Formation of Contract' (1948) 11 Mod L Rev 257 at 263–64.

17  *Saunders v Anglia Building Society (Gallie v Lee)* [1971] AC 1004 (HL), per Lord Pearson, at 1013.

18  [1950] 1 KB 671.        19  [2002] EWJ No 4397.

20  *Riverlake Properties, Ltd v Paul* [1975] 1 Ch 113 (CA 1974).

21  See generally: Ferrand, F, *Droit privé allemand*, 1997, Paris: Dalloz; Witz, op cit.

objectivism are very much apparent in the code's treatment of contractual mistake.

While in principle there is no relief for mistake in motive under the BGB, s 119(2), an exception is made in cases where the error concerns 'such characteristics of a thing or a person as are considered essential in business practice'. Applying this test, the oats being old might arguably be considered 'essential' provided that the relevant 'business practice' here is described as a horse breeder buying food for his breed, and not just any sale of oats, particularly not a sale of oats by sample. Section 119 of the BGB thus, on the one hand, yields to subjectivism by allowing for the voiding of contracts in certain cases of mistake in the motive for contracting but, on the other hand, applies an objective test for purpose of assessing the essential or non-essential character of the mistake in these cases.

What is more, in all cases where the mistaken party decides to take advantage of s 119 in order to have the contract set aside, he is then under an obligation to compensate anyone who suffers damage as a result of the loss of the contract; compensation is payable to the other party to the contract or to a third party, so long as that party's loss is suffered in good faith. The amount of the compensation, however, is strictly capped by the amount of this party's reliance interest under s 122 of the code.

Here again the dialectic subjective/objective understanding of contract is apparent. A party is legally responsible from the moment from which she can objectively be construed as having made a declaration of contractual intention, regardless of whether the objective declaration turns out to be supported by a genuine subjective intention. Where it is found that the declaration was supported by intention, ordinary contractual liability is imposed, and the non-breaching party's expectation interest is protected. Where it is instead found that the declaration was not supported by the requisite intention, only the reliance interest of the non-breaching party is protected. This is the compromise position prescribed by the BGB and it is also more or less the position which German courts have followed since this Code's enactment.[22]

This brief survey thus reveals that while the French, English, and German judicial practices on mistake in assumptions suggest understandings of contract that all sit somewhere around the middle of the objective/subjective spectrum, French, English, and German doctrinal perceptions of contract vary greatly. Whereas French jurists cling to the belief that their law understands contract as primarily subjective, and correspondingly tend to dismiss the objective dimension of it that emerges from judicial practice, English jurists like to believe that their law understands contracts objectively, and correspondingly tend to dismiss its subjective dimension. As for German

---

22  Ewald, W, above n 1 at 2086.

jurists, they have been content to view contract for what it is in judicial practice, that is, as a dialectic combination of subjective and objective.

In order to explain these different perceptions of contract by French, English, and German jurists it is necessary to examine the larger intellectual contexts that bred French, English, and German private law.

## Intellectual contexts of French, German, and English private law

### French context

The Napoleonic Code is a child of the French Revolution and the philosophical rationalism that animated it.[23] Rousseau and the School of Natural Law had taught that the world was made up of two, hierarchically ordered, watertight compartments: first, the compartment of ideas – pure, aspirationally perfect, since inherently subservient to Reason; second, the compartment of facts – contingent, messy, and unruly facts. Ideas were seen as logically prior, and qualitatively superior, to facts; they would accordingly be made to rule over facts, to rein them in. A better world, it was thought, would be a world in which facts consistent with ideas had been preserved, and from which disobedient facts had been eliminated. Consistently with this view of the relation of facts to ideas, French revolutionaries undertook to erase France's feudal past, to rid it of all existing institutions, and to start afresh. Their aim was to reinvent France as a democratic, republican state; it would be one that would speak to all citizens equally, regardless of class, privilege, or money; one that would abstract from the citizens' material, variable, contingent circumstances, and address them as essentially free and equal rational beings.

Law and all political institutions accordingly had to be created out of thin air through a Cartesian process of rational deduction from first principles. The resulting intellectual edifice would have to be flawlessly coherent, since it would be grounded in logic alone. This entailed, *inter alia*, that the principles constituting this edifice could present no exceptions. Principles could only be right or wrong, they could not be both. Right principles would be included, wrong ones would be excluded. And logic demanded further that, once included as being right, principles could not be subsequently qualified by exceptions, for that would have suggested that the principles were not entirely right.

For this reason, the judiciary (a remnant of French feudalism) was highly

---

23 See generally: Wieacker, F, *A History of Private Law in Europe*, 2003, Oxford: Clarendon Press; Watson, A, *The Making of the Civil Law*, 1981, Cambridge: Harvard University Press; Merryman, JH, *The Civil Law Tradition*, 1985, Stanford, California: Stanford University Press.

mistrusted. Scholars, on the other hand, were revered, for their only task consisted of revelling in unadulterated rational reasoning, sheltered as they were from the distorting effects which contact with the real world might have had on their thinking.

This also explained the French legal scholars' perception of contract as subjective. 'Consent' as a pure idea in the legal actor's mind is in their view necessarily juridically prior and superior to the materialisation of this idea through words and actions. Put simply, subjective contract is consistent with the primacy of ideas over facts.

### German context

What happened to make German law take such a different course from French law? Like France, Germany embraced the civil law tradition, but its legal system was codified a century after the French. Many intellectual developments occurred in the intervening period.[24] On the philosophical front, Immanuel Kant fundamentally challenged the dualistic account of the relation of facts to ideas put forward by the rationalists.[25] Kant was the first scholar to seriously question the wisdom of fact-free reasoning, of reasoning based exclusively on formal logic. He was the first to attempt to bridge the rationalistic fact/idea divide; to find some kind of middle course between pure idealism and pure empiricism, to work dialectically between facts and ideas and to take facts seriously. All this he did most prominently in his theory of knowledge which he later transposed into law.[26] At Hegel's hands, the bridging of facts and ideas undertaken by Kant became synthesis proper.[27] In summary, by the end of the nineteenth century, when the German Civil Code was being drafted, the philosophical agenda had changed dramatically. The aim was no longer to preserve the purity of theory by relegating resistant facts to the status of 'exceptions', for there were no longer 'principles' and 'exceptions'. The philosopher's venture was now to find some form of equilibrium between facts and ideas, one that would treat them as interacting equals.

As Germany was a very scholarly society, the dialectic thought-structure of German idealism made its way into all domains of social life: culture, politics and literature, as well as law and legal theory. The issues that so troubled the German idealists resonated through the writings of Savigny, unquestionably the most important German legal scholar of all times and the founder of the

24 See generally: Wieacker, F, op cit; Ewald, W, above n 1.
25 Kant, I, *Groundwork for the Metaphysics of Morals*, Ellington, WJ, trans, Indianapolis, Hackett Publishing, 1981.
26 Kant, I, 'Doctrine of Right', Part I of *The Metaphysics of Morals*, Gregor, M (ed), 1991, Cambridge: New York; Cambridge University Press.
27 Hegel, GWF, *Philosophy of Right*, Knox, TM, trans, 1967, Oxford: Oxford University Press.

famous Historical School. His influence upon German private law has been monumental,[28] and the fact/idea, history/reason, Germanist/Romanist, and objective/subjective dualities indeed permeate German private law to this day. On the institutional front this is reflected in Germans being much more deferential than the French towards judicial practice, and German law being generally less strictly compartmentalised than French law. In particular, the private/public distinction being more elusive; German judges have achieved a much greater level of integration between German private and public law than French private and public law will ever have.

This may help explain why it is that German jurists, unlike their French counterparts, have always self-consciously endorsed the dialectic subjective/ objective understanding of contract suggested in the judicial practice on mistake in assumptions – an understanding of contract that sits somewhere in the middle of the subjective/objective spectrum.

## English context

English law originated from a dramatically different context. As we just saw, French and German law both emerged from heavily intellectual contexts. English law in contrast was bred by a context that was altogether atheoretical. The story is well known.[29] Like ancient Roman law, early English law was highly formalistic. And whereas in other Western European territories Roman law was (due to the efforts of continental scholars) reborn in the form of an intellectual tradition – the *Ius Commune* – this tradition never made its way across the English Channel. By the time that Roman law began its second life, England indeed was already politically unified, and English common law firmly entrenched as an administrative and procedural structure so tight as to be almost entirely impermeable to outside ideas. What is more, the system was applied by individuals who were not particularly inclined towards abstract forms of reasoning. Laypeople at first, later to be replaced by the famous 'counters', whose only claim to their lofty professional positions lay in their fine elocutionary skills, all shared a clear preference for concrete facts over abstract ideas.[30]

In its early days English law was nothing but institutions, techniques, strategies – a succession of procedural frameworks filled with custom, tradition and history. Early English law was entirely made up of facts. Ideas – explicit

---

28 See generally: Kantorowicz, H, 'Savigny and the Historical School of Law' (1937) 53 LQ Rev 326.
29 See generally: Milsom, SFC, *Historical Foundations of the Common Law*, London; Boston: Butterworths, 2nd edn, 1981; Pollock, F, Sir and Maitland, FW, *The History of England before the Time of Edward I*, Vol I, 2nd edn, 1968, London: Cambridge University Press.
30 Postema, G, 'Classical Common Law Jurisprudence (Part I)' (2002) 2 OU Comm LJ 155 at 160–61.

and openly acknowledged ideas – played no role in its early development. Only later on, with the advent of the Chancery, did explicit ideas begin to play a role in the development of English law. The Chancellor was a cleric, schooled and versed in continental writings, and the more flexible procedure of the Chancery had been deliberately designed to make room for ideas. In time, rules and principles of substantive law began to emerge from the common law as well, but this process was far from deliberate or even conscious; these rules and principles had to seep out from beneath the maze of forms of actions and their rigid procedural apparatus.[31]

In this context it is hardly surprising that English lawyers would traditionally have preferred to see contract as concrete words and actions, rather than as abstract ideas. In the view of these lawyers, only objective, material manifestations of intention were externally observable, and thus recognisable in legal practice. So it is that English lawyers have resisted the pull of equity away from the objective end of the spectrum towards some point closer to the middle.

### Conclusion

This discussion shows that although the understandings of contract suggested by French, English, and German judicial practice on mistake in assumptions is in the final analysis similar, being somewhere in the middle of the subjective/objective spectrum, this similarity belies a significant difference in the jurists' perceptions of contract, consistent with the different contexts which fostered the emergence of their national law. Whereas French and English jurists like to think of contract as being respectively purely subjective and purely objective, and resist the movement towards the middle of the spectrum forced upon them by judicial decision-making, German jurists are happy to see contract as sitting in that middle point. This is consistent with French law having grown out of the Age of Reason, German law being a child of German idealism, and English law having emerged from a strongly anti-intellectual environment.

My aim has been to underscore the connection between law and its larger intellectual environment. To the extent that the ideals, attitudes, and perceptions of jurists can be considered a part of 'law', this aim appears to be fulfilled. Yet it could be argued that the upshot of this contribution is exactly the opposite; for it also stands for the proposition that legal practice will ultimately drive law to where it is meant to be (whatever that means) regardless of the jurists' own agenda. To that extent, my conclusions arguably contradict the very thesis which I had set out to defend.

---

31  As Maine famously explained, they were 'secreted in the interstices of procedure'. Maine, HS, 1901, *Dissertations on Early Law and Custom*, London: Murray, 389.

Part IV

# Certainty and discretion in property, equity and unjust enrichment

# Chapter 8

# Estoppel, discretion and the nature of the estoppel equity

*Elizabeth Cooke**

## Introduction

The subject of this chapter is the inchoate equity in estoppel, topical as it is because of the prominence and new status given to it by s 116 of the Land Registration Act 2002, which states:

> It is hereby declared for the avoidance of doubt that, in relation to registered land, ... an equity by estoppel ... has effect from the time the equity arises as an interest capable of binding successors in title (subject to the rules about the effect of dispositions on priority).

In order to get a clear view of the equity by estoppel, and to make any assessment of the effect of s 116, we have to begin one step away, by looking at the remedial discretion in estoppel; and that is indeed only one step away because, as will be seen, the fact that estoppel gives rise to an 'equity' is the result of the existence of that remedial discretion.

### Decisions in estoppel: creation not discovery

It has been said that '[t]he court has a very wide discretion in satisfying an equity arising under the doctrine of proprietary estoppel'.[1] There has been

---

* Professor of Law, University of Reading. When this paper was written, I benefited enormously from having had sight of Nick Hopkins' paper before completing my work. The paper appears here as it was written in 2004, and does not take account of a number of fascinating estoppel cases and important academic writings on the subject which have appeared since that date.
1 *Campbell v Griffin* [2001] EWCA Civ 990, per Walker, Robert LJ at [36].

considerable debate as to how that discretion is normally exercised,[2] but very little doubt that it exists.[3]

Discretion is exercised in the law of proprietary estoppel[4] as follows: where A is the owner of land, and assures B that B will be able to live there, or lets B build a garage there on the assumption that it is B's own (or whatever) and B acts to his detriment in reliance on that assurance, then A will be estopped from going back on his assurance, because it is unconscionable for him to do so.[5] The court, on B's application, will decide how to 'satisfy the equity'.[6] The 'equity' is B's right to relief, which arises after the detriment is incurred and once it becomes unconscionable for the defendant to go back on his assurance;[7] and the court will satisfy the equity on the basis of its own view as to what would be the fair way to do so. Normally, and despite the rhetoric of the need to award 'the minimum equity to do justice',[8] the court's decision takes the form of awarding B whatever interest, proprietary or otherwise, he was

2   Thompson, MP, 'From Representation to Expectation: Estoppel as a Cause of Action', [1983] CLJ 257; Davis, C, 'Estoppel: An Adequate Substitute for Part Performance?' (1993) 13 OxJLS 99; Finn, PD, Equitable Estoppel' in Finn, PD (ed.), *Essays in Equity*, 1985, Sydney: The Law Book Co, at 59; Smith, R, 'How Proprietary is Proprietary estoppel?' in Rose (ed.), *Consensus Ad Idem*, 1996, London: Sweet and Maxwell; Gardner, S, 'The Remedial Discretion in Proprietary Estoppel' (1999) 115 LQR 438; Cooke, E, 'Estoppel and the Propection of Expectations' (1997) 17 LS 258; Robertson, A, 'Reliance and Expectation in Estoppel Remedies' [1998] LS 360; Wright, D, 'Giumelli, Estoppel and the new law of remedies' [1999] CLJ 476; Robertson, A, 'The Statute of Frauds, equitable estoppel and the Need for "Something More" ' [2003] 19 JCL 173; F. Burns, '*Giumelli v Giumelli* Revisited: Equitable Estoppel, the Remedial Constructive trust and Discretionary Remedialism' (2001) 22 Adelaide Law Review 123; Jensen, D, 'In Defence of the Reliance Theory of Equitable Estoppel' (2001) 22 Adelaide Law Review 157.

3   Moriarty, S, 'Licences and Land Law: Legal Principles and Public Policies' (1984) 100 LQR 376; Edelman, J, 'Remedial Certainty or Remedial Discretion in Estoppel after *Giumelli*' (1999) 15 JCL 179; McFarlane, B, in 'Proprietary Estoppel and Third Parties after the Land Registration Act 2002', [2003] CLJ 661, where he argues for a 'new model' of proprietary estoppel which would assimilate estoppel to the common intention constructive trust.

4   The label is used to denote cases where estoppel is used as a cause of action; and currently in England and Wales that encompasses only claims to an interest in land. The question whether or not estoppel should be a cause of action in a wider context is not discussed in this chapter.

5   This is an adaptation of the summary of the doctrine offered by the Law Commission for England and Wales in *Land Registration for the Twenty-First Century: a Consultative Document*, Law Com No 254 London: The Stationery Office, (1998) 'Law Com 254'.

6   *Crabb v Arun DC* [1976] 1 Ch 179, CA, per Scarman LJ at 193: 'the court has . . . to answer three questions. First, is there an equity established? Secondly, what is the extent of the equity, if one is established? And, thirdly, what is the relief appropriate to satisfy the equity?'

7   Law Com 254, at 3.36, referring to *Lim v Ang* [1992] 1 WLR 113, 118. As Nick Hopkins explains in his chapter, it is difficult to be precise about when the equity comes into being.

8   The oft-quoted dictum of Scarman LJ in *Crabb v Arun DC* [1976] 1 Ch 179, CA, at 198; it is not always pointed out that Scarman LJ said this while justifying an award that matched the claimant's expectation.

led to expect to get. This is generally agreed to be the usual exercise of the discretion both in England and in Australia.[9] Thus B might get the easement he was promised;[10] or an order might be made that the property be conveyed to him, thus giving him the home which he had been told was to be his, or partly his;[11] or be given the right to stay there for life as a licensee,[12] or the monetary equivalent of such a right of occupation.[13]

This is the courts' usual, but not invariable, choice; expectation relief is not invariably awarded. Instances of relief that did not match expectation, in the English cases, used to be rare;[14] but in a series of recent decisions less than the expectation measure of relief has been awarded, for a variety of reasons,[15] and with a renewed stress on the need for proportionality between detriment and remedy.[16]

Whatever the substance of the decision, it is important to note the role

---

9 See the references at nn 2 and 3 above.

10 *Crabb v Arun District Council* [1976] Ch 179.

11 *Pascoe v Turner* [1979] 1 WLR 431; *Gillett v Holt* [2001] Ch 210. Hayton, D, in 'Equitable Rights of Cohabitees' [1990] Conv. 370, observes that the court may order that A must hold the home on constructive trust for B and himself, perhaps in equal shares, and states that this can be seen as the creation of a remedial constructive trust; but the trust arises at the point of the court's decision, and is not retrospective, so that it does not excite the controversy associated with that term in recent debate; see n 36 below. Unfortunately, it is not possible to find an English estoppel decision where precisely this happens, simply because the courts can clearly see the difficulty in ordering two people, who *ex hypothesi* have fallen out, to share a home: *Dodsworth v Dodsworth* (1973) 228 EG 1115. Hayton cites *Muchinski v Dodds* [1985] 160 CLR 583, which may be close to what Hayton envisages, but of course the property was going to be sold in that case, and in any event the decision does not seem to be based on estoppel.

12 *Williams v Staite* [1979] Ch 291; *Maharaj v Chand* [1986] AC 898.

13 *Baker v Baker* [1993] 2 FLR 247.

14 They were collected in Cooke, E, 'Estoppel and the protection of expectations', (1997) 17 LS 258. It is important to appreciate just how few such decisions there had been at that date; thus the four decisions there cited (*Unity Joint Stock Mutual Banking Association v King* (1858) 25 Beav 72; *Hussey v Palmer* [1972] 1 WLR 1286; *Dodsworth v Dodsworth* (1973) 228 EG 1115; *Cushley v Seale* 28 October 1986) are the only ones the writer could find. It is wholly misleading to cite them as *examples*.

15 Prominent recent decisions of this nature are *Sledmore v Dalby* (1996) 72 P & CR 196; *Gillett v Holt* [2001] Ch 210; *Campbell v Griffin* [2001] EWCA Civ 990; *Jennings v Rice* [2003] 1 P & CR 8; *Ottey v Grundy* [2003] EWCA Civ 1176, as to which see Thompson, MP, 'Estoppel and proportionality' [2004] Conv. 137. The various instances are discussed, and the important roles of unconscionability and proportionality explored, in Nick Hopkins' chapter.

16 See in particular *Jennings v Rice* [2003] 1 P & CR 8, per Aldous LJ at 109; Robert Walker LJ, at [50], said: '. . . there is a category of case in which the benefactor and the claimant have reached a mutual understanding which . . . does not amount to a contract. . . . In such a case the court's *natural response* is to fulfil the claimant's expectations. But if the claimant's expectations are uncertain, or extravagant, or out of all proportion to the detriment which the claimant has suffered, the court can and should recognise that the claimant's equity should be satisfied in another (and generally more limited) way' (emphasis added).

played by the court's discretion. It is the judge's, or judges', decision that brings the claimant's right into being. Whatever he is awarded – fee simple, equitable interest, compensation – did not exist, and therefore was not his, immediately before the court's decision. The court's own choice brings the remedy into being, even though we can predict with reasonable accuracy (because of the general preference for expectation-based awards) what that remedy will be. 'It is only by the judge's order . . . that the inchoate rights created by proprietary estoppel have crystallised into a defined proprietary interest'.[17] Nick Hopkins' chapter[18] has discussed the complexity of 'unconscionability' within estoppel, and it is upon this complex of moral and practical factors that discretion operates, evaluating and assessing the remedy needed.

With this we must contrast what is supposed to happen in the common intention constructive trust. English law insists that this trust is institutional, not remedial; arising from the facts themselves (when the parties have agreed to share the beneficial ownership of a house, for example)[19] and not created by the court's discretion. Thus the facts are as above,[20] but instead of a representation by A to B, A and B have an agreement or common intention,[21] on which B subsequently acts to his detriment. When A seeks to renege on the agreement, denying the rights B was to obtain, the court will declare that the facts gave rise to a beneficial interest in B at the point when he relied on the agreement. At that point, he acquired the equitable fee simple in the garage land, or a share in the family home, or whatever. The scope for discretion is therefore limited, because the court is discovering B's interest, not deciding what it is; and the decision is not supposed to be the cause of the rights that emerge from it.[22] Between its arising

---

17  *Habermann v Koehler* [2000] EGCS 125 at [23]. See also *Bawden v Bawden* 7 November 1997, CA, per Robert Walker LJ: 'I cannot accept that . . . that once the factual basis for some proprietary estoppel is put in place that a right of enjoyment for life is more or less automatically established. On the contrary, that ignores the court's insistence on it being the minimum equity that is to be satisfied and on the need for the court to adopt a flexible approach.'
18  'Unconscionability, Constructive Trusts and Estoppel'.
19  *Gissing v Gissing* [1971] AC 886; *Grant v Edwards* [1986] Ch 638; *Midland Bank plc v Cooke* [1995] 4 All ER 562.
20  Text at n 5.
21  Expressed in words; or inferred from a direct contribution to the purchase price of the house: *Lloyds Bank plc v Rosset* [1991] 1 AC 107. The difficulties in analysing some of these situations as agreements are exposed by Gardner, Simon in 'Rethinking Family Property' (1993) 109 LQR 263.
22  Cf the points made on causation and timing in Birks, P, 'The End of the Remedial Constructive Trust' [1998] Trust Law International 202 at 203; and O'Connor, P, 'Happy Partners or Strange Bedfellows: the Blending of Remedial and Institutional Features in the Evolving Constructive Trust' (1996) 20 Melbourne University Law Review 735 at 738.

and its 'discovery' by the court, B's interest may of course have bound a third party.[23]

However, as is well known, the cases are contradictory. There is authority for the proposition just rejected by this rather traditional account, namely that the facts giving rise to the proprietary estoppel claim give rise to a full property right in B;[24] such cases assert that the claimant's right predates the litigation, and is there for the court to discover, not to create. The effect of this would be to assimilate proprietary estoppel to the institutional constructive trust. Unfortunately, many of the cases that make up this body of authority were decided at a stage when licences were regarded as proprietary interests. Any case decided at that era must be treated with great caution because in such cases the claimant, *ex hypothesi* and as part of the facts giving rise to the cause of action in estoppel, had a proprietary right antedating the court's decision. Perhaps the strongest authority is *Re Sharpe*[25], where there was an overwhelming need to protect the claimant against the representor's trustee in bankruptcy.

The authorities for the view that estoppel creates a fully-fledged proprietary interest before the court's decision are not especially strong, but sufficient to create a significant contradiction within the law.[26] Which view is correct? Is there discretion, and therefore an inchoate equity? Or does the claimant's interest arise automatically, to be discovered later by the court? The authorities are contradictory. It is not hard to see why the contradictions arise, given the closely linked factual basis of proprietary estoppel, on the one hand, and the constructive trust, on the other.[27] The discretionary analysis is preferred here; it appears to accord most closely with what the courts declare they are doing,[28] and with recent trends in the English cases.[29] And the discretion, provided it is exercised in a well-controlled manner,[30] is valuable. It is

---

23  This was the effect the claimant wanted in *Midland Bank v Dobson* [1986] 1 FLR 171 and in *Lloyds Bank plc v Rosset* [1989] Ch 350.

24  Perhaps *Unity Joint Stock Mutual Banking Association v King* (1858) 25 Beav 72; *Pennine Raceway v Kirklees MBC* [1983] QB 382. The latter treats a licence as a proprietary interest, and would probably be decided quite differently today.

25  [1980] 1 WLR 219. *Voyce v Voyce* (1991) 62 P & CR 290 may also support this view, but see below, text at n 73. *Birmingham Midshires Mortgage Services Ltd v Sabherwal* 17 December 1999, CA, is also supportive; but the difference between estoppel and a constructive trust was not explored in the case, the *ratio* being simply that by whichever means the claimant's right, if any, had arisen, it could be overreached.

26  Another difficulty is that some cases, while capable of being read as consistent with this view, may equally be saying, at most, that the inchoate equity has a proprietary effect: *Lloyd v Dugdale* [2002] 2 P & CR 13; *Habermann v Koehler* (1996) 73 P & CR 515; *Singh v Sandhu* 4th May 1995, CA. Hopkins in his chapter notes the weakness of the authorities in this context, at n 171.

27  See text at n 50 below.        28  See nn 1 and 6 above.        29  N 15 above.

30  Text at n 40 below.

worth looking back at the debate between David Hayton and Patricia Ferguson a few years ago.[31] They disagreed, essentially, as to whether or not institutional constructive trusts should be assimilated to the estoppel model, whereby property rights do not come into being except as a result of the court's decision; but there was no disagreement between them – they treated the point as beyond question – that the remedial process in estoppel is discretionary, and that the court creates rights rather than discovering them. Hayton's enthusiasm for the assimilation of constructive trusts with estoppel arose from his wish to bring into common intention constructive trusts the overt remedial discretion found in proprietary estoppel – even though that must mean that the courts would no longer be discovering pre-existing rights in the trust cases, so that the potential for protecting claimants from third parties must therefore be limited. As we shall see, English jurisprudence has stood firm, at least in theory, on the institutional rather than remedial nature of common intention constructive trusts; but in the estoppel cases the courts have found, and the legislature has now recognised, a way of both having the discretionary cake and eating an effect upon third parties.

### The exercise of discretion in estoppel

Before we look at that particular manoeuvre, it is useful to situate this discretion on the spectrum of discretionary decision-making exercised by the courts, for the word 'discretion' has a very wide scope.

The first thing to say is that this is a 'foreground' rather than a 'background' discretion. The terms are used in Simon Gardner's analysis,[32] and he explains that whereas there is a background discretion throughout the judge's task, 'necessarily embedded in . . . the business of determining the relevant facts, and interpreting the terms of the applicable rule',[33] including such broad terms as 'reasonableness', 'estoppel features the less endemic "foreground" kind of discretion which is present when the law, not even appearing to assert a firm standard, overtly invites and requires the judge to make a personal choice'.[34] That element of personal choice means that a value judgement is invited, and that the judge's own views have an influence.[35]

---

31  Hayton, D, 'Equitable Rights of Cohabitees', [1990] Conv. 370; Ferguson, P, 'Constructive Trusts – A Note of Caution', (1993) 109 LQR 114; Hayton, D, 'Constructive Trusts of Homes – A Bold Approach', (1993) 109 LQR 485. See also Evans, PT 'Choosing the Right Estoppel' [1988] Conv. 346 at 351.
32  Above, n 2.      33  Ibid 442.
34  Ibid 442. Gardner refers to Hawkins, K, *The Uses of Discretion*, 1992, Oxford: Clarendon Press.
35  Thus in the exercise of discretion upon the facts giving rise to estoppel, it is not simply the case that the judge is having a look at those facts alone, and deciding that they give rise to a property right; the judge's own views, practical and moral, are part of the ingredients that go

To that we must immediately add that the exercise of this foreground discretion in estoppel is not entirely untrammelled. English law, at any rate, has not evolved any formal rules about how the claimant's estoppel equity is to be satisfied, but, as has been said, the courts usually (by which is meant far more often than not) meet the claimant's expectation. Any mention of remedial discretion conjures up the current debate about discretion in the context of the constructive trust;[36] and it has to be stressed that in the English law of estoppel – and, so far as this writer can see, Australian – there is no question of the courts having a completely open, free choice between a range of remedies so that none is more likely or more predictable than any other.[37] The courts have a foreground discretion but exercise it within self-imposed constraints, showing a clear preference for one particular kind of remedy, enabling us to predict, within reason, what the outcome will be[38] and giving the claimant a degree of control over the outcome.[39] Fiona Burns has called this a 'moderate discretionary remedialism',[40] where the court is constrained by precedent and the claimant's own expectations and preference rather than constructing 'an obligation or a remedial response *de novo*'.[41]

There are examples of this type of discretion elsewhere in the law. An interesting parallel, in English law, is the discretion used in financial provision on divorce, through the Matrimonial Causes Act 1973. This gives the court an apparently very broad foreground discretion to award financial provision,

into the decision making. Thus the writer ventures to disagree with Peter Birks' view, expressed in the context of the remedial constructive trust, that a discretionary decision cannot generate a conclusion which does not arise automatically from the bare facts themselves: Birks, P, 'The end of the common intention constructive trust', (1998) 12 Trust Law International, 202 at 206. His view would entail that there is no such thing as 'foreground' discretion.

36  The current literature on this is so vast that one can only cite a sample: Wright, D, *The Remedial Constructive Trust*, 1998, Sydney: Butterworths; Birks, P's, review of Wright's book, (1999) 115 LQR 681 and Burns, F's, review of the same, (2000) 29 WALR 143; Birks, P, op cit n 35 above; Evans, S, 'Defending Discretionary Remedialism' (2001) 23 Sydney Law Review 463; Wright, D 'Giumelli, Estoppel and the New Law of Remedies' [1999] CLJ 476.

37  The account of remedies given in McGhee, J's, *Snell's Equity*, 30th edn 2002, London: Sweet and Maxwell at 641–2 suggests that the discretion is untrammelled: 'If the equity is established, effect is given to it in whatever is the most appropriate way taking into account all relevant circumstances including the conduct of the parties.' The difficulty with this position is apparent when it is seen that the passage in *Snell's Equity* lists the range of remedies available but neglects to mention the correlation between expectation and remedy in virtually every case.

38  This meets the concern about uncertainty; Edelman, J, n 3 above.

39  Because one major reason why the reliance rather than the expectation measure of relief has been given has been the claimant's own choice: *Unity Joint Stock Mutual Banking Association v King* (1858) 25 Beav 72, *Hussey v Palmer* [1972] 1 WLR 1286.

40  F. Burns, '*Giumelli v Giumelli* revisited: Equitable Estoppel, the Constructive Trust and Discretionary Remedialism', (2001) 22 Adelaide Law Review 123 at 154.

41  Ibid.

giving no guidelines at all as to how or to what end that discretion is to be exercised (save by prescribing a 'menu' of orders; the court is not told how to choose between them). Nevertheless, financial provision awards have been very predictable indeed because the courts have moderated their discretion by imposing upon themselves a norm which does not derive from the statute. Thus, until recently awards could be predicted by the 'reasonable requirements' test. When pressure upon that test became too great – i.e., when the judges came to appreciate the need to use a standard that did not involve discrimination against those who care for children – the standard was changed, in *White v White*,[42] to the 'yardstick of equality'. The discretion remains, but still we have predictability.

### Digression: why the preference for expectation-based relief?

It is difficult to move away from this description of the remedial discretion in estoppel without commenting, briefly, on the question *why* the courts have chosen to moderate their discretion in this particular way; that is, why is there such a strong preference for expectation-based rather than reliance-based relief?[43] There has been a huge amount of debate about this,[44] and there is no knock-down argument in either direction. The argument that the maintenance of a principle of reliance-based relief in estoppel (in order to keep distinct the territories of estoppel and contract) is extremely persuasive in principle. Perhaps the most interesting ingredient in the debate in the last few years is the fact that *even after* the authoritative encouragement given to reliance-based relief in *Waltons Stores (Interstate) Ltd v Maher*[45] and *Commonwealth v Verwayen*,[46] the Australian courts have chosen, with remarkable consistency, to award expectation-based relief. These landmark decisions could have kick-started a change, and therefore the preference cannot be ascribed largely to conservatism.[47] Andrew Robertson has observed that very often, reliance loss in estoppel cannot be compensated without meeting the expectation;[48] difficulties in calculation may otherwise be insuperable. This is particularly so in view of the unique nature of land, its permanence, and its

---

42 [2000] 3 WLR 1571, HL.

43 This is not the place for a more general discussion of the virtues of a moderated, rather than an entirely untrammelled, foreground discretion, or indeed of foreground discretion versus rule-based decision-making. See the extensive literature of which n 36 above represents only a sample.

44 See the literature at n 2 above, and Neyers, J, 'Towards a Coherent Theory of Estoppel' (2003) Journal of Obligations and Remedies 25.

45 (1988) 164 CLR 387.        46  (1990) 170 CLR 394.

47 My own account of the problem has veered in this direction. Cooke, E, *The Modern Law of Estoppel*, 2000, Oxford: Oxford University Press, 165–169.

48 Robertson, A, op cit, n 2 above and 'Satisfying the Minimum Equity: Equitable Estoppel Remedies after *Verwayen*', (1996) Melbourne University Law Review 805.

development and investment potential, and of the especially unique nature of the family home. The reliance loss in estoppel may consist in lost opportunity (for example, to invest in other property); compensating accrued loss may truly be no compensation at all for the loss of an expectation.

Another factor that may be important is the overlap between proprietary estoppel and the common intention constructive trust. It is clear, at least in the English cases dealing with family property, that the same facts may very easily give rise to both causes of action – they just need to be described a little differently for each.

Consider the assurance given by the defendant to the claimant in *Hammond v Mitchell*.[49] This was a typical home-sharing case where a girlfriend came to live with her partner in his house. His words were: 'Don't worry about the future because when we are married it will be half yours anyway and I'll always look after you and the boy.'[50] The case was pleaded and decided as one of common intention constructive trust; but this was no more obviously an agreement, supporting the trust argument, than an assurance/representation which would support the estoppel model. Either model could have been used. It could indeed be disastrous if the common intention constructive trust gives, as it must by definition, the expectation measure of relief, whereas estoppel gives only the reliance measure. This in itself provides a strong incentive for the courts to continue giving expectation-based relief in estoppel; it is hardly surprising that it is in the context of this sort of case that there have been dicta to the effect that the two doctrines are identical, and that it is in this context that estoppel claims have slithered into the constructive trust category, with the courts asserting the close similarity of the two doctrines.[51]

Equally, it is not surprising that the doctrines of constructive trust and proprietary estoppel have been run together to a considerable extent in the area of disappointed contractual expectations. The typical fact pattern is that A has told B that A will sell his land to B; B has done work on the land in reliance on that assurance; but no contract has materialised. The quirk here is that s 2 of the Law of Property (Miscellaneous Provisions) Act of 1989 gives an exception, in s 2(5) for the creation of 'resulting, implied or constructive trusts', but gives no explicit exception for rights arising by estoppel.

---

49  [1991] 1 WLR 1127: See Clarke, L and Edmonds, R, '*H v M*: Equity and the Essex Cohabitant' (1992) 22 Family Law 523. Cf the *dicta* in *Re Basham* [1986] 1 WLR 1498 at 1504, linking estoppel with the common intention constructive trust; and *Juggins v Brisley* [2003] All ER (D) 319.

50  [1991] 1 WLR 1127.

51  The classic *dictum* to this effect is that of Sir Nicholas Browne-Wilkinson V-C in *Grant v Edwards* [1986] Ch 638 at 656. Cf *Chan v Leung* 2002 EWCA Civ 1075. The distinction between the two doctrines is asserted in *Stokes v Anderson* [1991] 1 FLR 391 per Nourse LJ at 399, where he emphasised the lack of argument on this point in *Grant v Edwards*.

Accordingly, in cases where estoppel has been pleaded, it is not surprising that the courts have given in to the temptation to emphasise the closeness of the two doctrines.[52] Again, the courts therefore have every incentive to treat the remedial consequences as being very similar in measure.[53]

Equally, it is unsurprising that the two doctrines have refused to merge, for several reasons. First, there is the entrenched conservatism of pleadings. If a case can be made in two ways rather than one, it will be pleaded both ways.[54] Second, if estoppel merges with the common intention constructive trust then, given the refusal of English courts to countenance the remedial constructive trust, the remedial discretion in estoppel would be lost.[55] And that discretion is highly prized. The loss of it, by assimilation to the constructive trust model where the claimant's interest is discovered rather than created, would render impossible a sensitivity to moral and economic factors which the courts use, however sparingly and carefully, in estoppel.[56]

Perhaps the most important reason why proprietary estoppel persists as a legal model, separate from the common intention constructive trust, is that it operates in circumstances where it is even more difficult to find or infer an agreement than it is in the home-sharing cases, so that the facts really do fit the pattern appropriate to estoppel rather than to the common intention constructive trust.[57] This is particularly relevant in situations where there has

---

52  *Yaxley v Gotts* [1999] 3 WLR 1217. Dixon, M explores the importance of the use of estoppel in this context in 'Proprietary Estoppel and Formalities in Land Law and the Land Registration Act 2002: A Theory of Unconscionability', in Cooke, E (ed), *Modern Studies in Property Law*, Vol II, 2003, Oxford: Hart Publishing Ltd, p 165.

53  However, in these cases the courts have not addressed the adjacent issue of the timing of the relief in the two cases. Accordingly these cases are not of assistance in addressing the issue of whether or not the remedy in estoppel is discretionary, arising only as a result of the court's decision.

54  Hence the multiplicity of forms of estoppel asserted in the traditional textbooks and in practitioner works such as Wilken, S, *The Law of Waiver, Variation and Estoppel*, 2002, Oxford: Oxford University Press, Cf. Feltham, P, Hochberg, D, Leech, T, *Spencer Bower, Estoppel by Representation*, 4th edn, 2004, London: LexisNexis UK. An example is *Edwin Shirley Productions Ltd v Workspace Management Ltd and others* (2001) 23 EG 158, where the two doctrines were pleaded; both claims failed, and the difference in remedial structure was not discussed.

55  Not entirely. The institutional constructive trust is supposed to operate without 'foreground' discretion. But the approach to quantum found in *Midland Bank plc v Cooke* [1995] 4 All ER 561 demonstrates that that claim is not entirely plausible.

56  If the facts of *Sledmore v Dalby* (1996) 72 P & CR 196 are fed into the institutional constructive trust machinery, an equitable fee simple for the claimant might well be generated, since at one stage the owner intended to give the property to the claimant and his wife. Only a discretionary jurisdiction could be sensitive to the changes in circumstances, and nuances of behaviour, involved in a case like this.

57  Even in home-sharing cases we can find assertions that an equity by estoppel has arisen, alongside the insistence that no trust has yet come into existence *Pascoe v Turner* [1979] 1 WLR 431, per Cumming-Bruce LJ at 435. At 438 the discretionary and creative nature of the

been a promise of a testamentary gift. Such an assurance really is a promise not an agreement; and simply cannot, by any stretch of the imagination, be supposed to give rise to an immediate proprietary interest or indeed anything immediate except expectation[58] – sometimes because there is not sufficient certainty in the promise and in all cases because the promise is of a *future* interest.[59] It is interesting to note that it is in such cases that the remedial discretion has most conspicuously been exercised, in departing from the expectation norm, among recent English cases.

Accordingly, we have to continue to regard proprietary estoppel and the common intention constructive trust as separate legal concepts, even though they operate, frequently, upon similar situations and give, generally, the same measure of relief. Nick Hopkins has discussed the difference in the reasoning employed within the two concepts. They are unlikely to coalesce. It may be that the use of the common intention constructive trust and of estoppel to resolve family property disputes will become obsolete in England and Wales when a new statutory jurisdiction is put in place to regulate, by a statutory discretion,[60] the property rights of cohabitants.[61] Such a move would leave estoppel to operate in circumstances where overlap with the constructive trust is less likely, but leaves unresolved the confusion caused by the indiscriminate mixing of the two concepts in the cases on pre-contractual expectations.

### What is an 'equity by estoppel'?

Back, then, to the estoppel equity. To recap: the claimant's 'equity', arising after detrimental reliance and before the court grants relief, is germane to the proprietary estoppel model, described above, and not to the common intention constructive trust model. It is the existence of the court's discretion, and the causative role played by that discretion, that precludes any insistence that the factual basis of estoppel brings property rights into being, to be

court's decision is asserted: 'We are satisfied that the problem of remedy on the facts resolves itself into a choice between two alternatives: should the equity be satisfied by a licence to the defendant to occupy the house for her lifetime, or should there be a transfer to her of the fee simple?'

58  See the cases at n 15 above; the point is considered in *Jiggins v Brisley* [2003] All ER (D) 319.
59  Certainly the 'new model' proposed by McFarlane ([2003] CLJ 661, see n 3 above) will not operate in these circumstances, for that reason – a point which surely cannot be met by his suggestion that in such cases a proprietary interest generated by estoppel may subsequently diminish or increase over time; op cit, at 683. If that were the case, presumably it would not be free to metamorphose after the court's decision: see *Williams v Staite* [1979] Ch 291 per Goff LJ at 300.
60  Which of course offends nobody; see text at n 42 above.
61  Sarah Worthington advocates this as a way out of the difficulties of the common intention constructive trust, in *Equity*, 2003, Oxford: Oxford University Press, at 241. Trends in English family law indicate that this is likely to happen in the not-too-distant future.

discovered rather than created later by the court. Up to the point of the court's decision the claimant has not a property right, but an equity.

The next thing to say is that the claimant has not merely a cause of action, but an equity. And we have to ask a further question: why there is an equity at all? Why do we insist that the factual basis of estoppel brings an 'equity' into existence, and what is the 'equity'?

The estoppel claimant's equity has often been described as an 'equitable right to go to court to seek relief',[62] or similar; it has been pointed out[63] that this is not a helpful description, as anyone has a right to go to court. Can we describe it more accurately? What is intended is something more than a cause of action; we might describe it as an expectation of equity's intervention or, perhaps, as a right to satisfaction. This fits with what the courts say they do once an equity is found to exist: the court must then decide how the equity is to be satisfied.[64] In some cases, for example, the court has decided to make no award because the equity has *already* been satisfied.[65]

The word 'equity' has, of course, a meaning beyond this context, more generally, as a weak form of equitable proprietary interest.[66] Such a right is more than merely personal; the benefit of an equity can be transmitted to successors in title, and so can the burden, although it is more easily defeasible than an equitable interest in that it will not bind the purchaser of an equitable interest in the property without notice of the equity. The estoppel equity cannot fit squarely into this category, but clearly, it is something very similar.[67]

As such, it does have proprietary effect, even though it cannot meet the traditional criteria for being a property right, in that its nature is uncertain;[68] when the claimant has an equity we do not know what remedy the court will award.[69] Equitable property rights are well known to be directly linked to, and

---

62  Harpum, C, *Megarry and Wade, The Law of Real Property*, 6th edn, 2000, London: Sweet & Maxwell, 13–028.

63  McFarlane, B, 'Proprietary Estoppel and Third Parties after the Land Registration Act 2002' [2003] CLJ 661 at 663.

64  See n 6 above. Heffey, P, Patterson, J and Robertson, A in *Principles of Contract Law*, Sydney: Lawbook Co, 2002 at 168 put it like this: 'The word "equity" in this context means an entitlement to some equitable relief, the determination of which is within the court's discretion. The "equity" raised by the estoppel is said to be an undefined equity, since the relying party cannot assert a right to a particular remedy, but must persuade the court to fashion a remedy to suit the facts of the particular case.'

65  *Sledmore v Dalby* (1996) P & CR 196, CA, per Roch LJ at 205.

66  *Latec Investments Ltd v Hotel Terrigal Pty Ltd* (1965) 113 CLR 265; *Blacklocks v JB Developments (Godalming) Ltd* [1982] Ch 183.

67  Thus s 116 of the Land Registration Act 2002 distinguishes an equity by estoppel and a mere equity, but is of no assistance on the question as to precisely what the difference is.

68  *National Provincial Bank Ltd v Ainsworth* [1965] AC 1175.

69  In this respect it differs from, say, an equity to have a document rectified: *Blacklocks v JB Developments (Godalming) Ltd* [1982] Ch 183.

defined by, the remedy that equity is prepared to grant.[70] But it has been shown that the uncertain resolution of the equity is not a bar to its having proprietary effect;[71] and it is well established that it can bind successors in title to the land while the equity remains unsatisfied; a trustee in bankruptcy, for example, will take on the burden of an equity, so that he will have to hold the land subject to any proprietary right the court awards in satisfaction of the equity.[72] So will a donee of the land; *Voyce v Voyce*[73] is the classic example of this. There, the claimant had been allowed to live in a cottage on his mother's farm, and had been promised that he could have it, with some land, as a gift, provided that he renovated it to his mother's satisfaction, which he did. His mother then gave the whole farm to the claimant's brother, who took the farm knowing of the claimant's position. Later there was a dispute, and the owner of the farm sought to exclude the claimant from part of the land he (the claimant) had occupied; so that the claim came to a head in litigation. What is clear from the Court of Appeal's decision is *both* that before the court's decision the claimant did not have anything but an equity, to be satisfied by whatever interest the court chose to award, *and* that the defendant, as a donee, must then be in no better position than his mother had been. The court's order was that the fee simple in the cottage must be conveyed to the claimant; thus the defendant suffered, in the loss of that land, the satisfaction of the equity out of the land.[74]

There are no English cases, so far as the writer is aware, where a purchaser for value of the land has been bound by an estoppel equity (although it was assumed, without argument, that this was so in *J T Developments Ltd v Quinn*),[75] but the reasoning employed in the cases concerning other successors in title imply that this must be so.[76] However, it must equally be clear that a

---

70  Thus one who has contracted to purchase land has an equitable interest in it because of his entitlement to specific performance.

71  Smith, R, 'How Proprietary is Proprietary Estoppel?' in Rose, F (ed) *Consensus Ad Idem*, London: Sweet & Maxwell 1996.

72  *Re Sharpe (a bankrupt), ex parte the trustee of the bankrupt v Sharpe and another* [1980] 1 WLR 219.

73  (1992) 62 P & CR 290.

74  There is no suggestion in the judgment of Nicholls LJ that at the point of the court's decision the claimant already held the equitable fee simple in the cottage. Dillon LJ at 294 refers to the fact that the claimant's 'equitable rights . . . had accrued long before', and that he was already the equitable owner. But this point is made in order to establish that an easement of light could be asserted against the claimant as owner of the cottage; it is made without any evaluation of the authorities on estoppel. Indeed, the case could equally be taken to widen the category of persons against whom such an easement can be claimed, by including among them the holder of an estoppel equity. The point, and the distinction between these two readings, is not explored in the judgment.

75  (1990) 62 P & CR 33.

76  Note that we must distinguish those cases where successors in title to the original estopped party are bound, not by succession, but by a fresh liability of their own, by their own

purchaser for value of a legal estate without notice of the equity must take free of it; so, presumably, would a purchaser of an equitable interest without notice, by analogy with equities generally; and it is established that an equity by estoppel can be overreached.[77]

The equity is then defined in two directions. It is *greater than* a cause of action, being proprietary in nature and capable of binding a successor in title, although, being without the certainty that property rights must have, it is *less than* a property right.[78] And both those limiting factors can be seen as statements about the court's discretionary power. The equity has proprietary status because of the strength of the court's power to grant a remedy. Just as a contract to purchase land gives the purchaser an equitable interest in the land because of the strength of the remedy available to him, namely specific performance, so the estoppel claimant has an equity because of the strength and range of proprietary interests that the court can award. In the other direction, however, the equity is not a full, defined property right for precisely the same reason: that the court insists upon the range of choice available to it at the point of decision. It has a foreground discretion and has the power to create personal or property rights and the flexibility to mould them to the circumstances in response to unconscionability and to all the facts; therefore the claimant has, until that point, no more than an equity. The equity, therefore, plays an important role in maintaining the decision-making power and flexibility of the courts, and in enabling them to respond powerfully to unconscionability.

It is in this respect that the courts have found a way to have their cake and eat it too. They have found a remedial model which preserves their discretionary decision-making power, but which can bind successors in title, so enabling the courts to give an especially powerful protection to claimants.

### The significance of s 116

Against this background, s 116 of the English Land Registration Act 2002 states:

> It is hereby declared for the avoidance of doubt that, in relation to

---

conduct. Thus Graham Battersby has analysed the very difficult case of *ER Ives Investments Ltd v High* in this way: 'Contractual and Estoppel Licences as Proprietary Interests in Land' [1991] Conv. 36 and 'Informal Transactions in Land, Estoppel and Registration' (1995) 58 Mod L Rev 637.

77  *Birmingham Midshires Mortgage Services Ltd v Sabherwal* (1999) 80 P & CR 256. The reasoning is that if an equitable interest can be overreached, so, *a fortiori*, can an equity.

78  An interesting parallel can again be found in family law. The spouse's right of occupation of the matrimonial home, now conferred by s 30 of the Family Law Act 1996, is not a property right but it behaves like one if registered (s 31).

registered land, . . . an equity by estoppel . . . has effect from the time the equity arises as an interest capable of binding successors in title (subject to the rules about the effect of dispositions on priority).

Title registration has many purposes; among the most important is the regulation of the circumstances in which a purchaser of land can be bound by third-party rights in the land. So it is not surprising to find in a registration statute a provision regulating the potency of a third-party right vis-à-vis a purchaser of land. What exactly is this section doing with the estoppel equity?

What the section does not mean, in view of what has been said above, is that the estoppel claimant has, from the point when he incurs his detrimental reliance on the representation, a full proprietary interest in the property; a fee simple, a lease, an easement, or whatever he expected. The weight of authority is against this. Where the equity binds successors in title, it does so by placing them in the position in which A would have found himself had B sued A himself; vulnerable to the court's discretion, and therefore likely to have an order made against him.[79] Equity acts *in personam* as ever; but B's equity, while it can bind a successor in title, remains inchoate.

Section 116 purports to be declaratory. It does not claim to change anything, so existing law continues to define the current position. However, the 'rules about the effect of dispositions on priority' are those contained in the new Act itself, and so we must regard those as having been pasted on top of the existing case law or rules.

Moving to the words of the section, these require some unpacking. Taking the easy part first. What sort of successor in title? That is going to depend upon 'the rules about the effect of dispositions on priority', and these are contained in ss 28 and 29 of the Land Registration Act 2002. Section 28 simply states that, except as provided by s 29,[80] the priority of an interest affecting a registered estate is not affected by a disposition of the estate, whether or not the interest is registered. Section 29 goes on to give the rules about the effect of registrable dispositions of a registered estate *made for valuable consideration.*[81] So s 29 is relevant only to purchasers for value; and s 28 must therefore preserve the position already established for purchasers other than for value. In particular, the position established in *Re Sharpe*[82] and in *Voyce v Voyce*[83] for donees of the land and for a trustee in bankruptcy will

---

79 But note that the discretion and the exercise of moral judgment is against A himself, and is then transferred to P. There is no basis in law for a fresh discretion exercised on the basis of P's conduct. The writer agrees entirely with McFarlane's point about this (op cit, n 3 at 691–3).

80 Emphasis added.

81 And 30, which deals with dispositions of registered charges, which are ignored here for the sake of simplicity.

82 [1980] 1 WLR 219.      83 (1991) 62 P & CR 290.

remain the same; they are bound by the equity. Turning to s 29, the 'rules about the effect of dispositions on priority' are found to be that interests will bind a purchaser if *either* they are protected by notice on the register *or* they are overriding interests. Overriding interests are listed in Sched 3 of the Land Registration Act 2002; these are interests which will override a registered disposition even though they do not appear on the register.[84] Examples are legal easements or local land charges; there is no explicit mention of an equity by estoppel, but para 2 of the Schedule states (leaving aside the details) that an interest held by someone who is in actual occupation of the land will be overriding by virtue of that occupation.

An estoppel interest is unlikely to be protected by notice, and so it is the protection of the estoppel equity by actual occupation that is relevant to us here.[85] The consequence of this part of the 'rules about the effect of dispositions on priority' is that estoppel equities unprotected by notice or occupation will *not* bind a purchaser; those that are so protected are *capable of* doing so. Accordingly, a claimant who has been caring for the representor in the estoppel situation, without actually living in the representor's home, or who has moved out of the property, will not prevail against a purchaser (although he may still do so against other successors, as happened in *Re Sharpe*[86] and in *Voyce v Voyce*,[87] and in *Wayling v Jones*[88] where the defendant was the representor's executor).

So far, this is fairly straightforward. But there is more to analyse. First, what of 'has effect from the time the equity arises'? We do not know what time that is. This issue is explored in Nick Hopkins' paper and is not considered further here; Hopkins points out that the Law Commission's own analysis of the timing is contradictory.[89] Accordingly, there is an issue here for the courts to decide.

Second, what happens to a successor in title when he has been bound by an equity? We still do not know how the equity will be satisfied. The equity may be satisfied by a proprietary right, or by something less, and it is not hard to guess that the nature of the right eventually granted is going to have a bearing upon its potential effect on third parties. Again, we have to bear in mind that a great many estoppel cases were decided in the pre-*Ashburn Anstalt*[90] era when a licence was regarded as a property right. We now know that it is not.

---

84 Schedule 1 lists interests which will override first registration. The lists are just slightly different, and the differences do not concern us here; Schedule 1 is ignored for the sake of
   simplicity.
85 Note that in *Lloyd v Dugdale* [2002] 2 P & CR 13 it was held *obiter* that an estoppel equity
   could be an overriding interest under the equivalent provision of the Land Registration Act
   1925, s 70(1)(g).
86 [1980] 1 WLR 219.       87 (1991) 62 P & CR 290.
88 (1995) 69 P & CR 170; *Inwards v Baker* [1965] 2 QB 29.
89 Hopkins, text at nn 189–90 *et seq.*       90 *Ashburn Anstalt v Arnold* [1988] 2 WLR 706.

Therefore, although the equity is 'capable of binding' successors in title, the position must be that, if the court takes the view that the equity is best satisfied by the award of a licence to occupy the premises, the court *is thereby deciding* that the claimant will not be protected against a successor in title.[91] The successor was bound by the equity, in that the property remained vulnerable, in his hands, to whatever proprietary right the court might decide to award. But if the court does not make such an award, the purchaser is then free of the claimant's claim.

Equally, if the court makes an award such as the one in *Voyce*,[92] to the effect that the claimant is to have a legal or equitable interest in the land, the purchaser holds the land subject to the claimant's award, and must hold on trust for him, or make a transfer, as appropriate. More difficult is the case where the court makes a monetary award, giving compensation rather than a proprietary right, either because an expectation award *in specie* is not practicable, or as a way of making a reliance-based award. Prima facie the section means that the successor in title will be subjected to that money judgment. But it is worth remembering that this is proprietary estoppel, involving claims to land, and that this is a title registration statute regulating third-party rights *in land*. Perhaps the most natural interpretation of this set of circumstances in this context is that the land is made security for the money judgment, if the purchaser cannot meet it out of his other resources. But that is not entirely clear from the section itself, and it is to be hoped that the courts in making the order will make this clear, as was done in *Jennings v Rice*.[93]

What has been said about s 116 here is, to some extent, conjectural. The section is not as clearly expressed as might be hoped; or, rather, it preserves the unfinished principles of the existing law, and leaves to the courts the task of refining and developing those principles. The principal message of this chapter is that it is to be hoped that the courts will do so in a way which is consistent with existing law and, in particular, with the inchoate nature of the estoppel equity. If they do not do so – if s 116 is used to redefine that equity as a ready-made proprietary interest – then the remedial discretion in estoppel will be lost.

---

91  And if the action was brought against a successor in title, the court would simply not make an order against him.

92  (1991) 62 P & CR 290.       93  [2002] EWCA Civ 159, [2003] 1 P & CR 100.

## Chapter 9

# Unconscionability, constructive trusts and proprietary estoppel

*Nicholas Hopkins**

## Introduction

The relationship between the common intention constructive trust and proprietary estoppel has generated considerable judicial and academic interest in English law. The central suggestion that has been made is that in some situations the doctrines may be merged.[1] However, despite numerous references to the relationship between the doctrines, as Nield notes, their 'confused interrelationship' has not been addressed.[2] Indeed, the case law displays a range of possibilities, not all of which are mutually exclusive. Arguments for the merger of the doctrines thus find resonance in suggestions that the doctrines are almost indistinguishable[3] and in their joint discussion and interpretation.[4] Yet pronouncements of their relationship have been combined

* Senior Lecturer in Law, University of Southampton, UK. This chapter draws on research carried out as a visitor at the University of Sydney and the University of Melbourne during May and June 2004 and at Victoria University of Wellington, where the author was a visitor from January to September 2004. I would like to thank those institutions and, additionally, the British Academy and the Society of Legal Scholars whose financial support for the visits to Sydney and Melbourne (British Academy) and Wellington (Society of Legal Scholars) is gratefully acknowledged. Thanks are also extended to Andrew Robertson, University of Melbourne, for his helpful comments on a draft of this paper and to Lizzie Cooke, University of Reading, for her many useful insights. Any remaining errors are the author's responsibility.
1  *Yaxley v Gotts* [2000] Ch 162; *Jennings v Rice* [2003] 1 FCR 501; *Chan v Leung* [2003] 1 FLR 23.
2  Nield, Sarah, 'Constructive Trusts and Estoppel' (2003) 23 Legal Studies 311, 313.
3  *Austin v Keele* (1987) 10 NSWLR 283; *Birmingham Midshires Mortgage Services Ltd v Sabherwal* ('*Sabherwal*') (2000) 80 P&CR 256.
4  *Edwin Shirley Productions v Workspace Management Ltd* ('*Edwin Shirley Productions*') [2001] 2 EGLR 16.

with a separate and distinct application of each,[5] or the application of one in preference to the other.[6]

Interest in the relationship between these doctrines stems, in particular, from Browne-Wilkinson V-C's judgment in *Grant v Edwards*. He explained that the common intention constructive trust and proprietary estoppel 'have been developed separately without cross-fertilisation between them: but they rest on the same foundation and have on all other matters reached the same conclusions'.[7] He perceived the relationship between the doctrines to lie both in the similarities between the elements of each (a common intention and detrimental reliance for a constructive trust; an assurance of rights and detrimental reliance for estoppel) and their common basis in preventing a legal owner's unconscionable assertion of his or her rights. The similarities of the constituent elements of the doctrines provided the focus of opposing academic views of their relationship by Hayton and Ferguson.[8] This chapter is concerned with the other aspect of the relationship; the common foundation of the principles in unconscionability.

Unconscionability has enjoyed a renaissance of interest in the common law world.[9] It appears indisputable that there is no single principle of unconscionability; 'the conscience of equity must not be given a life of its own, independent of the specific doctrines through which it finds expression'.[10] Therefore, the renaissance of the concept brings a need to analyse its use in specific contexts. In relation to both constructive trusts (together with all trusts) and proprietary estoppel, the same thesis of unconscionability has been separately advanced. This thesis (referred to in this chapter as the knowledge thesis of unconscionability) suggests that unconscionability relates to a requirement of knowledge of particular facts on the part of the person against whom intervention is sought. In the context of constructive trusts,

---

5 *Lloyds Bank plc v Carrick* [1996] 4 All ER 630, 640; *Mollo v Mollo* (Unreported, High Court of England and Wales, HH Judge Hunter, 8 October 1999); *Jiggins v Brisley* [2003] EWHC 841 (Unreported, High Court of England and Wales, HH Judge Elleray, 16 April 2003).

6 *Stokes v Anderson* [1991] 1 FLR 391, 399. Further, as is noted in that case, despite Browne-Wilkinson V-C's comments in *Grant v Edwards* the court in that case in fact applied an orthodox trust analysis.

7 [1986] Ch 638, 656.

8 Hayton argued that the supposed distinction between the doctrines is illusory while Ferguson urged caution in merging the doctrines. See Hayton, David, 'Equitable Rights of Co-habitees' [1990] Conveyancer and Property Lawyer 370 and (responding to Ferguson) Hayton, David, 'Constructive Trusts of Homes – A Bold Approach' (1993) 109 Law Quarterly Review 485. Ferguson, Patricia, 'Constructive Trusts – A Note of Caution' (1993) 109 Law Quarterly Review 114.

9 See, eg, Parkinson, Patrick, 'The Conscience of Equity' in Patrick Parkinson (ed), *The Principles of Equity*, 2nd edn 2003, Sydney: Lawbook Co, Ch 2, 29. In this regard, England may readily be added to the list of jurisdictions Parkinson specifically refers to (Australia, Canada, New Zealand and the US).

10 Ibid 53.

Lord Browne-Wilkinson interpreted conscience as a requirement of knowledge in his judgment in *Westdeutsche Landesbank Girozentrale v Islington LBC* ('*Westdeutsche*').[11] In relation to estoppel, Robertson has argued that where the courts have required something more than satisfaction of the elements of a claim to establish unconscionability, that has in fact related to the representor's knowledge or intention.[12] If correct, the existence of this common thesis of unconscionability would enable that concept to cement the relationship between estoppel and the common intention constructive trust.

The argument advanced in this chapter, however, is that as a result of recent developments in our understanding of unconscionability in the context of proprietary estoppel, that concept may now in fact serve to distinguish between the two doctrines, rather than cement their relationship. Further, it is argued that a requirement of knowledge does not explain the role of unconscionability in relation to either of these doctrines. In relation to the common intention constructive trust, the authorities do not convincingly establish that any requirement of knowledge exists. As regards proprietary estoppel, in cases subsequent to Robertson's analysis, conscience has now been attributed with a wide evaluative role. While knowledge may be of relevance in determining unconscionability, establishing unconscionability may include a consideration of other factors beyond the core elements of a claim.

The relevance of the relationship between the common intention constructive trust and proprietary estoppel may initially appear to be of marginal interest in Australian law. In Australia, the common intention constructive trust has been overshadowed by recognition of the remedial trust. Notably, however, Dal Pont suggests that in the line of cases stemming from *Allen v Snyder*,[13] where English doctrine was followed, the courts 'ultimately generated something little removed from a proprietary estoppel'.[14] More recently, there is some evidence of a renewed interest in the common intention trust.[15] At a broader level, unconscionability is sufficiently central to our understanding of the operation of equity that lessons can be learnt from studying its use across jurisdictions. Robertson's knowledge thesis is drawn from English as

11  [1996] AC 669.
12  Robertson's thesis is summarised in Robertson, Andrew, 'Knowledge and Unconscionability in a Unified Estoppel' (1998) 24 Monash University Law Review 115, 117. It is developed in other articles. See, in particular, 'Towards a Unifying Purpose for Estoppel' (1996) 22 Melbourne University Law Review 1; 'Situating Equitable Estoppel Within the Law of Obligations' (1997) 19 Sydney Law Review 32; 'Reliance, Conscience and the New Equitable Estoppel' (2000) Melbourne University Law Review 7 (a review of Spence, Michael, *Protecting Reliance: The Emergent Doctrine of Equitable Estoppel* (1999)).
13  [1977] 2 NSWLR 685.
14  Dal Pont, GE, 'Timing, Insolvency and the Constructive Trust' (2004) 24 Australian Bar Review 262.
15  *Parsons v McBain* (2001) 109 FCR 120 (discussed by Dal Pont ibid); *Parianos v Melluish (Trustee for the Estate of Parianos)* [2003] FCA 190.

well as Australian case law. Further, as will be seen,[16] English courts' developing use of unconscionability in exercising remedial discretion in estoppel appears to have its origins in Australian law.

This chapter is structured as follows. The knowledge thesis of unconscionability is first discussed in 'The Knowledge Thesis of Unconscionability'. 'The Use of Unconscionability in Proprietary Estoppel and the Common Intention Constructive Trust' then considers how unconscionability is used by the courts in relation to the common intention constructive trust and proprietary estoppel. It is argued that unconscionability is used differently in relation to each of these doctrines. 'The Relationship between the Common Intention Constructive Trust and Proprietary Estoppel' examines the consequences of these different uses for the relationship between the doctrines. The arguments will then be summarised and concluded.

## The knowledge thesis of unconscionability

The link between knowledge and unconscionability has been developed primarily in relation to determining the basis on which the court intervenes. It is at this level that conscience is considered to provide the common foundation of proprietary estoppel and the common intention constructive trust. However, in the context of proprietary estoppel, an additional issue arises as regards the use of unconscionability in relation to the courts' exercise of its remedial discretion once a successful claim to estoppel has been made out.

### Outline of the knowledge thesis

In *Westdeutsche*[17] Lord Browne-Wilkinson advanced two propositions. First, that all trusts are based on conscience; and second that conscience, in turn, is based on the trustee's knowledge of the matters affecting his or her conscience. The underlying purpose of Lord Browne-Wilkinson's judgment, as Birks explains, is to provide a 'single foundational principle' for the whole of the law of trusts.[18] Lord Browne-Wilkinson rejected the contention that a trust necessarily arises whenever legal and equitable entitlement to property is split; on his view there is no trust unless and until the conscience of the trustee is affected by having the requisite knowledge.

The foundation upon which Lord Browne-Wilkinson rests the link between conscience and knowledge appears far from clear. In forwarding his thesis on trusts, Lord Browne-Wilkinson emphasised the general principle that 'equity operates on the conscience of the owner of the legal interest'.[19] This general

---

16 See the discussion below commencing n 75.      17 [1996] AC 669
18 Birks, Peter, 'Trusts Raised to Reverse Unjust Enrichment: the *Westdeutsche* Case' [1996] Restitution Law Review 3, 9.
19 [1996] AC 669, 705.

principle provides, at best, equivocal support for a link between conscience and knowledge. There are circumstances in which equity is described as operating on the conscience when the knowledge of the defendant is not necessarily in issue. An example is provided by the notion of 'equity's darling'; the bona fide purchaser for value without notice against whom, in the development of the equity jurisdiction, trusts and other equitable interests were not enforceable. The non-enforcement of equitable interests against such a third party is rationalised on the basis that the conscience of such a person is not affected by the interest.[20] Included among those whose conscience *is* affected (and who are therefore bound by trusts) is a donee, regardless of whether the donee has knowledge of the trust. Equitable interests are also enforceable against a purchaser with constructive notice and, as is considered below, this form of *notice* may not be sufficient to establish *knowledge*.[21] However, while as a composite expression the non-enforcement of interests against equity's darling is explained in terms of the reach of conscience, this explanation is not given for each component part. For example, Maitland does not explain the enforcement of trusts against donees, or purchasers with constructive notice, explicitly on the grounds of conscience.[22] He confines this explanation to the enforcement of trusts against a purchaser with actual knowledge of the trust.[23]

Lord Browne-Wilkinson's judgment has received widespread criticism. Some commentators reject his conscience-based theory of trusts without overtly questioning his interpretation of conscience.[24] These commentators reject the proposition that trusts are founded on conscience by accepting (or at least not challenging) the proposition that conscience is necessarily concerned with the trustee's knowledge. Other commentators directly challenge the link between conscience and knowledge. Swadling, for example, argues that conscience has a technical meaning, divorced from knowledge and wrongdoing.[25] Worthington notes that 'equity does not regard a recipient's

---

20  See, eg, *Midland Bank Trust Co v Green* [1981] AC 513, 528 'the character in law known as . . . [equity's darling] was the creation of equity. In order to affect a purchaser for value of a legal estate with some equity or equitable interest, equity fastened upon his conscience and the composite expression was used to epitomise the circumstances in which equity would or rather would not do so' (Lord Wilberforce).

21  This is discussed below, n 41, and accompanying text.

22  Maitland, FW, *Equity*, 2nd edn, 1936, Cambridge: Cambridge University Press, 113. No specific explanation is given for enforcement against a donee, while the inclusion of constructive notice is seen as an 'inevitable step' from actual notice.

23  Ibid 113: '[t]he ground [of enforcement against a purchaser who knew of the trust] is fraud or something akin to fraud. It is unconscientious – "against the conscience" – to buy what you know to be held on trust for another'.

24  See, eg, Birks above n 18, 19–21; Chambers, Robert, *Resulting Trusts*, 1997, Oxford: Clarendon Press; New York: Oxford University Press, 203–09.

25  Swadling, William, 'The Law of Property' in Birks, Peter and Rose, Francis (eds), *Lessons of the Swaps Litigation*, 2000, London: Mansfield Press, Chapter 9, 258–9.

conscience as affected only when there is some appropriate degree of knowledge'.[26] On this view, it is possible to accept conscience as providing the single foundational principle of the law of trusts, by accepting a definition of conscience broader than the mere presence or absence of knowledge.

Of Lord Browne-Wilkinson's two propositions, this chapter is primarily concerned with the second; that conscience requires the trustee to have knowledge of particular factors. It will be argued below that there is insufficient support in the case law to suggest that conscience is linked to a requirement of knowledge in relation to the common intention constructive trust.[27] This argument does, however, have consequences for Lord Browne-Wilkinson's first proposition; that all trusts are based on conscience. The result of the argument advanced in this chapter is that this first proposition (and therefore the use of conscience as a foundational principle for trusts) can be accepted only if seen as separate from the second, so that conscience is not necessarily linked to a requirement of knowledge.

In relation to estoppel, the link between conscience and knowledge is developed by Robertson in the context of discussing a unified doctrine of (common law and equitable) estoppel[28] and through a discussion of taxonomy.[29] The link is drawn through an analysis of case law. Robertson suggests that in estoppel cases involving a positive representation the unconscionability requirement is (generally) fulfilled by the existence of the core elements of a claim; (on his analysis) assumption, inducement, detrimental reliance and reasonable reliance.[30] Only in cases involving acquiescence have the courts required something more to establish unconscionability and that something more relates to the 'knowledge and state of mind of the representor'.[31] Having linked unconscionability with the knowledge and conduct of the representor, Robertson then rejects the concept as providing the focus of estoppel. He concludes:

> [w]hile the rhetoric of unconscionability has dominated the recent cases and commentary on equitable estoppel, claims that the doctrine is organised around the concept of unconscionability are not supported by the

---

26  Worthington, Sarah, *Proprietary Interests in Commercial Transactions*, New York: Clarendon Press, 1996, Addendum, xv.
27  See the discussion below commencing n 104.
28  'Towards a Unifying Purpose for Estoppel', above n 12; 'Knowledge and Unconscionability in a Unified Estoppel', above n 12.
29  'Situating Equitable Estoppel Within the Law of Obligations', above n 12.
30  'Knowledge and Unconscionability in a Unified Estoppel', above n 12, 117. Robertson explains at 116 that reasonable reliance requires the representee to have acted reasonably in adopting and acting upon the assumption. This issue is explored further in Robertson, Andrew, 'The "Reasonableness" Requirement in Estoppel' (1994) 1 Canberra Law Review 231.
31  'Knowledge and Unconscionability in a Unified Estoppel', above n 12, 117.

approach taken in these cases. The characterisation of the representor's conduct as unconscionable justifies the intervention of equity in estoppel cases, but ... questions of conscience have a limited role to play in the operation of the doctrine. The knowledge and conduct of the representor are only relevant to the threshold question whether the representor bears responsibility for the representee's adoption of the relevant assumption. Questions of liability and remedy are otherwise determined by reference to the representee's reliance.[32]

On Robertson's view, estoppel is focused on the reasonableness of the representee's reliance; an issue to be judged by reference to the conduct and knowledge of the representee, not that of the representor.[33] In the context of a unified estoppel, Robertson's analysis aims at demystifying unconscionability to discover the real extent of differences between the common law and equitable doctrines. By reducing unconscionability to a requirement of knowledge, he argues that the concept does not preclude reconciling the different doctrines; all that is required is for the courts to be explicit about the elements of the claim.[34] As a doctrine based on reliance, Robertson situates equitable estoppel in the category of equitable wrongs.[35] Combined with his support for a reliance-based approach to remedies,[36] Robertson offers a view of estoppel in which reliance provides both the basis of intervention and the measure of relief. Conscience, as a concept linked to the representor's knowledge, is marginalised insofar as it provides no more than the underlying justification for intervention. Robertson's view of estoppel is attractive in providing congruence between the basis of intervention and the measure of relief[37] but, it is argued, his approach does not explain cases decided after the publication of his theory.

A reliance-based approach to estoppel and its resulting place in legal taxonomy remain matters of debate. Robertson's views are challenged, in particular, by the High Court decision in *Giumelli v Giumelli*.[38] Edelman has argued that that case marks a move towards establishing estoppel as a cause of action to enforce promises, in which expectations provide the measure of

---

32 'Situating Estoppel Within the Law of Obligations', above n 12, 64.
33 'Towards a Unifying Purpose for Estoppel', above n 12. Robertson provides a useful summary of his argument in 'Reliance, Conscience and the New Equitable Estoppel' above n 12.
34 'Knowledge and Unconscionability in a Unified Estoppel' above n 12, 117.
35 'Situating Equitable Estoppel Within the Law of Obligations', above n 12.
36 Robertson, Andrew, 'Reliance and Expectation in Estoppel Remedies' (1998) 18 Legal Studies 360.
37 A point acknowledged by Jensen, Darryn, 'In Defence of the Reliance Theory of Equitable Estoppel' (2001) 22 Adelaide Law Review 157, 176.
38 [1999] 161 ALR 473. A reliance approach continues to attract support. For a recent example see Bright, Susan & McFarlane, Ben, 'Proprietary Estoppel and Property Rights' [2005] CLJ 449.

relief. Rejecting a reliance analysis, Edelman suggests that estoppel is an 'orphan' falling outside the traditional taxonomic classification of the law of obligations as involving contract, wrong and unjust enrichment.[39] As will be seen below, recent developments have established a role for unconscionability in estoppel beyond a requirement of knowledge. Further, the development of the use of unconscionability in the exercise of remedial discretion has led to an approach based neither on reliance nor on enforcement of expectations.[40] However, before these issues are addressed, a practical difficulty with the knowledge thesis will be discussed, namely how such a requirement may be fulfilled.

### Applying a knowledge requirement

If the requirement of unconscionability in constructive trust and estoppel is dependent upon the representor's or trustee's knowledge, then two additional questions arise: what must the representor or trustee have knowledge of; and what type of knowledge is sufficient? As regards both doctrines the former question is more readily answered than the latter. In *Westdeutsche*, Lord Browne-Wilkinson explained that in a constructive trust the requisite knowledge must be of the factors alleged to affect the trustee's conscience; that is, knowledge of the facts on which the imposition of the trust is based. As regards estoppel, Robertson suggests that in all cases of estoppel (by acquiescence) knowledge of the assumption adopted by the representee is required, while knowledge of the true position and of the detrimental reliance may also be relevant.[41]

The more difficult question is that of identifying the nature of the knowledge that is required: must the representor have actual knowledge, or is something less than that sufficient? This in turn raises the question of the relationship between knowledge and notice. Those concepts are generally thought to be distinct, though the point of departure between them is difficult to pinpoint. Ultimately, as Howell explains, '[a]lthough "knowledge"

---

39 Edelman, James, 'Remedial Certainty or Remedial Uncertainty in Estoppel after *Giumelli?*' (1999) 15 Journal of Contract Law 179, 198. A more cautious approach to *Giumelli* is adopted by Burns, Fiona, '*Giumelli v Giumelli* Revisited: Equitable Estoppel, the Constructive Trust and Discretionary Remedialism' (2001) 22 Adelaide Law Review 123. She accepts, at 125 that it is 'probably a correct' interpretation of *Giumelli* that it confirms expectation relief as the 'benchmark' in estoppel, though argues, at 154–5 that the courts' approach constitutes a form of 'moderate discretionary remedialism'. An expectation approach to estoppel is advocated by Cooke, Elizabeth, 'Estoppel and the Protection of Expectations' (1997) 17 Legal Studies 258 and Cooke, Elizabeth, *The Modern Law of Estoppel*, 2000, Oxford: New York: Oxford University Press, 150–69. See also Pratt, Michael, 'Identifying the Harm Done: A Critique of the Reliance Theory of Estoppel' (1999) 21 Adelaide Law Review 209.
40 See the discussion below commencing n 76.
41 'Knowledge and Unconscionability in a Unified Estoppel' above, n 12, 141.

and "notice" are said to be different, it seems that they are rather points on a scale of awareness, with actual knowledge (or notice) at one end, and constructive notice at the other'.[42] The nature of the knowledge requirement is not addressed by Lord Browne-Wilkinson. He does, however, implicitly treat knowledge as distinct from notice.[43] The type of knowledge required is addressed by Robertson in relation to estoppel, though he does so by reference to notice without distinguishing between the two concepts.[44]

In relation to estoppel, Robertson argues that the knowledge requirement is satisfied where the representor has actual notice or constructive notice in a narrow sense of wilful ignorance: 'deliberately abstaining from inquiry in order to avoid knowledge'.[45] He argues, further, that a 'strong case' can be made for accepting the requirement as being satisfied by constructive notice in a broad sense of a 'mere failure to make reasonable inquiries or a finding that the representor ought to have known of the representee's assumption and detrimental reliance'.[46] Robertson uses evidence of courts acting on the basis of constructive knowledge to strengthen his argument that unconscionability does not in fact provide the basis of estoppel.[47] He considers a broad approach to knowledge to indicate that the real focus of the court is on the position of the representee, not the knowledge (conscience) of the representor. In support of this, he cites a comment by Duggan, made in relation to unconscientious dealing that for the court to act on the basis of constructive knowledge 'marks an important shift in the philosophical underpinnings of the unconscientious dealing doctrine. Relief of A's misfortunes replaces prevention of B's wrongdoing as the basis for intervention'.[48] However, in the context of unconscientious dealing, the possible acceptance of constructive knowledge is not considered by Duggan to change the basis of intervention away from unconscionability, but to mark a shift (which he considers to be undesirable) in the nature of the unconscionability in issue: from unconscionability directed at procedural fairness to unconscionability directed at substantive outcomes.[49]

In relation to trusts, the meaning of knowledge and its relationship with notice has been considered by the courts in the context of determining the scope of the personal liability to account as constructive trustee imposed on a

---

42  Howell, Jean, 'Notice: A Broad View and a Narrow View' [1996] Conveyancer and Property Lawyer 34, 35–6 (fns omitted).

43  [1996] AC 669, 705. Having explained the relevance of knowledge to the existence of a trust, Lord Browne-Wilkinson explains that once the trust is established the beneficiary has a proprietary interest enforceable against all except a purchaser for value without notice. Some of the difficulties arising from this distinction are outlined by Swadling above n 25, 259–60.

44  'Knowledge and Unconscionability in a Unified Estoppel' above n 12, 141–2.

45  Ibid 142.        46  Ibid 142.        47  Ibid 142–3.

48  Ibid 142 citing Duggan, Anthony, 'Unconscientious Dealing' in Parkinson, Patrick (ed), *The Principles of Equity*, 1996, Sydney: LBC Information Services, 121, 139.

49  Ibid 137.

person who 'knowingly' receives trust property. In that context, there was an attempt to define the nature of the knowledge required. A fivefold classification of types of knowledge was accepted (in a case involving knowing assistance rather than knowing receipt)[50] by Peter Gibson J in *Baden v Société Générale pour Favoriser le Developpment du Commerce et de L'Industrie en France SA ('Baden').*[51] By reference to that classification, in *Re Montagu's Settlement Trusts* Megarry V-C provided a tentative definition of knowledge as including: (i) actual knowledge; (ii) wilfully shutting one's eyes to the obvious; and (iii) wilfully and recklessly failing to make such inquiries as an honest and reasonable man would make.[52] He excluded imputed notice (actual and constructive notice of an agent) and considered it doubtful that more expansive forms of constructive notice would be included.[53] However, referring to developments in estoppel (in *Taylors Fashions Ltd v Liverpool Victoria Trustees Co Ltd ('Taylors Fashions')* )[54] Megarry V-C noted the current trend in equity towards placing greater weight on underlying ideas than on detailed rules drawn from them.[55] In that respect, he commented that while the categorisation of knowledge provided useful guidelines they should be approached as an aid in determining the underlying issue; whether 'the [recipient's] conscience was affected in such a way as to require him to hold any or all of the chattels that he received on a constructive trust'.[56] The attempt at definition now seems to have been abandoned in favour of a more flexible test. In *Akindele*, Nourse LJ (further reflecting the trend identified by Megarry V-C) suggested that if the only purpose of categorisation was to determine the issue of conscience, then there was no need to categorise. He considered that there 'ought to be a single test of knowledge' for determining liability for knowing receipt.[57] The test Nourse LJ proposed is that 'the recipient's state of knowledge must be such as to make it unconscionable for him to retain the benefit of the receipt'.[58]

The adoption of unconscionability as the basis of liability appears to have been welcomed,[59] in particular for the element of flexibility in the concept.[60] However, it is submitted that, considered together, *Westdeutsche* and *Akindele* produce circularity. In *Westdeutsche*, Lord Browne-Wilkinson explains that the creation of a trust is dependent on conscience and therefore on the

---

50 See the explanation in *BCCI (Overseas) Ltd v Akindele ('Akindele')* [2001] Ch 437, 454.
51 [1992] 4 All ER 161.        52 [1992] 4 ER 308, 323.
53 Megarry V-C therefore omitted the fourth and fifth *Baden* classifications: (iv) knowledge of circumstances which would indicate the facts to an honest and reasonable man; and (v) knowledge of circumstances which would put an honest and reasonable man on inquiry.
54 [1982] QB 133.        55 [1992] 4 All ER 308, 324.        56 Ibid 324.
57 [2001] Ch 437, 455.        58 Ibid 455.
59 See, eg, Martin, JE, *Hanbury & Martin Modern Equity*, 16th edn, 2001, London: Sweet & Maxwell, 313.
60 See, eg, Barkehall-Thomas, S, ' "Goodbye" Knowing Receipt. "Hello" Unconscientious Receipt' (2001) 21 Oxford Journal of Legal Studies 239.

knowledge of the trustee. In *Akindele*, however, Nourse LJ's test for determining whether a recipient has knowledge is to consider whether his or her conscience is affected. In other words, *Westdeutsche* raises the question as to what knowledge a person must have for his or her conscience to be affected by a trust. The answer, through *Akindele*, is that the individual must have sufficient knowledge that his or her conscience is affected. The underlying difficulty is that the terms 'knowledge' and 'conscience' have been defined by reference to each other.[61] Problems in defining knowledge and in understanding its relationship with notice are not the creation of Lord Browne-Wilkinson's judgment. However, by providing knowledge with a central role in the application of the law of trusts his judgment perpetuates them and serves to heighten their significance.

### The use of unconscionability in proprietary estoppel and the common intention constructive trust

As the preceding analysis shows, there are difficulties in accepting the knowledge thesis of unconscionability. In relation to the constructive trust, the general principle from which the thesis is derived does not provide a convincing foundation. In estoppel the thesis is drawn principally in the context of an analysis which has the underlying purpose of presenting a reliance-based approach to the doctrine: an approach which itself is inconsistent with more recent jurisprudence. In addition, there is an overriding difficulty in understanding the nature of the knowledge required. As a result, even if it is accepted that conscience relates to knowledge, it is uncertain how the requirement is fulfilled. In this part of the chapter, the actual use of unconscionability by the courts is discussed, and through this analysis the extent to which the knowledge thesis is supported by authority is considered.

#### Proprietary estoppel

A link between conscience and knowledge is fundamental to Robertson's views on estoppel. It is because of this link that he considers a ground of intervention based on conscience as necessarily focused on the representor and therefore rejects it as the basis of estoppel because of the perceived focus of that doctrine on the representee's reliance. However, a significant factor in Robertson's rejection of unconscionability as providing the focus of estoppel claims is the inability of the concept to explain the appropriate remedial relief. He considers that it is in the context of determining the remedy that

---

61 In this respect doubt is cast on the economic analysis of unconscionability proposed by Barkehall-Thomas, S, ibid. Any definition of the concept, at least in a context where a trust is imposed, must tackle the *Westdeutsche* judgment.

unconscionability, expectations and reasonable reliance, as alternative bases for estoppel, most clearly conflict.[62] The use of unconscionability in relation to estoppel needs to be discussed both in relation to the initial finding of estoppel and the court's exercise of remedial discretion.[63]

## Conscience and establishing the estoppel

The central role of conscience in a claim to estoppel has been recognised at least since Oliver J's judgment in *Taylors Fashions*.[64] There, as is well known, Oliver J liberated estoppel from restrictions imposed by Fry J's probanda in *Willmott v Barber*,[65] but which have their origins in the judgment of Lord Cranworth in *Ramsden v Dyson*.[66] In *Ramsden v Dyson* two distinct concepts of estoppel were developed. A narrow principle, envisaged by Lord Cranworth, was directed at situations in which the legal owner did no more than acquiesce in the claimant's acts. Such acquiescence would preclude the assertion of entitlement by the legal owner only if maintained in the face of knowledge of his or her own rights and of the mistaken belief as to entitlement held by the claimant. A broader principle, envisaged by Lord Kingsdown, was directed at situations where the legal owner's conduct goes beyond mere acquiescence and where he or she 'created or encouraged' the claimant's expectations. In such a case, the only knowledge required of the legal owner was knowledge of the claimant's expenditure (in reliance on the expectation). In *Willmott v Barber*, the five probanda provided by Fry J adopted Lord Cranworth's formulation for *all* claims to proprietary estoppel; in particular, the requirement that the legal owner have knowledge of his or her own entitlement and of the claimant's mistake. This appeared to preclude the application of estoppel to cases where the parties act on the basis of a shared belief or expectation as to the claimant's entitlement, even where the legal owner has actively 'created or encouraged' the claimant's expectation. In such cases, by definition, the legal owner is unaware of his or her entitlement.

Against this background, the impetus to the adoption of a broad approach to estoppel based on unconscionability was to establish that the strict requirement of knowledge contained in Fry J's probanda is not required in all cases. In *Taylors Fashions* Oliver J explained:

the more recent cases indicate, in my judgment, that the application of the *Ramsden v Dyson* principle ... requires a very much broader

---

62 'Towards a Unifying Purpose for Estoppel', above n 12, 19.
63 A detailed discussion of the development and use of unconscionability in proprietary estoppel is provided by the current author in 'Understanding Unconscionability in Proprietary Estoppel' (2004) 20 Journal of Contract Law 210.
64 [1982] 1 QB 133.    65 (1880) 15 Ch D 96.    66 (1866) LR 1 HL 129.

approach which is directed rather at ascertaining whether, in particular individual circumstances, it would be unconscionable for a party to be permitted to deny that which, knowingly, or unknowingly, he has allowed or encouraged another to assume to his detriment than to inquiring whether the circumstances can be fitted within the confines of some preconceived yardstick for every form of unconscionable behaviour.

So regarded, knowledge of the true position by the party alleged to be estopped, becomes merely one of the relevant factors . . . in the overall inquiry.[67]

There is no doubt (as is indicated by Oliver J's formulation) that the knowledge of the legal owner may be a relevant factor in determining whether it is unconscionable for him or her to renege on the assurance. Further, knowledge is more likely to be of relevance in cases of acquiescence. Where the legal owner has actively created or encouraged the claimant's expectation, the court is able to focus on his or her acts rather than merely his or her knowledge. The role of unconscionability in estoppel has, however, developed significantly in a number of recent cases stemming from the Court of Appeal's decision in *Gillett v Holt*.[68] These cases demonstrate that unconscionability cannot be reduced to a knowledge requirement applicable in cases of estoppel by acquiescence. Unconscionability is an issue to be determined in all claims to estoppel. While it is related to the core elements of the claim unconscionability is not simply fulfilled by establishing the existence of those elements, but plays an active role in their determination.

In *Gillett v Holt*, Robert Walker LJ explained the approach that courts should take to estoppel. He said:

> it is important to note at the outset that the doctrine of proprietary estoppel cannot be treated as subdivided into three or four watertight compartments . . . the quality of the relevant assurances may influence the issues of reliance, [. . .] reliance and detriment are often intertwined . . . Moreover the fundamental principle that equity is concerned to prevent unconscionable conduct permeates all the elements of the doctrine. In the end the court must look at the matter in the round.[69]

His judgment has established unconscionability as providing an overriding or umbrella element of an estoppel claim. It feeds in to the assessment of an assurance, reliance and detriment (as it 'permeates all the elements of a claim') but it also provides a general evaluative tool through which the court considers the claim 'in the round'. This approach has been influential in a number of cases. The question as to whether it is unconscionable for the legal

---

67 [1982] 1 QB 133, 151–2.        68 [2001] Ch 210.        69 Ibid 225.

owner to renege on the assurance actively feeds into the assessment of whether the core elements of the claim are present so that the subsistence of those elements cannot be isolated from the overriding question of unconscionability. This is illustrated by the approach of the court to the element of detrimental reliance in *Gillett v Holt* itself and in *Campbell v Griffin*.[70] In both cases, the Court of Appeal (led by Robert Walker LJ) assessed the claimant's detriment by reference to the overriding question of whether it was unconscionable for the legal owner to renege. Adopting this approach, the court accepted as a sufficient detriment acts that had been considered inadequate (assessed in isolation from unconscionability) at first instance. A similar approach can be seen in *Lloyd v Dugdale*. There, by reference to the approach to detriment in *Gillett v Holt*, the court emphasised the consequence to the claimant of his detrimental reliance in finding that it was unconscionable for the legal owner to renege on the assurance.[71] The claimant had moved into commercial premises and incurred expenditure on building works prior to the formal grant of rights. As a result, the claimant was 'effectively locked in'.[72] He had foregone the opportunity to find alternative premises and enjoy 'all the contemplated advantages of ownership'.[73]

In other cases, unconscionability has been used as the basis of an overall evaluation of the claim 'in the round'. The determination of unconscionability through this evaluation has been treated as an additional issue to establishing the core elements of the claim. For example, in *Jennings v Rice* HH Judge Weeks explained that after considering the elements of the claim he would 'step back, look at the matter in the round and consider whether it was unconscionable for [the legal owner] to go back on any assurance she gave to [the claimant]'.[74] Applying this approach, and evaluating the claim in the round, unconscionability was related specifically to the legal owner's 'deliberate disappointment' of the claimant's expectation after accepting the benefit of his services. Where the courts have specifically addressed unconscionability through an 'in the round' evaluation of the claim, that evaluation has included a consideration of factors that are not related to establishing the core elements of the claim. In *Parker v Parker*, for example, rejecting the

---

70 [2001] EWCA 990 (Unreported, Dame Elizabeth Butler-Sloss, Robert Walker and Thorpe LJJ, 27 June 2001).

71 [2002] 2 P&CR 13; (2002) 84 P&CR 167, 177–9.          72 Ibid 179.

73 Ibid 179. Although the initial claim to estoppel succeeded, the claimant's inchoate equity was held to have been defeated by a subsequent transfer of the land. The estoppel arose in favour of the claimant personally, but the premises were occupied by the claimant's company. In the absence of actual occupation by the claimant in his personal capacity the inchoate equity did not bind the transferee under the (then) provisions of the Land Registration Act 1925 (UK) c 21, s 70(1)(g).

74 Unreported, High Court of England and Wales, HH Judge Weeks, 20 March 2001. The subsequent appeal, reported at [2003] 1 FCR 501, concerned only the remedy awarded by the judge. His finding of estoppel was not challenged.

principal claim to estoppel, Lewison J emphasised the 'wholly uncontemplated' financial burdens that would be imposed on the legal owners by holding them to the claimant's expectation.[75]

### Conscience and remedial discretion

Robertson's principal criticism of unconscionability as providing the focus of estoppel is the inability of the concept to assist in determining the appropriate remedy. He explains:

> [t]he most significant problem with a conscience-based approach, however, is that the representor's conscience does not provide sufficient guidance in the difficult, but fundamental, question of the relief to be provided to give effect to an estoppel in a particular case . . . in most cases the nature of the representor's conduct will not provide clear guidance in choosing between reliance and expectation relief.[76]

As Robertson notes (even where courts have referred to unconscionability in the context of determining the remedy) relief is not generally determined by the knowledge or conduct of the representor.[77] Where conscience has been referred to in the context of remedial discretion, it has generally been linked with a requirement of proportionality between the detriment and the remedy. This use of unconscionability has been given new impetus by recent English case law. Through this development, the courts have reasserted the discretionary nature of estoppel remedies, the determination of which is not seen as a stark choice between expectations and reliance.

The link between unconscionability and proportionality has its origins in Australian courts. In *Waltons Stores v Mayer* Brennan J explained:

> the element which both attracts the jurisdiction of the court of equity and shapes the remedy to be given is unconscionable conduct on the part of the person bound by the equity . . . [In] moulding its decree, the court,

---

75 [2003] EWHC 1846 (Unreported, Lewison J, 24 July 2003) [241]. The principal claim to estoppel, by the Earl of Macclesfield, was for a life interest or a long lease in Shirburn Castle, his ancestral home. Following the failure of this claim, a more limited claim was upheld to provide the claimant with two years' notice to leave the Castle. The notice period allowed for the claimant to remove his extensive chattels, which included three libraries.
76 'Situating Equitable Estoppel Within the Law of Obligations', above n 12, 55.
77 Ibid 54. However, while not providing the principal measure of relief, the representor's conduct may affect the remedy awarded. See, eg, *Crabb v Arun DC* [1976] Ch 179 where the representor's conduct was considered to preclude the award of compensation for an easement awarded to the claimant that might otherwise have been appropriate.

as a court of conscience, goes no further than is necessary to prevent unconscionable conduct.[78]

This was cited by Mason CJ in *Commonwealth v Verwayen* ('*Verwayen*') in holding that 'a central element of [estoppel] is that there must be proportionality between the remedy and the detriment . . . It would be wholly inequitable and unjust to insist upon a disproportionate making good of the relevant assumption'.[79] The focus on proportionality in that case was a key factor in the court's assertion of a reliance-based approach to remedies. Mason CJ suggested that to do more than prevent the claimant's detriment 'would sit uncomfortably with a general principle whose underlying foundation was the concept of unconscionability'.[80]

Robertson notes that in this initial use of unconscionability the courts were in fact concerned with the representee's reliance and not the representor's knowledge of the detriment.[81] This lends support for his view that estoppel is focused on reliance rather than unconscionability. In *Giumelli v Giumelli* the High Court expressly acknowledged that *Verwayen* and subsequent authorities support a broader view of remedial discretion than the reversal of the claimant's detriment.[82] The Full Court had awarded the estoppel claimant a constructive trust over land that had been the subject of assurances. The High Court qualified this award 'both to avoid injustice to others [particularly the claimant's bother who had improved the land] and to avoid relief which went beyond what was required for conscientious conduct by [the representors]'.[83] Instead of the award of expectation *in specie*, the claimant was awarded a financial sum representing the value of his expectation but reduced to take into account those other factors.[84] Hence, taking the claimant's expectations as a starting point, the remedy was expressly reduced by virtue of what was required (*inter alia*) by reference to the representor's conscience.[84a] Robertson argues that the award of expectations in fact is not inconsistent with a reliance-based approach. He notes that 'in most cases the only way to ensure that the relying party suffers no harm is to require the

---

78  (1988) 164 CLR 387 at 419. Cf. Bright & McFarlane, n 38 above, who consider proportionality to support a reliance-based approach, and Gardner, Simon, 'The Remedial Discretion in Proprietary Estoppel–Again', (2006) 122 LQR 492, 499, suggesting that proportionality indicates a remedy between expectation enforcement and reliance but is unable, of itself, to explain where exactly the remedy should be pitched.

79  (1990) 170 CLR 394, 413.        80  Ibid 411.

81  'Towards a Unifying Purpose for Estoppel', above n 12, 23 and 25–26.

82  (1999) 161 ALR 473 [33].        83  Ibid [50].

84  Ibid [58]. In determining the sum to be awarded the judge was directed to take into account 'all considerations for which allowance should be made . . . so as to do equity between the parties to the action and all relevant third parties'.

84a  This approach is noted in *Vukic v Gubin* [2006] NSWSC 41 [33] and *Young v Lilac* [2006] NSWSC 18 [101–102].

representor to make good the relevant assumption'.[85] This is an argument that requires us to accept that the theoretical purpose of the remedy may in most cases be achieved only by an award that in fact produces a different measure of relief. A rationalisation of estoppel remedies that emphasises the actual measure of relief has been argued by other commentators to be preferable.[86] In any event, it is clear that in *Giumelli v Giumelli* the measure of relief was not determined by the prevention of harm to the claimant. The courts' focus was on the conscience of the representors and the broader requirements of justice as regards third parties.

In English law, the approach to determining the remedy was considered by the Court of Appeal in *Jennings v Rice*.[87] The court emphasised the central role of proportionality (derived from unconscionability) in the exercise of remedial discretion. Aldous LJ suggested that the proportionality of the remedy to the detriment is 'the most essential requirement'.[88] However, this supposed primacy of proportionality was asserted in the context of a discretionary approach to remedies. Aldous LJ explained (immediately prior to his reference to proportionality) that, 'the value of [the equity derived from estoppel] will *depend upon all the circumstances* including the expectation and the detriment. The task of the court is to do justice'.[89] There are echoes in this statement of the 'in the round' evaluation conducted to establish an estoppel. Robert Walker LJ indicated that in most cases the courts enjoyed a 'wide judgmental discretion',[90] though acknowledging that 'the court must take a principled approach, and cannot exercise a completely unfettered discretion according to the individual judge's notion of what is fair in any particular case'.[91] On the facts of that case, the Court of Appeal upheld a financial remedy provided by HH Judge Weeks at first instance which he had based on the cost of care the claimant had provided to the representor. In doing so, the Court of Appeal rejected an argument that the award of expectations was the 'basic rule' in estoppel.[92] The award of expectations had been rejected by HH

85 Robertson, Andrew, 'The Statute of Frauds, Equitable Estoppel and the Need for Something More' (2003) 19 *Journal of Contract Law* 173, 187. See further, Robertson above n 36. This is described by Burns above n 39, 132 as a 'hybrid' approach to the remedy.

86 See, eg, Cooke, *The Modern Law of Estoppel* above n 39, 164 and Pratt above n 39, 217.

87 [2003] 1 FCR 501.

88 [2003] 1 FCR 501 [36]. Proportionality had previously been referred to (by reference to *Verwayen*) in the context of remedial discretion by the Court of Appeal in *Sledmore v Dalby* (1996) 72 P&CR 196. However, it is only since *Jennings v Rice* that the concept has become of central importance in the exercise of that discretion.

89 Ibid [36] (emphasis added).

90 Ibid [51]. This discretion is considered to exist outside those cases in which the representor's assurance and the representee's detrimental reliance 'have a consensual character falling not far short of an enforceable contract': Robert Walker LJ [45]. In such cases the award of the representee's expectations is 'the court's natural response': Robert Walker LJ [50].

91 Ibid [43].        92 Cf: Counsel's argument summarised ibid [16].

Judge Weeks partly on the basis that it was out of proportion to the claim-ant's detriment. Robert Walker LJ had provided a financial remedy in a claim to estoppel by a carer (though without specifying the basis on which the award had been calculated) in the earlier case of *Campbell v Griffin*.[93] He rejected an argument for the award of expectations (occupation of the repre-sentor's house for life) on the basis that such an award would be 'dis-proportionate'.[94] The *Jennings v Rice* approach to the remedy was followed in *Ottey v Grundy (Andreae's Executor)* ('*Ottey v Grundy*').[95] There, as in the previous cases, a financial remedy was provided to the claimant who had provided care to the representor (a chronic alcoholic). In determining the remedy at first instance, HH Judge Langan (whose remedy was upheld on appeal)[96] noted that the expectation and detriment were 'wholly out of pro-portion'.[97] He highlighted the need to 'make such award as will do justice between the parties'.[98] The approach he adopted was, first, to calculate the financial value of the claimant's expectation, and then determine the final (lesser) award by taking into account a number of specified factors.[99]

Despite the emphasis placed on proportionality these cases indicate that the real concern of the courts in this regard is simply to prevent a *dis-proportionate* remedy. Beyond this, the courts' focus appears to be on the discretionary nature of the award. Although Robert Walker LJ noted the need for a 'principled approach' the basis on which remedies are determined is not necessarily explicit. In *Campbell v Griffin* the remedy appeared to be directed at providing a 'fair' distribution of a modest estate. Although not offering any explanation for the sum (£35,000) awarded, Robert Walker LJ noted that the claimant's claim on the property 'is not so compelling as to

---

93  [2001] EWCA 990 (Unreported, Dame Elizabeth Butler-Sloss, Robert Walker and Thorpe LJJ, 27 June 2001).

94  Ibid [34]. Robert Walker LJ noted the administrative inconvenience such an award would create as it would require a trust of land governed by the *Trusts of Land and Appointment of Trustee Act 1996* (UK) c 47, incurring legal expenses and the possibility of further disputes.

95  [2003] EWCA 1176 (Unreported, Arden, Laws and Pill LJJ, 31 July 2003).

96  [2002] EWHC 2858 (Unreported, HH Judge Langan, 1 November 2002) [38]–[48]; [2003] EWCA 1176 [57]–[62].

97  [2002] EWHC (Unreported, HH Judge Langan, 1 November 2002) 2858 [48].

98  Ibid [38].

99  The claimant's expectation related to a life interest in a houseboat in Chelsea and to owner-ship of an apartment in Jamaica. The total value of the expectation was £240,000–£250,000. The final remedy awarded was £50,000 plus the apartment (or a further £50,000 in default of transfer). The assurances had been made in the context of a cohabiting relationship which had terminated prior to the representor's death. The circumstances taken into account by the judge included the termination of the relationship that the termination was not the fault of the claimant and the effect the termination had on her lifestyle. In addition to the care she had provided, the claimant was also held to have suffered detriment by virtue of an interrup-tion to her career. Insofar as the judge started with the expectation value and reduced the award in light of other circumstances, his approach is comparable to that in *Giumelli v Giumelli* (1999) 161 ALR 473.

demand total satisfaction, regardless of the effect on other persons with a claim on the . . . estate'.[100] In *Ottey v Grundy* the extent of the financial award, though generous on the facts, represented a modest part of a substantial estate.[101] Arguably, the remedy represented the court's perception of a 'fair' distribution of the representor's assets in light of the parties' previous relationship, and the contrast between the claimant's prevailing circumstances and the lifestyle she had enjoyed with the representor.[102]

Although the courts are not explicit in this regard, they appear in fact to determine the appropriate remedy through a broad evaluation of the circumstances. In this respect, the courts' approach to the exercise of remedial discretion increasingly appears to mirror the 'in the round' evaluation conducted to establish the estoppel. The prevailing view of the courts as to the purpose of the estoppel remedy is perhaps most accurately summarised by Arden LJ in *Ottey v Grundy*. She explained, 'the purpose of proprietary estoppel is not to enforce an obligation which does not amount to a contract [that is, expectations] nor yet to reverse the detriment which the claimant has suffered [that is, reliance] but to grant an appropriate remedy in respect of the unconscionable conduct'.[103] If this approach continues, unconscionability will be recognised as performing a central role in estoppel claims not only in determining whether the estoppel is established, but also in measuring the relief to be awarded. At neither stage is unconscionability confined to an assessment of the representor's knowledge, but it provides the basis of a wide evaluation of the claim.

### Common intention constructive trust

The common intention constructive trust developed as a means of determining proprietary entitlement where land (typically the parties' home) has been acquired during the course of a familial or quasi-familial relationship. More recently, the application of the trust, or of an analogous concept, has arisen in the commercial sphere. In the context of the family home, the trust has its

---

100 [2001] EWCA 990 [34].
101 The claimant was awarded a maximum of £100,000 out of an estate with a net value of approximately £1.5 million. The parties had cohabited for a little over three years and their relationship continued for just over two years from the time of the assurance. They had separated several months before the representor's death. Compare the award of £200,000 based on the cost of alternative care for eight years in *Jennings v Rice* (where, again, the value of the estate exceeded £1 million). In *Campbell v Griffin* the claimant had provided significant care for at least seven years.
102 In determining the appropriate remedy, the judge explained that the claimant had 'passed from an extremely comfortable mode of life to one which is economically on the margin': [2002] EWHC (Unreported, HH Judge Langan, 1 November 2002) 2858 [47].
103 [2003] EWCA 1176 (Unreported, Arden, Laws and Pill LJJ, 31 July 2003) [61].

origins in the House of Lords decisions in *Pettitt v Pettitt*[104] and *Gissing v Gissing*.[105] Its modern formulation is derived from *Lloyds Bank plc v Rosset* (*'Rosset'*).[106] In the commercial sphere claims to an interest in land arising on the failure of negotiations conducted on a 'subject to contract' basis have been made through a constructive trust. However, these claims have been made jointly with estoppel, and a constructive trust has not yet successfully been claimed.[107] In a separate development, the *'Pallant v Morgan*[108] equity' recognised by the Court of Appeal in *Banner Homes Group plc v Luff Developments Ltd* (*'Banner Homes'*)[109] has been described by Thompson as an extension of the common intention constructive trust.[110] That trust is not discussed here, however, as its relationship with the common intention constructive trust remains doubtful.[111] Indeed, Nield suggests that it is 'confusing' to equate the two.[112] In any event, the nature of the unconscionable conduct in issue is clearly distinguishable, as the trust derived from the *Pallant v Morgan* equity can apply where the reliance confers an advantage (or gain) on the acquiring party with no corresponding disadvantage (detriment) to the non-acquiring party.[113]

The common intention constructive trust, like all constructive trusts, has its foundation in unconscionable or inequitable conduct.[114] This is reflected in Lord Diplock's formulation of the trust in *Gissing v Gissing*. He explained:

---

104 [1970] AC 777.     105 [1971] AC 886.     106 [1991] 1 AC 107.
107 A common intention constructive trust was claimed in *Edwin Shirley Productions* [2001] 2 EGLR 16 and in *James v Evans* [2000] 3 EGLR 1. The objection to the application of the trust (and estoppel) is not the commercial context per se but the existence of the 'subject to contract' clause which expressly acknowledges either party's right to withdraw.
108 [1953] Ch 43.     109 [2000] Ch 372.
110 Thompson, Mark, 'Constructive Trusts and Non-Binding Agreements' [2001] Conveyancer and Property Lawyer 265, 265–6.
111 The requirements for the *Pallant v Morgan* equity are explained by Chadwick LJ in *Banner Homes* [2000] Ch 372, 397–9. It is apparent from the requirements that the trust applies to a narrower range of circumstances than the common intention constructive trust. For example, it applies only to an agreement or understanding reached prior to the acquisition of land to the effect that one party will take steps to secure the acquisition and, if successful, the other will have an interest. It is not anticipated that the non-acquiring party will make any contribution to the acquisition other than refraining from seeking to acquire the land on its own account.
112 Above n 2, 329.
113 The gain-based nature of the doctrine is discussed by the current author in 'The *Pallant v Morgan* "Equity"?' [2002] Conveyancer and Property Lawyer 35.
114 See, eg, *Paragon Finance plc v DB Thakerar & Co* [1999] 1 All ER 400, 409. Millett LJ explained, 'A constructive trust arises by operation of law whenever the circumstances are such that it would be unconscionable for the owner of the property ... to assert his own beneficial interest in the property and deny the beneficial interest of another.' He made the same point extra-judicially in Millett LJ 'Restitution and Constructive Trusts' (1998) 114 Law Quarterly Review 399, 400.

A resulting, implied or constructive trust . . . is created by a transaction between the trustee and the cestui que trust in connection with the acquisition by the trustee of a legal estate in land, whenever the trustee has so conducted himself that it would be inequitable to allow him to deny the cestui que trust a beneficial interest in the land acquired. And he will be held so to have conducted himself if by his words or conduct he has induced the cestui que trust to act to his own detriment in the reasonable belief that by so acting he was acquiring a beneficial interest in the land.[115]

The basis of the trust in conscience was further acknowledged by Browne-Wilkinson V-C in *Grant v Edwards*.[116] However, the modern formulation of the trust by Lord Bridge in *Rosset*[117] is notable for the absence of any reference to unconscionability.

In *Rosset*, Lord Bridge distinguished between an express agreement constructive trust, arising where 'there has at any time prior to acquisition, or exceptionally at some later date, been any agreement, arrangement or understanding reached between [the parties] that the property is to be shared beneficially'; and an inferred agreement constructive trust, where 'the court must rely entirely on the conduct of the parties both as the basis from which to infer a common intention to share the property beneficially and as to the conduct relied on to give rise to a constructive trust'.[118] In the former category, Lord Bridge explained that once the agreement has been established, all the claimant must show is that 'he or she has acted to his or her detriment or significantly altered his or her position in reliance on the agreement'.[119] The latter trust arises only on the basis of 'direct contributions to the purchase price . . . whether initially or by payment of the mortgage instalments'.[120]

The absence of an express reference to unconscionability in Lord Bridge's formulation calls into question the significance of the concept in relation to a claim. In *Grant v Edwards*, Browne-Wilkinson V-C explained that to establish that it was inequitable for the legal owner to claim sole beneficial ownership was dependent upon the two factors of a common intention and detrimental reliance.[121] On this basis, the omission of an express reference to unconscionability by Lord Bridge may be explained on the basis that his formula incorporates the grounds on which unconscionability is determined: the existence of a common intention and detrimental reliance. This suggests a simple formula for the determination of unconscionability: the trust arises because it is unconscionable for legal entitlement to be asserted; it is unconscionable to do so because of the existence of a common intention and the claimant's detrimental reliance.

---

115 [1971] AC 886, 905.    116 [1986] Ch 638.    117 [1991] 1 AC 107.    118 Ibid 132–3.
119 Ibid 132.    120 Ibid 133.    121 [1986] Ch 638, 654.

There is no indication within this formula of a requirement of knowledge on the part of the legal owner. Applying *Westdeutsche*, the factors alleged to affect the trustee's conscience (and therefore the factors of which the trustee must have requisite knowledge) are the existence of the common intention and the claimant's detrimental reliance. In *Grant v Edwards*, in drawing a comparison between the common intention constructive trust and proprietary estoppel, Browne-Wilkinson V-C himself suggested that the claimant must have acted 'to the knowledge of' the legal owner in the belief that he or she has or will acquire an interest in the property.[122] No explanation is given as to the source of the knowledge requirement. The absence of stronger authority would not be insurmountable were it possible to assume that the legal owner would necessarily have such knowledge.[123] As regards the existence of a common intention, such an assumption may safely be made. In an inferred agreement constructive trust it may readily be assumed that the legal owner has knowledge of the source of direct contributions to the purchase on which the trust is founded. In an express agreement trust it is inherent in the existence of an express *common* intention that the legal owner has knowledge of the facts on which the intention is based. However, it is conceivable that he or she may have no knowledge of the facts constituting the claimant's detrimental reliance. This may be the case, for example, where the claimant's acts are carried out on land not currently occupied by the parties, or during a period of the legal owner's absence.[124]

Further, there is little evidence that the more expansive role for unconscionability that has been developed in the context of proprietary estoppel has been carried over to the common intention constructive trust. There is an increased tendency to emphasise the relevance of unconscionability to the constructive trust when the trust is discussed jointly with proprietary estoppel. However, this seems to be the consequence of comments made in *Yaxley v Gotts* concerning the relationship between the doctrines rather than in response to developments in estoppel.[125] In applying the constructive trust, courts generally continue to follow an 'orthodox' approach of treating unconscionability as no more than the underlying rationale for intervention. This is illustrated by a number of recent decisions. In *Driver v Yorke*, HH Judge Bowsher noted 'whether the claim is put in terms of a constructive

---

122  Ibid 656.
123  Such an approach is taken by Chambers above n 24, 204. He suggests that the common intention constructive trust is one in which the facts giving rise to the trust necessarily involve the trustee's knowledge, though the point is not developed.
124  Both of these examples are drawn from the facts of *Rosset*. There the claimant's claim to detrimental reliance included acts carried out on a semi-derelict property prior to the parties' occupation while, in addition, the legal owner had spent some of the time abroad. No question of his knowledge of these acts is raised though the claim failed on other grounds.
125  [2000] Ch 162. The case is considered below n 156 and text.

trust or proprietary estoppel, a fundamental ingredient is that the legal owner of the property has acted unconscionably'.[126] The case involved an attempt by the sons of the legal owner of a house to exclude their sister from inheriting an equal share. The claim failed on the facts as there was insufficient evidence of a common intention or of contributions to the mortgage by the sons. Unconscionability was not further discussed. In *Jiggins v Brisley*, constructive trust and estoppel were again raised in the context of a disputed inheritance.[127] HH Judge Elleray noted the relationship between the two doctrines,[128] but his application of each was distinct. The claim to a constructive trust failed as there was no agreement that the claimant would have an immediate interest.[129] The claim to estoppel (which can apply to a promise of a future interest) succeeded. Adopting the approach to unconscionability from *Gillett v Holt*, the judge concluded that in light of the agreement and detrimental reliance and 'viewing the circumstances in the round' it was unconscionable to deny the claimant the flat.[130] A constructive trust of the flat was imposed as a remedy for the estoppel. However, the judge noted that such a trust is 'remedial' and based on the unconscionability established in the estoppel claim. He distinguished this trust from the common intention constructive trust, which he explained as being based on an agreement and contribution to the purchase.[131] In *McKenzie v McKenzie*, the claimant sought to establish an interest in a house in the sole legal ownership of his father on the basis of a constructive trust.[132] It was noted at the outset that no alternative claim was made through estoppel.[133] Approaching the claim solely on the basis of constructive trust, unconscionability was mentioned only as providing the rationale for intervention.[134]

There are two exceptional cases in which unconscionability appears to have been interpreted more expansively. First, in *Chan v Leung* the judge at first instance approached the question of detriment in the context of a constructive trust claim by reference to whether it was unconscionable for the legal

---

126 [2003] EWHC 746 [28] (Unreported, HH Judge Bowsher, 7 April 2003).
127 [2003] EWHC 841 (Unreported, HH Judge Elleray, 16 April 2003).      128 Ibid [73]–[76].
129 The claimant and her late husband had contributed financially to the cost of acquisition of a flat by her parents-in-law who had been entitled to a substantial discount as local authority tenants under 'right to buy' legislation. The parties initially agreed that the flat would be transferred to the claimant after a specified time and subsequently amended this agreement to a promise of inheritance. The reason for the delay was a prevailing concern at the time of the purchase that an immediate trust would trigger the application of discount repayment provisions.
130 [2003] EWHC 841 [95].      131 Ibid [83].
132 [2003] EWHC 601 (Unreported, HH Judge Hildyard, 12 February 2003).      133 Ibid [5].
134 Ibid [69]. The rationale for the trust was discussed in the context of distinguishing the constructive trust from a resulting trust. The judge explained: 'a constructive trust is equity's method of enforcing conscience; a resulting trust is equity's response to the failure of a gift or proof of lack of intention to make one'. Insofar as the explanation distinguishes a resulting trust from intervention based on conscience it is inconsistent with *Westdeutsche*.

owner to renege on the parties' common intention.[135] This test was derived from the proprietary estoppel case of *Gillett v Holt* and was applied to the constructive trust without further comment. The judgment is unsatisfactory insofar as the novelty of the approach adopted is not acknowledged. A subsequent appeal was dismissed and while the judge's finding of detriment was upheld, his approach to the matter was not discussed.[136] However, the Court of Appeal classified the case as one in which the constructive trust and estoppel are indistinguishable. This view, which may explain the adoption of an estoppel analysis, is discussed below.[137]

Secondly, in *Edwin Shirley Productions v Workspace Management Ltd*, constructive trust and proprietary estoppel were jointly used as the basis of a claim to an interest in land following the failure of negotiations conducted on a 'subject to contract' basis.[138] The joint basis of the claim appears to be a consequence of *Yaxley v Gotts*.[139] There, Robert Walker LJ suggested that in some circumstances where an estoppel claim arises from an informal agreement between the parties, constructive trusts and estoppel 'coincide'.[140] This was to prevent estoppel claims derived from an agreement from failing as a matter of course as a result of the Law of Property (Miscellaneous Provisions) Act 1989 (UK) 2(1). The case concerned a joint venture for the acquisition of land and it was in that context that Robert Walker LJ considered the two doctrines to coincide. In *Edwin Shirley Productions* the source of the claim in an 'agreement' probably resulted in the dual basis of the claim despite the different factual context. The 'subject to contract' provision was considered to be decisive in defeating both the constructive trust and estoppel. Lawrence Collins J explained that both required detrimental reliance and unconscionable conduct. There could be no question of reliance or of unconscionable conduct where the parties were free to withdraw. This common interpretation of unconscionability therefore relates specifically to the application of these principles in a 'subject to contract' context. Prior to *Yaxley v Gotts*, claims in this context appear generally to have been based solely on proprietary estoppel.[141] A claim to a constructive trust appears

---

135  Unreported, High Court of England and Wales, HH Judge McGonigal, 30 November 2001.

136  The judge referred to *Gillett v Holt* in the context of the claim to detriment relating to the 'Wo Mei' and 'Ho Chung' properties. The Court of Appeal's discussion of this issue is reported at [2003] 1 FLR 23 [89].

137  Below n 162 and text.          138  [2001] 2 EGLR 16.

139  [2000] Ch 162. In *Edwin Shirley Productions* ibid [42] the court noted that the basis of the claim to a constructive trust had not been fully articulated. (The case was considered on an application for an interim injunction.)

140  [2000] Ch 162, 176.

141  The constructive trust does not generally seem to have been regarded as a possible basis for determining claims in this context. See, eg, the review by Barker, Kit, 'Coping with Failure – Reappraising Pre-Contractual Remuneration' (2003) 19 Journal of Contract Law 105. He discusses estoppel, together with contract, tort, unjust enrichment and redistribution.

to have been 'bootstrapped' to estoppel as a result of the agreement-based context of the claim.

### Summary

In applying the common intention constructive trust and proprietary estoppel the courts address the same issue: whether it is unconscionable for a legal owner to assert his or her rights and, in so doing, renege on an agreement or assurance relating to the claimant. However, the courts' approach to determining the issue of unconscionability differs between the doctrines. In relation to proprietary estoppel the existence of the core elements of a claim (and in particular the finding of detrimental reliance) is assessed by reference to the overriding question of whether it is unconscionable for the legal owner to renege on an assurance. Unconscionability also provides the basis of an overall evaluation of the claim 'in the round'. While the representor's knowledge may be a factor in determining unconscionability, particularly in claims to estoppel by acquiescence, it cannot be reduced to that requirement. Although less developed, a similar evaluative approach is being adopted in the exercise of remedial discretion through the concept of proportionality as a concept linked with unconscionability. In contrast, in relation to the common intention constructive trust, unconscionability is treated as the *consequence* of the existence of a common intention and detrimental reliance. It is not addressed as a specific requirement of the claim nor is it reflected in the courts' determination of the existence of the common intention and detrimental reliance. There is insufficient evidence of a requirement of knowledge reflecting that suggested by Lord Browne-Wilkinson's formula.

These differences in approach reflect different roles attributed to unconscionability in each doctrine. Bamforth and Finn have separately identified a number of different roles that may be attributed to unconscionability.[142] In light of their discussions, three broad uses of the concept can be identified.[143] First, unconscionability may provide an underlying rationale for intervention so that intervention is justified and informed by conscience in circumstances in which no explicit finding of unconscionability is required. Second, unconscionability may develop into a separate cause of action. Third, and between these extremes, unconscionability may play an active role where intervention

---

142  Bamforth, Nicholas, 'Unconscionability as a Vitiating Factor' (1995) Lloyds Maritime and Commercial Law Quarterly 538; Finn, Paul, 'Unconscionable Conduct' (1994) 8 Journal of Contract Law 37.

143  Bamforth ibid 539–42 discusses three senses in which unconscionability is used in the context of vitiating a contractual agreement. Finn ibid identifies four roles for the concept. Three of those reflect the roles identified here. The other (Finn's third role) relates specifically to unconscionable dealings in which he considers that unconscionable conduct has crystallised into a discrete doctrine.

is 'conditional upon the explicit finding of unconscionable conduct' and is used to channel the intervention or the relief.[144] The English courts' use of unconscionability in a claim to proprietary estoppel in cases stemming from *Gillett v Holt* reflects this active role for the concept. In contrast, the passive use of unconscionability in a common intention constructive trust equates with the first role.

While these different roles can be identified with some certainty, less clear is the extent to which they translate into differences in substance in determining when it is unconscionable for the representor or trustee to renege. In relation to determining detriment, reference to the overriding question of unconscionability in estoppel has appeared particularly significant in the context of assessing non-financial acts of the claimant. In *Gillett v Holt*[145] the claimants had subordinated their wishes to those of the legal owner over a long period of time and had devoted much of their lives to the legal owner and to his business interests. In *Campbell v Griffin*[146] and *Ottey v Grundy*[147] unconscionability was referred to in assessing claims to detriment that centred on care provided in the context of a quasi-familial relationship. Such claims to detriment are particularly difficult for the courts to assess. They may be explicable, in part, by the nature of the parties' relationship and may not be readily quantifiable in financial terms.[148] In the context of constructive trusts, without drawing on unconscionability, courts have considered claims to detriment based on non-financial contributions by reference to the context in which they have been provided. The courts generally look for conduct beyond that expected of a person in the claimant's position.[149] The test derived by the courts in estoppel by reference to unconscionability may in substance be the

---

144  Cf: Finn ibid 38.
145  [2001] Ch 210.
146  [2001] EWCA 990 (Unreported, Dame Elizabeth Butler-Sloss, Robert Walker and Thorpe LJJ, 27 June 2001).
147  [2003] EWCA 1176 (Unreported, Arden, Laws and Pill LJJ, 31 July 2003).
148  This difficulty was acknowledged by Robert Walker, LJ in *Jennings v Rice* [2003] 1 FCR 501 [51]. He explained that 'detriment can be quantified with reasonable precision if it consists solely of expenditure on improvements to another person's house . . . But the detriment of an ever-increasing burden of care for an elderly person, and of having to be subservient to his or her moods and wishes, is very difficult to quantify in money terms'. The remedy awarded in that case at first instance (and upheld on appeal) was based on the cost of care the claimant had provided the representor during the last eight years of her life. Robert Walker LJ [53]–[54] noted the 'detailed computational approach' that had been adopted by the Supreme Court of Tasmania in *Public Trustee v Wadley* [1997] 7 Tas LR 35 and attributed this to the (then prevailing) Australian preference for reliance-based remedies. Although he doubted that such an approach would be appropriate in English courts he accepted that 'the going-rate for live-in carers can provide a useful cross-check in the exercise of the court's discretion'.
149  Hopkins, Nicholas, *The Informal Acquisition of Rights in Land*, 2000, London: Sweet & Maxwell, 112–14.

same. The one guideline to emerge from *Ottey v Grundy* and *Campbell v Griffin* is for the courts to consider whether the claimant's acts go beyond those that could be expected of him or her by virtue of the parties' relationship. In *Ottey v Grundy* the Court of Appeal accepted the conclusion of the judge at first instance that the claimant had performed tasks 'well beyond anything that could be expected of her as a carer and girl friend'.[150] Similarly, in *Campbell v Griffin*, where the claimant had initially moved into the house of the representors, an elderly couple, as a lodger, Robert Walker LJ explained that he 'was doing much more for [the representors] than could be ascribed to even the most friendly lodger'.[151] However, substantive differences may arise as a result of the 'in the round' evaluation of unconscionability undertaken in estoppel. This is particularly because the evaluation enables a consideration of factors not necessarily related to establishing the core elements.

The consequence of these differences for the relationship between the concepts can now be discussed.

### The relationship between the common intention constructive trust and proprietary estoppel

The practical consequences of the different uses of unconscionability for the relationship between the common intention constructive trust and proprietary estoppel are twofold. First, the differences appear to belie suggestions that the two doctrines can be merged. Second, they may have overriding consequences for the timing of the claimant's interest under each doctrine.

#### The merger of the doctrines

A supposed merger of the common intention constructive trust and proprietary estoppel has been a consistent feature of the discussion of their relationship.[152] In *Austin v Keele*, Lord Oliver (delivering the Opinion of the Privy Council) suggested that the common intention constructive trust is 'in essence . . . an application of proprietary estoppel' for the purpose of establishing that the trust could post-date acquisition.[153] This is a point subsequently confirmed by the formula in *Rosset*.[154] In *Sabherwal* Robert Walker LJ suggested that estoppel is 'almost interchangeable' with the constructive trust (and the purchase money resulting trust) for the purposes of

---

150 [2003] EWCA 1176 (Unreported, Arden, Laws and Pill LJJ, 31 July 2003) [59].
151 [2001] EWCA 990 (Unreported, Dame Elizabeth Butler-Sloss, Robert Walker and Thorpe LJJ, 27 June 2001) [27].
152 The strongest academic proponent of this view is Hayton in his writings listed above n 8.
153 (1987) 10 NSWLR 283, 290.      154 Above n 118 and accompanying text.

applying statutory overreaching provisions.[155] In these cases the relationship between the principles was drawn on to achieve a particular purpose. A potentially broader and more significant suggestion is that there exists a category of case in which the doctrines merge or coincide. The principal line of authority for this view has its origins in Robert Walker LJ's judgment in *Yaxley v Gotts*.[156]

In *Yaxley v Gotts*, the Court of Appeal considered the application of estoppel to an oral agreement for an interest in land in light of the Law of Property (Miscellaneous Provisions) Act 1989 (UK), s 2(1). Under that provision an oral contract for sale of land is void and not merely unenforceable. Section 2(5) saves the operation of resulting, implied and constructive trusts but does not refer to estoppel. Robert Walker LJ rejected a general assertion that s 2 is a 'no-go area' for estoppel.[157] However, he considered that 'in the area of a joint enterprise for the acquisition of land . . . the two concepts [common intention constructive trust and proprietary estoppel] coincide'.[158] Therefore the findings on which the judge at first instance had applied estoppel could equally provide the basis for the imposition of a constructive trust.[159] By applying a constructive trust Robert Walker LJ relied on the statutory saving in s 2(5).

While Robert Walker LJ's comments were concerned specifically with the joint acquisition of land, as has been noted the case has led to a similar discussion of claims to a constructive trust and proprietary estoppel arising from failed negotiations conducted 'subject to contract'.[160] In *Jennings v Rice*, in a discussion of the remedial discretion in estoppel, Robert Walker LJ noted the consensual character of some claims to estoppel, 'falling not far short of an enforceable contract'. He made the general observation, by reference to *Yaxley v Gotts*, that 'if the only bar to the formation of a contract is non-compliance with s 2 of the Law of Property (Miscellaneous Provisions) Act 1989, the proprietary estoppel may become indistinguishable from a constructive trust'.[161] In *Chan v Leung* (although s 2 was not in issue) the Court of Appeal considered the facts of the case to fall within the consensual category identified in *Jennings v Rice* in which estoppel and constructive

---

155 (2000) 80 P&CR 256. There Robert Walker LJ distinguished between 'family' and 'commercial' equitable interests, suggesting that the former are subject to overreaching regardless of whether they are claimed through a constructive (or resulting) trust or proprietary estoppel. This is different from his suggestion in the other cases discussed in this part that constructive trusts and estoppel coincide where the estoppel claim arises in a consensual or agreement context. For example, an estoppel claim arising from a unilateral assurance would be treated as indistinguishable from a constructive trust through *Sabherwal* for the purpose of applying overreaching. However, such a claim falls outside the consensual situation identified in other cases as the situation in which the doctrines coincide.

156 [2000] Ch 162.        157 Ibid 174.        158 Ibid 176.        159 Ibid 177.

160 Above n 138 and accompanying text.        161 [2003] 1 FCR 501 [45].

trusts are indistinguishable.[162] In *Kinane v Mackie-Conteh* Neuberger LJ identified the 'essential difference' between situations where estoppel arises on its own, and those in which it gives rise to a constructive trust, as lying in the presence or absence of a common intention.[162a] Collectively, the emerging suggestion is that where a claim to estoppel arises in the context of an 'agreement' (and therefore potentially runs into the difficulty of non-compliance with s 2(1)) the doctrine merges with that of constructive trust (to enable reliance on s 2(5)).

On examination, however, it is apparent that there are difficulties with this developing argument. First, the authority for the merger is far from conclusive. It is founded on Robert Walker LJ's judgment in *Yaxley v Gotts* and on his own comments in *Jennings v Rice*. While the distinction had gathered momentum and reached a level of authority through *Chan v Leung* and *Kinane v Mackie-Conteh*, it rests on weak foundations. Robert Walker LJ's broad statement in *Yaxley v Gotts* is not supported by the judgments of Beldam and Clarke LJJ. Their judgments appear to accept that s 2(1) does not preclude the application of estoppel, without the imposition of a constructive trust, as long as the result does not run contrary to the public policy underlying the section,[163] a view recently approved in *Yeoman's Row Management Ltd v Cobbe* where a narrower view of the overlap in agreement cases appeared to be taken.[163a] Robert Walker LJ's comment in *Jennings v Rice* is *obiter* and based on his own (minority) judgment in *Yaxley v Gotts*. These weaknesses, in turn, detract from the authority of *Chan v Leung* and subsequent decisions. Second, while these cases represent the most developed idea of a category of case in which the doctrines coincide it is not the only suggestion to have been made. There remains a lack of coherence in identifying when a merger is appropriate. In *Oxley v Hiscock* Chadwick LJ supported the merger of the doctrines in circumstances in which the court is determining cohabitees' property rights in their home.[164] His argument is driven by the coincidence in the outcome of the principles when applied in such cases rather than the basis on which the court intervenes.[165] However, claims to property rights in a home may involve an agreement (and therefore fall within the same category of case identified in *Yaxley v Gotts*) or be based on a unilateral assurance (and thus fall outside the *Yaxley v Gotts* category).

---

162 [2003] 1 FLR 23 [91].     162a [2005] EWCA 45 [51].
163 The difference in the approach of the judges is acknowledged in *James v Evans* [2000] 3 EGLR 1. See further, eg, Smith, Roger J, 'Oral Contracts for the Sale of Land: Estoppels and Constructive Trusts' (2000) 116 Law Quarterly Review 11.
163a [2006] EWCA 1139, 31 July 2006. The Court of Appeal considered s 2(1) to be irrelevant to a claim in estoppel arising from pre-contractual expenditure pursuant to an agreement 'in principle' on the basis that the estoppel did not depend on a 'concluded agreement'.
164 [2004] 3 WLR 715 [66].     165 Ibid [66]–[71].

Even if these issues are resolved, however, it is submitted that the idea of a merger of the doctrines is ultimately irreconcilable with other case law which has seen the development of an active role for unconscionability in estoppel while a passive role has been maintained in constructive trusts. The different use of unconscionability in each doctrine appears to preclude any merger. The doctrines cannot be merged as the courts' approach to determining unconscionability in each differs.

### The timing of the claimant's interest

In relation to both the common intention constructive trust and proprietary estoppel the question arises as to the time at which the claimant's interest takes effect. As both doctrines are based on unconscionable conduct, consistency requires that the claimant cannot acquire an interest until the unconscionability is established. This point is made by Dal Pont in relation to the question of timing of the remedial constructive trust. He notes that as it is the finding of unconscionable conduct that attracts intervention, where no intervention is otherwise justified, 'this clearly must impact upon the timing of the relevant equitable interest'.[166] Without recognition of this link 'equity courts could intervene, and create or recognise equitable interests in property, whenever justice and fairness so dictated, without regard to principle'.[167] Dal Pont notes the difficulty this presents for a beneficial interest under a remedial constructive trust to be held to pre-date the judgment and, on this basis, he advocates the common intention trust as a means of providing the claimant with an interest pre-dating the claims of third parties.[168] As regards the remedial constructive trust, debate as to the timing of the interest has focused on whether the interest can pre-date the court's judgment. Rotherham has

---

166  above n 14, 265.

167  ibid 265. He notes that this statement assumes, in this instance, that the concept of unconscionability is grounded in principle.

168  Dal Pont notes, ibid 268, that in *Re Sabri* (1996) 21 Fam LR 213, where priority over a third party was accorded to the beneficiary under a remedial trust, the interest pre-dated the unconscionability. Contrast, Levine, J, 'Does Equity Treat as Done that which Ought to be Done? The Consequences Flowing from the Timing of the Imposition of a Constructive Trust' (1997) 5 Australian Journal of Property Law 74. She argues that the claimant's interest under a trust imposed through *Baumgartner v Baumgartner* (1987) 164 CLR 137 should date from the time of contributions to provide the beneficiary (in a family context) with priority. However, unconscionability is not present at that time: the unconscionability that forms the basis of the doctrine is the breakdown of the relationship without attributable fault and an unconscionable attempt by one party to then assert legal rights to property acquired in the course of and for the purposes of the relationship. (See, eg, *West v Mead* [2003] NSWSC 161 [84].) Despite this logical difficulty, in *Parianos v Melluish (Trustee for the Estate of Parianos)* [2003] FCA 190 [60] the Federal Court considered that the same approach to the timing of the trust could be taken regardless of whether the trust was based on a common intention or on the *Baumgartner v Baumgartner* principle.

suggested that 'the debate over the point at which the constructive trust takes effect is rather bizarre. The constructive trust is not an observable physical phenomenon. Rather, it is a purely juridical construct. As such it arises whenever the courts say it does'.[169]

The link between the timing of the interest and the foundation of the remedial constructive trust in unconscionability suggests that the question of timing is in fact central to the coherence of the doctrine. The same point applies *mutatis mutandis* to the common intention constructive trust and proprietary estoppel. However, in relation to these doctrines, the issue of timing does not revolve around pre- or post-judgment imposition of interests. As regards both, it is now established that the claimant acquires an interest prior to the judgment that is capable of being enforced against third parties. The question that arises is from what (pre-judgment) event the interest takes effect: the claimant's detrimental reliance or the time at which the legal owner reneges on the agreement or assurance? As regards the constructive trust, the interest acquired at the disputed time is the claimant's beneficial interest. In the context of estoppel, the question relates to the time at which the claimant acquires an inchoate equity that represents the existence of the estoppel claim. The (previously) uncertain proprietary status of the inchoate equity has been resolved (for the purpose of registered land) by the Land Registration Act.[170]

Under both doctrines the unconscionability relates to the trustee or representor reneging on the agreement or assurance. Therefore, the foundation of the doctrines in unconscionability suggests that the interest must date from that time. This is the view taken by Gray and Gray.[171] However, most

---

169 Rotherham, C, 'Proprietary Relief for Enrichment for Wrongs: Some Realism about Property Talk' (1996) 19 University of New South Wales Law Journal 378, 400.

170 This is the orthodox analysis of estoppel which distinguishes the inchoate equity from the interest awarded by the court in the exercise of its remedial discretion. The latter interest itself dates from the court's judgment. An alternative analysis is suggested by McFarlane, B, 'Proprietary Estoppel and Third Parties after the Land Registration Act 2002 (UK) c 9, s 116' (2003) 62 Cambridge Law Journal 661. Under his 'unitary' analysis the interest awarded by the court should exist retrospectively from the time the estoppel arises and its enforceability against third parties should be determined by its personal or proprietary status (as a matter of general law) rather than its mode of acquisition through estoppel. Adopting this approach, it is still necessary to identify the time at which the claimant acquires his or her interest, though the nature of the interest acquired at that date (and therefore its ability to bind third parties) would be dependent on the court's judgment. McFarlane does not address the issue of the time at which the interest arises beyond a general proposition, at 663 that the interest should exist 'as soon as all the requirements of the estoppel are made out'.

171 Gray, K and Gray, SF, *Elements of Land Law*, 3rd edn, 2000, London: Butterworths, 773 (in relation to estoppel) and at 724 (constructive trusts). In relation to estoppel see further Pawlowski, M, *The Doctrine of Proprietary Estoppel*, 1996, London: Sweet & Maxwell, 128–31 and Sparkes, Peter, *A New Land Law*, 2nd edn, 2003, Oxford: Hart Publishing,

commentators suggest that under both doctrines the claimant's interest dates from the time of the detrimental reliance.[172] One advantage of this interpretation is that the date is relatively identifiable. This enables certainty in determining the timing of the interest and also provides a trigger for the claimant to take action to protect the interest by, for example, entering a caution (or caveat) against the registered title. Whether the latter is of practical significance is dependent upon the likelihood of such interests being entered on the register. Given the informal nature of arrangements that lead to claims to estoppel or constructive trusts, it seems more likely that priority will be dependent on a claim to an overriding interest (where the claimant is in actual occupation). As a result of the different roles attributed to unconscionability this view of the timing may be sustainable in relation to the constructive trust but not as regards estoppel.

In the context of constructive trusts, *Re Sharpe* is generally cited as authority for the claimant's interest dating from the detriment,[173] but the case is unsatisfactory in this regard. There, the question was whether the claimant had rights in a home she shared with her nephew, the legal owner, enforceable against a third party (the nephew's trustee in bankruptcy). The claimant had provided a loan to enable the purchase of the house and was considered by the court to have an irrevocable licence to occupy until repayment of the loan. The case arose at a time when the legal status of licences remained uncertain and (in reasoning that no longer represents the accepted legal position) Browne-Wilkinson J held that the licence was a proprietary interest which took effect behind a constructive trust.[174] The importance of the judgment lies in how Browne-Wilkinson J determined the timing of the interest under the constructive trust. For the interest to be enforceable against the trustee in bankruptcy it was necessary to establish that it pre-dated the bankruptcy. Browne-Wilkinson J held that the interest dated from the time of the transac-

[23–31]. Sparkes explains the inchoate equity as arising on proof of the expectation, inducement and detrimental reliance. This includes unconscionability, which Sparkes considers to be the test of inducement.

172  In relation to estoppel see Wilken, S, *Wilken and Villiers: The Law of Waiver, Variation and Estoppel*, 2nd edn, 2002, Oxford; New York: Oxford University Press [11–79]; Ferguson above n 8, 122; Simon Baughen 'Estoppels Over Land and Third Parties: An Open Question?' (1994) 14 Legal Studies 147, 147, 154; Smith, RJ, *Property Law*, 4th edn, 2003, Harlow: Longman 189. This approach is also adopted in the context of explaining the operation of the Land Registration Act 2002 (UK) c 9 s 116 by Harpum, C, and Bignell, J, *Registered Land – The New Law*: a Guide to the Land Registration Act 2002, 2002, Bristol: Jordans [3–41] and Abbey, Robert and Richards, Mark, *Blackstone's Guide to the Land Registration Act 2002*, 2002, Oxford: Oxford University Press. In relation to the common intention constructive trust see Ferguson above n 8, 121.

173  [1980] 1 WLR 219. See, eg, Ferguson above n 8, 122.

174  The status of licences as personal interests in land was subsequently authoritatively established in *Ashburn Anstalt v Arnold* [1989] Ch 1.

tion (the purchase of the house). On the facts, as the claimant had provided a loan in connection with the purchase, this coincided with the time of her detriment. However, importantly, that is not the basis of Browne-Wilkinson J's reasoning. His reasoning is wholly negative as it is based on explaining why the claimant's interest could not be derived from other events. The interest could not date from the time of the parties' oral agreement as regards her occupation as such an agreement was unenforceable (under the then-applicable formality requirement in the Law of Property Act)[175] for lack of writing. Browne-Wilkinson J rejected an argument that the trust was remedial and that consequently the claimant's interest dated only from the time of his judgment, on the general basis that 'in order to provide a remedy the court must first find a right which has been infringed'.[176]

In relation to estoppel, no single authority is commonly cited as demonstrating that the inchoate equity arises at the time of the detrimental reliance, and the existence of differing views is rarely acknowledged.[177] Wilken cites *Pascoe v Turner*[178] in support of his view that the claimant's interest dates from the detriment.[179] There, however, the court did not state that the claimant's interest dated from that time. The detriment provided the basis of a claim to estoppel in circumstances in which, it was explained, the claimant would otherwise have remained a tenant at will.[180] The timing of her interest was not in issue, as her claim arose when the legal owner reneged on his assurance by bringing an action for possession. Wilken also cites a number of cases in which courts have treated the estoppel claimant as having an ownership interest in the land, or have said that a constructive trust arises in his or her favour at the time of the detriment. These authorities are not necessarily strong on their merits.[181] For example, in relation to the imposition of a trust,

---

175 (1925) UK c 20, s 40.   176 [1986] 1 WLR 219, 225.
177 An exception is Wilken above n 172, [11–79] n 318 where the author notes his disagreement with the analysis provided by Gray and Gray (though without stating reasons).
178 [1979] 1 WLR 431.   179 Above n 172, [11–79] n 318.   180 [1979] 1 WLR 431, 435–6.
181 In relation to the claimant being recognised as having ownership rights other than under a constructive trust the author cites *Unity Joint Stock Mutual Banking Association v King* ('*Unity Joint Stock*') (1858) 25 Beav 72; 53 ER 563; *Pennine Raceway v Kirkless MBC* ('*Pennine Raceway*') [1983] QB 382; *Voyce v Voyce* (1991) 62 P&CR 290. *Unity Joint Stock* is an early case and the basis of the principle was not discussed. In *Pennine Raceway*, the claimants had acted to their detriment pursuant to a contract with the local authority for use of land for motor racing. In upholding a claim to compensation against the local authority following revocation of planning permission the court said, *obiter*, that the claimant's interest would constitute an interest in the land if this had been a requirement for compensation. The interest was not explained in terms of estoppel but as a contractual licence made irrevocable by the claimant's acts. In *Voyce v Voyce*, the question in issue was the enforcement of an estoppel claim against the representor's successor under her will. The claimant's detriment was one aspect in establishing that prior to the representor's death the point had already been reached whereby it would have been unconscionable for her to renege on the assurance. Nicholls LJ, at 296 summarised the conclusion of the judge that 'by

the leading authority cited is *Re Basham*.[182] There, HH Judge Nugee suggested that where a claim to estoppel concerns a future interest, it gives rise to a species of constructive trust based on the claimant's detriment. The constructive trust envisaged (being institutional, as distinct from a constructive trust imposed as a remedy for estoppel)[183] was explained as being distinct from the common intention constructive trust but shared a 'common theme' with that and other constructive trusts so as to raise an expectation that the general principles applicable will be the same.[184] However, the imposition of a constructive trust has not been followed in subsequent estoppel claims involving future interests.[185] In any event, the case serves only to reiterate the underlying issue. If, as HH Judge Nugee states, the constructive trust (including one imposed in a claim to estoppel) 'is the concept employed by a court of equity to prevent a person from relying on his legal rights where it would be unconscionable for him to do so',[186] on what basis could the trust pre-date the unconscionability on which it is based?

The issue of timing of the inchoate equity is not resolved by the Land Registration Act.[187] Section 116 of that Act provides that the equity acquired by estoppel 'has effect *from the time the equity arises* as an interest capable of binding successors in title'.[188] The provision is derived from a Law Commission report, but the report itself is contradictory as regards the time at which the inchoate equity arises. The Law Commission initially explains that an equity that gives the claimant the right to go to court and seek relief arises when the legal owner 'refuses [the claimant] the anticipated right or interest in circumstances that make the refusal unconscionable'.[189] However, the Law Commission subsequently notes that its concern is with the status of the

---

reason of what [the representor] had said and done and what [the claimant] had done in reliance thereon, [the representor] would have been estopped herself'.

182 [1986] 1 WLR 1498. Wilken also cites *Sen v Headley* [1991] Ch 425 and *Re Dale* [1993] 4 All ER 129. Neither of those cases concerned claims to estoppel and in neither is the timing of a constructive trust discussed. In *Sen v Headley* (a claim to *donatio mortis causa*) the court suggested that where estoppel gives the claimant the right to call for a conveyance, that right could exist under a constructive trust. In *Re Dale* (a claim based on mutual wills) the court simply noted that the trust referred to in *Re Basham* was not based on the receipt of property.

183 See the discussion by Nield above n 2, 312–13.

184 [1986] 1 WLR 1498, 1504.

185 Eg, those arising in the same factual context as *Re Basham* of testamentary promises: *Gillett v Holt* [2001] Ch 210; *Jennings v Rice* [2003] 1 FCR 501; *Ottey v Grundy* [2003] EWCA 1176 (Unreported, Arden, Laws and Pill LJJ, 31 July 2003); *Jiggins v Brisley* [2003] EWHC 841 (Unreported, HH Judge Elleray, 16 April 2003).

186 [1986] 1 WLR 1498, 1504.        187 2002 (UK) c 9, s 116        188 Emphasis added.

189 Law Commission for England and Wales, *Land Registration for the 21st Century – A Conveyancing Revolution*, Report No 271 (2001) [5–29] (quoting from its consultative document).

inchoate equity 'that arises after [the claimant] has acted to his or her detriment but before the court can make an order giving effect to it'.[190]

In the context of the common intention constructive trust the passive role of unconscionability makes it possible to treat the claimant's interest as arising from the time of the detrimental reliance despite the initial logical difficulty in the interest pre-dating the unconscionable denial of the right. Applying the formula for unconscionability in *Gissing v Gissing* and *Grant v Edwards*, once a common intention and detrimental reliance have been established, the legal owner's conscience is affected because it is *necessarily* unconscionable for him or her to deny the claimant's interest. In relation to estoppel, however, the active role of unconscionability precludes a similar analysis. The existence of detrimental reliance is insufficient to establish whether it is unconscionable for the legal owner to renege. That question requires an examination of the claim 'in the round' which, as has been seen, may involve consideration of factors beyond the existence of the detriment. In light of the active role of unconscionability in estoppel there is a logical bar to recognising the inchoate equity as arising prior to establishing that it is unconscionable for the legal owner to renege.

### Conclusion

The principal conclusion reached is that, while the common intention constructive trust and proprietary estoppel are both founded on unconscionability, the courts' use of that concept in each doctrine differs. On this basis, unconscionability may serve to differentiate between the doctrines rather than to reinforce their relationship. The secondary conclusion is that the knowledge thesis of unconscionability that has been separately advanced to explain the role of unconscionability in each of these doctrines does not accurately explain its role in either.

These conclusions have consequences both for our understanding of the relationship between the common intention constructive trust and proprietary estoppel and, in the broader context, for our understanding of unconscionability. The conclusions do not put an end to the question of the relationship between these doctrines, but they inform and refocus that debate. The different use of unconscionability in each of the doctrines belies the developing idea that the doctrines can be merged. Debate as to their relationship should take as a starting point that the courts are applying two distinct doctrines. The different use of unconscionability may affect the timing of the claimant's interest under each doctrine and, in particular, the active role of unconscionability in estoppel precludes the claimant's interest from pre-dating the unconscionable assertion of the representor's legal rights.

190  Ibid [5–30].

In broader terms, the analysis re-emphasises the importance of examining unconscionability in each context in which the concept is invoked and highlights the difficulty in attempting to reduce the concept to any particular requirement. Unconscionability is 'too chameleon' a concept to be so confined.[191] Even in doctrines in which the courts are addressing the same question (whether it is unconscionable to renege on an agreement or assurance as to the claimant's rights) unconscionability has been shown to be playing different roles. This, in turn, casts further doubt on Lord Browne-Wilkinson's attempt to use conscience as a requirement linked to knowledge as a foundational principle for the law of trusts. If conscience is to provide such a foundational principle, it must be recognised that in some trusts (including the common intention constructive trust) it is not connected to a requirement of knowledge.

---

191 A description coined by Finn, Paul, 'Australian Developments in Common and Commercial Law' [1990] Journal of Business Law 265, 269.

# Chapter 10

# Constructive trusts from a law and economcs perspective

*Anthony Duggan**

## Introduction

The constructive trust is a court order declaring that the defendant (D) holds a disputed asset on trust for the plaintiff (P). Langbein says that the constructive trust is 'a species of equitable remedy, comparable in function to the injunction or decree of specific performance. The constructive trust is imposed coercively, as a means of correcting wrongdoing or preventing unjust enrichment'.[1] By contrast, he goes on to say, 'the ordinary private trust is a consensual relationship voluntarily assumed by the trustee'.[2] The constructive trust remedy is a proprietary one. It gives P a claim to the disputed asset itself. The alternative is a personal remedy for damages or an account of profits. A personal remedy gives P a money claim against D but nothing more. The difference matters particularly if D is bankrupt, but it is trite law that D's bankruptcy is neither a necessary nor a sufficient condition for granting P constructive trust relief.[3]

What are the factors that determine the availability of constructive trust relief? Langbein's statement suggests that the constructive trust remedy may serve either a deterrence function or a restitutionary function. The implication is that the deterrence function and the restitutionary function together account for all cases of constructive trust relief. However, as Chambers points out, sometimes the constructive trust serves what he calls a 'perfectionary' function: the court grants the remedy to enforce an express or implied bargain

* Iacobucci Chair, Faculty of Law, University of Toronto. Thanks to Amanda Darrach for research assistance, to Michael Bryan for many instructive discussions and to Ed Iacobucci, Rick Bigwood and Robert Chambers for comments on an earlier draft. All errors are mine. This paper was completed while I was on sabbatical leave at the University of Auckland Faculty of Law. My thanks to generous hosts.

1 Langbein, John, 'The Contractarian Basis of the Law of Trusts' (1995) 105 Yale Law Journal 625 at 631.
2 Ibid.     3 See the bankruptcy aspect section at p 261, below.

between P and D.[4] For example, constructive trusts are commonly imposed to perfect an agreement for the transfer of an asset by D to P.[5] The law and economics literature to date has given the constructive trust scant attention. Langbein analyses the express trust from a law and economics perspective, but he pointedly leaves the constructive trust out of account.[6] Levmore discusses the law of restitution from a law and economics perspective, but his focus is on the cause of action and not the choice of remedy.[7] This chapter aims to fill the gap. The section of this chapter titled 'Five illustrative cases' analyses five leading Australian, Canadian and English cases: *Hewett v Court*;[8] *Soulos v Korkontzilas*;[9] *Daly v Sydney Stock Exchange Ltd*;[10] *Chase Manhattan Bank NA v Israel-British Bank (London) Ltd*;[11] and *Baumgartner v Baumgartner*.[12] The argument, taking Chambers one step further, is that all constructive trusts are perfectionary at heart: in all cases (not some) the function of the remedy is to reproduce the outcome P and D themselves are likely to have agreed on upfront if bargaining had been costless. The deterrence and restitutionary functions Langbein identifies are subsidiary to the perfectionary function. Given the constructive trust's perfectionary function, it is untrue or at least an over-simplification to say that the constructive trust is 'imposed coercively'. As it happens, the constructive trust is subject to more or less the same kind of contractarian analysis that Langbein applies to express trusts and that Easterbrook and Fischel apply to fiduciary relationships at large.[13] 'The bankruptcy aspect' section of this chapter discusses bankruptcy with reference back to the cases as outlined in the previous section.

4 Chambers, Robert, 'Constructive Trusts in Canada' (1999) 37 Alberta Law Review 173. The terminology comes from Gbolhan Elias, *Explaining Constructive Trusts*, 1990, Oxford: Clarendon Press.

5 See, eg, *Lysaght v Edwards* (1876) 2 Ch.D. 499. Sir George Jessel MR said:

'it appears to me that the effect of a contract of sale has been settled for more than two centuries ... [T]he moment you have a valid contract for sale the vendor becomes in equity a trustee for the purchaser of the estate sold, and the beneficial ownership passes to the purchaser, the vendor having a right to the purchase-money, a charge or lien on the estate for the security of the purchase-money, and a right to retain possession of the estate until the purchase-money is paid, in the absence of express contract as to the time of delivering possession' (p 506, quoted in Chambers, op cit 186).

6 Langbein, op cit.

7 Levmore, Saul, 'Explaining Restitution', (1975) 71 Virginia Law Review 65. See also Beatson, J and Bishop, W, 'Mistaken Payments in the Law of Restitution', (1986) 36 University of Toronto Law Journal 149 republished in Beatson, Jack, *The Use and Abuse of Unjust Enrichment: Essays on the Law of Restitution*, 1991, Oxford: Clarendon Press, Ch 6.

8 (1983) 149 CLR 639.     9 [1997] 2 SCR 217.     10 (1986) 160 CLR 371.

11 [1981] Ch 105.     12 (1987) 164 CLR 137.

13 Langbein, op cit; Easterbrook, Frank H and Fischel, Daniel, R, 'Contract and Fiduciary Duty' (1993) 36 Journal of Law and Economics 425.

The chapter focuses on Australian, English and Canadian cases. There are differences in constructive trusts doctrine between the three countries. In Canada, the courts following the United States lead, have developed the remedial constructive trust to prevent unjust enrichment. The test for unjust enrichment depends on proof of: (1) D's enrichment; (2) P's corresponding deprivation; and (3) the absence of a 'juridical justification' for the enrichment.[14] The remedy is discretionary in the sense that even if the case satisfies all three elements of the test, the court will still not necessarily impose the trust. The court may refuse to impose the trust on the ground that there are other remedies available to P 'which make the declaration of the constructive trust unnecessary or inappropriate'.[15] The remedial constructive trust is not part of English or Australian law.[16] For the courts in England or Australia to impose a constructive trust, P must establish a pre-existing proprietary entitlement in the disputed asset. The constructive trust simply declares P's entitlement. By contrast, in Canada the remedial constructive trust is more than just declaratory of P's pre-existing right. It is the source of the right. The expression 'institutional' constructive trust distinguishes the Anglo-Australian variety from the North American remedial variety.[17] The difference between the institutional constructive trust and the remedial constructive trust is not as large as it seems. In Canada it ought to follow from the explicitly remedial character of the remedial constructive trust that P's entitlement dates only from the making of the order. However, the courts have not followed this path. The general rule is that the remedial constructive trust is retrospective to the date P's claim arose.[18] The rule is anomalous given the supposedly remedial character of the remedial constructive trust and it blurs the distinction between the remedial constructive trust, and the institutional constructive trust. Conversely, in England and Australia it ought to follow from the institutional character of the institutional constructive trust that P's entitlement dates from the event that gives rise to P's claim. However, the courts do not always follow this path. Depending on the circumstances, a court may frame the order so that it is operative only from the judgment date.[19] The rule is anomalous given the supposedly institutional character of the institutional constructive trust. It blurs the distinction between the institutional constructive trust and the remedial constructive trust. The dating of P's entitlement matters in the context of a potential priority dispute between P and a third party who acquires an equitable interest in the disputed asset

14  *Pettkus v Becker* (1980) 117 DLR (3d) 257.

15  *Rawluk v Rawluk* (1990) 65 DLR (4th) 161 at 185–186 per McLachlin J.

16  *Westdeutsche Landesbank Girozentrale v Council of the London Borough of Islington* [1996] AC 669; *Muschinski v Dodds* (1985) 160 CLR 583.

17  Dewar, JL, 'The Development of the Remedial Constructive Trust', (1982) 60 Canadian Bar Review 265.

18  *Rawluk v Rawluk* (1990) 65 DLR (4th) 161.   19  *Muschinski v Dodds* (1985) 160 CLR 583.

between the date P's claim arose and the judgment date.[20] In principle, the third party should have priority given that P's interest was undiscoverable at the date of P's dealing with the third party and in both institutional constructive trusts and remedial constructive trusts jurisdictions, the courts, in the manner just described, have retained for themselves sufficient discretion to achieve this outcome. Subject to this point, the institutional-remedial constructive trust distinction is an arid one in policy terms.[21] The key question is not how the courts rationalise the constructive trust doctrinally, but what considerations drive the outcomes of the cases. That question is common to all jurisdictions, regardless of which doctrine the courts apply, and it is the question this chapter addresses.

### Five illustrative cases

### 1 *Hewett v Court*[22]

#### Case summary

In *Hewett v Court*, P (the customers) contracted with D (the builder) for the construction of a transportable house. The arrangement was that D would construct the house at its premises and, upon completion, transport the house and install it on P's land. The contract price was $34,116, made up as follows:

| | |
|---|---:|
| Twenty per cent deposit on execution of contract | $ 6,823 |
| On pitching of roof | 13,646 |
| Seven days prior to delivery | 12,647 |
| Practical completion on site – ready for occupation | 1,000 |
| | $34,116 |

Clause 8 of the contract provided that the house was to be at D's risk from commencement to practical completion and that it remained D's property until P paid the whole of the contract price. Clause 10 provided that if P terminated the contract D could recover from P a proportion of the contract price equivalent to the value of the work D had already done.

D became insolvent while P's house was still under construction. D agreed

---

20 See Goode, R, 'Proprietary Restitutionary Claims' in Cornish, WR, Nolan, R, O'Sullivan, J and Virgo, G (eds), *Restitution Past, Present and Future: Essays in Honour of Gareth Jones*, 1998, Oxford: Hart Publishing, 63 at 72–73.

21 Paciocco, DM, 'The Remedial Constructive Trust: A Principled Basis for Priorities Over Creditors' (1989) 68 Canadian Bar Review 315 at 319

22 (1983) 149 CLR 639. For two similar Canadian cases, see: *Waselenko v Touche Ross Ltd* [1983] 2 WWR 352 affirmed [1985] 3 WWR 38 (Sask. CA) and *Re Kenyon Homes Ltd* [1985] 3 WWR 18 (Sask. CA)

to hand over the partly completed house to P in exchange for a payment ($6,411) representing the difference between the value of the partly completed house ($26,880) and the amounts P had already paid D under the contract ($20,469). D's liquidator attacked the transaction, claiming it was a preference because P received a house valued at $26,880 in return for a payment of only $6,411. Wickham J in the Supreme Court of Western Australia held that there was no preference and that P was entitled to keep the house. The Full Court reversed his decision on appeal. The High Court, on further appeal, by a majority (Gibbs CJ, Murphy and Deane JJ, Wilson and Dawson JJ dissenting) reversed the Full Court and restored Wickham J's decision. The basis for the decision was that P had an equitable lien on the partly completed house to secure repayment of the deposit and instalments P had paid under the contract. The equitable lien gave P a right to the partly completed house ahead of D's other creditors in bankruptcy and so D's delivery of the house to P did not amount to a preference. An equitable lien is a form of judicially created security interest. It gives the lienee 'a positive right to obtain, in certain circumstances, an order for the sale of the subject property or for actual payment from the subject fund'.[23] The lienee must account to the lienor for any surplus. In *Hewett v Court*, P's total payments equalled the value of the house and so there was no surplus. To all intents and purposes, therefore, the court's ruling was the same as if it had declared a constructive trust over the house in P's favour.

Clause 8 of the contract stated unequivocally that property was to remain in D until P paid the whole of the contract price. According to the majority judgments, this meant legal title only and it did not preclude P from acquiring an equitable interest at an earlier time. It was 'a fundamental assumption of the contract that, from the time construction commenced, a particular home in the course of construction would be identified as the home being constructed for installation on [P's] land'.[24] The majority implied the equitable lien to give effect to this assumption. One indicator of the assumption was the parties' use of the word 'home' to describe the subject matter of the contract: '[D] covenanted that it would complete the construction of "the home" in accordance with identified plans and specifications "within 60 days of the date of commencement"' and 'the design of the home accorded with the plans and specifications which had been agreed between [P and D] and which, to some extent, were the product of their joint intellectual activity'.[25] A second indicator was clause 10 (the termination provision) which, the majority said, 'is plainly based upon mutual recognition that circumstances could arise in which, upon [P's] rescission or termination of the contract . . . they

---

23  (1983) 149 CLR 639 at 664 per Deane J.  24  (1983) 149 CLR 639 at 661 per Deane J.
25  (1983) 149 CLR 639 at 661 per Deane J.

would be entitled to the partly completed house'.[26] Wilson and Dawson JJ, dissenting, held that no property in the construction passed to P until completion and there was no obligation on D's part to transfer that particular house to P: 'they might have constructed an identical house to fulfil their contractual obligations to [P]'.[27] Furthermore, there was no reason in principle for preferring P to D's other creditors in D's bankruptcy: 'the other creditors may have included persons who paid moneys by way of deposit or otherwise for transportable houses but who were unable to identify, or sufficiently identify, a particular house as the one which was being constructed pursuant to the contract between them and the company.'[28] The correct approach, Wilson and Dawson JJ said, was to disregard D's financial position and to ask whether, if D had been solvent, P would have had a claim to the uncompleted house. The answer, they said, was 'no'. P and D's contract was not specifically enforceable. It was a construction contract and 'as a general rule, the Court will not compel the building of houses'.[29] There was no reason to suppose that damages would not have been an adequate remedy for P.[30] Giving P an equitable lien would 'introduce unnecessary complexity into the ascertainment of the rights of the parties and would be destructive of that certainty which is the basis of sound commercial practice'.[31]

### Analysis

The majority judgments in *Hewett v Court* assume that the parties by implication intended P to have a proprietary interest in the house from the time construction commenced. Is this a plausible assumption? The answer depends on the net costs and benefits to P and D jointly of such a provision. Outside D's bankruptcy, the main benefit to P is that if D breached the contract at any stage P could claim the uncompleted house as an alternative to suing D for damages. P might prefer a proprietary remedy to damages if the construction has sentimental or other special value for P. In advance of the contract, P might worry that if the remedy is damages, a court may assess the claim solely by reference to the construction's market value, leaving P's special attachment out of account. A key consideration for the majority in *Hewett v Court* was that the contract described the construction as 'a home', not a house. By implication, a home has sentimental or like value for the purchaser, but a house does not. If this was what P and D really meant, then the distinction

26  (1983) 149 CLR 639 at 661–662 per Deane J.
27  (1983) 149 CLR 639 at 658 per Wilson and Dawson JJ.
28  (1983) 149 CLR 639 at 658 per Wilson and Dawson JJ.
29  (1983) 149 CLR 639 at 658 per Wilson and Dawson JJ, quoting *Wilkinson v Clements* (1872) 8 Ch App 96 at 112 per Mellish LJ.
30  (1983) 149 CLR 639 at 658 per Wilson and Dawson JJ.
31  (1983) 149 CLR 639 at 659 per Wilson and Dawson JJ.

the majority drew is readily understandable in economic terms. The question is whether it *was* what they really meant. Clause 8 of the contract clearly stated that property was to remain in D until completion. The 'house-home' distinction is at best flimsy evidence of a contrary intention.[32] Wilson and Dawson JJ reached the opposite conclusion. They said that damages would have been an adequate remedy for P. This implies a finding that P did not value the uncompleted construction at higher than its market value. Clause 8 of the contract supports Wilson and Dawson JJ's construction. It is plausible to suppose that if P really did have a special interest they wanted to protect, they would have bargained for the removal or modification of clause 8 rather than leaving the question to be determined by implication from vague hints in other parts of the contract. In any event, a ruling against P would have reduced contractual uncertainty in future cases by forcing parties who want an equitable lien to say so explicitly.

The main cost to D of an equitable lien, as Wilson and Dawson JJ recognised,[33] is that D loses the right of substitution from the moment the roof is pitched. D may have wanted a right of substitution to guard against the risk of unexpected delays in other similar projects. Call D's contract with P 'Project A'. Call D's contract with Customer 2 'Project B'. Project A and Project B are similar. Assume that D is on schedule with Project A but behind with Project B. Customer 2 values timely completion more highly than P does. The economically efficient solution is for D to substitute the Project A construction for the Project B one and to pay P damages for loss the delay causes. Then all parties are better off, or at least no worse off: Customer 2, because it gets timely completion; P, because D compensates P for loss the delay causes; and D, because D saves on the difference between the damages it would otherwise have paid Customer 2 and the damages it pays P. An equitable lien in P's favour might prevent this outcome. If P has an equitable lien, D will have to purchase the right of substitution from P. Other things being equal, D will purchase for any price equal to or lower than the amount of damages it will have to pay Customer 2 if Project B is delayed. P will sell at any price equal to or higher than the loss P will suffer if Project A is delayed. In practice, though, P or D may make strategic bargaining mistakes: in an effort to secure a larger share of the post-bargaining surplus, P or D may make wrong estimates about what the other party will do: P may hold out for a

---

32  The majority also relied on clause 10 (the termination provision), asserting that it was 'plainly based' on P and D's understanding that in certain circumstances P would have a claim to the construction while work was still in progress. However, clause 10 was expressly subject to any other rights or remedies D might have. The provision could be read as meaning simply that in the case of P's repudiation, D might, at its election, force P to purchase the partly completed house for a proportion of the total price. On this construction, property in the house would pass to P upon payment of the required amount, but not before.

33  (1983) 149 CLR 639 at 658.

higher price than D is willing to pay and D may hold out for a lower price than P is willing to accept. Negotiations may break down as a result.[34] In advance of the contract, D may worry about the risks associated with strategic behaviour if P has an equitable lien and D's preference may be for P not to have one.

In summary, the majority judgments in *Hewett v Court* are open to question because: (1) they assume, on the basis of flimsy evidence and contrary to what the contract expressly said, that P had a sentimental or like attachment to the house from the time construction began and that P would have wanted an equitable lien to protect that interest; and (2) they disregard the costs to D of an equitable lien and the possibility that, given the costs, an equitable lien might not have been in P and D's joint interests.[35] In addition, the decision has costly implications for future cases because it increases contractual uncertainty. The reach of the decision is uncertain. It may not apply to contracts for the sale of goods because the sale of goods legislation precludes equitable interests arising by operation of law[36] and it does not apply to a building contract where the construction takes place on P's own site because in that case '[P] needs no lien to protect him once the work for which he pays has become a fixture'.[37] However, numerous other contracts for work and materials may now be subject to a default rule implying an equitable lien in P's favour. It is hard to predict which contracts the default rule applies to or at what stage of the work in progress a court might say the lien arises. If parties do not want an equitable lien, they will have to say so expressly. Even this may not be enough if the court decides, as in *Hewett v Court* itself, that the express term is not sufficiently explicit or that other features of the contract point to an overriding contrary intention. The upshot is that, in future cases, D cannot be certain about its right of substitution. Uncertainty causes mistakes: D may bargain with P for a right of substitution only to discover later that P never had an equitable lien in the first place. The consequence is to increase needlessly the parties' transactions costs. Alternatively, D may neglect to bargain with P, only to discover later that P did have an equitable lien after all. The likely consequence is costly litigation to determine the parties' rights.

---

34  See Ulen, Thomas H, 'Specific Performance' in Peter Newman (ed), *The New Palgrave Dictionary of Economics and the Law*, 1998, London: Macmillan, III, p 481 and references cited there.

35  Note Murphy J's lament: 'as so often happens in commercial and conveyancing cases, the court was not assisted by any "commercial impact statement", that is, of what would be the effect in commerce generally, of charges arising in such circumstances': (1983) 149 CLR 639 at 651.

36  (1983) 149 CLR 639 at 646 per Gibbs CJ and 662 per Deane J.

37  (1983) 149 CLR 639 at 647 per Gibbs CJ.

## Recapitulation

To recapitulate, with reference to this chapter's main themes, the judgments in *Hewett v Court* all focus explicitly on P and D's likely joint intention with respect to the passing of property in the house. Where they part company is on the secondary question as to what that likely intention might be. The court clearly saw the granting or withholding of the proprietary remedy in perfectionary terms. Deterrence and restitutionary considerations did not enter into the matter.

## 2  *Soulos v Korkontzilas* [38]

## Case summary

In *Soulos v Korkontzilas*, P and D were both members of the Toronto Greek community. D was a real estate broker and P was his client. D negotiated on P's behalf for the purchase of a commercial property. After some toing and froing, the vendor agreed to a price of $265,000. Instead of passing this information on to P, D arranged for his wife to purchase the property. She later transferred the property to D and herself as joint tenants. D told P that the sale had gone off because the vendor had changed its mind about selling the property. Three years later, P learned that D had purchased the property for himself. He brought an action against D alleging breach of fiduciary duty giving rise to a constructive trust. P's claim was for the property to be transferred to him for the price D had paid subject to adjustments for changes in value and losses incurred on the property since purchase. The market value of the property had decreased since the date of D's purchase. However, the property held special value for P because its tenant was P's banker and being one's banker's landlord was a source of prestige in the Greek community. The trial judge rejected P's claim, holding on the basis of *Pettkus v Becker* [39] that there must be unjust enrichment before the court can award a constructive trust. In the present case, there was no unjust enrichment because the market value of the property had decreased and so D had lost money on the deal. The judge also said that it would be 'disproportionate and inappropriate to utilize the drastic remedy of a constructive trust where the plaintiff has suffered no damage'. [40] The Ontario Court of Appeal reversed the trial judge. The Supreme Court by a majority (La Forest, Gonthier, Cory, McLachlin and Major JJ, Sopinka and Iacobucci JJ dissenting) upheld the Court of Appeal's decision.

McLachlin J delivered judgment on behalf of the majority. She held that the law of constructive trust embraces the situations in which English courts

---

38  [1997] 2 SCR 217.        39  (1980) 117 DLR (3rd) 257 (SCC).
40  Quoted by McLachlin J [1997] 2 SCR 117 at 225.

of equity traditionally found a constructive trust in addition to cases of unjust enrichment like *Pettkus v Becker*. 'Good conscience' was the unifying concept. Cases where good conscience requires the imposition of a constructive trust fall into two general categories: (1) where D obtains property by a wrongful act, notably breach of fiduciary duty or breach of a duty of loyalty D owes P; and (2) where D has not acted wrongfully in obtaining the property, but D would be unjustly enriched at P's expense by being permitted to keep the property himself.[41] In the present case, a constructive trust was required: (1) to remedy the non-monetary deprivation P had suffered as a consequence of D's wrongful conduct; and (2) to ensure that agents and others in positions of trust remain faithful to their duty of loyalty. There were no special features that would make imposition of a constructive trust unjust. No third parties were affected. Nor would D be treated unfairly because P was prepared to reimburse D for his outlay on the property. Sopinka and Iacobucci JJ dissented. They held that: (1) the constructive trust remedy depends on proof of unjust enrichment; (2) the trial judge rejected P's contention that the property held special value for him and there was no basis for interfering with this conclusion; and (3) given (2), there was no unjust enrichment because P had suffered no loss.[42]

### Analysis

Fiduciary relationships raise monitoring cost problems.[43] P (the principal) or T a third party (such as the creator of a trust) entrusts D (the fiduciary) with an enterprise to control and manage on P's behalf. The enterprise may comprise assets (land, investments and the like) (as in the case of a trust where

41  This statement overlooks the perfectionary function of the constructive trust: see Chambers, op cit.
42  Proposition (1) is open to question on the ground that it does not adequately account for the bribe cases (eg, *Reading v The King* [1947] 2 All ER 27) or the conflict of interest cases (eg, *Canadian Aero Services Ltd v O'Malley* [1974] SCR 592). To fit these cases into the unjust enrichment mould one has to say that the profits D earned in breach of fiduciary duty belong in equity to P whether or not P could have earned those profits in the absence of the breach: *Soulos v Korkontzilas* [1997] 2 SCR 217 at 253 per Sopinka J. However, the analysis begs the question: if D's profits belong in equity to P, the reason must be because D holds the profits on trust but the existence of the trust is the point in issue. Proposition (1) is 'an attempt to shoehorn disgorgement of the profits of wrongdoing into a model based on subtractive unjust enrichment': Smith, Lionel D, 'Constructive Trusts – Unjust Enrichment – Breach of Fiduciary Obligation: *Soulos v Korkontzilas*', (1997) 76 Canadian Bar Review 539 at 547.
43  Easterbrook and Fischel, op cit. See also: Cooter, RJ and Freedman, BJ, 'The Fiduciary Relationship: Its Economic Character and Legal Consequences' (1991), 66 New York University Law Review 1045; Smith, DG, 'The Critical Resource Theory of Fiduciary Duty', (2002) 55 Vanderbilt Law Review 1399; Ribstein, LE, *The Structure of the Fiduciary Relationship* Illinois Law and Economics Working Paper Series, Working Paper No LE03–003, January 2003.

D is the trustee and P is the beneficiary), a business (as in the case of a company where D is a director and P is a shareholder) or an acquisition (as in the case of an agency arrangement where P is a prospective buyer and D acts on P's behalf). The separation of ownership from management and control of the enterprise gives D an incentive to cheat P. The incentive to cheat arises because of the costs to outsiders associated with monitoring D's inputs. Monitoring costs are high because D's management and control of the enterprise gives D exclusive access to information that may be relevant to the assessment of D's inputs. This means that D's outputs may be all outsiders have to go on as evidence of D's inputs. However, D's outputs themselves may be ambiguous to outside eyes in the absence of information about D's inputs. A loss to the enterprise may signal misconduct on D's part or it may be just bad luck. Likewise, a gain to the enterprise may occur despite D's inputs. Fiduciary law's response to this information imbalance is to assume the worst. As a general rule, D must disgorge all personal gains made in the course of office and P does not have to prove that D actually cheated. In the landmark case of *Keech v Sandford*,[44] D, having failed to obtain the renewal of a lease on P's behalf, took the lease in his own name. There was no way for the court to know whether D deliberately caused his negotiations on P's behalf with the landlord to fail so that he could pick up the lease for himself. The court held that proof of D's intention to cheat was immaterial and it declared a constructive trust of the leasehold interest in P's favour. The *Keech v Sandford* rule forces D either to give up all thought of taking the gain for himself or alternatively to disclose to P all relevant information about D's inputs and obtain P's consent to the dealing.

In *Soulos v Korkontzilas*, it was in P and D's joint interests at the outset of their relationship for P to have some kind of remedy if D cheated P in the way he did. A remedy was in P's interests as a precaution against D's incentive to cheat and it was in D's interests because it promoted P's trust. Without P's trust, the value of D's services to P would have been substantially lower. The main choice of remedy was: (1) a constructive trust order; and (2) a personal remedy for compensation or an account of profits. P had a special attachment to the disputed property, or so the majority was prepared to hold. A personal remedy would require the court to put a money value on P's special attachment, but this is hard to do. The court may undervalue P's special attachment or it may leave P's special attachment out of account altogether and assess P's claim solely by reference to the property's market value.[45] If that happens, the remedy will be insufficient both to: (1) compensate P; and (2) deter D.

For example, assume the market value of the disputed property at all relevant times is $5. P values the property at $7. D values the property at $6.

44  (1726) 25 ER 223.
45  This is effectively what the minority did in *Soulos v Korkontzilas*.

If D wants the property for himself, the *Keech v Sandford* rule requires him to obtain P's informed consent. In the example, P is unlikely to consent because he would want at least $7 from D in return whereas D would be prepared to pay no more than $6. The alternative is for D to go behind P's back, as happened in *Soulos v Korkontzilas*. If the court awards P a money remedy limited to the property's market value, the net result will be a gain to D of $1 ($6 – $5) and a loss to P of $2 ($7 – $5). This outcome means that D is better off going behind P's back. The reason is straightforward: if D is honest, he will have to pay P at least $7 in order to acquire the property (which, presumably, he would not be prepared to do), whereas if he is dishonest he can have the property for $5 (the amount of the money remedy the court awards P). A constructive trust addresses both the under-compensation problem and the under-deterrence problem. It addresses the under-compensation problem because, by giving the disputed property itself to P, the remedy necessarily captures the full value of P's special attachment. The constructive trust addresses the under-deterrence problem because it internalises to D the full cost of D's wrongdoing.

In the above example, a constructive trust remedy makes both P and D better off in at least two respects: (1) it avoids a joint $1 loss (the difference between P's $2 loss and D's $1 gain); and (2) assuming the remedy deters D's breach, it saves litigation costs. If P and D had written a fully specified contract at the outset of D's engagement, it is reasonable to suppose that they would have made provision for a constructive trust remedy with a view to capturing these benefits. A constructive trust provision would have enabled D to charge P a higher price for his services. Correspondingly, without a constructive trust, P would be likely to have insisted on a price reduction to compensate for the increased risk of D's wrongdoing. Note that the constructive trust remedy does not preclude D from acquiring the property for himself provided he values the property more highly than P does. For example, assume that the market value of the property at all relevant times is $5. P values the property at $6. D values the property at $7. If the remedy for going behind P's back is a money remedy limited to the property's market value then, as in the previous example, D will be better off going behind P's back. If D is honest, P will insist on a payment of at least $6 whereas if D is dishonest, the court will make him pay P only $5. On the other hand, if the remedy is a constructive trust, there is no benefit to D in going behind P's back and so D will deal with P upfront. If D deals with P upfront then, other things being equal, P will trade the entitlement to D for a price of between $6 and $7.

The majority in *Soulos v Korkontzilas* justified the constructive trust remedy on two grounds: (1) to remedy the non-monetary deprivation P had suffered as a consequence of D's wrongful conduct; and (2) to ensure that agents and others in positions of trust remain faithful to their duty of loyalty. Ground (2) suggests that the court may award a constructive trust remedy for deterrence reasons, regardless of unjust enrichment. The bribe cases provide a useful illustration. In *Lister v Stubbs*,[46] D was P's purchasing officer. T, a supplier, bribed D to put P's business T's way. D profitably invested the bribe money and P claimed a constructive trust over D's investments. The court declined the constructive trust remedy, restricting P to a money claim for the amount of the actual bribes. On the other hand, in *Attorney-General for Hong Kong v Reid*,[47] a similar case, the court awarded P a constructive trust relying on deterrence considerations in support of its decision. The court could not justify the constructive trust remedy on restitutionary grounds because although D's gains were unquestionably wrongful, he did not take them from P: P did not previously own the bribe money or the investments.

The case for a constructive trust remedy in the bribe cases turns on more or less the same considerations as before. The alternative to a constructive trust is a personal remedy for compensation or an account of profits. However, in the bribe cases P's loss bears no necessary relation to D's gain and it may be unquantifiable.[48] Therefore, a personal remedy is likely to result in systematic under-compensation. Given the risk of under-compensation, P's likely *ex ante* preference is for a remedy to deter D's wrongdoing so that the compensation issue does not arise. For effective deterrence, the remedy must capture all D's gains from the wrongdoing. The *Lister v Stubbs* remedy falls short in this regard because it captures only the bribe money itself, leaving D's profitable investments out of account. A possible alternative might be a more expansive account of profits remedy, covering not only the bribe money itself but also the market value of any traceable proceeds. However, even this may result in under-deterrence if D has a special attachment to the property in question or if there is a chance that the value of the property will increase after the judgment date. The only sure-fire way of extracting all D's gains is to impose a constructive trust on the bribe money and its traceable proceeds. *Ex ante*, the availability of a constructive trust remedy makes both P and D better off because it increases the value of D's services to P and presumably also the price P is prepared to pay for them. *Attorney-General for Hong Kong v Reid* has been criticised on the ground that, if D becomes bankrupt, the burden of the remedy will fall on D's unsecured creditors and not D personally.[49] From an *ex post* perspective, it may seem that the constructive trust remedy makes D's other creditors worse off. However, from an *ex ante* perspective, the creditors are probably better off because the availability of the

---

46 (1890) 45 ChD 1.      47 [1994] 1 AC 324.

48 As in *Attorney-General for Hong Kong v Reid* itself: see [1994] 1 AC 324 at 331 per Lord Templeman.

49 See, eg, Goode, Roy, 'Proprietary Restitutionary Claims' in Cornish, W et al (eds), *Restitution Past Present and Future: Essays in Honour of Gareth Jones*, 1998, Oxford: Hart Publishing, p 63.

remedy increases D's income-earning potential by improving the marketability of his services.[50]

### Recapitulation

*Soulos v Korkontzilas* speaks of restitution and deterrence, but the true function of the remedy the court granted was a perfectionary one. The purpose was to protect the integrity of P and D's fiduciary relationship. In this connection, a constructive trust was in both P and D's interests upfront and it reflects the kind of provision that, but for transactions costs, they are likely to have bargained for themselves.[51]

## 3 *Daly v Sydney Stock Exchange Ltd*[52]

### Case summary

In *Daly v Sydney Stock Exchange Ltd*, P (Dr Daly) had inherited some money from his father's estate and he wanted to invest it. He approached D (Patrick Partners, a firm of stockbrokers) for investment advice. D's client adviser told P that it was not a good time to buy shares and that P should put his money on deposit with D until the stock market improved. The adviser said that D was 'as safe as a bank'. Acting on this advice, P made two deposits with D, totalling $29,000 at an interest rate of 14 *per cent per annum*. P assigned his interest in the deposits to his wife (P1). As it happened, D was in financial difficulty at the time and three months later it went into liquidation. D's partners knew about the financial problems but, in an effort to improve the firm's liquidity, they had instructed their employees that they should encourage clients to invest funds on interest-bearing deposits with the firm. P1 made a claim on the securities industry fidelity fund. The purpose of the fund was to compensate clients who lost money due to defalcation by a broker in relation to money which was entrusted to or received by the broker as a trustee.[53] The issue was whether D was entrusted with or received P's money as trustee. If so, P1 would have a claim on the fund. The deposit was a loan by P to D. A loan contract does not normally give rise to a trust relationship. The borrower receives the money on its own account. It is a debtor, not a trustee. P1 argued that in the present case there was a trust because D obtained the loan in breach of fiduciary duty and this meant that D held the loan money on constructive trust, first for P and later for P1.

---

50 On the bankruptcy implications of the constructive trust, see further 'The bankruptcy aspect' section at p 261 below.
51 See Easterbrook and Fischel, op cit.      52 (1986) 160 CLR 371.
53 Securities Industry Act 1970 (NSW), ss 58 and 59; Security Industry Act 1975 (NSW), ss 97 and 98.

The High Court unanimously rejected P1's argument. Brennan J held that D was in a fiduciary relationship with P: 'whenever a stockbroker or other person who holds himself out as having expertise in advising on investments is approached for advice on investments and undertakes to give it, in giving that advice the adviser stands in a fiduciary relationship to the person whom he advises. The adviser cannot assume a position where his self-interest might conflict with the honest and impartial giving of advice.'[54] D breached the duty by failing to warn P about D's financial difficulties and by telling P that D was 'as safe as a bank'. D's wrongdoing gave P a right of rescission. The parallel case is where D (the fiduciary) buys land from P (the principal) in breach of fiduciary duty. In that case, if P elects to avoid the contract, D has a duty to retransfer the land to P at the original contract price. In the meantime, D holds the land on constructive trust for P. Typically, D will have purchased the land from P at an undervalue. However, that is not a requirement for the remedy: 'a conveyance or transfer on sale may be set aside though the terms of the contract are fair if it appears that the fiduciary has failed to give the advice which he was bound to give in respect of that contract'.[55] The same principles apply to a loan contract, subject to the requirement that the loan money or its proceeds are still traceable in D's hands: 'a person lending money to a fiduciary who obtains the loan without discharging his fiduciary duty is entitled in equity to avoid the contract of loan and to recover, by tracing if need be, the money lost'.[56] The constructive trust arises when P elects to avoid the contract, not before: 'where property has been sold and conveyed, the purchaser's beneficial title must be ascertained by reference to the sale so long as it stands; the vendor cannot insist on an equitable interest in the property if he does not choose to enforce his equity to avoid the sale'.[57] 'Similarly, until the lender elects to avoid the contract of loan, he cannot assert an equitable title to the money lent. He cannot at once leave the contract on foot and deny the borrowers the title to the money which the contract confers.'[58] Applying these principles to the present case, P1's claim on the fidelity fund failed because it did not meet the statutory requirements: there was no trust over the deposit at the time D received it.

Gibbs CJ reached the same conclusion but on different grounds. He held that P would not have been entitled to constructive trust relief in any event because the normal creditor's remedies were sufficient to protect P: 'the existence of a constructive trust was on the one hand unnecessary to protect [P's legitimate interests] and on the other hand would have led to consequences unjust both to [D's creditors] and D itself'.[59] Dawson J agreed with Gibbs CJ. Wilson J agreed with Gibbs CJ and Brennan J. There is no question that

54 (1986) 160 CLR 371 at 385.     55 (1986) 160 CLR 371 at 387.
56 (1986) 160 CLR 371 at 388.     57 (1986) 160 CLR 371 at 389.
58 (1986) 160 CLR 371 at 389.     59 (1986) 160 CLR 371 at 380.

P had a right of rescission for breach of fiduciary obligation. The division of opinion in *Daly v Sydney Stock Exchange Ltd* was over what the consequences of rescission would have been. Brennan J's judgment suggests that if P had rescinded the loan contract before D went into liquidation, D would have held the money or its traceable proceeds on constructive trust for P. On the other hand, according to Gibbs CJ, P would have had only a personal claim against D for recovery of his deposit.

### Analysis

For reasons that have already been discussed, D (the fiduciary) has an incentive to cheat P (the principal). In *Daly v Sydney Stock Exchange Ltd* P relied on D for good investment advice. P's reliance was implicit because P lacked the information he would have needed to test the truth and accuracy of D's statements. This information imbalance was the reason why P consulted D in the first place. If P knew enough to monitor D effectively, P could have made his own investment decisions and he would not have needed D. It was P's implicit reliance on D that gave D the opportunity for cheating P. Removing the incentive to cheat helps preserve the integrity of the market for investment advice. The client must be able to trust the adviser. Otherwise, the value of investment advisory services will fall and both advisers and clients will suffer. Demand for investment advisory services will drop and advisers may have to lower their fees. Clients will want to either: (1) look elsewhere for more reliable information but at a higher cost; (2) take the risk of investing on the basis of sub-optimal information; or (3) forego potentially profitable investment opportunities because the costs of obtaining reliable information and the risks of investing without it are too high. In *Daly v Sydney Stock Exchange Ltd*, P and D at the outset of their relationship are likely to have wanted P to have a constructive trust remedy, in the circumstances of the case, as a way of promoting P's trust in D. Without the constructive trust remedy, P could not confidently deposit funds with D on the strength of D's assurances alone. To be on the safe side, P would have to run an independent check on D's financial situation but the need for such precautions is inconsistent with P and D's supposed relationship of trust.

In *Baltman v Melnitzer*,[60] an Ontario case, P (a bank) opened an eight million dollar line of credit in D's favour. P took various kinds of security from D to secure repayment of the debt. D drew on the line of credit and used the money to purchase paintings. D went bankrupt owing P approximately $2.5 million. P's security was insufficient to cover this amount. It turned out that, in negotiating for the line of credit, D had lied to P about his creditworthiness. P sued D's trustee in bankruptcy claiming a remedial constructive

---

60  (1996) 43 CBR (3d) 33 (Ont. Gen. Div. – Bkrcy).

trust over the paintings as proceeds of the loan money. The court disallowed P's claim. According to *Pettkus v Becker*, to qualify for the constructive trust remedy, P must prove that: (1) D was unjustly enriched; (2) P was correspondingly deprived; and (3) there was no juristic reason to support D's enrichment. In *Baltman v Melnitzer*, P failed to satisfy the third requirement. The court held that the loan contract was a sufficient juristic reason to support D's enrichment, despite D's lies. Anglo-Australian law does not recognise the remedial constructive trust. How would a case like *Baltman v Melnitzer* be pleaded under Anglo-Australian law? P would rescind the loan contract on account of D's fraud and claim a constructive trust over the paintings as the traceable proceeds of the loan money. At first glance, *Daly v Sydney Stock Exchange Ltd* seems to suggest that P might win.[61] However, the two cases are distinguishable. In *Baltman v Melnitzer*, there was no fiduciary relationship. P and D's relationship was an arm's-length commercial one. P had no basis for implicitly trusting D. P could have protected itself by taking additional security or running more thorough credit checks on D before contracting with him. By contrast, in *Daly v Sydney Stock Exchange Ltd*, P justifiably assumed that D was acting in P's best interests and that precautions were unnecessary. If precautions had been necessary, the value of the relationship to P would have been substantially diminished.

In a *Baltman v Melnitzer*-type case, a constructive trust in P's favour would be equivalent to a security interest in the paintings over and above the security P and D had expressly bargained for. It is unlikely that P and D intended P to have the additional security because otherwise they would have said so.[62] A constructive trust would give P an unbargained-for benefit and P's entitlement to the remedy would become the default rule for future cases. Parties in future would have to bear the additional costs of bargaining for and incorporating express provisions to exclude the remedy if they did not want it. They would also bear the costs of uncertainty about how a court might interpret their wishes as expressed in the contract. To justify these additional costs, it would have to be shown that borrowers and lenders at large are more likely than not to want a constructive trust so that it is cheaper for the court to imply the remedy across the board than it is for parties themselves to write in the remedy on a case-by-case basis. Given the availability to institutional

---

61 See, eg, *El Ajou v Dollar Land Holdings Ltd* [1993] 3 All ER 717. There P was induced by D's fraud to buy shares from D. P rescinded the contract and claimed a constructive trust over the proceeds of the purchase price. Millett J allowed P's claim, citing *Daly v Sydney Stock Exchange Ltd* as authority.

62 The judge said: 'What were the legitimate or reasonable expectations of the parties when the deal or occurrences took place? Surely, at the time of the advances in question the Bank had no expectation whatsoever that it would or could acquire a proprietary interest in the paintings which Mr Melnitzer was purchasing. It was content with its credit-line arrangements and the collateral it had received': *Baltman v Melnitzer* (1996) 43 CBR (3d) 33 at para 43.

lenders of routine and relatively low-cost precautions against D's default, this seems unlikely. To summarise, in *Baltman v Melnitzer*, there is no question that P was entitled to rescind the loan contract. However, the consequence of rescission, as the judgment implies, was to give P no more than a personal claim against D for restitution of the loan amount. The court was right to deny the constructive trust.

### Recapitulation

Where D contracts with P in breach of fiduciary duty, P can rescind the contract. The better view is that in the case of a loan contract, following rescission, D holds the money on constructive trust for P. At one level, the remedy can be justified by reference to either deterrence or restitutionary considerations. At another level, though, the remedy serves a perfectionary function. It is a gap-filling device, like fiduciary law at large.[63] In granting or withholding the remedy, the courts give effect to P and D's likely joint preferences at the outset of their relationship. In *Daly v Sydney Stock Exchange Ltd*, P and D are likely to have wanted the constructive trust remedy to promote P's trust in D. By contrast, in *Baltman v Melnitzer*, P and D's relationship was an arm's-length commercial one and P had relatively low-cost precautions open to it against the risk of D's insolvency, including the taking of security. As it happens, P did take security and a constructive trust remedy would have been inconsistent with the terms of the security agreement.

### 4  *Chase Manhattan Bank NA v Israel-British Bank (London) Ltd*[64]

### Case summary

In the *Chase Manhattan Bank* case, P bank in New York by mistake made a payment of just over two million dollars to D bank in London. D discovered the mistake soon afterwards but it went into liquidation without having repaid the money. P sued for a declaration that D held the money on constructive trust for P from the date D received it. In earlier proceedings P had successfully established a claim against D for money had and received, and it had proved in D's liquidation in respect of this entitlement. The point of the constructive trust claim was that, if successful, it would allow P to trace the mistaken payment and to recover the proceeds from D. The case was fought on the assumption that there were in fact traceable proceeds. It was common ground that the governing law was the law of the State of New York. Goulding J held in P's favour. Story says that 'the recovery of money which consistently with conscience cannot be retained is, in Equity, sufficient to raise a trust in

---

63  See Easterbrook and Fischel, op cit.      64  [1981] Ch 105.

favor of the party for whom or on whose account it was received'.[65] Likewise, Scott says that: 'where chattels are conveyed or money is paid by mistake, so that the person making the conveyance or payment is entitled to restitution, the transferee or payee holds the chattels or money upon a constructive trust'.[66] Goulding J held that these statements correctly represented New York law and that the same general principles apply in England.[67] D argued that P's claim should fail because English law requires proof of a fiduciary relationship before the court can impose a constructive trust. Goulding J.'s response was that the payment into wrong hands was itself enough to create a fiduciary relationship. The payment was impressed with a trust from the moment D received it.[68]

The *Chase Manhattan Bank* case is a textbook example of circular reasoning: P was entitled to a constructive trust because P and D were in a fiduciary relationship and there was a fiduciary relationship because D held the money on trust. In *Westdeutsche Landesbank Girozentrale v Council of the London Borough of Islington*,[69] Lord Browne-Wilkinson disagreed with Goulding J's reasons but cautiously agreed with the result. Among other things, Lord Browne-Wilkinson said that 'the equitable jurisdiction to enforce trusts depends upon the conscience of the holder of the legal interest being affected' and so 'he cannot be a trustee of the property if and so long as he is ignorant of the facts alleged to affect his conscience'.[70] In support of the actual result in the *Chase Manhattan Bank* case, he said: '[D] knew of [P's mistake] within two days of the receipt of the moneys … The judge treated this fact as irrelevant … but it may well provide a proper foundation for the decision. Although the mere receipt of the moneys, in ignorance of the mistake, gives rise to no trust, the retention of the moneys after [D] learned of the mistake may well have given rise to a constructive trust.'[71] On the other hand, Birks argues that, though D's obligation to account may depend on knowledge of the mistake, the constructive trust itself does not: a 'causative mistake' attracts equitable intervention *in rem*. Legal title passes to D, but an equitable interest arises in P's favour straight away.[72]

In the *Chase Manhattan Bank* case, P's entitlement to the constructive trust remedy mattered because D was bankrupt. However, the constructive trust

65 *Story's Commentaries on Equity Jurisprudence* 2nd edn, 1839, Vol 2, para 1255.
66 Scott, AW, *The Law of Trusts*, 3rd ed, 1967, *Boston: Little, Brown*, p 3428.
67 [1981] Ch 105 at 118. This proposition is contentious because New York law recognises the remedial constructive trust, whereas English law does not: *Westdeutsche Landesbank Girozentrale v Council of the London Borough of Islington* [1996] AC 669 at 714 per Lord Browne-Wilkinson.
68 [1981] Ch 105 at 119.        69 [1996] AC 669.        70 [1996] AC 669 at 705.
71 [1996] AC 669 at 715.
72 Birks, Peter, 'Trusts Raised to Reverse Unjust Enrichment: The *Westdeutsche* Case' [1996] Restitution Law Review 3 at 24. See further, text at n 80, below.

remedy may matter outside bankruptcy as well. Assume P makes a mistaken payment to D. D pays the money into its account with T bank. The account is in credit. D has another account with T bank which is in debit. T bank has a right of set-off, which it purports to exercise by consolidating the two accounts. P can defeat T bank's set-off, at least if T bank has knowledge of P's mistake: *Neste Oy v Lloyds Bank plc*.[73] On the same principles as underlie the *Chase Manhattan Bank* case, D holds the mistaken payment on construc- tive trust for P and P's equitable interest has priority over T bank unless T bank is a bona fide purchaser for value without notice. In the *Neste Oy* case, P, a shipowner, made payments to D, a shipping agent, so that D could pay suppliers for services they had provided to P (jetty and river dues, pilotage, towage, berth fees and the like). Unknown to P, at the time of the last pay- ment, D had resolved to cease trading and it had no funds of its own to pay P's bills. D's bank asserted a right of set-off. Bingham J concluded that D held the money on constructive trust for P: 'given [D's] situation when the last payment was received, any reasonable and honest directors of that company (or the actual directors had they known of it) would, I feel sure, have arranged for the repayment of that sum to [P] without hesitation or delay. It would have seemed little short of sharp practice for D to take any benefit from the payment, and it would have seemed contrary to any notion of fairness that the general body of creditors should profit from the accident of a payment made at a time when there was bound to be a total failure of consideration'.[74]

### Analysis

The general rule is that P can recover overpayments from D. Once D finds out about P's mistake, D must give back the money or account for its traceable proceeds. P's negligence makes no difference, assuming D has not already spent the money. Levmore says that if, contrary to prevailing law, debtors could not retrieve overpayments, debtors would protect themselves with more paperwork: 'the flat denial of restitution would lead to an inefficiently high level of care'.[75] The overpayment is a loss to P, but restitution is no loss to D. If P owes D $100 but P pays $150, D 'cannot, without straining credulity, claim that receiving fifty dollars is worth less than giving up that amount'.[76] The law encourages D to return the overpayment voluntarily. In cases where P tells D about P's mistake before P spends the money, as in the *Chase Manhattan Bank* case itself, giving the money back is a virtually costless way

---

73 [1983] 2 Lloyds LR 658.
74 [1983] 2 Lloyds LR 658 at 666. Bingham J went on to hold that the bank was on notice because it knew about D's decision to cease trading and this put it on inquiry.
75 Op cit at 69.    76 Ibid 77–78.

of avoiding P's loss and it reduces the need for costly additional precautions on P's part. Assume P plans a $100 transfer to D. There is a 1/50 chance that P will overpay D $50 and a 7/10 chance if this happens that P will notify D of the mistake while D still holds the money or its traceable proceeds. If the law flatly denies restitution, P's expected loss is $1 ($50 × 1/50) and P will spend up to this amount on precautions. On the other hand, if the law requires restitution subject to a change of position defence,[77] P's expected loss is reduced to 30 cents ($1 − $1 × 7/10) and P will want to spend no more than this amount to avoid the loss. The net result is a 70 cents saving on P's precautions.[78]

The *Chase Manhattan Bank* case holds that P has both a personal and a proprietary remedy against D. P can sue to recover the money. Alternatively, P can ask for a constructive trust over the money or its traceable proceeds. The constructive trust remedy matters in cases like the *Chase Manhattan Bank* case and *Neste Oy* where D is on the verge of bankruptcy at the time of P's payment. The rationale for the remedy is to prevent 'sharp practice' on D's part: *Neste Oy*. Why would it be sharp practice for D to keep the money? The answer the *Neste Oy* case gives is that 'honest and reasonable directors of [D] would have arranged for . . . repayment to [P] without delay', but this is circular. A better explanation is that it would be inconsistent with P and D's implied bargain for D to keep the money. In cases where P notifies D of the mistake before D spends the money, the cheapest loss-avoidance strategy is simply for D to give the money back. A no restitution rule would encourage P to take wasteful upfront precautions.[79]

A rule promoting the cheapest loss-avoidance strategy reduces P and D's joint costs and it is in both their interests to agree on the rule at the outset. A personal claim for restitution does not eliminate the need for P to take wasteful precautions because it does not guarantee recovery if D is insolvent. P will still want to spend money upfront to cover the risk of D's insolvency, even though restitution is the cheaper loss-avoidance strategy. The constructive trust remedy avoids the need for this expenditure. The constructive trust remedy is costless to D: given D's insolvency, it will be indifferent to the remedy. Instead, the cost of the remedy falls on D's other creditors: it reduces their prospects of payment by subtracting P's money from D's estate. From an *ex post* perspective, D's creditors might seem worse off. However, from an *ex ante* perspective, they are probably better off: the benefit of the constructive

---

77  The change of position defence applies where D's position 'has so changed that it would be inequitable in all the circumstances to require him to make restitution, or alternatively to make restitution in full': *Lipkin Gorman v Karpnale Ltd* [1991] 2 AC 548 at 580 per Lord Goff. See also *Restatement, Restitution* (1937), ss 69(1) and 142.

78  The focus here is on the case where D knows about P's mistake. For consideration of the case where D spends the money before discovering P's mistake, see Beatson, J and Bishop, W, op cit.

79  See text at n 75, above.

trust remedy to D's creditors lies in the savings it achieves on D's costs of doing business with P.

In the *Chase Manhattan Bank* case, Goulding J held that there was a constructive trust as soon as D received the money and it was irrelevant that D did not learn about P's mistake until afterwards. Lord Browne-Wilkinson in the *Westdeutsche Bank* case disagreed. Assume P makes an overpayment of $50 to D. Before discovering P's mistake, D loses the money in a bad investment. If the trust arises as soon as D receives the money, D is liable to make good the loss out of its own pocket because the money is trust money. This outcome appears to contradict the change of position defence. However, as Birks explains, the change of position defence applies to personal and proprietary claims for unjust enrichment alike. In the case under consideration, D's personal liability and its liability as trustee are equally subject to the defence.[80] At issue is the question of whether it is cheaper: (1) for P to take precautions for discovering its own mistake before it pays the money to D; or (2) for D to take precautions for discovering P's mistake before D spends the money. The availability and scope of the change of position defence reflect the courts' assessment of where the comparative advantage lies.[81]

### Recapitulation

Levmore insightfully says about the relationship between torts, contracts and the law of restitution that tort law deals with unbargained-for harms, contract law deals with bargained-for harms and benefits, and the law of restitution deals with unbargained-for benefits.[82] The granting of a constructive trust remedy in mistaken payment cases can be explained on one level in either restitutionary or deterrence terms. However, the remedy also enforces a Coasean bargain between the parties and in this sense it serves a perfectionary function. The constructive trust remedy gives D the incentive to repay P without delay once D learns of P's mistake. This is the outcome P and D in a *Chase Manhattan Bank* case scenario are likely to have agreed on themselves if they had bargained in advance about mistaken payment entitlements. The reason is that if P tells D about the mistake before D spends the money, the cheaper loss-avoidance strategy is simply for D to give back the money rather than for P to invest resources up front in additional precautions to prevent the mistake from happening.[83]

---

80 Op cit pp 25–26.     81 See generally, Beatson and Bishop, op cit.     82 Op cit 67.

83 'This is not to assert, as did the old implied contract theory . . ., that unjust enrichment is a subordinate or at any rate not an independent category of claim. Rather it is to say that it is likely in a developed system of unjust enrichment claims that the remedies based on such claims will not simply restore to [P] a benefit that [D] has acquired at [P's] expense but will look to the social cost of the "transaction" between the two in quantifying the amount to be restored': Beatson and Bishop, op cit 184–185.

## 5 *Baumgartner v Baumgartner* [84]

*Case summary*

In *Baumgartner v Baumgartner*, P and D were in a de facto relationship. They lived for a while in D's home unit. Later, D bought some land to build a house on (the 'Leumeah property'). D put the Leumeah property in his own name. He refused to put it in both their names because they weren't married. D sold his home unit and P and D lived in rented accommodation for a time while the house on the Leumeah property was being finished. From the time they started living together, P had given D her pay packet. P and D regarded this as a pooling of resources. D paid rent, mortgage instalments and other expenses. He also paid the day-to-day living expenses. At the time D bought the Leumeah property, D still owed money on his home unit. He made double payments out of P and D's pooled earnings on four occasions. P and D's pooled earnings over the period of their relationship totalled approximately $89,000. P's share was $38,000 and D's share was $51,000. P's share was less partly because she spent 3 months out of the workforce following the birth of their child. P and D separated. They had been together for four years and had lived in the house on the Leumeah property for about two years. P sued D claiming that D held the Leumeah property on constructive trust for P and D in equal shares. The case ended up in the High Court of Australia. The court made an order declaring that D held the property on constructive trust for P and D, not equally, but in proportion to their contributions to the earnings pool. It was agreed that, after crediting P with the amount she would have earned during the period she was off work, P and D's contributions were 45 *per cent* and 55 *per cent*, respectively. [85]

Mason CJ and Wilson and Deane JJ delivered the leading judgment. They relied on a 'general equitable principle' which restores to a party contributions which he or she has made where the substratum of a joint endeavour fails without attributable blame: 'the content of the principle is that, in such a case, equity will not permit [D] to assert or retain the benefit of the relevant property to the extent that it would be unconscionable for him so to do'. [86] The constructive trust is 'a remedy which equity imposes regardless of actual or presumed agreement or intention "to preclude the retention or assertion of beneficial ownership of property to the extent that such retention or assertion

---

84  (1987) 164 CLR 137.

85  The court also ordered a number of adjustments in D's favour. Specifically, it said that if the Leumeah property was sold, D should receive from the sale proceeds repayment of the contributions effectively made by him before and after the period during which the parties were living together and pooling their resources. The court also said that D was entitled to an adjustment in respect of the furniture, which P had taken with her when she and D separated.

86  (1987) 164 CLR 137 at 148 quoting *Muschinski v Dodds* (1985) 160 CLR 583 at 620 per Deane J.

would be contrary to equitable principle" '.[87] In the present case, P and D pooled their earnings to meet the family's living expenses. They did not allocate their individual contributions to any particular category of expenditure. The acquisition of the Leumeah property and the building of the house was a family endeavour: 'together [P and D] planned the building of the house. Together they inspected it in the course of its construction. Together they moved into it and made it their home after it was built'.[88] P and D's pooled earnings contributed directly and indirectly to the acquisition of the property and the building of the house. In these circumstances, it was unconscionable conduct for D to claim the Leumeah property solely for himself and a constructive trust was the appropriate remedy.

*Baumgartner v Baumgartner* is in the same vein as the *Pettkus v Becker*[89] line of cases in the Supreme Court of Canada.[90] According to *Pettkus v Becker*, the purpose of the constructive trust remedy is to prevent D's unjust enrichment at P's expense. According to *Baumgartner v Baumgartner*, the purpose is to prevent D's unconscionable conduct. However, as Toohey J pointed out in *Baumgartner v Baumgartner*, the results of the cases are equally explicable either way.[91] The Canadian cases recognise that a constructive trust may not always be necessary to prevent D's unjust enrichment and that a compensation order in P's favour may be enough. In *Sorochan v Sorochan*, the justification for the constructive trust remedy was '[P's] desire to devise an interest in the land she had worked for 42 years to her children'.[92] In *Peter v Beblow*, Cory J held that a constructive trust was appropriate in part because 'it would not have been unreasonable to infer' that P had formed an emotional attachment to the property, whereas D clearly had none.[93] *Rawluk v Rawluk* and *Peter v Beblow* also suggest that a constructive trust may be imposed to give P a share in any property value increase between the date P and D separated and the trial date.

### Analysis

In *Baumgartner v Baumgartner*, P and D could have written a contract, at the outset of their relationship or later on, specifying how their assets were to be divided between them if the relationship broke down. The court would

---

87 *Baumgartner v Baumgartner* (1987) 164 CLR 137 at 148 per Mason CJ and Wilson and Deane JJ, quoting *Muschinski v Dodds* (1985) 160 CLR 583 at 614 per Deane J.

88 *Baumgartner v Baumgartner* (1985) 160 CLR 137 at 149 per Mason CJ and Wilson and Deane JJ.

89 (1980) 117 DLR (3d) 257.

90 *Pettkus v Becker* (1980) 117 DLR (3d) 257; *Sorochan v Sorochan* (1986) 29 DLR (4th) 1; *Rawluk v Rawluk* (1990) 65 DLR (4th) 161; *Peter v Beblow* (1993) 101 DLR (4th) 621.

91 (1987) 164 CLR 137 at 153–154.        92 (1986) 29 DLR (4th) 1 at 12.

93 (1993) 101 DLR (4th) 621 at 641.

presumably have enforced the contract, provided it was not affected by fraud, undue influence or the like. An express property sharing arrangement benefits the parties by: (1) saving litigation costs; and (2) reducing the uncertainty of litigation outcomes.[94] Given these advantages, it might seem surprising that parties do not enter into property sharing arrangements as a matter of course. The reason they do not is because property sharing arrangements are costly to negotiate. The costs of negotiating a property sharing arrangement are high at the outset of the relationship and they increase as the relationship progresses. At the outset of the relationship P and D are likely to discount the risk of breakdown. Self-interested negotiations over who is to get what in the event of breakdown are inconsistent with the 'communality and trust'[95] that typify marital and marriage-like relationships. To a greater or lesser extent, acknowledging the possibility of breakdown signals a lack of confidence on P or D's part in the long-term prospects of the relationship and they may worry about the consequences. Consistently with these considerations, in *Peter v Beblow*, Cory J said that 'the parties entering a marriage or common law relationship will rarely have considered the question of compensation for benefits. If asked, they might say that because they loved their partner, each worked to achieve the common goal of creating a home and establishing a good life for themselves'.[96] The costs of negotiating a property sharing arrangement are likely to be higher still once the relationship gets under way; as time goes by, P and D's capital contributions to the partnership accumulate. P's contributions are more likely to be of a non-refundable kind: childcare, housekeeping and the like. This means that, in the absence of judicial intervention, P stands to lose progressively more than D if the relationship breaks down. P may worry increasingly that D will leave her if she keeps asking for a share of the property: better not to stir the pot and keep the relationship intact. On breakdown the prospects of a bargained-for settlement are remoter still because *ex post* it is against D's interests to give P a share of the property. D will already have received the benefit of P's contributions to the partnership and there is no economic incentive left for him to give her anything in return.

To quote Cory J again in *Peter v Beblow*: 'As I have said, it is unlikely that couples will ever turn their minds to the issue of their expectations about their legal entitlements at the outset of their marriage or common law relationship. If they were specifically asked about their expectations, I would think . . . they would say, if the relationship were ever to be dissolved, then

---

94  See Trebilcock, MJ and Keshvani, R, 'The Role of Private Ordering in Family Law', (1991) 41 University of Toronto Law Journal 533.

95  The expression derives from Trebilcock, MJ and Elliott, S, 'The Scope and Limits of Legal Paternalism: Altruism and Coercion in Family Financial Arrangements', in Peter Benson (ed), *The Theory of Contract Law*, 2001, Cambridge: Cambridge University Press, 45.

96  (1993) 101 DLR (4th) 621 at 635.

they would expect that both parties would share in the assets or wealth that they had helped to create'.[97] As this statement suggests, the purpose of the constructive trust in cases like *Baumgartner v Baumgartner* and the *Pettkus v Becker* line of cases is to remedy contract failure. The constructive trust reproduces the kind of property sharing agreement P and D are likely to have agreed on themselves if bargaining between them had been costless. Matrimonial property legislation serves a similar purpose in relation to marriage breakdowns.[98] It is true that in *Baumgartner v Baumgartner*, the majority judgment says that equity imposes the constructive trust 'regardless of actual or presumed intention'.[99] However, the overall tenor of the judgment belies this statement.[100] Likewise in relation to the *Pettkus v Becker* line of cases. As Chambers points out, while the courts use the language of unjust enrichment to explain the constructive trust, it is clear from the cases read as a whole that the real purpose is to perfect the parties' likely expectations at the outset of the relationship: 'the trust is not possible unless [D] is (or ought to be) aware that [P] expected to receive an interest'. '[P's] expectation is the key ingredient and the constructive trust arises to perfect it'.[101]

The property sharing regime *Baumgartner v Baumgartner* and like cases imposes acts as a default rule for future cases. The rule applies unless the parties explicitly contract for a different rule. If D wants an arrangement that is less generous to P, he will have to tell her. D's disclosure gives P the opportunity to walk away. If she elects to stay, it will be with her eyes open.[102] Compensation for P's contributions is a possible alternative remedy to the constructive trust. However, compensation merely reverses P's inputs,

---

97  (1993) 101 DLR (4th) 621 at 639.

98  See *Nova Scotia (Attorney-General) v Walsh* [2002] 4 SCR 325, where the Supreme Court of Canada in the context of a Charter challenge to provincial matrimonial property legislation applying only to married couples, analysed both marriage and common law relationships in explicitly contractarian terms. The court held that, in deciding to marry, couples subscribe to the sharing rules the matrimonial property rules provided for in the event of marriage breakdown, while in deciding not to marry, couples opt out of the statutory regime in favour of a different set of rules represented in part by the law of constructive trusts.

99  (1987) 164 CLR 137 at 148 per Mason CJ and Wilson and Deane JJ.

100  For example, the judgment says that 'the land at Leumeah was acquired and the house on it was built in the context of and for the purposes of [the] relationship' and 'it would be unreal and artificial to say that the respondent intended to make a gift to the appellant' and 'their contributions . . . were on the basis of, and for the purposes of [the] joint relationship': ibid at 149.

101  Op cit 201. The *Pettkus v Becker* test of unjust enrichment depends on proof of: (1) D's enrichment; (2) P's corresponding deprivation; and (3) the absence of a juristic reason in support of D's enrichment. The test of juristic reason is whether P reasonably expected to receive an interest in the disputed asset and whether D knew or ought to have known about P's expectation: *Sorochan v Sorochan* (1986) 29 DLR (4th) 1 at 12 per Dickson CJ.

102  On the role of background entitlements in facilitating express contracts in the family law context, see Trebilcock and Keshvani, op cit.

whereas the aim in many cases is to ensure that 'both parties share in the assets or wealth that they had helped to create'.[103] 'A straight reversal of inputs may be the appropriate response to the break-up of some family relationships, such as those of short duration or where the parties maintained financial independence throughout. However, there are others in which that approach is unacceptable due to the presence of detrimentally relied upon expectations'.[104]

*Recapitulation*

According to *Baumgartner v Baumgartner*, the purpose of the constructive trust remedy in family property cases is to prevent unconscionable conduct on D's part. This implies that the remedy serves a deterrence function. According to the *Pettkus v Becker* line of cases, the purpose of the remedy is to reverse unjust enrichment. In other words, the remedy serves a restitutionary function. However, as Chambers says, in truth 'the trusts in [these] situations are perfectionary'.[105] The court's underlying concern is to reproduce the outcome the parties themselves are likely to have bargained for in the absence of transactions costs. 'The expectation of sharing the beneficial ownership of the family home ... might now be regarded as a normal feature of most stable family relationships' and the court imposes the constructive trust to enforce this understanding.[106]

## The bankruptcy aspect

*Introduction*

The five illustrative cases above focus on P's claim for constructive trust relief outside D's bankruptcy. Should P's claim survive D's bankruptcy and, if so, under what circumstances? The following discussion: (1) identifies three main theories that inform the inquiry (the property rights theory, the relative entitlements theory and the prevention of unjust enrichment theory); (2) demonstrates, by reference back to the cases previously discussed, how these three theories can lead to different case outcomes; and (3) compares the theories normatively.

*Three competing theories*

*(i)  The property rights theory*
The property rights theory focuses on the nature of P's entitlement outside bankruptcy. If P had a property right in the disputed asset before D became

---

103  *Peter v Beblow* (1993) 101 DLR (4th) 621 at 639 per Cory J.
104  Chambers, op cit 206–7.       105  Op cit 205.       106  Ibid 207.

bankrupt, P should have the same entitlement inside D's bankruptcy. More specifically, if P would have been entitled to a constructive trust remedy outside D's bankruptcy, the court should not use D's bankruptcy as a basis for refusing the remedy. The rationale is that the constructive trust removes the disputed asset from D's estate so that it does not form part of the property that is available for distribution among creditors. D's trustee has bare legal title to the asset but no beneficial interest and so she must turn over the asset to P.[107] Goode says that the first principle of corporate insolvency law is that 'corporate insolvency law recognizes rights accrued under the general law prior to liquidation' and he describes this as a 'principle of cardinal importance'.[108] Goode's statement reflects the property rights theory.

*(ii)   The relative entitlements theory*
The relative entitlements theory rests on the premise that the purpose of bankruptcy law is to solve a common pool problem.[109] Outside bankruptcy, as a general rule, unsecured creditors are entitled to satisfaction of their claims on a first-come, first-served basis. The first-come, first-served rule gives an unsecured creditor the incentive to stake its claim as quickly as possible: being first increases the chances of payment. On the other hand, a race to judgment between individual creditors is likely to result in the piecemeal dismantlement of D's estate. This will be contrary to the interests of the creditors as a group if D's assets are worth more together than separately. Bankruptcy laws maximise the overall value of D's estate to the unsecured creditors by substituting a system of collective debt enforcement for the individual debt enforcement system that operates outside bankruptcy. Bankruptcy law conserves D's estate by restraining self-interested behaviour on the part of individual creditors, in much the same way as fisheries laws conserve fish stocks by restraining individual fishers from over-fishing.

Premature bankruptcy is against the interests of creditors collectively. While D remains solvent, there is always the prospect that it will be able to trade its way out of trouble. Putting a firm into bankruptcy reduces the prospect of all creditors being paid in full because bankruptcy proceedings set the sharks circling: suppliers may refuse further credit, the bank may want to call in its overdraft, and so on. To reduce the incidence of premature bankruptcies, creditors' relative entitlements should be the same inside D's bankruptcy as they are outside. If Creditor 1 can improve its position relative

---

107  Sherwin, Emily L, 'Constructive Trusts in Bankruptcy', [1989] University of Illinois Law Review 297 at 313–316.
108  Goode, R, *Principles of Corporate Insolvency Law*, 2nd edn, 1997, London: Sweet & Maxwell, p 54.
109  Jackson, TH, *The Logic and Limits of Bankruptcy Law*, 1986, Cambridge, Mass: Harvard University Press, Chs 1 and 2.

to Creditor 2 in D's bankruptcy, Creditor 1 will have an incentive to use the bankruptcy laws opportunistically – to put D into bankruptcy for its own benefit even if bankruptcy is not in the collective interests of the creditors as a group. Changing creditors' relative entitlements in bankruptcy conflicts with the collectivisation goal of the bankruptcy laws because it encourages self-interested behaviour on the part of individual creditors, whereas the goal is to subordinate individual self-interest to the interests of the group.

The relative entitlements theory involves asking not how non-bankruptcy law would treat P's claim relative to D but, rather, how non-bankruptcy law would treat P's claim relative to the claim of a hypothetical execution creditor on the eve of D's bankruptcy. The question is one of priorities, not property.[110] Jackson claims that in the United States, state debt recovery laws by and large favour the execution creditor over the holder of an undisclosed equitable interest in the disputed asset.[111] The upshot of applying the relative entitlements theory on this basis is that P's constructive trust claim will not prevail over unsecured creditors in D's bankruptcy.[112] Contrast the Canadian position. In Canada, the sheriff cannot seize or sell better title to an asset than the judgment debtor possessed.[113] Dunlop says that the rule is firmly established and it represents a fundamental limitation on the reach of the judgment creditor.[114] The upshot of applying the relative entitlements theory on this basis is that since P's constructive trust claim would have had priority over the claim of an execution creditor outside D's bankruptcy, it prevails over unsecured creditors inside D's bankruptcy. Coincidentally, this outcome is the same as the outcome the property rights theory leads to.

*(iii)   The prevention of unjust enrichment theory*
Sherwin argues on corrective justice grounds that P should be entitled to a constructive trust in D's bankruptcy if the remedy is necessary to prevent the unjust enrichment of D's general creditors at P's expense.[115] She identifies

---

110  Jackson, op cit pp 65–66.
111  Ibid p 66. See also Baird, Douglas, G, *The Elements of Bankruptcy Law*, 3rd edn, 2001, New York: Foundation Press, pp 107–108. Cf Kull, A, 'Restitution in Bankruptcy: Reclamation and Constructive Trust' (1998), 72 American Bankruptcy Law Journal 265 at 270.
112  Ibid.
113  *Wickham v NB & Can Rwy Co* (1865) 16 ER 158 (PC). The rule is the same for both personal property and realty: CRB Dunlop, *Creditor-Debtor Law in Canada*, 2nd edn, 1995, Toronto: Carswell, pp 267–268 (personalty) and 355–356 (realty).
114  Ibid pp 267–8.
115  Op cit. See also Paciocco, DM, 'The Remedial Constructive Trust: A Principled Basis for Priorities Over Creditors' (1989), 68 Canadian Bar Review 315; Andrew Burrows, 'Proprietary Restitution: Unmasking Unjust Enrichment' (2001) 117 Law Quarterly Review 412 at 423–429.

three requirements for the remedy: (1) proof of unjust enrichment; (2) the identification of assets that represent D's unjust enrichment in the bankruptcy estate; and (3) P's status as an involuntary creditor in D's bankruptcy. Requirement (1) implies a correlation between D's gain and P's loss: 'this correlation of gain and loss gives the restitutionary claim strong appeal in terms of fairness and corrective justice'.[116] Requirement (2) means that there must be a connection to specific property. The specific connection makes it possible to say that the constructive trust will prevent unjust enrichment of creditors: 'tracing the claim to particular assets demonstrates that the unjust enrichment is still present among the assets to be divided among competing parties. The constructive trust remedy avoids unjust enrichment of other creditors by denying them a share of property that would not be available for distribution but for [D's] unjust gain at [P's] expense'.[117] Requirement (3) focuses on whether P voluntarily accepted the risk of D's bankruptcy or, more precisely, whether P had the 'opportunity to demand compensation for the risk of bankruptcy in the form of price or interest, or protection by means of collateral'.[118]

### Applications

#### (i) Hewett v Court

In *Hewett v Court*, Wilson and Dawson JJ say that '[D's] insolvency is no reason of itself for placing [P] in a secured position so as to achieve an advantage over other creditors'.[119] This statement suggests that the majority judgments may have been motivated by a concern to protect P from the consequences of D's bankruptcy. However, as Wilson and Dawson JJ go on to say, any such concern is misplaced because it gives P an unprincipled advantage over other creditors who may be equally deserving of protection. The proper analysis is 'to look at [P's] position, disregarding [D's] financial position . . . and to look at it before the events took place which are said to constitute the preference'.[120] This statement is consistent with both the property rights theory and the relative entitlements theory. Both theories support the conclusion that if P has no property right in the disputed asset outside D's bankruptcy, P's claim should not have priority over D's other creditors in bankruptcy. The prevention of unjust enrichment theory points to the same conclusion: P were voluntary creditors because, being in a direct contractual relationship with D, they had the opportunity to demand compensation for the risk of bankruptcy or protection in the form of a security interest.

---

116 Sherwin, op cit 330.    117 Ibid 332.    118 Ibid 336.
119 (1983) 149 CLR 639 at 658.    120 (1983) 149 CLR 639 at 658.

## (ii) Soulos v Korkontzilas

In *Soulos v Korkontzilas*, the court imposed the constructive trust: (1) to remedy P's non-monetary deprivation; and (2) to deprive D of his non-monetary gains. Should P still have the remedy if D is bankrupt? *Attorney-General for Hong Kong v Reid*[121] suggests that the answer should be yes. The government of Hong Kong (P) employed Reid (D) as a prosecutor. D accepted bribes in return for obstructing the prosecution of cases. He invested money in New Zealand real estate. P sued D for breach of fiduciary duty, claiming a constructive trust over the real estate. The court granted the remedy on deterrence grounds. D argued that the court should not impose a constructive trust because if D became insolvent, D's unsecured creditors would be deprived of their right to share in the proceeds of the property. The court's response was to say that 'the unsecured creditors cannot be in a better position than their debtor'.[122] This response is consistent with the property rights theory. The relative entitlements theory leads to the same conclusion, assuming the rule outside bankruptcy is that execution creditors are subordinate to P's undisclosed equitable claim. Contrast the prevention of unjust enrichment approach. Sherwin argues that where the purpose for granting the constructive trust remedy outside bankruptcy is deterrence, the court should not grant the remedy if D is bankrupt. Inside bankruptcy, the impact of the remedy does not fall on D personally and so it can have no deterrent impact on him: 'when the contest for assets is between the restitution claimant and other creditors, a remedy that allocates property to one claimant in favour of others has no deterrent effect on the wrongdoer [D]'.[123] For this reason, 'any instance or incident of the constructive trust remedy based solely on deterrence should be eliminated in bankruptcy, no matter how egregious [D's] conduct'.[124] This approach discounts the costs of changing creditors' relative entitlements in bankruptcy. If P loses the constructive trust remedy when D becomes bankrupt, other creditors will have an incentive to put D into bankruptcy so they can capture P's entitlement for themselves.

## (iii) Daly v Sydney Stock Exchange Ltd

Brennan J's judgment in *Daly v Sydney Stock Exchange Ltd* suggests that if P rescinds a loan contract before D goes into liquidation, D holds the loan money or its traceable proceeds on constructive trust for P. Does the same result hold if D is bankrupt? 'Warts and all' is the governing principle: 'in asserting rights in D's name, the liquidator stands in no better position than [D] himself; he takes them as they stand, warts and all'.[125] 'Warts and all'

---

121 [1994] 1 AC 324.   122 [1994] 1 AC 324 at 331 per Lord Templeman.
123 Op cit 339.   124 Ibid.
125 Goode, Roy, *Principles of Corporate Insolvency Law*, 2nd edn, 1997, London: Sweet & Maxwell, 56.

includes equities in P's favour. 'A typical equity is a right to rescind a contract by reason of some external vitiating factor such as fraud, misrepresentation or undue influence'.[126] The 'warts and all' principle derives from the property rights theory of bankruptcy entitlements. The relative entitlements theory points to the same conclusion, assuming the rule outside bankruptcy is that P's undisclosed claim on the fund has priority over execution creditors. The outcome under the prevention of unjust enrichment theory may vary depending on the nature of D's fraud: 'if the fraud is such that [P] did not and could not fairly be expected to perceive the risk of loss, [P] should be treated as an involuntary creditor'.[127] In a case like *Daly v Sydney Stock Exchange Ltd*, a court is likely to say that P is an involuntary creditor given the fiduciary relationship between P and D and P's implicit reliance on D's advice.

### (iv)   Chase Manhattan Bank NA v Israel-British Bank (London) Ltd

The justification for the constructive trust remedy in mistaken payment cases outside bankruptcy is based on lowest-cost avoider considerations. The property rights theory indicates that P's claim should survive D's bankruptcy. So does the relative entitlements theory, assuming the rule outside bankruptcy is that P's claim on the fund has priority over execution creditors. The prevention of unjust enrichment theory points to the same conclusion. P is an involuntary creditor because it had no intention of making the payment to D in the first place and a constructive trust over the money or its traceable proceeds is necessary to prevent the unjust enrichment of D's other creditors at P's expense.[128] Should P's carelessness affect its right to a constructive trust in D's bankruptcy? Sherwin mentions a mistaken payment case where the bankruptcy court denied P constructive trust relief, holding that P should not 'profit from its own negligence at the expense of those who have dealt with the debtor in a more diligent fashion'.[129] Sherwin argues that the case was wrongly decided because P's negligence generally does not negate its status as an involuntary creditor in P's bankruptcy.[130] An alternative explanation is to say that outside D's bankruptcy, P's carelessness does not affect P's claim because if D finds out about the mistake before spending the money, it is more cost-effective for D to make restitution than it is for P to take additional precautions against mistakes. D's bankruptcy should not make any difference to P's entitlement.

### (v)   Baumgartner v Baumgartner

Outside D's bankruptcy, the constructive trust remedy in cases like *Baumgartner v Baumgartner* serves a perfectionary function. The cases

---

126  Ibid citing *Re Eastgate* [1905] 1 KB 465 and *Tilley v Bowman Ltd* [1910] 1 KB 745.
127  Sherwin, op cit 350–351.        128  Ibid 357–360.
129  *In Re Vichele Tops, Inc* 62 Bankr. 788 (Bankr. EDNY 1986), discussed Sherwin, op cit 358.
130  Ibid.

suggest that P's entitlement remains enforceable in D's bankruptcy.[131] This outcome is consistent with the property rights theory (D's trustee takes subject to equities[132]) and also with the relative entitlements theory, assuming the rule outside bankruptcy is that P's undisclosed claim has priority over execution creditors. Under the prevention of unjust enrichment theory, the main consideration is whether P qualifies as an involuntary creditor: did P have the opportunity to demand compensation for the risk of D's bankruptcy or protection by means of collateral? The answer is probably, 'no', for the same reason that P had no opportunity to bargain with D about how the assets of the relationship should be divided between P and D in the event of breakdown.

## Evaluation

It will be clear from the foregoing that P's entitlement in D's bankruptcy may be different depending on which theory the court applies. Which theory should the court apply? Jackson says that the property rights approach is flawed because it focuses on the wrong attribute of P's entitlement. From a bankruptcy perspective, the question is not whether P has a property claim vis-à-vis D but, instead, whether P's claim has priority over D's other creditors. The relevant question is, how would non-bankruptcy law treat P's claim to the disputed asset versus an execution creditor on the eve of D's bankruptcy? Assuming the execution creditor has priority, to recognise P's entitlement in D's bankruptcy, as the property rights theory does, is to change creditors' relative entitlements. This outcome is contrary to sound bankruptcy policy because it encourages strategic behaviour by individual creditors. [133]

Conversely, if the hypothetical execution creditor's claim does not have priority over P outside bankruptcy, the relative entitlements theory dictates that the claim should not have priority inside bankruptcy either. In that case, the property rights theory and the relative entitlements theory coincidentally lead to the same outcome. There may be good policy reasons for saying that P's undisclosed equitable interest should not prevail over other creditors.[134] However, this is a matter for reform of the relevant non-bankruptcy laws. Changing the parties' relative entitlements solely as a matter of bankruptcy law involves costly trade-offs against bankruptcy's collectivisation function.

The prevention of unjust enrichment theory, too, in some cases may lead to a change in creditors' relative entitlements upon bankruptcy. The relative

---

131  See, eg, *Re Sabri; ex parte Australia and New Zealand Banking Group Ltd* (1996) 31 Family LR 213.
132  Ibid 222 and 230.        133  Op cit 65–66.        134  Ibid 66.

entitlements theory promotes economic efficiency considerations. The prevention of unjust enrichment theory promotes corrective justice considerations. Sherwin favours the prevention of unjust enrichment theory because,
she says, corrective justice considerations are more important than efficiency
considerations: the prevention of unjust enrichment theory may be, 'to some
degree, inefficient. But it promotes the integrity of the constructive trust
remedy, because the bankruptcy proceeding brings into focus the interests
actually affected by specific restitution'.[135] In short, economic consequences
do not matter. The prevention of unjust enrichment theory is vulnerable on
this score. Sherwin defines the integrity of the constructive trust remedy using
corrective justice as the benchmark. However, as the previous five illustrative
cases show, economic efficiency is an alternative benchmark and it is by no
means self-evident that the integrity of the constructive trust remedy, if
defined using efficiency as the benchmark, requires the bankruptcy measures
Sherwin favours. In any event, others might argue with at least equal legitimacy that the integrity of the bankruptcy system trumps the integrity of the
constructive trust remedy. Moreover, the prevention of unjust enrichment
theory is open to charges of indeterminacy, particularly in its application to
cases of fraud, mistake and the like. In these cases, the question is whether
D's fraud sufficiently impaired P's assessment of the credit risk to justify
saying that P was an involuntary creditor. This is a question of degree requiring
determination on a case-by-case basis, and parties may have trouble predicting
in a given case which way the court will decide.

## Conclusion

Bryan laments the lack of 'an adequate conceptual framework' for determining the availability of proprietary remedies as an alternative to personal
restitution'.[136] My aim in this chapter has been to develop a theory of the
constructive trust based on economic considerations. It is commonly said
that the constructive trust serves two functions: (1) a deterrence function (the
prevention of unconscionable conduct); and (2) a restitutionary function
(the reversal of unjust enrichment). This taxonomy overlooks the constructive trust's perfectionary function, namely the enforcement of express and
implied bargains. Some constructive trusts serve an explicitly perfectionary
function: the constructive trust to perfect an agreement to transfer is a case in
point. Other constructive trusts appear to serve a deterrence or restitutionary
function. However, on closer examination these constructive trusts turn out
to be perfectionary as well.

135  Op cit 364.
136  Bryan, Michael, 'Unravelling Proprietary Restitution: An Australian Perspective', (2004),
      40 Canadian Business Law Journal 339 at 346–347.

To recapitulate on the cases analysed: in *Hewett v Court*, the judgments are explicitly in perfectionary terms and neither deterrence nor restitutionary considerations entered into the matter; *Soulos v Korkontzilas, Daly v Sydney Stock Exchange Ltd* and *Chase Manhattan Bank N.A. v Israel-British Bank (London) Ltd* can all be explained in deterrence or restitutionary terms, but the deterrence and restitutionary functions are subsidiary to the perfectionary function; in *Baumgartner v Baumgartner*, the court justified the constructive trust remedy on deterrence grounds (preventing unconscionable conduct) while in *Pettkus v Becker* the court resorted to the language of unjust enrichment, but in both cases the court's rhetoric masks the underlying objective which is a perfectionary one. In all the cases discussed, the primary objective in granting or withholding the remedy is to reproduce the outcome P and D are likely to have agreed on upfront if bargaining between them had been costless. Express or implicit cost-benefit analysis is an indispensable part of the decision-making process.

Inside D's bankruptcy, there are three main theories a court may apply to determine P's entitlement: (1) the property rights theory; (2) the relative entitlements theory; and (3) the prevention of unjust enrichment theory. The theories lead to different case outcomes on certain sets of facts. They also involve important policy trade-offs, in particular between economic efficiency and corrective justice concerns. The policy tension helps to explain why the determination of property rights in bankruptcy is such a thorny question. In any event, the courts need to be aware of what the policy choices are, as the first step towards the development of a coherent body of case law.

# Chapter 11

# The criteria for the award of proprietary remedies: rethinking the proprietary base

*Michael Bryan\**

## Introduction

What criteria ought to govern the award of a proprietary remedy?[1] The question is deceptively simple, so it should come as no surprise that attempts to answer it have resulted in a complex and inconclusive theoretical literature. The difficulties involved in identifying coherent criteria for the award of proprietary remedies are well known. First, the creation of new property rights by court order is not always clearly distinguishable from the enforcement of pre-existing property rights.[2] Second, assuming that a proprietary order can be made, it is uncertain when it will be preferred to a personal remedy. Finally, if a proprietary remedy is preferable, will the claimant be entitled to a proportionate share of the disputed property (either a resulting or constructive trust) or only to a security interest over the property (the equitable lien)? The cases give little help in answering these questions; they are mostly 'a wilderness of individual instances', being for the most part decisions on their own facts from which few general propositions can be derived.

Interest in proprietary remedies has been stimulated by recent academic writing on the law of unjust enrichment. Some North American theory even

---

\* Professor of Law, University of Melbourne.

1 For the purposes of this chapter, proprietary remedy is used as a generic name for the imposition of a constructive trust, resulting trust or equitable lien. As to whether resulting trusts reverse unjust enrichment see Chambers, R, *Resulting Trusts*, 1997, Oxford: Clarendon Press; New York: Oxford University Press, and Grantham, RB and Rickett, CEF, *Enrichment and Restitution in New Zealand*, 2000, Oxford: Hart Publishing Ch 13.

2 Birks, P, Property and Unjust Enrichment [1997] New Zealand Law Review 623; Grantham, R and Rickett, C, Property and Unjust Enrichment: Categorical Truths and Unnecessary Complexity [1997] New Zealand Law Review 668; Grantham, R and Rickett, C, *Enrichment and Restitution in New Zealand*, Ch 3 and 403–435; Virgo, G, *Principles of the Law of Restitution*, 1999, Oxford: Clarendon Press, 8, 11–16; Burrows, A, Proprietary Restitution: Unmasking Unjust Enrichment, 117 (2001) LQR 412, 412–423 (Burrows, Proprietary Restitution); Grantham, RB and Rickett, CEF, Property Rights as a Legally Significant Event, 62 (2003) CLJ 717.

assumes that proprietary remedies can *only* be awarded as a response to unjust enrichment.[3] The reversal of unjust enrichment is an important function of proprietary remedies but, in Anglo-Australian law at least, it is not the only function they perform. Not all proprietary remedies are restitutionary, in the sense of restoring property to its original titleholder.[4] They also enforce a plaintiff's reasonable expectations, perfect legally incomplete or imperfect transactions, and enable the proceeds of wrongdoing to be recovered.[5]

It is unlikely that any meta-principle or 'overarching concept', such as the prevention of unjust enrichment or the avoidance of unconscionable conduct, could ever adequately explain all the situations in which proprietary remedies can be imposed. Certainly no explanation at this level of generality would have any predictive value. A more promising approach is to isolate specific applications of proprietary relief and then to identify the criteria for their award. This has in fact been the method adopted by most recent scholarship.

The only proprietary remedies to be considered in this chapter are those that reverse unjust enrichment. This is not because there is any objection in principle to imposing proprietary relief in order to further other aims.[6] This needs emphasising as some restitution writing conveys the (perhaps unintentional) impression that the reversal of unjust enrichment is a stronger reason for granting a proprietary remedy than (say) the enforcement of expectations. An assumption on which the argument of this paper rests is that there is nothing to be gained by trying to create a hierarchy of proprietary remedial objectives since reversing unjust enrichment and enforcing expectations are simply different methods of achieving corrective justice. This chapter focuses exclusively on proprietary remedies for unjust enrichment, partly for reasons of space and partly because recent decisions have made these remedies topical. But it is not part of the argument that a restitutionary constructive trust effectuates corrective justice more fully than the 'common intention' constructive trust, the constructive trust imposed upon a vendor of land, secret trusts, mutual wills or the various other trusts imposed by court order.

---

3   Sherwin, EI, Constructive Trusts in Bankruptcy, [1989] Illinois Law Review 297, 299 (Sherwin, Constructive Trusts in Bankruptcy); Paciocco, DM, The Remedial Constructive Trust: A Principled Basis for Priorities over Creditors, 68 (1989) Canadian Bar Review 315, 318–319 (Paciocco, The Remedial Constructive Trust).

4   *Stephenson Nominees Pty Ltd v Official Receiver* (1987) 76 ALR 485, 501–506, Gummow J. For overviews of the various functions of the constructive trust see G. Elias, *Explaining Constructive Trusts*, 1990, Oxford: Clarendon Press, Chambers, Robert, Constructive Trusts in Canada, 37 (1999) Alberta Law Review 173.

5   See G. Elias, *Explaining Constructive Trusts*, fn 4 above.

6   Although the imposition of a constructive trust in cases of wrongdoing where the criteria of unjust enrichment have not been met, as in *Attorney – General for Hong Kong v Reid* [1994] 1 AC 324 (PC), is controversial. See Goode, Roy, 'Proprietary Restitutionary Claims' in WR Cornish *et al* (eds), *Restitution Past, Present & Future*, Oxford: Hart Publishing, 1998, 63.

This chapter revisits the analysis of proprietary remedies proposed by the late Professor Peter Birks which goes by the unlovely shorthand of 'proprietary base theory'.[7] Put shortly, proprietary base theory holds that a proprietary remedy reversing unjust enrichment will be imposed only where the plaintiff can show:

(1) a legally recognised ground of restitution, such as mistake or failure of consideration,
(2) that the plaintiff has or, immediately before its receipt by the defendant, had beneficial title to the property, and
(3) that the defendant has acquired title to the property or to its traceable substitute.[8]

Although Birks never wavered from his conviction that a finding of a proprietary base was an essential precondition to the imposition of a restitutionary proprietary remedy he disapproved of the direction taken by the English authorities over the last decade. In his final book, he concluded that '[t]he law as to the incidence of rights *in rem* in response to unjust enrichment is in a very poor state'.[9]

From his perspective there were two grounds for pessimism. First, the House of Lords in *Foskett v McKeown*[10] held that the tracing rules belonged to property law, and not to the law of unjust enrichment. As a result, proprietary remedies imposed following the application of the tracing rules enforce existing property rights and do not create new property rights which reverse unjust enrichment. Second, an earlier House of Lords decision, *Westdeutsche Landesbank Girozentrale v Islington London Borough Council*[11] had treated the distinction between an initial and a subsequent failure of consideration as being irrelevant to the award of a proprietary remedy. As will be shown, the distinction is fundamental to determining entitlement to a proprietary remedy where property has been transferred on an assumption which turns out to be false. Birks responded to the decision by arguing that the substitution of 'absence of basis' for the nominate 'unjust factors' such as mistake and

---

7 Birks, P, *An Introduction to the Law of Restitution*, Oxford; New York: Clarendon Press, revised edn 1989, (*Introduction*) Ch 11, esp. 378–385. Birks examined proprietary restitution in many later articles, among them Birks, P, 'Mixing and Tracing: Property and Restitution', [1992] Current Legal Problems 69; Birks, P, 'Property in the Profits of Wrongdoing', 24 (1994) University of Western Australia Law Review 8.

8 These criteria are extrapolated from *Introduction*, fn 7, at 378–379. The important question as to whether a proprietary remedy for unjust enrichment is available when the plaintiff has retained beneficial title to the property will be considered later.

9 Birks, Peter, *Unjust Enrichment*, 2003, Oxford; New York: Oxford University Press, Clarendon Law Series, (*Unjust Enrichment*) 162.

10 [2001] 1 AC 102.        11 [1996] AC 669.

failure of consideration would establish a more rational analytical framework for awarding proprietary, as well as personal, restitution for unjust enrichment.[12] But, as his discussion of proprietary remedies makes clear, 'absence of basis' does not remove the need to distinguish between initial and later failures of consideration. It is the latter distinction which determines whether an unjustly enriched recipient who is subject to a personal restitutionary claim can still deal with the property as his own, or alternatively must return it to the claimant.

The thesis of this chapter is that a finding of a proprietary base, in addition to a finding of a recognised ground of unjust enrichment, is still the most satisfactory method of determining the availability of a proprietary remedy. It is true that the application of the proprietary base is not always straightforward, and some of the difficulties will be explored in this chapter. But the proprietary base approach is superior, in point of both principle and predictive value, to alternative criteria for determining the availability of proprietary relief. It is to these that we now turn.

### Proprietary relief: the competing approaches

Two other approaches to the imposition of proprietary remedies have been canvassed in the cases and in academic writing. They are the 'conscience' and 'assumption of risk' approaches.

#### The conscience approach

This approach is well established in Australian law. In contemporary equity it derives its authority from the judgment of Deane J in *Muschinski v Dodds*.[13] In a much cited passage Deane J identified some of the circumstances in which common law and equity ordered restitution of payments made pursuant to a failed joint endeavour, and continued:

> The *prima facie* rules respectively entitling a fixed term partner to a proportionate repayment of his or her premium and a contractual joint venturer to a proportionate repayment of his or her capital payment contribution on the premature dissolution of the partnership or collapse of the joint venture are properly to be seen as instances of a more general principle of equity. That more general principle of equity can also be readily related to the general equitable notions which find expression in the common law count of money had and received and to the rationale of the particular rule of contract law to which reference has been made

12  *Unjust Enrichment*, fn 9, 166.
13  (1985) 160 CLR 583, 612–617. See also *Baumgartner v Baumgartner* (1987) 164 CLR 137.

... Like most of the traditional doctrines of equity, it operates upon legal entitlement to prevent a person from asserting or exercising a legal right in circumstances where the particular assertion or exercise of it would constitute unconscionable conduct . . .[14]

Later authority has qualified this pronouncement in one respect. Even where it would be unconscionable for the defendant to assert sole beneficial title to the disputed property,[15] a proprietary order will not be made if 'there are other means available to quell the controversy'.[16]

Conscience and unjust enrichment are not mutually exclusive organising categories. An unconscionable assertion of title can sometimes amount to an unjust enrichment. There are some examples in the authorities of an unjust enrichment being reversed under the guise of preventing unconscionable conduct.[17] But for a court to declare that it would be unconscionable for a defendant to retain the sole beneficial title to property is only to state a conclusion. The grounds for reaching that conclusion must still be spelt out. The 'unconscionable assertion of beneficial title' mantra has been invoked to achieve a variety of remedial objectives. Most commonly it gives effect to a plaintiff's reasonable expectations[18] but there are also cases where it has protected a plaintiff's reliance interest[19] or compelled a wrongdoer to hold the fruits of his crime on trust for the victim.[20]

The conscience approach directs the court's inquiry to the state of the defendant's 'conscience'. It might be thought that this refers to the defendant's motive in obtaining title to the property, but equitable entitlement has usually been determined by reference to the plaintiff's contributions to the purchase or improvement of that property without much attention being paid to the defendant's intention or motive in taking title.[21] What is unconscionable is the defendant's failure to give effect to the expectations generated by the plaintiff's making of the contributions. The ambiguity

---

14  Ibid 619–620 (references omitted).
15  Or, as in *Muschinski v Dodds*, to assert a larger share in the property than his contributions justify.
16  *Bathurst City Council v PWC Properties Pty Ltd* (1998) 195 CLR 566, 585.
17  *Muschinski v Dodds* is an example: the constructive trust restored to the plaintiff, the value of the financial contributions which she and her de facto had intended at the time to be an arts and crafts centre. Query whether, as a case of subsequent failure of consideration, proprietary relief should have been granted at all, as opposed to the contribution order preferred by Gibbs CJ: (1985) 160 CLR 583, 596–598, Gibbs CJ.
18  *Baumgartner v Baumgartner* (1987) 164 CLR 137.
19  *Giumelli v Giumelli* (1998) 196 CLR 101 (where, however, a personal remedy was preferred).
20  *Zobory v Commissioner of Taxation* (1995) FCR 86.
21  Contributions may be financial or homemaker: see *Baumgartner v Baumgartner*, fn 18; *Parij v Parij* (1997) 72 SASR 153; *Read v Nicholls* [2004]VSC 66; cf *Bryson v Bryant* (1992) 29 NSWLR 188.

between unconscionability, in the sense of exploitative conduct (or *ex ante* unconscionability), and unconscionability, in the sense of a judicial finding that it would be unfair for the defendant to retain sole beneficial title to property (or *ex post* unconscionability) is largely unresolved in the caselaw and theoretical writing. Most Australian property cases use 'conscience' in the former sense, but examples of the latter rationalising sense can be found.[22]

But there is a more fundamental objection to the application of con-science-based criteria for the award of proprietary relief. It is that these criteria place settled property rights at risk of a potential exercise of judicial discretion in situations in which there is no convincing reason for unsettling them. Examples of constructive trust claims based on unjust enrichment include cases where a contract, gift or bequest has been vitiated by fraud, mistake, misrepresentation, undue influence or exploitative conduct. Assuming that no recognised defence such as change of position or good faith purchase applies, claimants who have entered into transactions where the consent to transfer property has been vitiated for any reason should not be placed at risk of losing their property, in the event of the defendant's insolvency, by the exercise of a generalised discretion favouring the wrongdoer's creditors.[23]

It is of course unlikely that property rights will be lost in such a case; courts are usually averse to exercising a discretion so as to disturb accrued property rights, or to subordinate them to the interests of wrongdoers and wrong-doers' creditors.[24] But there is no reason why a claimant should be subjected to any exercise of discretion if a rule can be formulated that ensures that he will never lose established property rights. Security of title is more effectively preserved by automatically enforcing a claimant's proprietary base, subject to the application of recognised defences, than by making enforcement depend on the outcome of some kind of equitable balancing exercise.

A review of the numerous authorities on the application of the conscience approach discloses no tendency on the part of Australian judges to interfere with claimants' established property rights. 'Conscience' is for the most part synonymous with the enforcement of a claimant's proprietary base. The dif-ference between the two approaches has mattered most in a few cases in which the award of a proprietary remedy has been made to turn on the existence or absence of actual creditors who will be affected by a decision to award a proprietary remedy.[25] In refusing a proprietary order on the ground that the defendant has actual creditors whose claims will be placed in jeopardy by the making of the order courts have confused the criteria for

---

22  See the cases in fn 25 for illustrations.
23  Failure of consideration raises different issues and is discussed below at 282–285.
24  Evans, Simon, 'Defending Discretionary Remedialism', 23 (2001) Sydney Law Rev 463.
25  Compare *Katingal Pty Ltd v Amor* [1999] FCA 317, [9]–[11] with *Robins v Incentive Dynamics Pty Ltd* [2003] NSWCA at [71].

imposing a constructive trust with the consequences of its imposition. While it is true that proprietary remedies withdraw the subject matter of the trust from the pool of assets available for distribution to the defendant's creditors in the event of the latter's bankruptcy, it does not follow that relief to a plaintiff who has an unqualified beneficial title to property should be made conditional on the absence of any personal claims third parties may have against the defendant.

### The assumption of risk approach

The second alternative to proprietary base analysis is the 'assumption of risk' approach to determining the availability of proprietary remedies. Writers adopting this perspective[26] differ on matters of detail, but there is broad agreement on the following criteria for the award of a proprietary remedy:

(a) the defendant has been unjustly enriched at the expense of the plaintiff;
(b) the defendant has property which traceably represents the property of which the plaintiff has been deprived; and
(c) the plaintiff has not assumed the risk of the defendant's insolvency.

The 'assumption of risk' approach combines elements of corrective and distributive justice. The first two requirements (being corrective) restate the criteria of proprietary base theory. The third requirement (being distributive) introduces an explicit normative justification for imposing a proprietary remedy. There is no uniform formulation of this requirement. Emily Sherwin, for example, advocates granting proprietary relief where 'the claimant did not extend credit voluntarily to the debtor',[27] whereas Andrew Burrows argues that 'the law should not create proprietary rights where, analogously to an unsecured creditor, the unjust enrichment creditor has taken the risk of the defendant's insolvency'.[28]

Although 'assumption of risk' analysis has been proposed as an alternative to 'proprietary base', the two approaches are very similar in practice. Subject to one exception, to be discussed later, the distinction which 'assumption of risk' analysis draws between voluntary lenders and involuntary creditors reflects the line drawn by 'proprietary base' theory between cases of initial and subsequent failure of consideration. The latter articulates in terms of legal doctrine a distinction that the former draws in terms of economic risk analysis.

But where 'assumption of risk' theory differs from 'proprietary base' is in denying proprietary restitution in a few cases where consent to the transfer

---

26 Burrows, Proprietary Restitution, fn 2; Paciocco, The Remedial Constructive Trust, fn 4; Sherwin, Constructive Trusts in Bankruptcy, fn 4.
27 Sherwin, Constructive Trusts in Bankruptcy, fn 4 at 336.
28 Burrows, Proprietary Restitution, fn 2 at 425.

has been vitiated and the plaintiff can prove the existence of a proprietary base. Burrows gives an example of such a case:

> Say, for example, a claimant has made a payment to the defendant by reason of a mistake of law in believing that a purported contract under which he was to confer credit without security, was valid whereas, as a matter of law, it was void. Although the claimant has a personal action for the recovery of the money paid by mistake of law, that mistake plainly does not hide the risk taken by the claimant as to the defendant's insolvency. In that situation, the mistake of law should not trigger proprietary restitution so as to confer priority on the defendant's insolvency.[29]

A difficulty with this example is that it is not at all clear that the claimant should be denied a proprietary remedy on these facts. The argument for withholding proprietary relief emphasises the failure of the mistaken payer to take security in return for extending credit. A possible counter-argument might be that a mistaken payer only takes the risk of non-payment where the contract is legally enforceable, since a rational decision to take security from a borrower can only be taken in the context of a valid contract. A mistake as to the validity of a contract which entitles a payer of money under the contract to personal restitution may also cause the payer to mis-assess the risk of taking security and entitle him to proprietary restitution.

The example also highlights an unjustifiable distinction between money paid under void and voidable contracts. Had the contract in this example been voidable, for example because a material misrepresentation had been made, the payer would be entitled to rescind the contract and to have a constructive trust imposed over the traceable proceeds of the payment. The remedy restores both parties to their pre-contractual position.[30] It is inconsistent to apply different principles to void and voidable contracts where in both cases the payer has extended credit without taking security. The application of 'assumption of risk' analysis to property transferred under a voidable contract ought logically to result in denying a proprietary remedy to a transferor who has taken the risk of the transferee's insolvency. But this solution is contrary to the well-established equitable principle of restoring both parties to the 'status quo ante', and suggests that the application of this analysis to voidable contracts may not be straightforward.

The distinction between void and voidable contracts creates no problems for proprietary base theory. In both the Burrows case and the example put forward in the previous paragraph the payer can show that he had title to the

---

29  Ibid 427.
30  *Daly v Sydney Stock Exchange* (1986) 160 CLR 571; *Guinness plc v Saunders* [1990] 2 AC 663.

property immediately before it was transferred under the contract. If the contract is voidable the plaintiff must elect to treat the contract as at an end as a precondition of an award of equitable rescission. Once the election has been made, however, proprietary restitution will be available, unless a recognised defence, such as change of position or good faith purchase, bars recovery.

## Defending and refining proprietary base

Judicial and academic analysis of the proprietary base approach has not stood still since Peter Birks first gave currency to the notion in *Introduction*. Much of the later work on the application of proprietary base to specific cases was done by Birks himself. Three issues merit brief discussion.

The most critical challenge to proprietary base theory has come not from the formulation of alternative models of proprietary restitution (of the kind discussed in the previous section) but from the argument, accepted by the House of Lords in *Foskett v McKeown*,[31] that a claim to the restitution of specific property or to its traceable proceeds enforces pre-existing property rights and is not a claim in unjust enrichment. From one point of view, the positioning of proprietary relief within the law of property reinforces the importance of finding a proprietary base, since the central concern of property law is the identification and enforcement of proprietary rights. But from another point of view the House of Lords decision amounts to a rejection of proprietary base theory because it denies that proof of the existence of such a base can entitle a claimant to a proprietary remedy in unjust enrichment.

A second development concerns the application of proprietary base theory to the 'unjust factor' of failure of consideration (or basis of payment). Following the House of Lords decision in *Westdeutsche Landesbank Girozentrale v Islington London Borough Council*[32] academic writers have elaborated a distinction between initial failures of consideration (or basis), which attract proprietary restitution if all other criteria for relief are satisfied, and subsequent failures of consideration. A proprietary remedy will not be ordered in a case of subsequent failure because by the time of the failure the recipient will have obtained full beneficial title to the money or other property received, and can deal with it as he likes. The only exception is where a payee is a trustee or has otherwise assumed a fiduciary obligation to segregate the payment from his own funds. In such a case the trustee or other fiduciary owner does not take as beneficial owner, and is under a fiduciary duty to make restitution of the specific money received (or its traceable substitute) by

---

31 [2001] 1 AC 102.
32 [1996] AC 669.

way of account to the payer.[33] Robert Chambers identified the critical distinction between subsequent and initial failures of consideration in his book *Resulting Trusts*.[34] It captures in doctrinal terms the distinction between property intended to be at the free disposal of the recipient, reserving no title to the transferor, and property which is not intended to be enjoyed by the recipient as he pleases and to which the transferor (upon proof of a legally recognised ground of restitution) can assert a proprietary claim. Birks emphasised this distinction in his analysis of proprietary remedies in *Unjust Enrichment*.[35]

The *Introduction* also drew attention to another distinction. This is between proprietary remedies which confer proportionate shares in property on the claimant, such as resulting and constructive trusts, and the equitable lien, which entitles the claimant to a security interest. The House of Lords in *Foskett v McKeown* was divided on the appropriateness of awarding a proprietary share or security interest to the plaintiff in that case, and it cannot be said that judicial or academic analysis has so far succeeded in shedding much light on how the choice between trust and lien should be made.

All three issues will be briefly considered.

### Property and unjust enrichment

In *Foskett v McKeown* a majority of the House of Lords held that, where the trustee of an investment trust had, acting in breach of trust, applied some of the trust money towards purchase of premiums of a life insurance policy taken out in favour of his children, the trust beneficiaries were, upon the death of the trustee, entitled to a proportionate share of the proceeds of the policy paid to the children. While the House was divided on the question whether the appropriate remedy for the beneficiaries was a proportionate share of the proceeds of the policy or an equitable lien to secure repayment of the amount misapplied, it was unanimously held that the purpose of both remedies was to enforce the beneficiaries' property rights and not to reverse unjust enrichment. In the words of Lord Millett, '[t]he transmission of a claimant's property rights from one asset to its traceable proceeds is part of our law of property, not of the law of unjust enrichment'.[36]

*Foskett v McKeown* therefore constitutes binding authority in English law for the proposition that interests created as a result of the application of equitable tracing principles vindicate the beneficiaries' pre-existing property rights, and are not new rights in unjust enrichment. It will also be highly

---

33 This proviso covers, among others, the Quistclose authorities: *Barclays Bank Ltd v Quistclose Investments Ltd* [1970] AC 567; *Twinsectra Ltd v Yardley* [2002] 2 AC 164.

34 Oxford: Clarendon Press, 1997, 147–163.    35 *Unjust Enrichment*, fn 9 at 166–178.

36 [2001]1 AC 102, 127.

persuasive authority in other common law jurisdictions where the question has not so far been directly considered. The decision has not, however, settled the long-running debate on where the boundary between property law and the law of unjust enrichment should be drawn.

The academic literature on the 'property versus unjust enrichment' controversy is extensive.[37] The nature of the relationship between the two private law organising categories has been described, with only slight exaggeration, as 'the last great unsolved mystery for those working in the law of restitution'.[38] It is not the purpose of this chapter to solve the mystery or to offer a critique of the arguments advanced on either side. In *Introduction*, Birks included within his definition of proprietary restitution for unjust enrichment cases where the defendant acquires title to property which had previously belonged to the plaintiff (for example where P pays $100 to D in the mistaken belief that she is under a legal obligation to do so) as well as cases where, in spite of the transfer, the plaintiff retains title to the property (as where P transfers $100 to D as a result of a mistake of identity).[39] The inclusion of the latter was defended on the ground that D is factually enriched by the receipt of the mistaken payment even if he has obtained no title to the money.[40] P will be entitled to restitution for unjust enrichment in order to capture D's factual benefit.[41]

Not every unjust enrichment theorist would agree with Birks that the definition of enrichment includes cases of factual benefit where the enrichee has received no title to the enrichment.[42] But some unjust enrichment writers still insist, contrary to the House of Lords, that a successful claim made through tracing to an exchange-substitute of the plaintiff's original property is one in unjust enrichment, and does not enforce pre-existing property rights. The proprietary remedy entitles the plaintiff to new property, not being the 'old' property of which he has been deprived. While property law permits a titleholder to vindicate title to pre-existing property interests, only the law of unjust enrichment can explain why a claimant should be

37 It includes all the chapters and journal articles cited in fn 2. See also Grantham, R and Rickett, C, 'Tracing and Proprietary Rights: The Categorical Truth', 63 (2000) Mod L Rev 905; Virgo, G, *The Principles of the Law of Restitution*, 1999, Oxford: Clarendon Press, Chs 1, 20; Virgo, G, 'Vindicating Vindication: *Foskett v McKeown*' in, Hudson, A, ed, *New Perspectives on Property Law, Obligations and Restitution*, 2004, London: Cavendish Publishing, Ch 10 (*Vindicating Vindication*).

38 Burrows, Proprietary Restitution, fn 2 at 412.      39 *Introduction* 378

40 Birks, P, 'Property and Unjust Enrichment: Categorical Truths', [1997] NZ LRev 623, 654–656. See also Burrows, Proprietary Restitution, fn 2 at 419.

41 Cf, *Kuwait Airways Corp v Iraqi Airways Co (Nos 4 and 5)* [2002] 2 AC 883, 1093 at [79] where Lord Nicholls characterised the vindication of the plaintiff's property right to capture gains as involving unjust enrichment.

42 Swadling, W, 'A Claim in Restitution?' [1996] LCMLQ 63, 65.

entitled to a new asset obtained by the defendant in substitution for the old one.[43]

One consequence of classifying tracing claims to exchange-substitutes in terms of the enforcement of subsisting property rights is that the defence of change of position will not be available to the honest recipient of the plaintiff's property who deals with the property, or with other property, on the faith of the validity of the receipt.[44] The disallowance of the defence could create tactical opportunities for claimants relying on equity's tracing rules. Some claimants, upon proof of a recognised ground of unjust enrichment will have a choice between a personal claim in restitution, attracting the application of the defence,[45] and a proprietary claim to which the defence does not apply. In addition to satisfying the natural preference many claimants have for the return of their property *in specie* the proprietary claim will on this analysis also enable a claimant to avoid a successful plea of change of position.[46]

This undesirable outcome could be avoided by extending the change of position defence to proprietary claims based on tracing, but an objection to this solution is that it would fragment the structure of property law. It would create an artificial distinction between proprietary claims to which change of position does not apply, being the greater part of property law, and proprietary claims to which the defence does apply.

It is hard to see the merits of this kind of fragmentation. The difficulties of fitting change of position into the scheme of personal and proprietary claims based on tracing would be avoided if, contrary to the decision in *Foskett* all claims based on the application of tracing principles were to be characterised as claims in unjust enrichment.

### Initial and subsequent failure of consideration

A proprietary remedy is in principle available where any factor vitiating consent to a legal transaction, such as mistake or duress, has been established, provided that the enrichment is traceably identifiable and that the plaintiff

---

43  Cf, Virgo, G, *Vindicating Vindication*, fn 37, 219, arguing that property law allows the claimant to assert title to the exchange-substitute.

44  In *Foskett v McKeown* Lord Millett assumes that the defence will be unavailable: [2001] 1 AC 102, 129. Some Australian decisions have applied the defence to claims based on tracing but they have been claims to personal restitution: *Gertsch v Atsas* [1999] NSWSC 898, Foster AJ; *Port of Brisbane Corp v ANZ Securities* [2002] QCA 158.

45  *Lipkin Gorman v Karpnale* [1991] 2 AC 548, 580, Lord Goff.

46  For the argument that change of position should apply to proprietary claims in order to prevent plaintiffs with personal claims avoiding its application, see Birks, P, 'Change of Position: The Nature of the Defence and its Relationship to Other Restitutionary Defences' in Mitchell McInnes (ed), *Restitution: Developments in Unjust Enrichment*, 1996, LBC Sydney 55–56.

can show the necessary proprietary base in the property claimed. Failure of consideration (or basis) differs from these grounds in that relief is not granted on the basis that any intention to confer a benefit on the recipient was vitiated; rather, the intention was made subject to some condition or assumption which has not been fulfilled. It is a matter of construction of the agreement between the parties, or of the circumstances surrounding the conferral of the benefit, as to whether the provider of the benefit should be entitled to the specific recovery of the property (as opposed to its value in a personal claim) upon the failure of the condition or assumption.

In assessing the availability of proprietary restitution a critical distinction has been drawn between cases of initial failure of consideration and cases of subsequent failure of consideration. The general rule is that proprietary relief is limited to cases of initial failure of consideration, unless the property claimed is trust property or property subject to some other fiduciary obligation which can be recovered even where there has been a subsequent failure of consideration.[47] The significance of the distinction between initial and subsequent failure of consideration was explored in detail by Dr Robert Chambers in his work *Resulting Trusts*.[48]

Where a recipient of property has, upon transfer, obtained unfettered beneficial ownership of that property before the failure of the basis on which the transfer was made the transferor will be entitled to personal restitution of the value of the property transferred but not to a proprietary remedy. This is a case of subsequent failure of consideration. The transferor loses his proprietary base as soon as the recipient obtains full beneficial title. Conversely, if the basis of the transfer fails before the recipient has obtained full beneficial title, the case is one of initial failure of consideration and the transferor will be entitled to proprietary restitution. The transferor's proprietary base has not been lost in this case.

The distinction between initial and subsequent failure of consideration is easier to state than to apply. It will not always be clear from the documentation of many sales or loans contracts whether the beneficial ownership in the subject matter of the contract was intended to pass under the contract at the time of the physical transfer of the subject matter or at a later date. The leading 'swaps' case of *Westdeutsche Landesbank Girozentrale v Islington London Borough Council*[49] highlights the practical difficulties involved in giving effect to the distinction.

The case concerned an interest-rate swap agreement under which the parties made reciprocal loans to each other, one at a fixed rate of interest and the other at a floating rate. After it was discovered that the agreement was *ultra*

---

47 *Introduction*, fn 7, 385. *Unjust Enrichment*, fn 9, 166–178.
48 Chambers, R, *Resulting Trusts*, 1997, Oxford: Clarendon Press, 151–163.
49 [1996] AC 669.

*vires* the council's statutory borrowing powers,[50] the bank claimed restitution from the council of the difference between the amount it had lent the council and the amount it had received in return. A majority of the House of Lords held that the bank was entitled to personal restitution of the amount claimed but that it was not entitled to a proprietary remedy.[51]

The ground of unjust enrichment in *Westdeutsche* was failure of consideration: the consideration (or basis) for the bank's payment to the council had failed after the contract of loan had been held to be *ultra vires*. But if the bank was to be entitled to a proprietary remedy, two other conditions had to be satisfied. First, the property to be included within the court order had to be identifiable. In *Westdeutsche* the proceeds of the bank loan had been spent and were no longer traceable.[52] Secondly, the basis of the payment must have failed no later than the time when the council obtained full beneficial title to the money paid under the loan agreement so that the case qualified as one of initial, and not subsequent, failure of consideration.

Was *Westdeutsche Landesbank Girozentrale v Islington London Borough Council* a case of initial failure of consideration? In *Unjust Enrichment* Birks accepted that the decision to deny the bank a proprietary remedy was defensible only if the failure of consideration was subsequent; but he nonetheless insisted that the swaps cases 'were not cases of subsequent failure'.[53] This was because the ground of restitution, being the failure of consideration of money paid under the void contract of loan, existed at the moment the council received the money.

It is submitted that this is not the right way to determine whether a failure of consideration is initial or subsequent. The critical question is whether the money paid under the loan agreement is intended to be at the free disposal of the borrower. A borrower who is entitled to apply the proceeds of a loan for any lawful purpose enjoys full beneficial title to the money lent. Upon the occurrence of the failure of consideration the lender will be entitled only to personal restitution. Conversely, where the payment is not intended to be at the free disposal of the borrower, and the basis for making the payment ceases to exist, the payer will have retained property in the payment and will be entitled to a proprietary remedy over the payment if it is traceable.[54]

50  *Hazell v Hammersmith and Fulham LBC* [1992] 2 AC 1.
51  A successful proprietary claim would have entitled the bank to payment of compound interest. C f, the different principles applied to govern the award of compound interest in *Hungerfords v Walker* (1989) 171 CLR 125 (HCA).
52  'The money initially received by Islington from Westdeutsche was spent by Islington on its ordinary purposes': [1994] 4 All ER 890, 966, Dillon LJ.
53  *Unjust Enrichment*, fn 9, 172.
54  *Twinsectra Ltd v Yardley* [2002] 2 AC 164, 184, Lord Millett. The restrictions may fall short, in a variety of ways, of preserving the lender's equitable interest. For a comprehensive analysis

As already noticed, the distinction between initial and subsequent failure of consideration, drawn in this way, restates in doctrinal terms the principle that only a claimant who has not taken the risk of the recipient's insolvency should be entitled to proprietary restitution. Lenders who do not impose restrictions on the use of the money lent, and who do not take security for repayment, have taken the risk of the borrower's insolvency.

In the *Westdeutsche* case the council was entitled to apply the bank loan for any purpose authorised by local government legislation. The 'swaps' arrangement imposed no restrictions on the application of the money which would have reserved to the lender a proprietary base. Put another way, the money had not been lent on *Quistclose* terms. The basis of the loan contract failed when the contract itself was held to be void.[55] At that time the bank had no retained interest entitling it to proprietary relief. It was a case of subsequent failure of consideration, occurring after the council had received the money as full beneficial owner.

### Proportionate shares and security interests

*Foskett v McKeown* makes an important contribution to the debate on the conceptual basis of tracing but the actual decision turned on a different issue. There was no disagreement among the judges who decided *Foskett* that the investors were entitled to trace their money into the proceeds of a life insurance policy paid out to the children of the deceased trustee. Opinion was, however, divided on the amount that the investors could recover. The majority held that the investors were entitled to a proportionate share of the proceeds representing the insurance premiums which their money had been used to buy.[56] The minority judges, on the other hand, would have limited recovery to repayment of the misappropriated money secured by an equitable lien imposed over the proceeds.

*Foskett v McKeown* is authority for the proposition that a trust beneficiary who is entitled to trace trust money into a substitute property can elect

---

of restrictions on loans see Chambers, Robert, 'Restrictions on the Use of Money', in Swadling, W (ed), *The Quistclose Trust: Critical Essays*, 2004, Oxford: Hart Publishing, Ch 5.

55  The effect of *Hazell v Hammersmith and Fulham LBC* [1992] 2 AC 1 was to hold the swaps contract void 'ab initio', so it would be incorrect to treat the failure of consideration as being subsequent, in the sense of taking effect from the date of the House of Lords decision in that case. But this is a separate issue from whether the loan is intended to be at the free disposal of the borrower.

56  There was also a difference of opinion between Lord Browne-Wilkinson and Lord Hoffman, on the one hand, and Lord Millett, on the other, as to how the proportionate share should be valued. See [2001] 1 AC 102, 111 (Lord Browne-Wilkinson), 115–116 (Lord Hoffman), 142–145 (Lord Millett). See also Virgo, G, *Vindicating Vindication*, fn 37, 208.

between a proportionate share of that property and an equitable lien to secure repayment of the misapplied money. But it is not clear from the decision whether plaintiffs who are not trust beneficiaries can also claim proportionate share remedies. The Court of Appeal in *Foskett*, applying earlier authority, had held that trust money used by the trustee, acting in breach of trust, to improve property attracts only the application of an equitable lien to secure its recovery.[57] As Birks remarked, '[t]he principle underlying these cases is difficult to articulate. It has to explain not only why a lien is an appropriate response but also why a beneficial interest is not'.[58]

The key to the distinction between a proportionate share of property acquired through the application of misappropriated funds and a security interest to secure repayment of the amount misappropriated can be found in another distinction, namely that between breaches of trust and other wrongs, including other breaches of fiduciary obligation. Where misapplied trust money is traceable into a substitute asset, the beneficiaries (or the trustee, or a replacement trustee claiming on behalf of the beneficiaries) can claim a proportionate share in the substitute asset. Unless the trust instrument provides to the contrary, trustees are under a duty to invest trust monies so as to promote the financial interests of the beneficiaries.[59] A trustee's misappropriation of the trust fund deprives the beneficiaries not only of the settled capital but also of any appreciation in the value of the fund due to successful investment. Corrective justice considerations suggest that the beneficiaries ought to be entitled to the profit and to any appreciation in the trust property. Had the breach not been committed the profit or appreciation would have accrued to the beneficiaries.[60] Of course the proportionate share remedy will only be appropriate where tracing establishes that the profit was made, or asset acquired, by the trustee. Where trust money has been paid by the trustee to an innocent volunteer who uses that money, as well as his own, to make the profit or buy the valuable asset, the beneficiaries will be limited to an equitable lien to secure repayment of the trust money.[61]

The position is otherwise where the claimant is not a trust beneficiary but some other victim of wrongdoing (whether or not the wrongdoer was a

---

57 [1998] Ch 265, 278; *Unity Joint Stock Mutual Banking Association v King* (1858) 25 Beav 72, 53 ER 563.

58 *Unjust Enrichment*, fn 9, 181.      59 *Cowan v Scargill* [1985] Ch 270.

60 Query whether the beneficiaries should be permitted to claim a profit which the trustee, acting prudently and in conformity to the terms of the trust instrument, could not have obtained on behalf of the trust. If the analogy of the beneficiaries' right to adopt a successful investment made in breach of trust is apt the beneficiaries should be entitled to claim the profit even in this case.

61 *Re Diplock* [1948] 1 Ch 465.

fiduciary).[62] The appropriate proprietary remedy in such a case will be the imposition of an equitable lien over the property traced. The wrongdoer will have been under no obligation to invest on behalf of the claimant, nor will the claimant have looked to the wrongdoer to promote his economic interests. No trust should be imposed over the appreciated value of the property, or over any profit made as a result of the wrongdoing, as the claimant will have had no expectation of obtaining that profit or appreciation for himself. Moreover, the proprietary remedy will have been asserted by the claimant in order to obtain priority over the wrongdoer's unsecured creditors. While the claimant's proprietary base entitles him to the award of a remedy restoring the property or its traceable product of which he has been deprived, there is no good reason for allowing him, as against the wrongdoer's creditors, to make a proprietary claim to any profits derived from the misapplied property or to its appreciated value.

Confining the application of the proportionate share remedy to the traceable proceeds of a breach of trust is consistent with the application of the unjust enrichment principle in order to achieve corrective justice. If the defendant has been unjustly enriched at the expense of the plaintiff, corrective justice considerations justify restoring to the claimant the value of the enrichment of which she has been deprived, but to no more than that value. Birks vigorously argued, to the contrary, that the plaintiff's loss need not correspond to the defendant's gain, and that the gain could include profits generated from the initial enrichment.[63] But even if there is a case for breaking the arithmetical link between loss and gain in the context of personal restitution the argument is less persuasive when applied to proprietary restitution. It is appropriate to recognise a claimant's traceable property interest in an insolvent's estate, but there can be no convincing policy justification, in an unjust enrichment claim, for awarding her property to which she never had title prior to the defendant's enrichment. The claim by a non-trust claimant should be limited to an equitable lien to restore the value of the misapplied property at the time of the enrichment.

The only situation in which a claimant should be entitled to a proportionate share remedy is where she would have made the profit, or have been entitled to the appreciation, but for the unjust enrichment of the defendant.[64]

---

62  A fiduciary relationship is no longer a precondition to tracing in equity: *Foskett v McKeown* [2001] 1 AC 102, 113 (Lord Steyn), 128–129 (Lord Millett). Where a fiduciary other than a trustee is under a duty to invest the principal's funds, the principal should, by analogy with the trust, be entitled to a proportionate share remedy. This will be relevant to some cases of agency.

63  *Unjust Enrichment*, fn 9, 64–66. Cf Grantham, RB and Rickett, CEF, 'Disgorgement for Unjust Enrichment' [2003] CLJ 159; M.McInnes, 'At the Plaintiff's Expense: Quantifying Restitutionary Relief' [1998] CLJ 471.

64  Burrows, Andrew, Proprietary Restitution, fn 2, 418.

This includes the natural fruits of property such as mining rights. But in all other cases the conclusion must be that 'beyond the degree of his actual loss, the plaintiff has no higher claim to the defendant's property than do the defendant's general creditors'.[65]

## Conclusion

The modest, revisionist purpose of this chapter is to reaffirm the basic proposition – perhaps so basic as to be banal – that a precondition for the award of a proprietary remedy for unjust enrichment is that the claimant can establish a proprietary base in the property being claimed. On the assumption that one of the objectives of private law is to accomplish corrective justice, the aim will be more fully realised by the application of the proprietary base theory than by conscience-derived or assumption of risk approaches. Insofar as these other approaches ignore the requirement of a proprietary base, they are little more than unacknowledged experiments in distributive justice.

It is important, though, to reiterate the principal limitation of proprietary base theory: it only purports to explain the criteria for the award of proprietary remedies for unjust enrichment. The theory is irrelevant to the imposition of constructive trusts or equitable liens on other grounds, such as the enforcement of expectations or the disgorgement of the fruits of wrongdoing.

In unjust enrichment scholarship the proprietary base is associated with the name of Peter Birks. The association is deserved inasmuch as Birks, more than any other academic writer of his generation, set the debate on the criteria for proprietary restitution running, but he did not invent the proprietary base. As elsewhere in his scholarship he identified a pattern inherent in the law which had previously been overlooked until he drew attention to it. Recent authorities have confirmed the existence of this pattern. Authority and analysis both establish that there is no more convincing criterion for the award of a proprietary remedy for unjust enrichment than a finding that the plaintiff can establish a proprietary base in the property claimed, or to its traceable substitute.

---

65  Paciocco, D, The Remedial Constructive Trust, fn 3, 351.

## Chapter 12

# Change of position, good faith and unconscionability

*Susan Barkehall-Thomas* *

## Introduction

Two recent English Court of Appeal decisions deal with the change of position defence, applicable in cases of restitution for unjust enrichment.[1] The decisions are *Niru Battery Manufacturing Company v Milestone Trading Limited*[2] (the *Niru Battery* case) and *Jones v Commerzbank AG*[3] (the *Commerzbank* case). In both, the conclusions reached are within accepted principle, and thus not startling. What is remarkable, however, is the breadth of discussion on the operation of the defence.

The most notable feature of the decisions is the formulation of a test based on inequity or unconscientousness as the touchstone for the application of the defence. The flexibility this concept introduces into the defence, and its implications, will be examined. Given the recent statements by Justice Gummow in the High Court[4] on the relationship between unconscionability and unjust enrichment, this formulation of the defence may be particularly appropriate for the Australian version of the defence.

However, it will be argued that the way in which the unconscionability test should be applied must be very carefully considered in order to prevent broad notions of unjustness destroying the predictive value of the defence. Part of this analysis involves consideration of whether Australia should retain a reliance-based model of the defence. In recent cases it has been confirmed that English law has moved to a 'broad' version of the defence. Australian courts, on the other hand, have consistently adopted a 'narrow' version of the defence, based on the requirement that the defendant act 'on the faith' of

* BA LLB LLM(Mon), Senior Lecturer, Faculty of Law, Monash University. I wish to thank the participants of the conference session for their comments on the earlier version of this work. Any errors are, of course, my own.
1 Birks, P, *Unjust Enrichment*, 2nd edn, 2004, Oxford: Oxford University Press.
2 [2003] EWCA Civ 1446, Court of Appeal, 23 October 2003.
3 [2003] EWCA Civ 1663, Court of Appeal, 21 November 2003.
4 *Roxborough v Rothmans Pall Mall* (2001) 208 CLR 516.

the receipt. This produces quite different versions of the defence, particularly if an unconscionability touchstone is a characteristic of the former. It will be argued that the narrow version of the defence is to be preferred.

The final issue for discussion is the relevance of the decisions for the equitable action of knowing receipt of trust property. In an interesting move, in formulating the change of position test the English decisions drew an analogy between the change of position defence and the equitable 'knowing receipt' action. This analogy needs careful analysis as it has some important (but probably unintended) ramifications for the knowing receipt action.

### The cases

Before turning to the cases it is necessary to outline the nature of the defence.

Change of position has been recognised as a defence to a restitutionary claim for unjust enrichment in both England and Australia for more than 10 years. However, its precise scope was deliberately left open in the cases which approved the existence of the defence. In *Lipkin Gorman v Karpnale*[5] (the case in which the House of Lords accepted change of position as a defence in the English law of unjust enrichment) Lord Goff[6] stated:

> I am most anxious that, . . . nothing should be said at this stage to inhibit the development of the defence on a case by case basis . . . It is, of course, plain that the defence is not open to one who has changed his position in bad faith, as where the defendant has paid away the money with knowledge of the facts entitling the plaintiff to restitution, and it is commonly accepted that the defence should not be open to a wrongdoer.[7]

In Australia, similar broad statements as to the scope of the defence were made by the High Court of Australia in *David Securities Pty Ltd v Commonwealth Bank of Australia*.[8] But the focus of the Australian defence was slightly different, as the court emphasised that the 'central element is that the defendant has acted to her detriment on the faith of the receipt'.[9]

Despite there being no explicit[10] reference in *David Securities* to a 'good faith' requirement, this has been seen to be part of the Australian defence.[11]

---

5 [1991] 2 AC 548.    6   With whom Lords Bridge, Ackner and Griffiths agreed.
7 [1991] 2 AC 548 at 580.
8 (1992) 175 CLR 353. The broad nature of preventing an 'unjust' recovery was emphasised.
9 Ibid at 385.
10 Although the Court referred, with apparent approval to the formulation in *Australia and New Zealand Banking Group Ltd v Westpac Banking Corp* (1988) CLR 662 which referred to good faith.
11 *Port of Brisbane Corp v ANZ Securities Ltd* [2001] 2 Qd R 51. Also in *Mercedes Benz (NSW) Pty Ltd v National Mutual Royal Savings Bank Ltd* (Unreported, Court of Appeal (NSW),

Thus, the Australian version of the defence contains three elements: the defendant must (i) act in good faith, (ii) act in reliance on the receipt, and (iii) incur detriment.

### Niru Battery Manufacturing [12]

The *Niru Battery* case is, in part, a mistaken payment case.[13] The change of position defence was raised by the fourth defendant Bank, Crédit Agricole Indosuez (CAI). CAI was the recipient of a mistaken payment, which was then paid away to a third party. At trial, it had been held that an employee of CAI was not acting dishonestly in paying the money away. However, it was clear from the facts that the employee had knowledge of the facts which themselves indicated the payer's mistake. The question was whether CAI could rely on the change of position defence if it paid away the money once it had obtained knowledge that the money had been paid to it under a mistake.

#### APPLICATION TO THE FACTS

Although it had not acted dishonestly, the defendant was denied the application of the defence. This was because of its knowledge of the mistaken payment. Thus, in application, this case sheds little light on Lord Goff's test; it is simply a case where bad faith existed because the defendant knew the facts entitling the payer to restitution.

#### THEORY

Nonetheless, the judgments contain some important analysis of the content of the defence. Counsel for CAI had argued that the defendant would only be acting in bad faith, so as to lose the benefit of the defence if it acted dishonestly. Counsel relied on an earlier decision of the Court of Appeal in which a lack of good faith was explicitly equated to dishonesty.[14] Clarke LJ rejected that proposition. His Lordship was of the view that although the defence would be precluded if the defendant acted dishonestly, the

Priestley, Sheller & Clarke JJA, 1 April 1996) the Court of Appeal affirmed the decision of Palmer J on the question of change of position, with apparent approval of His Honour's discussion of good faith.

12 [2003] EWCA Civ 1446.

13 It also involved, against other defendants, the tort of deceit, constructive trusteeship, and accessory liability for a breach of trust.

14 *Medforth v Blake* [2000] Ch 86. Sir Richard Scott VC (with whom Swinton Thomas and Tuckey LJJ agreed) said *obiter* at 103: 'breach of a duty of good faith should, in this area as in all others, require some dishonesty or improper motive.' The case involved the duty of good faith of a receiver of mortgaged property.

circumstances in which it would be lost were not confined to dishonesty or other wrongdoing.

Instead, he identified some broad underlying principles from the judgment of Lord Goff in *Lipkin Gorman*[15] as follows:

(i)   The question is whether it would be unjust to allow restitution (or restitution in full).

(ii)  It will be unjust to allow restitution where an innocent defendant's position has so changed that the injustice of requiring him to repay outweighs the injustice of denying the claimant restitution.

(iii) The defence of change of position is not, for example, available to a defendant who has changed his position in bad faith, as where he has paid away the money with knowledge of the facts entitling the claimant to restitution.

(iv)  Nor is it available to a wrongdoer.

(v)   In general terms, the defence is available to a defendant whose position has so changed that it would be inequitable to require him to make restitution or to make restitution in full.[16]

His Lordship also noticed references by Lord Templeman in *Lipkin Gorman* to 'good conscience', and drew the conclusion that 'the essential question is whether it would be inequitable or unconscionable, and thus unjust, to allow the recipient . . . to deny restitution to the payer'.[17]

## ANALOGY TO KNOWING RECEIPT

In what may be a controversial move His Lordship adopted the unconscionability test of Nourse LJ in *Bank of Credit and Commerce International (Overseas) Ltd v Akindele*.[18] In that case, Nourse LJ held that dishonesty is not an ingredient of the cause of action of 'knowing receipt of property in breach of trust'.[19] He held instead that the question is whether the defendant had such knowledge as to make his retention of the benefit unconscionable.[20]

Sedley LJ approached the operation of the defence somewhat differently.[21] He concluded that there was an intermediate stage of 'inequitability' which fell short of bad faith, but was sufficient to deny the defence.[22] He did not explicitly adopt the *Akindele* unconscionability terminology, although he used it as grounds to support his argument. He claimed that it would be:

---

15 [1991] 2 AC 548.   16 [2003] EWCA Civ 1446 at [147].   17 Ibid at [149].
18 [2001] Ch 437.
19 Derived from *Barnes v Addy* (1874) 9 Ch App 244. The twin action is 'dishonest assistance in a breach of trust or fiduciary duty'. See *Twinsectra v Yardley* [2002] 2 AC 164.
20 [2001] Ch 437 at 455.   21 Butler-Sloss P agreed with both Clarke and Sedley LJJ.
22 [2003] EWCA Civ 1446 at [181].

strange if the 'analogous' doctrines of knowing receipt and unjust enrichment carried different defences, the former defeasible simply by proof of material knowledge, the latter only by proof of dishonesty.[23]

## Jones v Commerzbank[24]

This is another mistaken payment case. The defendant was a bank executive who mistakenly believed he was entitled to two salary bonuses from his employer. He claimed he had changed his position as a consequence of his mistaken belief. At its core this was a case about what types of expenditure will attract the defence. There was no issue of the defendant knowing of the mistake or acting in bad faith. The case turned on whether the defendant had changed his position to the extent that he should not be required to make restitution. Mummery LJ (with whom Sedley LJ agreed) held that the defendant should be denied the defence as he had not been disenriched.

As in the *Niru Battery* decision, the conclusions in this case are not controversial. It is the *obiter dicta* of Munby J that give rise to interest.

Munby J considered it 'necessary and important' to address the broader question of how the defence is to be defined in order to deal with some of the submissions made in argument as to its desirable future direction. Without having read the *Niru Battery* decision handed down only weeks before, Munby J independently reached very similar conclusions on the nature of the defence. He stated:

> The focus of the debate is . . . to identify whether in the particular case it would in all the circumstances be an 'injustice' or 'inequitable' to require the overpaid recipient to make restitution . . . That is not, with all respect to those who might suggest otherwise, an exercise in judicial discretion. It is an exercise in judicial evaluation. The judge is required to make a value judgment in the light of all the relevant circumstances.[25]

## Issues for analysis

Discussion will focus on three aspects of these decisions. First, the 'unconscionability'-based test will be analysed, with reference to its possible adoption in Australia. Particular attention will be paid to the question of whether a defendant with actual knowledge of the facts requiring restitution will always be acting in bad faith by refusing to repay the plaintiff.

Second, the requirement of reliance established by the High Court in *David Securities* will be subjected to examination. The English decisions confirm a divergence between Australia and England on the width of the defence. The

23  Id.       24  [2003] EWCA Civ 1663.       25  [2003] EWCA Civ 1663, at [53].

desirability of retaining the reliance limitation or of moving to a broader version of the defence will be addressed.

The third issue to be examined is the explicit analogy drawn between change of position and the equitable knowing receipt action. Case studies will demonstrate the potential implications for the equitable action should the analogy be adopted.

### Unconscionability terminology

The language of unconscionability used by Clarke LJ and Munby J, although not frequently heard in English courts, is very familiar to Australian lawyers. The strong theme of prevention of unconscionable conduct which underlies many equitable actions has resulted in the High Court making numerous statements on the role of unconscionability. It is worthwhile restating some of the most famous passages in order to demonstrate the similarity of the language used by English judges to that of Australian judges in formulating notions of unconscionability in Australia.

Perhaps the most famous passage on unconscionability is the statement by Deane J in *Muschinski v Dodds*[26] that in assessing unconscionable conduct:

> One is not left at large to indulge random notions of what is fair and just as a matter of abstract morality. Notions of what is fair and just are relevant but only in the confined context of determining whether conduct should, by legitimate processes of legal reasoning, be characterized as unconscionable for the purposes of a specific principle of equity.[27]

Just as forceful is the statement of Brennan J (as he was) that:

> If unconscionability were regarded as synonymous with the judge's sense of what is fair between the parties, the beneficial administration of the broad principles of equity would degenerate into an idiosyncratic intervention.[28]

The reasoning of Munby J also resonates with the recent dicta of Gummow J in *Roxborough v Rothmans Pall Mall*.[29] In that case His Honour forcefully suggested that causes of action founded in unjust enrichment (such as the action for money had and received) are strongly informed by equity, with its attendant theme of preventing unconscionable conduct. Although the passage is quite long, it needs to be set out in full to see its force. His Honour stated:

---

26 (1985) 160 CLR 583.     27 (1985) 160 CLR 583 at 621.
28 *Stern v McArthur* (1988) 165 CLR 489 at 514.     29 (2001) 208 CLR 516.

In all of these areas, as in *Moses v Macferlan*, notions derived from equity have been worked into and in that sense have become part of the fabric of the common law. Hence the statement in *Baltic Shipping* by Deane and Dawson JJ where, after indicating that the indebitatus count for money had and received was framed in the traditional language of trust or use, their Honours continued:

'[I]n a modern context where common law and equity are fused with equity prevailing, the artificial constraints imposed by the old forms of action can, unless they reflect coherent principle, be disregarded where they impede the principled enunciation and development of the law. In particular, the notions of good conscience, which both the common law and equity recognized as the underlying rationale of the law of unjust enrichment, now dictate that, in applying the relevant doctrines of law and equity, regard be had to matters of substance rather than technical form.'

Earlier, in *Muschinski v Dodds* Deane J, after referring to *Moses v Macferlan*, and to 'the general equitable notions which find expression in the common law count for money had and received', identified the operation of most of the traditional doctrines of equity as operating upon 'legal entitlement to prevent a person from asserting or exercising a legal right in circumstances where the particular assertion or exercise of it would constitute unconscionable conduct'.[30]

Given the emphasis placed on equitable notions, it would be no surprise if an Australian court were to adopt the unconscionability test for change of position. What remains to be considered is the desirability of its acceptance.

### Application of the unconscionability-based change of position defence

In adopting this test Clarke LJ came down in favour of a very wide concept of the defence. Previously, bad faith and wrongdoing were regarded as the essential disqualifiers. However, using the 'unconscionability' test, the potential circumstances in which the plaintiff will be prevented from recovering (and thus in which the defendant will be able to rely on the defence) are at once broader and inherently more flexible. The basis of the test is freed from notions of 'bad faith' and its inherent link to knowledge.

Indeed, the most obvious question that the court of appeal's formulation raises relates to knowledge. Will knowledge of the circumstances giving rise to the right of recovery preclude the defendant from relying on the defence? Is it ever unconscionable or inequitable for the plaintiff to be permitted to recover if the defendant knows of the circumstances which ground the

30  (2001) 208 CLR 516 at 554–5.

plaintiff's right of recovery? Before these cases these questions were easy to answer. It was generally accepted that a defendant with knowledge of the mistake would be acting in bad faith if it paid away the funds. Thus in *Lipkin Gorman*, Lord Goff referred to actual knowledge as an example of bad faith.[31] Academic commentary also generally supported the view that actual knowledge is the paradigm case of bad faith, disentitling the defendant from relying on the defence.[32] In the *Niru Battery* case itself, the defendant's knowledge of the payer's mistake was sufficient to prevent its attempted reliance on the defence.

Yet the crux of Clarke LJ's formulation of the defence, and his careful choice of unconscionability as his governing criterion,[33] is that the matter is not that simple. An unconscionability test requires global consideration of the circumstances surrounding the payment, the receipt, and the defendant's current circumstances. A single factor of knowledge alone will not necessarily preclude reliance on the defence if, overall, it is not unconscionable or inequitable for the plaintiff to be denied recovery.

The facts of the New Zealand decision of *National Bank of New Zealand v Waitaki International Processing (NI) Ltd*[34] illustrate a situation where an English court might now hold it to be unconscionable or inequitable for the plaintiff to recover, despite the defendant's knowledge of the mistake which caused the payment to be made. In this case the defendant recipient of the payment knew the bank had acted in error by attributing a sum of US$500,000 to the defendant. Over a period of three months the defendant denied ownership of the funds, but eventually accepted them with a view to investing them until the bank realised its mistake, and sought repayment. The investment failed, and by the time the bank realised its error and tried to reclaim the funds, the money had been lost.

This is obviously a highly unusual situation. It differs from the more likely scenario where the defendant deliberately pays away the money to a third party knowing of the plaintiff's claim. Knowledge is more likely to be coupled with a deliberate (or reckless) intention to defeat the plaintiff's right to recovery. Instead, the defendant's actions were consistent with its knowledge and recognition of the plaintiff's right to the money. In the

---

31 [1991] 2 AC 548 at 580. See also the recent English decision of *Campden Hill Limited v Chakrani* [2005] EWHC 911 (Ch) (13 May 2005, Hart J) where a recipient was denied the defence of change of position because at the time he changed his position, he knew that he was not entitled to the money. He became aware of the claimant's entitlement to the funds after receiving the funds, but before paying them away.

32 Usually assuming that conscious spending of the money would follow. See, for example, Nolan, R 'Change of Position' in Birks, P (ed) *Laundering and Tracing*, 1995, Oxford: Clarendon Press. But see Birks, P, 'Change of Position: The Nature of the Defence and its Relationship to Other Restitutionary Defences' in McInnes, M, *Restitution: Developments in Unjust Enrichment*, 1996, Sydney: LBC Information Services.

33 Or inequitability, in the case of Sedley LJ.         34 [1999] 2 NZLR 211.

New Zealand Court of Appeal the defendant was able to rely on the defence notwithstanding its knowledge. Henry J asked the question: 'is it inequitable to require the defendant to repay?'[35] He concluded that it was.[36]

The English approach now permits a similar question to be asked. Is it 'unconscionable' or inequitable for the plaintiff to recover in the circumstances?[37] In the context of the broader question of deciding if the defendant is 'unjustly enriched' the global consideration of facts permitted by the unconscionability test is surely right. Nonetheless, careful application of the test will be required. The next section addresses the potential pitfalls associated with combining the 'unconscionability' test with the 'broad' version of the defence.

### Narrow and broad versions of the defence

Recent English authority confirms the continuing divergence between Australian and English law as to whether a 'narrow' or 'broad' version of the defence is to be preferred. The broad terminology used by Lord Goff in *Lipkin Gorman*[38] has been warmly received by the English courts. Thus in *Derby v Scottish Equitable plc*,[39] and most recently in the *Commerzbank*[40] decision, the reliance requirement has been rejected. The broad version of the defence is clearly established.

By comparison, the 'narrow' version of the defence is the preferred model in Australia. It requires the defendant to have 'acted to his or her detriment on the faith' of the receipt.[41] This version of the defence was expounded by the High Court in *David Securities*, and its correctness has never since been doubted. Most recently, the model was applied by the Queensland Court of Appeal in *Port of Brisbane Corp v ANZ Securities Ltd.*[42]

The crucial difference between the two versions of the defence is that the

---

35  Ibid 220. Note that Henry J felt this was the appropriate question regardless of whether the statutory test or general principles were being applied.
36  Although, because the New Zealand courts take relative fault into account under a statutory test, Waitaki remained liable for 10 per cent of the loss.
37  The converse question: 'Is it unconscionable for the plaintiff to be denied recovery' can also be asked. This is how Clarke LJ framed it in *Niru Battery*, although His Lordship started within Lord Goff's original framework of asking whether it is inequitable for the defendant to be required to make restitution.
38  'The defence is available to a person whose position has so changed that it would be inequitable in all the circumstances to require him to make restitution' [1991] AC 548 at 580.
39  *Scottish Equitable plc v Derby* [2001] 3 All ER 818 at 827, per Robert Walker LJ.
40  [2003] EWCA Civ 1663, Court of Appeal, 21 November 2003, per Munby J who stated at [54]: 'there is in law no warrant at all for saying, that proof of detrimental reliance is a prerequisite to making good a defence of change of position.'
41  See *David Securities* (1992) 175 CLR 353 at 385.
42  See also *State Bank of New South Wales v Swiss Bank Corp* (1995) 39 NSWLR 350.

Australian model requires the defendant to make a conscious decision about the use to which the money or property will be put, in relying on the correctness of the payment. In contrast, all that is required under English law is that the causation test be satisfied. This causation test has been broadly stated, with tests of 'referable to' or 'relevant connection' being applied.[43] A 'but for' test has been seen as sufficient.[44] Birks argues that the causation test should be: 'if by reason of an event which would not have happened but for the enrichment the defendant's wealth is reduced, his liability is to that extent extinguished.'[45]

The situation where the defendant has been deprived of the enrichment through no fault of her own illustrates the difference between the two versions of the defence. In the *Waitaki* case, the New Zealand Court of Appeal allowed the defence to the defendant who lost the money through a failed investment.[46] The defendant was disenriched, and it was 'inequitable' to require it to return the funds to the mistaken payer. There was a sufficient causal nexus between the mistaken payment and the disenrichment, as the disenrichment would not have occurred 'but for' the overpayment. The *Niru Battery* and *Commerzbank* cases suggest that a similar approach would now apply in England.

But in Australia it is quite likely that the defence would not be available to a defendant in a similar situation. Although the investment was causally related to the receipt it was not made on the 'faith' of the receipt, in the sense that the recipient believed that it had a right to the funds. In fact, this is the very opposite of what the defendant believed. Because the defendant knew the plaintiff would call for the return of its money, its aim was *not to alter* its own financial position.

Elise Bant and Peter Creighton have argued the reliance test may nonetheless be satisfied in Australia on the facts of the *Waitaki* case.[47] They argue that it is enough for the defendant to show that it 'acted consistently with its knowledge as to the terms or basis on which it received the benefit'. Thus they argue that 'a defendant who has received a payment while knowing that the payment ought to be refunded can still establish reliance on the receipt if it applies the funds for the payer's benefit.'[48]

---

43   *Phillip Collins Ltd v Davis* [2000] 3 All ER 808; *Jones v Commerzbank* [2003] EWCA Civ 1663.
44   *Scottish Equitable plc v Derby* [2001] 3 All ER 818.
45   Birks, *Unjust Enrichment*, n1, at 188.
46   Note that in *Waitaki*, the members of the New Zealand Court of Appeal were divided on the question as to whether the statutory defence of change of position, which requires reliance, was satisfied under s 94B Judicature Act 1908. Although the Australian defence as formulated by the High Court does not expressly include the words 'the validity of', such words must be implicit in the Australian formulation.
47   Bant, E and Creighton, P, 'The Australian Change of Position Defence' (2002) 30 WALR 208, 218.
48   Id.

Their interpretation is supported by the judgment of Henry J in *Waitaki*. His Honour was of the view that the statutory defence was satisfied. The test requires that the defendant changed its position 'in reliance on the validity of the payment'. His Honour concluded that Waitaki had changed its position by depositing the funds, and this was:

> for the express purpose of keeping the fund available and in identifiable form against the day when payment may be requested. The investment was therefore made in reliance on the payment being valid in the sense that although the fund belonged to the bank, it was validly in Waitaki's hands at the insistence of the bank and importantly with its actual knowledge that Waitaki was asserting the bank was mistaken ... Waitaki relied on its belief that it could validly hold the fund on appropriate security on behalf of the bank, without risk of challenge as to its entitlement to do so pending demand.[49]

With respect, this interpretation of the statutory defence is strained. The interpretation of Thomas J should be preferred. His Honour was of the view that there had been no reliance on 'the validity of the payment' as this requires the defendant to believe that the payment was 'validly made, that is, not made under a mistake of fact or law'.[50] He also held that the defendant had not changed its position because the money was invested 'for and on behalf of the bank'.[51]

I am also unable to agree with the analysis by Bant and Creighton of the scope of the defence in Australia. Change of position in Australia as currently formulated is, at its core, a defence related to conscious disenrichment. In *David Securities* the High Court stated: 'its central element is that the defendant has acted to his or her detriment on the *faith of the receipt*.'[52] It applies because the defendant changed *its own* financial position, by spending or committing the value received, because it believed that the value was its own to spend. Crucial to the operation of the defence is that the defendant's conscious action in reliance on the receipt was detrimental.

Although the defendant in *Waitaki* took conscious action with the money, it did not spend it. It consciously preserved it. In such a case, how can the defendant demonstrate the crucial element of 'detriment'? The detriment (losing the money) is independent of the defendant's conscious decision to preserve the value in the knowledge that the money is subject to a claim for recovery.

Bant and Creighton's test of 'acting consistently' with the terms on which the value was received does not take adequate account of the detriment

---

49 [1999] 2 NZLR 211 at 218.       50 Ibid 227.       51 Id.
52 (1992) 175 CLR 353 at 385.

requirement. Under the Australian version of the defence the defendant may suffer hardship as a consequence of being forced to return the value to the plaintiff, but it is not unjust to require it to do so.

## Directions for Australia

As I have already argued, the Australian Courts may well adopt the unconscionability or inequitability test derived from *Niru Battery* and *Commerzbank*. In fact the language of reliance and detriment already strongly suggests that considerations of 'unconscionability' were in the minds of the judges when they established the model of the defence.[53]

Nonetheless, due to the adoption in Australia of the narrow version of the defence, compared to the broad English version, unconscionability may well mean different things in the two countries. In Australia it will not be unconscionable for the plaintiff to demand repayment unless the defendant has acted to his detriment in reliance on the receipt. In England, on the other hand, the defendant merely needs to demonstrate that his or her position has so changed that it is now inequitable or unconscionable for the plaintiff to recover.

The merit of the English test is that it provides a solution for the controversial case of the innocent defendant. An example provided by Burrows illustrates the point. He suggests the case of 'a defendant who is mistakenly (perhaps even negligently) paid £100,000 by his bank, which is then immediately stolen from him.'[54] Burrows argues that this scenario supports the operation of the broad defence, and that it would be 'grotesque' if the defendant were to be held liable. He states: 'Even though the subsequent loss of the benefit cannot be blamed on the bank, the fact remains that the bank started the chain of events by first making the mistaken payment.'[55]

The English broad test of causation, in combination with the test of 'unconscionability' or inequitability, provides a court with enough flexibility to permit the defendant to rely on the defence. Given the defendant's innocence, as well as the loss of enrichment, it can be concluded that it would be unconscionable to permit the plaintiff to recover.

In Australia this defendant would not currently have the benefit of the defence, and it is hard to support this conclusion. However, the English approach also permits the aware, but well-intentioned defendant to claim the benefit of the defence. It is at this point that the English approach is arguably

---

53 Because of the similarity of this language to the language applied in equitable estoppel, a doctrine based on unconscionable behaviour.

54 Burrows, A, 'Change of Position: The View from England', (2003) 36 Loyola of Los Angeles Law Review 803 at 808.

55 Ibid.

too broad. Two examples illustrate my point. The first example is provided by Birks:

> Suppose that a businesswoman finds an unexplained credit of $10,000 on her bank statement. She knows at once that it must be a mistake and has no intention other than to have the matter set right. She is intensely busy. She does not get around to the matter for three days. In the meantime the bank stops trading, broken by severe losses overseas.[56]

The *Waitaki* facts provide the second example. The defendant knew it was not entitled to the funds. It chose to accept them, and invested them on behalf of the plaintiff. Through the defendant's poor choice of investment the money was lost. The English approach permits the conclusion to be drawn that it may be unconscionable for the plaintiff to recover the funds, given the defendant's change of circumstances.

I suggest that it is not necessarily unconscionable for the plaintiff to recover, despite the defendant's loss of enrichment in each case. It is not a simple case of holding that the enrichment has disappeared. In each of these examples the defendant knew that the money in question did not belong to it. There must be limits on the availability of the defence to the defendant who knew that the money was not its own to retain. Support for this conclusion comes from a number of sources.

In the United States the Restatement of Restitution para 142 sets out the 'change of circumstances' defence to a claim for restitution. The defence is broadly defined as follows:

> The right of a person to restitution from another because of a benefit received is terminated or diminished if, after the receipt of the benefit, circumstances have so changed that it would be inequitable to require the other to make full restitution.

However, the application of the defence is then made subject to a number of comments and limitations. Thus, para (3) of the rule provides:

> Change of circumstances is not a defence if . . . (b) the change occurred after the recipient had knowledge of the facts entitling the other to restitution and had an opportunity to make restitution.

Most particularly, the effect of knowledge is addressed in comment (e) as follows:

---

56  Birks, P, 'Change of Position' n 32 above, at 59.

If a person acquires property from another as the result of a mistake and has no reason to know of facts which caused the transaction to be voidable, he has no duty with respect to the subject matter and is discharged from liability if, while he knows of no interest which the other has in the subject matter, the subject matter is destroyed. *If, however, he subsequently learns facts from which he realizes the existence of a mistake, his failure to notify the other party prevents a subsequent change of circumstances from being a defense. In such cases he should realize that the other party would desire the return of the subject matter and it is fair that he should retain it at his own risk after he has had a reasonable opportunity to return it.* The same rule is applicable to a person who in any other way than by a transfer from the owner has acquired property innocently but not for value and subsequently discovers the fact that the owner is entitled to it.[57]

Both para (3) and comment (e) suggest that once knowledge and reasonable opportunity of returning the property can be proved against the defendant, the defence will be denied.

However, other parts of para 142 suggest that in cases where a loss must be borne by one of the parties, which is the case we are considering, the answer will not be so simple. Comments (a) and (b) together provide that a rule of relative fault will be applied where a loss must be borne by one of the parties, and that a loss should not be borne by the recipient where he 'is guilty of no greater fault' than the claimant.[58]

---

57  American Law Institute, 1937. See also para 69 which reinforces para 142. Para 69(3) states: 'Change of circumstances is not a defense if . . . (b) the change occurred after the recipient had knowledge of the facts entitling the other to restitution and had an opportunity to make restitution.' The paragraphs have been applied in Virginia, see *Hilliard v Fox* 735 F. Supp. 674 (Dist Ct West District Virginia, 1990) and *Fed Ins Co v Smith* 144 F. Supp. 2d 507 (Dist Ct East District Virginia, 2001) although they have not been applied to the disaster scenario in question. *Hilliard v Fox* is the closest example, where the recipients invested a mistaken payment in a company that became defunct. On the plaintiff's motion for summary judgment the judge considered whether the defendants had a defence of change of position. Williams J limited his consideration of the defence to the time before the defendants had knowledge of mistake, expressly stating at 679, n 7, that he did not need to consider 'at this time the consequences of a loss of value occurring after notice had occurred'.

58  Comment (a) states: 'Where events are such that a loss must be suffered by one of the parties either with or without the ability to obtain reimbursement from a third person, justice does not require that the recipient should bear this loss, where he is guilty of no greater fault than that of the claimant.' Comment (b) provides: 'Any change of circumstances which would cause or which would be likely thereafter to cause the recipient entire or partial loss if the claimant were to obtain full restitution, is such a change as prevents full restitution if the recipient were not guilty of a tort nor substantially more at fault than the claimant.' See also the caveat to (2) and (3) suggesting that the defence may still be available where a loss must be borne by one of the parties and the defendant's fault was a lack of care in not knowing facts or an innocent misrepresentation.

There appears to be no case in which the scenarios offered by the comments have been analysed and explained. There has been no discussion of whether an absolute or relative rule is to be applied where there is both (1) knowledge and a reasonable opportunity to return the property, which was not acted upon; and (2) a loss which must be borne by one of the parties. It is suggested that in the type of case under consideration the following analysis may be appropriate.

1.  Was there a change of circumstances? If yes, the inquiry must go on to consider whether it is equitable to permit the defendant to rely on the change to prevent recovery by the plaintiff.
2.  Did the defendant have knowledge of the claimant's mistake? If yes, this would prima facie prevent the recipient from relying on the defence.
3.  Will the consequence of 2. be that the recipient will be forced to bear a loss? If yes, the relative fault of both parties should be considered. The defendant will only be required to bear the loss if he is more at fault than the plaintiff.
4.  Once the relative fault of both parties is considered, the mistake by the claimant becomes relevant.[59]
5.  It is likely that the knowing defendant who did not return the property within a reasonable time will be regarded as being more at fault than the mistaken payer.

If this analysis is correct, the defendant will be under a continuing liability to make restitution to the payer despite the payer's mistake. This would, however, be subject to consideration of the exact circumstances of the case. For example, if the defendant did not have a reasonable opportunity to return the property before its destruction, and the claimant was guilty of a gross error, the balance could easily swing the other way.

A liability to repay despite loss of enrichment is also suggested by Jaffey, although he uses a different analysis. He suggests that a recipient who is no longer enriched and who has knowledge of the mistaken transfer can still make out the defence of change of position. However, because the defendant was aware of the restitutionary claim, the defendant incurs a tortious 'duty of preservation to preserve or repay the surviving value'.[60] Alongside the duty of preservation, Jaffey suggests that there should be a role for the contributory negligence principle to operate so as to reduce the defendant's liability to repay in cases where the plaintiff's own carelessness led to the transfer. The imposition on the defendant of some level of obligation over funds which it knows to belong to another also promotes the efficient operation of the law.

59  See comment (d).
60  Jaffey, P, *The Nature and Scope of Restitution*, 2000, Oxford: Hart Publishing, at 235.

If prior to the transfer the recipient was aware that it was not entitled to the property, it is the party best placed to prevent the transfer.[61] A simple low-cost precaution of refusing to take the property (if refusal is available) will prevent the mistake and the subsequent need to claim restitution. Liability rules should promote this policy. Requiring such a recipient to repay the value received would provide the necessary incentive to recipients with prior awareness of the mistake to refuse to accept the property.

The *Waitaki* facts are an example of this extreme scenario of the defendant having the power to refuse the money. The defendant should never have taken the money – it was not forced to do so, and was in a position to reject it. Its best and most efficient course of action was to refuse the payment.[62] But once it had accepted the funds, how could it then deny that it had accepted the risk of something happening to that money while in its possession?[63]

But, even accepting this analysis, the hardest question is how stringently the test should be applied to the aware recipient. Is the aware recipient liable for any loss in value, regardless of precautions taken? If the defendant did not have an opportunity to reject the payment, or was not aware of the mistake until after the payment had been received, strict liability would not be appropriate. The Restatement test of whether the recipient had a 'reasonable opportunity' to return the payment once knowledge was acquired suggests an efficient rule. The defendant has the chance to return the property and suffer no loss. If the destruction, or reduction in value of the disputed property, occurred before the defendant had a reasonable time to return it the payor should continue to bear the loss. The denial of the defence after a reasonable time has passed provides the necessary incentive for the defendant to act efficiently. She should then be treated as having taken the risk of loss of the value of the property if she continues to retain it.

### Options for Australia?

The essential difference between the cases of the innocent and the aware defendant is that the innocent defendant does not consciously take the risk of

---

61  See Mautner, M, ' "The Eternal Triangles of the Law" Toward a Theory of Priorities in Conflicts Involving Remote Parties' (1991) Michigan Law Review 95 at 116 where it is argued that a purchaser with knowledge of a conflicting claim should be denied priority and that this promotes an efficient rule, as the purchaser is the 'party best located to prevent the fraud by avoiding the transaction'.

62  Although Henry J in *Waitaki* said at [1999] 2 NZLR 211 at 218 that it was 'patently unreal to suggest that Waitaki's only option was to refuse to accept the money'.

63  This view is supported by Richard Nolan who argues: 'if the defendant knew of the plaintiff's right to restitution, he should not be able to rely on any destruction or diminution in value of the surviving enrichment which occurred while he had that knowledge and while he was in breach of his obligation to make restitution to the plaintiff.' Nolan, R, 'Change of Position' Ch 6 in *Laundering and Tracing*, n 32 above, at 154.

dealing with another's money. In 'Change of Position', Peter Birks argued that theft or casual destruction must count as change of position:

> The reason why thefts and casual destructions of the very thing received must count is not some woolly equity beyond articulation. It lies in the protection of security of receipts . . . That interest is only protected if we are all in general free to dispose as we please of whatever wealth appears to be at our disposition. If these losses did not count we would not have that freedom. Each of us would have to set up a contingency fund or insurance against the danger of double losses, to fire or theft and to a restitutionary plaintiff.[64]

The whole thrust of this approach is that people should be able to rely on a receipt that 'appears to be at [their] disposition'. The defendant who is aware that money does not belong to her is outside the scope of this formula. The aware defendant knows that the wealth is not at her disposal.

The English approach is simply too broad, and draws no distinction between a defendant who assumes the risk of loss of another's money and one who does not. It is insufficiently tied to the basis of the doctrine as one protecting security of receipts. Correspondingly, the current narrowly framed Australian test excludes the innocent defendant who deserves protection.

How should the defence be framed to take account of this differentiation? If the Australian High Court were to reorientate the defence so as to incorporate unconscionability as its basis, limits must be placed on the scope of the defence. One important restriction would be that, despite the loss of enrichment, it will not be unconscionable for the plaintiff to recover unless the defendant can show that she did not take the risk of dealing with another's funds. In the usual case that limitation will be demonstrated by the application of the reliance requirement. However, it will also protect the truly innocent defendant who does not know that the money is not hers, and who takes no risk in relation to its loss because she believes that she has lost her own money.

### Analogy to equitable receipt liability

The connection made by the Court of Appeal judges between unjust enrichment claims and the knowing receipt action will interest lawyers who have followed the debates on the relationship between the two. Restitution lawyers (and Professor Peter Birks in particular) have argued for some years that the equitable action of knowing receipt should be a strict liability restitutionary

---

64  Birks, n 32, at 62.

action, subject to defences.[65] It is currently for the plaintiff to prove that the defendant received the trust property 'knowingly' (or unconscionably, according to Nourse LJ in *Akindele*). This is consistent with the doctrine's equitable heritage. The unjust enrichment analysis would render the defendant liable upon receipt unless he or she could claim the benefit of a defence. Birks later resiled somewhat from his initial position. He still argued that the fact of receipt should trigger a strict liability claim but suggested that it should exist as an alternative to the equitable claim.[66]

The unjust enrichment analysis has received some judicial support.[67] The most vocal judicial proponent has been Lord Millett.[68] In *Twinsectra v Yardley* His Lordship stated *obiter*:

> Liability for 'knowing receipt' is receipt-based. It does not depend on fault. The cause of action is restitutionary and is available only where the defendant received or applied the money in breach of trust for his own use and benefit (see *Agip (Africa) Ltd v Jackson, Royal Brunei Airlines Sdn Bhd v Tan*). There is no basis for requiring actual knowledge of the breach of trust, let alone dishonesty, as a condition of liability. Constructive notice is sufficient, and may not even be necessary. There is powerful academic support for the proposition that the liability of the recipient is the same as in other cases of restitution, that is to say strict but subject to a change of position defence.[69]

The analysis of recipient liability in *Niru Battery* suggests that the members of the Court of Appeal do not favour the strict liability restitutionary approach. Although Sedley LJ referred to actions in unjust enrichment and equitable receipt as 'analogous', this is clearly different from suggesting that the receipt action is governed by unjust enrichment principles. Instead, his judgment treats the equitable and common law actions as distinct, although arising in similar circumstances. Thus, similar considerations should apply to

---

65  For a contrary view, see L Smith 'Unjust Enrichment, Property and the Structure of Trusts' (2000) 116 LQR 412.

66  Birks, P, 'Property and Unjust Enrichment: Categorical Truths' [1997] NZLR 623, and 'Receipt' Ch 7 in Birks, P and Pretto, A (eds), 2002, *Breach of Trust*, Oxford: Hart Publishers.

67  Lord Nicholls of Birkenhead *obiter* in *Royal Brunei Airlines Sdn Bhd v Tan* [1995] 2 AC 378. Extra-judicially see 'Knowing Receipt: The Need for a New Landmark' in Cornish, Nolan, O'Sullivan and Virgo (eds), *Restitution Past, Present and Future*, 1998 Oxford: Hart Publishing. See also Hansen J *obiter* in *Koorootang Nominees v ANZ* [1998] 3 VR 16, and Tobias JA in *Say-Dee Pty Ltd v Farah Construction Pty Ltd*, Mason P and Giles JA agreeing, [2005] NSWCA 309.

68  See also the recent judgment of Lord Nicholls of Birkenhead in *Criterion Properties plc v Stratford Properties LLC* [2004] UKHL which affirms his view that the strict liability unjust enrichment approach is the correct one.

69  [2002] 2 AC 164 at 194 (citations deleted).

govern the defendant's liability. Clarke LJ also clearly regarded the knowing receipt action as being independent from the law of unjust enrichment, acknowledging the 'differences between the problems associated with knowing receipt and those with which we are concerned'.[70]

### Akindele, *unconscionability and knowledge*

What is the significance of the analogy drawn by the judges in *Niru Battery* between unjust enrichment actions and knowing receipt actions? It is suggested that the ramifications lie not in the analogy itself but in the analogy combined with the court's acceptance of the unconscionability test as being the basis for change of position. In particular, if a defendant can rely on the change of position defence despite actual knowledge of the facts constituting the unjust enrichment claim, will a defendant in a knowing receipt case necessarily be acting unconscionably if the receipt was a 'knowing' one? To understand the significance of this question, it is necessary to backtrack a little to the elements of the knowing receipt action.

Liability is imposed where trust property, or property subject to a fiduciary obligation, is transferred to a third party in breach of the trust or fiduciary obligation. If the third party knows of the trust, and that the transfer to her was in breach of duty, a court of equity will hold her personally liable for the value of the money or property transferred, irrespective of whether she still retains it.[71] The defendant will also be liable if she received the property or money innocently, but became aware of the trust and its breach before dealing with the property.

There is a cognate equitable action, which renders liable to compensation a third party who assists a trustee or fiduciary in a breach of duty. Traditionally this was framed as the action of 'assisting in a dishonest and fraudulent design'. Now it has been settled, at least in England,[72] that the test is one of dishonestly assisting in a breach of duty. The breach need not be fraudulent.[73]

Before *Akindele*, the focus of the equitable action of receipt was on determining the necessary knowledge for liability. There were a number of different views regarding the 'type' of knowledge or notice sufficient to render the

---

70  [2003] EWCA Civ 1446 at [157].
71  Traditionally, it is stated that the defendant is liable 'as a constructive trustee'. This has led to much confusion, as there is no actual trust. It is not a proprietary claim. Millett LJ in *Dubai Aluminium v Salaam* [2002] UKHL 48, [2003] 2 AC 366 recently expressed at [142] a strong wish that the traditional terminology be abandoned completely in favour of the term 'accountable in equity'.
72  We are still awaiting a definitive statement by the High Court for Australia, although the High Court adopted the dishonesty terminology in *obiter dicta* in *Giumelli v Giumelli* (1999) 196 CLR 101.
73  Cf the test of the Supreme Court of Canada, retaining the fraudulent breach requirement, and knowledge: *Re Air Canada v M & L Travel* (1993) 108 DLR (4th) 592.

defendant liable. For our purposes that debate need not be explored further as it is clear that a defendant with actual knowledge of the breach will be held liable. In *Akindele* Nourse LJ attempted to enunciate a single test for the receipt action, in the same way that a single test of dishonesty had been adopted for the assistance action. 'Unconscientiousness' was intended to be the key concept, with questions of degrees of knowledge being incorporated into the conscience inquiry. A test based on unconscionability, rather than knowledge, permits consideration of context.[74] The defendant's knowledge will still be relevant, but each case will be considered on its merits. No longer can it be said that any one level of knowledge definitively is, or is not, determinative of liability. Unconscionability presumably contains more elements than knowledge alone. If Nourse LJ wanted a test of actual knowledge he would have used one.[75]

The aim of a test of dishonesty in *Royal Brunei* was to move away from a test based on knowledge as the sole criterion of liability. Thus Lord Nicholls of Birkenhead, stated, '[T]he court will also have regard to personal attributes of the third party such as his experience and intelligence, and the reason why he acted as he did.'[76] In *Twinsectra*, Lord Hutton, in adopting a mixed subjective/objective test of dishonesty for imposing personal liability for assistance, stated that knowledge of the breach of duty is not sufficient unless the defendant is also aware that the impugned conduct is wrongful. So, the defendant in that case who knew of the facts constituting the breach was not dishonest. Although Lord Millett rejected the dishonesty test favoured by the majority, he acknowledged its multifaceted nature. He stated: 'Account must be taken of subjective considerations such as the defendant's experience and intelligence and his actual state of knowledge at the relevant time.'[77]

So, as in the decisions on change of position, it has been held that unconscionability encompasses more than knowledge of wrongdoing. Nevertheless, the scope of 'conscience' in the knowing receipt cases is more limited. *Akindele* stands for the much less controversial proposition that actual knowledge of a breach of fiduciary obligation equates to unconscionability.[78] Given the his-

---

74  I have previously argued the benefit of such a test, applying loss allocation principles. See ' "Goodbye" Knowing Receipt. "Hello" Unconscientious Receipt.' (2001) 21 Oxford Journal of Legal Studies 239.

75  Certainly in *Waitaki* Thomas J thought it was possible for a knowing recipient of funds paid by mistake to have a clear conscience. Referring to examples offered by Professor Birks, His Honour stated at [1999] 2 NZLR 211, 228: 'The essential point is, notwithstanding his or her knowledge, the recipient's conscience is clear.'

76  [1995] 2 AC 378 at 391. But see now the Privy Council's reinterpretation of that judgment in *Barlow Clowes International Ltd v Eurotrust International Ltd* [2005] UKPC 37.

77  [2002] 2 AC 164 at 198.

78  Per Chambers QC in *Papamichael v National Westminster Bank plc* [2003] EWHC 164 (Comm) at para 246, approving the judgment of Hart J in *Criterion Properties plc v Stratford Properties plc* [2002] EWHC 496. In Australia the same proposition was expressed by Bryson J in *Maronis Holdings Ltd v Nippon Credit Australia Ltd* (2001) 38 ACSR 404.

tory of the action, and the link made in Nourse LJ's judgment between unconscionability and knowledge[79] this is not surprising. However, in *Criterion Properties plc v Stratford UK Properties LLC*[80] the Court of Appeal took another view of *Akindele*, with Carnwath LJ stating that to hold the defendant liable simply because it had actual knowledge of the facts which gave rise to the breach of duty was 'too narrow and one-sided a view of the matter'.[81] Instead, he stated that a proper application of the *Akindele* test required consideration of the defendant's 'actions and knowledge in the context of the commercial relationship of the parties as a whole'. He also added that, 'I do not see how one can consider the "conscionability" of the actions of one party to the agreement without considering the position of the other.'[82] This is the first clear statement that a defendant in an equitable receipt case, with actual knowledge of the facts giving rise to the breach, could escape liability. The explicit analogy drawn in *Niru Battery*, and the clear flexibility of the unconscionability test as it was applied to change of position, reinforce this notion.

If this is correct, the next stage in the analysis is to consider how the analogy drawn in *Niru Battery* potentially affects equitable receipt liability. The critical question is whether a defendant to an equitable receipt claim who has acted with knowledge of the breach of equitable duty could nonetheless not be held to be acting unconscionably, just as a defendant to a claim in unjust enrichment who has knowledge of the claim may nonetheless be able to rely on the change of position defence, at least under English law.

The question can be considered by reference to an example: the case of the aware businesswoman, used in the *change of position* discussion, illustrates the problem. However, a minor variation is needed in order to make the example pertinent to the knowing receipt action. Suppose that our businesswoman provided some professional investment advice to the trustee of a trust, in her capacity as trustee. She was entitled to payment from the trust but in fact had already received her payment. She knew that the payment in question was a mistake by the trustee because she had been double paid. The payment was a breach of duty by the trustee, albeit an innocent one.

---

79 'The recipient's state of knowledge must be such as to make it unconscionable for him to retain the benefit of the receipt' [2001] Ch 437 at 455.
80 [2003] BCLC 129.      81 Ibid.
82 This was an appeal on the issue of summary judgment, and certain facts were assumed for that purpose. The essential question was divided into two parts. First, whether the managing director of Criterion had acted outside his apparent authority in causing Criterion to enter an agreement, which gave the third defendant the right to be bought out of a joint venture with Criterion on terms that were highly unfavourable to Criterion. Second, could the defendant rely on the agreement, despite the lack of apparent authority on the part of the director of Criterion to enter into the agreement? The unconscionability test was regarded as relevant here. The House of Lords has now said that this was not a case about knowing receipt at all: *Criterion Properties plc v Stratford Properties LLC* [2004] UKHL 28.

This is the essence of an equitable receipt case. The defendant has actual knowledge of the facts constituting the breach of trust. She no longer has the funds, so no proprietary claim is available. The equitable receipt claim, being personal, can still be relied upon. Does the businesswoman have a personal liability to repay? Is her receipt unconscientious?

If the analogy between the common law and equitable claims holds good, English law will recognise that her receipt was not unconscientious. Her actions were consistent with attempting to return the property to the trust, and her conduct was entirely honourable. Nonetheless, it can be argued that the defendant should still be liable to make repayment. Two particular arguments are relevant. The first is that the recipient may have rights to sue a third party for recovery of the funds lost to her. If she can recover the lost funds she is not unduly inconvenienced by being required to return money she knows is not hers. Although recovery is not certain, the existence of those rights should be relevant to assessing liability.[83] The second argument is identical to one used in the change of position context. The recipient knew from the moment of receipt that the money was not hers and needed to be returned. As soon as she had a reasonable opportunity to return the money, she, and not the beneficiary, should carry the risk of its loss.

In relation to the second argument, it is interesting to note that para 142 of the American Restatement of Restitution, discussed earlier in relation to change of position, contains commentary relevant to this situation. In fact, the rule stated for a knowing recipient of trust funds is different from the rule applied earlier.

Paragraph 142 provides that the defence of change of circumstances is not available to a tortfeasor.[84] Comment (d) states in part:

> a person who received title to property from a trustee and who had notice, although no knowledge, of the interests of the beneficiary and who, therefore, was not a bona fide purchaser is not entitled to deny liability for the value of the property received, although subsequently it is destroyed or harmed without his fault, since he was guilty of an equitable tort in taking title to the property.[85]

Although the paragraph appears to allow a defendant a reasonable opportunity to return funds before disqualifying her from the benefit of the defence, this option does not appear to be available in the equitable context. This

---

83 If the money had been embezzled from the businesswoman's account, such a right would be clearly available to her.

84 See para 142(3).

85 Restatement of Restitution, n 53 above. Jaffey argues that liability in knowing receipt should be understood as a liability based on the failure to preserve property once a duty of preservation has arisen. See Jaffey, P, n 60 above at 328–330.

difference could have considerable impact. Changing the facts of our example highlights the issue.

Consider the case where the businesswoman, having seen her bank statement, sets out immediately to drive to the bank to arrange a transfer of the funds back to the trust. On the way she is involved in a collision and is hospitalised. Before her discharge from hospital the bank fails and the funds are lost.

The example raises the broader question of whether equity is going to hold the defendant to a stricter standard than the common law. If the businesswoman acknowledged the claim, does that render her conscience-bound in equity although it will not be bound at common law? This is the 'big' question. It asks whether trust or equitable claims should be treated in the same fashion as common law ones. Supporters can be found for both sides of the debate. Lord Nicholls of Birkenhead has argued that equity should follow the law.[86] Professor Lionel Smith has reached the opposite conclusion. In a closely reasoned article[87] he has argued for the necessity of continuing to treat legal and equitable claims differently, as equitable or trust claims are more vulnerable than common law ones by their very nature. Nonetheless, even an acceptance of Lionel Smith's argument that equitable claims should be treated differently does not tell us how to define the term 'unconscionable' in this context. It does, however, remind us that in undertaking this loss allocation exercise there are specific policy considerations that have to be kept in mind. The most obvious consideration is that the beneficiary can normally sue the trustee as the primary defendant responsible for recouping the loss. The example given assumes that no recovery will be forthcoming from the trustee. This could be for the simple and frequently occurring reason that the trust document contains a clause excluding the trustee from liability for all but fraudulent breaches of trust.[88]

It could be argued, by extension from Smith's argument, that as the purpose of trust law is to protect beneficiaries, preference should be given to the beneficiary if the two parties are otherwise innocent. It is the beneficiary who

---

86 Lord Nicholls of Birkenhead, 'Knowing Receipt: The Need for a New Landmark', n 67 above.

87 'Unjust Enrichment, Property and the Structure of Trusts' (2000) 116 LQR 412.

88 In Ford, HAJ and Lee, WA, *Principles of the Law of Trusts*, 1996, Sydney: LBC Information Services, (looseleaf), the learned authors state at 18060 'Nearly all professionally drawn trust instruments contain provisions exempting trustees from liability for breach of trust.' *Armitage v Nurse* [1998] Ch 241 affirms the effectiveness of these clauses. Millett LJ at 256 described such clauses as 'common' and added 'it must be acknowledged that the view is widely held that these clauses have gone too far, and that trustees who charge for their services and who, as professional men, would not dream of excluding liability for ordinary professional negligence, should not be able to rely on a trustee exemption clause excluding liability for gross negligence.' It would be extremely unfair to a third party if the trustee were able to rely on such a clause to avoid liability and place the risk of loss onto the third party.

is vulnerable to loss caused through the trustee's default, and has no other recourse. Most likely he did not consent to (or even know of) the settlor's decision to limit the trustee's liability in the trust document.

These considerations are not intended to be determinative. I offer them only as a counterweight to the intuitive emotional response that it is not fair to make the defendant liable. In fact, I suggest that the difficulty inherent in such a loss allocation exercise involving two innocent parties highlights the need for an alternative solution.

Litigation against third parties would be greatly reduced[89] if trustees were required to take out insurance protecting the trust from loss due to the trustee's breach. This requirement could also be coupled with a prohibition on trustee exemption clauses.[90] This solution would result in trustees being held liable for breaches of trust, but the existence of insurance would defray their personal costs.[91] Professional trustees could be expected to pass on the cost of the insurance premiums to the trust, in the form of higher fees. In the case of

---

89  Claims for third-party liability consequent upon breaches of fiduciary duty other than breaches of trust will not be reduced unless fiduciary insurance could be arranged to cover the risk of loss. There is of course the possibility that insurance will cover a solicitor's breach of duty, and insurance policies could be extended to cover company directors' breaches of fiduciary duty. This will, of course, come at a cost. Insurance would not easily be available in less formalised fiduciary relationships.

90  Trustee exemption clauses have been considered by the Law Reform Commissions in Ontario, England and New Zealand. In British Columbia they were considered by the Law Institute's Committee on the Modernisation of the Trustee Act. In each jurisdiction a different view has been taken as to the wisdom of prohibiting such clauses. The Ontario Law Reform Commission was the only Commission to recommend that all exculpatory clauses be deprived of effect. The New Zealand Commission recommended that such clauses not be available to trustees for reward. They recommended against removal of protection for lay trustees on the basis that they 'may well not either realise the need to insure or find it difficult to obtain cover'. New Zealand Law Commission, Report 79, 2002, *Some Problems in the Law of Trusts*. The British Columbian solution was to give the Court the right to override exclusion clauses. The provisional English solution, proposed in the Law Commission's Consultation Paper No 171, 2003, *Trustee Exemption Clauses* was to regulate trustee exemption clauses for professional trustees, but not for lay trustees. The proposed regulation involves a reasonableness test, and an inability to rely on clauses to protect against negligence. Interestingly, although the Law Commission provisionally proposes retaining exemption clauses in their full scope for lay trustees, their research indicated that it was the lay trustees who were the least concerned about these clauses. See the summary of the results of the socio-economic research undertaken as part of the preparation of the Consultation Paper at 3.10–3.35.

91  Note the English Trust Law Committee was of the view that it would be inappropriate for professional paid trustees to be permitted to exclude liability for negligence, and that there should be a corresponding expectation that they would take out insurance. The Committee would permit exclusion of liability, with no expectation of insurance, to be relied on by unpaid trustees. (See Trust Law Committee Trustee Exemption Clauses, Consultation Paper June 1999.)

unpaid trustees it may be appropriate for the trust to pay the premiums.[92] Although the end result in both cases would be that the beneficiaries pay for their own insurance, this may still be preferable to the beneficiaries suffering the risk of losing all the trust assets without being able to sue a trustee or third party for compensation for the loss.[93]

## Conclusion

The adoption of an unconscionability-based test for the application of the defence of change of position is unlikely to be controversial in Australia. Within the limitations of the narrow defence at present applied here, the 'unconscionability' test perhaps adds little. The situation in England is rather different, and there is now significant danger of the defence operating too broadly. It is suggested that this approach should not be followed in Australia. If reform is needed, it can be more closely calibrated.

The other issue canvassed in this chapter relates to the equitable action of knowing or unconscientious receipt. It can confidently be predicted that the implications of *Niru Battery* will be argued about for many years to come.

---

92 The English Law Commission provisionally recommended at p viii that 'all trustees should be given power to make payments out of the trust fund to purchase indemnity insurance'.

93 In England the Law Commission was concerned about the economic impact of prohibiting exclusion clauses, namely the rise in insurance premiums. It also discusses at 3.82–3.90 a number of potential concerns regarding the possible inadequacy of insurance cover, or the impossibility of some lay trustees obtaining insurance. A compulsory insurance system would need to be carefully considered. The Commission was not convinced by arguments that trustees would transfer their trusts to jurisdictions without regulation, citing the continuing trust practice in Jersey and Guernsey, although both of those jurisdictions have imposed statutory controls on the application of exclusion clauses.

# Index

For Product Safety Concerns and Information please contact our EU
representative  GPSR@taylorandfrancis.com
Taylor & Francis Verlag GmbH, Kaufingerstraße 24, 80331 München, Germany